MATERIALS AND METHODS
FOR
CONTEMPORARY CONSTRUCTION

MATERIALS AND METHODS
FOR
CONTEMPORARY CONSTRUCTION
Second Edition

CALEB HORNBOSTEL

Temple University
Philadelphia, Pennsylvania

and

WILLIAM J. HORNUNG

California State Polytechnic University
Pomona, California

PRENTICE-HALL, INC., *Englewood Cliffs, New Jersey 07632*

Library of Congress Cataloging in Publication Data

Hornbostel, Caleb.
    Materials and methods for contemporary construction.

    Includes index.
    1. Building materials. 2. Building. I. Hornung,
William J. II. Title.
TA403.6.H67 1982   693   81-19158
ISBN 0-13-560904-6   AACR2

Editorial/production supervision
   and interior design by James M. Chege
Manufacturing buyer: Joyce Levatino
Cover design by 20/20 Services

Printed in the United States of America

10 9 8 7 6 5 4 3 2 1

ISBN 0-13-560904-6

Prentice-Hall International, Inc., *London*
Prentice-Hall of Australia Pty. Limited, *Sydney*
Prentice-Hall of Canada, Ltd., *Toronto*
Prentice-Hall of India Private Limited, *New Delhi*
Prentice-Hall of Japan, Inc., *Tokyo*
Prentice-Hall of Southeast Asia Pte. Ltd., *Singapore*
Whitehall Books Limited, *Wellington, New Zealand*

CONTENTS

PREFACE TO
THE SECOND EDITION

The second edition of *Materials and Methods for Contemporary Construction* has been revised and expanded with new and up-to-date building materials and construction methods.

Students of architecture, architectural technology, or construction technology are provided with the basic knowledge and information they need as a first course in their field of study. Building materials and methods of construction, both current and standard, are discussed and studied as are the fundamental characteristics of the materials and the various methods of construction in which these materials are used in the construction industry.

Ten of the 32 chapters have had major revisions and a number of new units have been added. The new chapters deal with: Plastics in Construction; Insulation and Acoustical Materials; and a special chapter on metrication that forms the major part of the Appendix.

The book retains the best parts of the first edition and follows a special learning format for each chapter. For example: each unit has an *Introduction*, which provides an overall concept of the unit; *Technical Information*, which covers the body of the subject matter; a *Review Examination*, in which the students have the opportunity to test themselves; *Assignments* as additional practice and study of the subject matter; and *Supplementary Information*, which provides further enrichment of the students' understanding of the material.

The authors are indebted to the manufacturers of the many building materials, whose methods, applications, installation, and final treatments have greatly contributed to the value of the text.

Caleb Hornbostel

William J. Hornung

PREFACE TO
THE FIRST EDITION

This book provides the key to an understanding of modern materials and methods of construction. Every student of architecture, architectural technology, or construction technology should have the basic knowledge and information provided within this text. Building materials and methods of construction, both current and standard, are discussed and studied as are the fundamental characteristics of the materials and the various methods of construction in which these materials are used in the construction industry.

The text is composed of 32 study units requiring approximately two semesters of two-hour periods. Each unit is composed of the following:

Introduction, which provides the student with an overall picture of the contents of the unit; *Technical Information*, which covers the body of the subject matter; *Review Examination*, in which the student has the opportunity to test himself and discover how well he has learned and retained the subject material (answers for all Review Examinations are supplied at the back of the book); *Assignment*, which provides additional practice and study of the subject matter; and *Supplementary Information*, which provides further study and enrichment of the student's understanding of the subject. In addition the text includes not only suggested mid-term examinations for the first eight units and for units 17 through 24, but also suggested end-term examinations for units 9 through 16 and 25 through 32. Experience has shown that such mid-term and end-term review examinations often pro-

vide the necessary study stimuli for successful completion of the course (answers are supplied for both the mid-term and end-term examinations at the back of the book).

Materials and Methods for Contemporary Construction is intended as a required course in the study of architecture, architectural technology, and construction technology. It is by no means an all-inclusive text, but rather encompasses the most important materials and methods of construction in present-day use. The development of the text parallels to a large degree the actual construction of buildings, beginning with the building process — property, finance, professional services, contracts, and so forth — through the steps ordinarily taken by the contractor in constructing a building; and on up to the final completion and occupancy of the building.

The authors are indebted to the various manufacturers of the numerous building materials whose suggested methods and applications, installations, and final treatments have greatly contributed to the value of the text. Special consideration and appreciation is extended to Dana L. Harris for his assistance in the preparation of the drawings, to Dorothy M. Larkin for her patience and skill in preparing the manuscript through its many stages to the final copy, and to Barbara Hornbostel for editing and proofreading of the text.

Caleb Hornbostel
William J. Hornung

MATERIALS AND METHODS
FOR
CONTEMPORARY CONSTRUCTION

1

THE BUILDING PROCESS

INTRODUCTION

When an individual, group, company, firm, or corporation envisions the construction of a building or buildings, a process is set in motion which involves property, finance, professional services, consultants, lawyers, contractors, subcontractors, material suppliers, furnishing, decorating, site improvement, landscaping and planting, etc., until the building is ready for occupancy. This chapter will cover in broad general terms the entire building process.

TECHNICAL INFORMATION

The Property

The property on which the construction is to take place must be checked for size, easements, lot-block-section numbers, zoning, utilities, and the restrictions set by the town, county, city, state, and federal codes.

The legal description and the survey, including the title guarantee, will give the sizes, the easements, and the lot, block, and section numbers (see Figure 1-1). The building code and local building department will give the zoning and building restrictions. An architectural survey (see Figure 1-2) must be made in order to locate utilities, grades, levels, sidewalks, curbs, etc., and a series of soil tests will have to be performed to obtain the bearing capacity of the soil and subgrade conditions.

The Finance

Depending upon the type of building or buildings to be constructed, a financial feasibility study is usually made. For a family residence, this study is not complicated. The family knows the size of house they want, they can visit some builders' houses to check size and cost, they own the property, and can easily check on how much they can afford to spend for the residence and then set a budget.

A large building or group of buildings requires a complete feasibility study. For example, when a company contemplates building a group of garden apartments on a tract of land, the following considerations must be fully evaluated to determine

FIGURE 1-1 *Legal description*

the financial feasibility of the project as shown in Table 1-1.

Professional Services

Generally the owners, builders, or promoters make the feasibility study. In some cases the planners and architect or architects will make the feasibility study; in others they will be part of a team, utilized as consultants. When this study is completed, the professional services of planners and architect or architects are obtained in order to produce the drawings and specifications necessary for construction of the building. The general process for producing these drawings and specifications is as follows:

PHASE A:

1. Schematics, preliminary drawings, specifications, and estimates which include architectural, structural, mechanical, site planning, and landscaping work.

Only after approval of the preliminaries are the next steps taken.

2. Architectural working drawings and details.
3. Structural working drawings and details.
4. Heating, ventilating, and air conditioning working drawings and details.
5. Plumbing working drawings and details.
6. Electrical working drawings and details.
7. Site improvement working drawings and details.
8. Landscaping and planting working drawings and details.

9. Separate specifications for each of the above.

10. Final estimate, and final approval before bidding.

PHASE B:

1. Approval by the local building department.

2. Approvals by all the other departments and agen-cies which have specific jurisdiction over building construction.

3. Rendering or model of the project.

4. Preparing forms for competitive bidding. Time of com-pletion, bond, insurance, labor department wage scales, time for bidding, etc.

5. Receiving of bids; consultation and approval.

FIGURE 1-2 *Architectural survey*

TABLE 1-1 *Information necessary for a feasibility study*

Information Necessary for a Feasibility Study

Taxes	Town, city, county, state and federal
Cost of Land	Original cost and cost when developed
Building Costs	Sq. ft. and cu. ft. costs for this type of building
Size and Height of Buildings and Types of Apartments	Codes checked for zoning and restrictions
Site Improvement	Grading, excavating, landscaping, planting, roads, walks, etc.
Legal Fees	Lawyers, permits, and contracts
Utilities	Costs for supplying utilities
Insurance	Fire, theft, damage, liability, etc.
Landscaping and Planting	Roads, walks, sidewalks, curbs, parking, grading, seeding and planting
Promotion and Publicity	Advertisement, photographs, renderings, brochures, etc.
Renting and Sales	Staff, office, telephone, etc.
Professional Services	Architects, engineers, decorator, etc.
Maintenance	Costs for maintenance of buildings, painting, repairs
Furnishing and Decoration	Entrance lobbies, halls, stairs, etc.
Profit	Income per year, costs per year
Construction Supervision	Staff for supervision
Mortgages	Construction or investment types: 10, 20, or 30 years
Utilities	Yearly cost of utilities

PHASE C:

1. Preparing contracts for prime contractors: (a) general construction, (b) heating, ventilating, and air conditioning, (c) plumbing, (d) electrical, (e) site improvement, landscaping, and planting.

In many cases, during the preparation of the working drawings, an interior decorator will be engaged to decorate and furnish the public lobbies, entrances, and halls and to furnish several apartments. The decorator will work with the architect or, as in some cases, be employed by the architect. The furniture, carpets, wall hangings, curtains, etc., will be separately handled by the decorator under separate contracts.

In this entire professional service operation, the coordination between architectural, structural, and mechanical drawings requires very close checking and cross-checking to see that all these various components of a building do not interfere with one another. In Figure 1-3, the space between the hung ceiling and the underside of the concrete floor slab must be of sufficient depth so that duct

FIGURE 1-3 *Coordination of architectural, structural, and mechanical components*

work can pass under structural beams and girders. In a like manner the spacing between ducts and recessed lighting fixtures, as well as plumbing and heating pipes and electrical conduits, must be considered so as not to interfere with their installation.

In the example chosen, a garden apartment project, it is immediately obvious that area limits have to be set on the drawings to designate the limits of property areas that are for the construction of the buildings and under the control of the general contractor, and to mark off at what point he or she has no further responsibility. Then the site improvement, landscaping, and planting contractor takes over the responsibility of seeding, grading, planting, etc.

Construction

Once costs have been agreed upon and contracts have been signed, the construction operation commences. Because the contracts prepared by the architect give a completion date, it is immediately necessary for the contractor to submit a building construction production schedule in order that all the various building trades know when and at what stage the various parts of their work must be started or completed.

The architect must constantly supervise the construction to check materials, workmanship, and progress in order to issue certificates of payments for the various contractors; the owners usually employ a Clerk-of-the-Works to check these things on a daily basis.

During construction, the inspectors from the various departments having jurisdiction over construction constantly supervise the construction, and in many cases, certain types of work cannot start until approved by them. For example, a private sewage disposal system has to be approved by the Department of Health before work can commence and it cannot be covered with earth until approved by the field inspector.

The various subcontractors and suppliers to the prime contractors will submit samples of materials and shop drawings (fabrication drawings) to the architect for his approval. These drawings have to be checked against the contract working drawings and specifications to see that they meet the standards, materials, etc.

During the construction phase, job meetings are periodically called at which the architect's representative, the Clerk-of-the-Works, and the superintendents of the various prime contractors are present in order to iron out any problems and to check the progress of the job with the construction procedure schedule. At these meetings, the question of changes (change orders) due to job conditions are discussed and decided. For example, suppose that, during the excavating, it was necessary to dip deeper to arrive at the correct bearing soil and therefore more foundation wall, stepped footings, and labor than shown in the contract drawings were necessary. Credits are also discussed. For example, contract specifications may call for a specific type of brick at current cost of so much per thousand; however, the architect and owner select a brick that costs $10 less per thousand.

When the construction phase nears completion, the architect and the Clerk-of-the-Works make up lists of work still to be completed (known as *punch lists*). Here is an example of such an item in a punch list:

Room 208. Door closer missing, piece of base missing on North wall, light fixture frames not installed, sink faucets missing, window glass broken, and switch plates missing.

When all the items on the punch lists are completed and the building is ready for occupancy, a Certificate of Occupancy must be obtained from the building department. In general, there are always small items that have to be installed, checked, and replaced after the building is occupied.

As the job reaches completion, there is a final accounting of all extras and credits, and all certificates, guarantees, approvals, etc., must be turned over to the owners. For 1 year after occupancy, all contractors have guaranteed their work and are responsible for correcting any failure, malfunction, etc.

REVIEW EXAMINATION

1. To obtain the exact size of a piece of property, what should be checked?
2. The legal description and survey including title guarantee give what information concerning a piece of property?
3. In order to locate utilities and grades of a piece of property, what document must be obtained?
4. Name five items that should be considered when making a feasibility study.
5. What do preliminary drawings, specifications, and estimates include?
6. Are separate specifications prepared for architectural, heating, ventilating and air conditioning, and site improvement?
7. Are separate contracts made for general construction and plumbing?

8. Very close coordination between what things is necessary in preparing working drawings?

9. Who supervises the construction of a building?

10. Material samples must be approved by whom?

11. Shop drawings must be checked against what things?

12. When the building is nearing completion, what must the architect prepare?

ASSIGNMENT

1. Make a diagram showing the four main parts of the building process and show the connection of the main documents, studies, professional services, and prime contractors.

2. Draw a diagram of a piece of property and write a legal description.

SUPPLEMENTARY INFORMATION

Contour Lines on a Survey

In order to develop a site plan we must understand the significance of contour lines on a survey map. Contours permit the visualization of land in three dimensions by showing existing elevations of topography. A contour map which shows the characteristics of a site is made by a licensed surveying engineer. Architectural surveys use two systems for showing grades and elevations, either by contours or spot points, as shown in Figure 1-4.

Contours are lines of equal elevation above the same datum plane or reference plane. The datum

FIGURE 1-5 *Contours of uniform slopes*

plane is generally located at mean sea level. A contour interval is the vertical distance between contours. Common intervals are 1, 2, and 5 ft.

The contour lines shown evenly spaced in Figure 1-5 are of a uniform slope. When contour lines are close at the top of a slope and become wider at the bottom, they indicate a concave slope, as in Figure 1-6.

The purpose of changing existing contours is to direct runoff water away from the building site. This process is also known as grading.

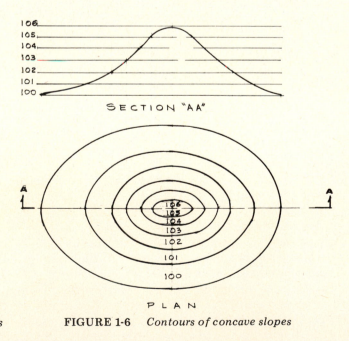

FIGURE 1-6 *Contours of concave slopes*

FIGURE 1-4 *Two methods of showing grades and elevations*

TABLE 1-2   *Typical fees for architectural services**

Building Type	Total Project Size in Thousands of Dollars						
	100	*250*	*500*	*1000*	*2500*	*5000*	*10,000*
Factories, garages, warehouses, repetitive housing	9.0%	8.0%	7.0%	6.2%	5.6%	5.3%	4.9%
Apartments, banks, schools, offices libraries, municipal buildings	11.7	10.8	8.5	7.3	6.7	6.4	6.0
Churches, hospitals, homes, laboratories, museums, research	14.0	12.8	11.9	10.9	9.5	8.5	7.8
Memorials, monumental work, decorative furnishings	—	16.0	14.5	13.1	11.3	10.0	9.0

*This information is copyrighted by Robert Snow Means, Co., Inc. It is reproduced from *1980 Building Construction Cost Data* with permission.

Easements and Subsurface Rights

In many cases public utilities, access to a property, and future right-of-way for roads or highways are part of the survey and the legal description of a piece of property (see Figures 1-1 and 1-2), but it is always advisable to check what limitations and restrictions are set by these easements. It is also necessary to check if mineral, oil, or gas rights exist as this could mean that the owner of the subsurface rights can at any time start a drilling or mining operation on the property.

Architectural Services Fees

Architectural professional service fees are generally based on a percentage of the cost of the building construction. The American Institute of Architects has prepared printed contract forms for owner and architect. They also have available printed contract forms of various types for owner and contractor such as lump sum, cost plus, fixed fee, etc. Table 1-2 shows typical percentage fees.

2

EARTH FORMATIONS
AND SOIL TESTS

INTRODUCTION

This chapter deals with the various kinds of soils that underlie building foundations and with the investigation of these soils which is done by means of soil tests.

In order to calculate the proper size of footing or foundation for a building, the bearing capacity of the soil on which the building is to be placed must be known. But first, the soil composition of the site must be determined.

The soils considered here are: rock, decayed rock, loose rock, shale, slate, boulders, hardpan, gravel, sand, both coarse and fine, clay, mud, silt, and quicksand. Other soils are also briefly described. The relation between type of soil and size of footings is then examined. Next, the bearing capacity of the soil on which the footings are to rest must be determined. Soil investigation will disclose the types of soil, the water table, the thickness of the bearing stratum, and the uniformity of soil deposits. Subsurface conditions and bearing capacities can be examined by various methods such as

1. Test pits
2. Loading platform

3. Test borings:
   Sounding rod
   Auger borings
   Wash borings
   Dry sample borings
   Rock drilling

This unit deals mainly with the loading platform and the test pit as means of determining bearing capacity and type of soil. It also gives general information on test borings.

TECHNICAL INFORMATION ON EARTH FORMATIONS

Soil

The word "soil" refers to a particular kind of earth or ground. It may be described as the unconsolidated material formed by the disintegration of rock and organic substances in varying proportions. This disintegration of rock masses is *chemical*, due to reaction and decomposition, and *mechanical*, due to frost, moving water, wind, ice, and movement of the earth's crust. The following definitions of the more commonly encountered soils are used in field identification. (Figure 2-1 illustrates these soils graphically.)

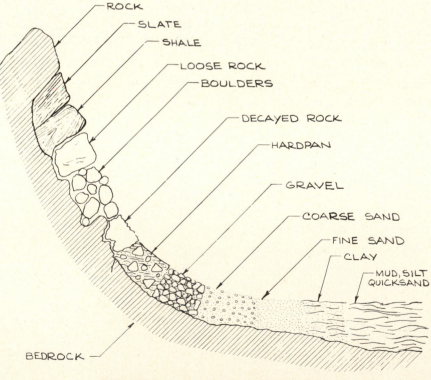

FIGURE 2-1 *Graphic definition of soils*

ROCK: Undisturbed, naturally formed rock masses which are part of the original rock formation. As used in building construction, the term identifies the solid material forming the earth's crust and is often referred to as "bedrock" or "ledge rock." Sound, hard rock is the best known support for the foundations of a structure.

SLATE: A dense, very fine-textured, soft rock which is readily split along cleavage planes into thin sheets and which cannot be reduced to a plastic condition by moderate grinding and mixing with water.

SHALE: A laminated, fine-textured, soft rock, composed of consolidated clay or silt, which cannot be molded without the addition of water but which can be reduced to a plastic condition by moderate grinding and mixing with water.

LOOSE ROCK: Rock masses detached from the ledge of which they originally formed a part.

BOULDERS: Detached rock larger than gravel, generally rounded and worn as a result of having been transported by water or ice a considerable distance from the original ledge.

DECAYED ROCK (rotten rock): Sand, clay, and other materials resulting from the disintegration of rock masses, lacking the coherent qualities but occupying the space formerly occupied by the original rock.

HARDPAN: A coherent mixture of clay with sand, gravel, and boulders, or a cemented combination of clay, sand, and gravel. "Hardpan," as the word is used in foundation engineering, suggests a degree of hardness caused by consolidation or cementation rather than any definite soil composition. Its removal often requires the use of tools operated by compressed air or even explosives.

GRAVEL: Detached rock particles 1/4 in. to 3 in. in size, rounded and waterworn.

SAND: Noncoherent rock particles smaller than 1/4 in. Sand has no plasticity or cohesion except along the seacoast and sometimes in beds of streams where sand, gravel, and boulders are generally mixed with other soils. In fact, sand is often referred to as a cohesionless soil. Coarse sand and gravel often furnish an excellent support for building foundations; fine sand is less reliable.

CLAY: A fine-grained, firm material resulting from the decomposition and hydration of certain kinds of rock. These finely divided minerals have a sheetlike crystal structure and a chemical composition which give clay its characteristics of slippage and plasticity. In other words, clay is malleable, plastic when wet, and relatively hard when dry. Clay also has elasticity—that is, the ability to regain its original form and dimensions when an applied load that has caused deformation is released. Clay, compared to sand, is relatively impermeable to water.

MUD: Sand, clay, and vegetable and animal matter with water, forming a soft, plastic, and sticky material.

SILT: A finely divided sedimentary material deposited from running water. It consists of sand, clay, and vegetable matter.

QUICKSAND: Sand mixed with water, forming a mass which yields easily to pressure and sucks down any object resting on its surface. Any uncemented sand, when subjected to the action of moving water, will move; thus any sand moving as the result of the action of water becomes a quicksand.

Other Soils

In addition to the soils defined, other soils are often mentioned in the building field. These are as follows:

DIRT: Word loosely used to describe any earthy material.

EARTH: Material capable of supporting vegetable life and generally limited to material containing decayed vegetable or animal matter.

LOAM: Earthy material containing a large proportion of vegetable matter.

PEAT: Compressed and partially carbonized vegetable matter.

SOIL: Earthy material suitable for growing plant life.

HUMUS: Earthy material containing a large proportion of decayed vegetable matter.

TOPSOIL: Earthy material capable of supporting vegetable life and generally limited to material containing vegetable or animal matter in large quantities.

SUBSOIL: Earthy material not capable of supporting vegetable life.

ALLUVIAL SOIL: Sand and clay deposited by flowing water, especially along the river bed.

TABLE 2-1 *Allowable bearing capacities of various foundation beds, in tons per sq. ft.* *

Hard rock	80
Loose rock	20
Hardpan or hard shale	10
Gravel and sand, well cemented	8
Gravel	6
Coarse dry sand	4
Hard clay	4
Fine dry sand	3
Sand and clay, mixed	2
Wet sand	2
Firm clay	2
Soft clay	1

*Figures given here should be considered as somewhat arbitrary maximums and should be checked by subsurface investigations in actual practice.

Effect of Soil on Size of Footings

Table 2-1 summarizes the allowable bearing capacities of various foundation beds. On the basis of these figures, we can now examine the relation between type of soil and size of footings.

The purpose of footings of buildings is to distribute the concentrated loads from columns, piers, or walls over a sufficient area of the soil so that they will not cause objectionable settlement. All foundations, except those on solid rock, will settle to some extent. Slight settlement is of no consequence provided the settlement is uniform, but uneven settlement of foundations may cause serious cracks in floors and walls.

Table 2-2 gives the weights of commonly used building materials.

Footings for Lightweight Buildings

Footings under foundation walls distribute the weight of the walls and buildings over a larger ground area, as shown in Figure 2-2. In lightweight construction, the thickness of the footing should be not less than 8 in., and generally 12 in. is used. Its projection on each side of the wall should be at

FIGURE 2-3 *Footing for stone walls*

least 6 in. and not more than one-half the thickness of the footing, in order to avoid undue bending moments and shearing or punching stresses. Footings may extend more than one-half the thickness of the footing when a larger ground area is required to support the loads, provided the footings have reinforcing.

The formula for finding the required number of square feet or area of the footing is *load divided by soil-bearing capacity.* Suppose a load of 40 tons per square foot were imposed on hardpan that has a bearing capacity of 10 tons per square foot—the size of footing would be calculated thus:

$$\frac{\text{Load}}{\text{Soil-bearing capacity}} = \frac{40}{10} = 4 \text{ sq. ft.}$$

EXAMPLE: Calculate the size of a plain concrete footing (Figure 2-3) under a masonry wall 2'-0" thick, bearing a load of 16,000 lbs. per lin. ft. The soil is firm clay that has a bearing value of 2 tons, or 4,000 lbs. per sq. ft.

$$\frac{\text{Load}}{\text{Soil-bearing capacity}} = \frac{16,600}{4,000} = 4 \text{ sq. ft.}$$

The footing must, therefore, be 4'-0" wide, giving a projection of 1'-0" on either side of the 2'-0" wall. Because the projection should not exceed one-half the depth of the footing, the footing will be 4'-0" wide and 2'-0" deep.

FIGURE 2-2 *Footings for foundation walls*

TABLE 2-2   *Weights of building materials*

Material	lbs. per cu. ft.	lbs. per sq. ft.	Material	lbs. per cu. ft.	lbs. per sq. ft.
Brickwork	120		Joists		
			2 X 8 @ 20″ o.c.		2
Cement finish	144		2 X 8 @ 14″ o.c.		3
			2 X 10 @ 12″ o.c.		4
Portland cement	94		2 X 10 @ 18″ o.c.		3
			2 X 12 @ 12″ o.c.		5
Cinder fill	60		2 X 12 @ 16″ o.c.		4
Concrete	108		Partitions		
Concrete plain stone	144		2″ clay tile,		
Reinforced	150		non-bending		16
			3″ clay tile,		
Ceilings			non-bending		18
Lath and 3/4″ plaster		8	4″ clay tile,		
Suspended metal lath			non-bending		20
and 3/4″ plaster		15	6″ clay tile,		
			non-bending		28
Floors			8″ clay tile,		
25/32″ hardwood finish		4	non-bending		34
3/8″ hardwood finish		2	10″ clay tile,		
25/32″ softwood under			non-bending		40
flooring		3	4″ structural clay tile,		
Terrazzo finish	144		load-bearing		22
Floor tile	144		2″ Hollow gypsum		
			block		10
			Gravel (dry)	105	
			Insulation		
			(loose fill)	10	

Slab and Pier Footings

When girders are supported on a wall, it often becomes necessary to thicken the wall and footing in order to support the concentrated load. The thickening forms what is known as a pier, as shown in Figure 2-4.

The additional areas required on each side of the wall together with the footing area for the wall lying between them should be arranged as a square around the center of gravity of the pier. The side of the square may be found from the following formula:

$$I = \frac{b}{2} + \sqrt{A + \left(\frac{b}{2}\right)^2}$$

in which

    I = side of square
    b = width of wall footing
    A = required area of pier footing

EXAMPLE: See Figure 2-4. A wall 2′-0″ thick has a footing 4′-0″ wide. A pier in the wall carries a con-

centrated load of 240,000 lbs. per sq. ft. The allowable bearing capacity of the soil is 8,000 psf (pounds per square foot). Find the size of the square footing for the combined pier and wall.

PIER AND WALL WITH FOOTING

SECTION A-A

FIGURE 2-4   *Footing for pier and wall*

$$A = \frac{240,000}{8,000} = 30 \text{ sq. ft.}$$

$$I = \frac{b}{2} + \sqrt{A + \left(\frac{b}{2}\right)^2}$$

$$I = \frac{4}{2} + \sqrt{30 + \left(\frac{4}{2}\right)^2}$$

$$I = 7.83$$

The length of the side of the combined square footing for wall and pier is 7.83 ft. or about 7'-10".

Frost Line

The National Building Code requires that footings be placed at least 1'-0" below the frost line. Frost line levels vary in different parts of the country, from 0 ft. to 6 ft. deep. In Chicago, the required footing depth is 4'-0" because the frost line can penetrate to a depth of 3'-0".

Table 2-3 shows the required depths of footings for different areas throughout the United States.

TABLE 2-3   *Footing depth required by building code*

Location	Below Grade
Atlanta, Ga.	1'-0"
Baltimore, Md.	3'-0"
Boston, Mass.	4'-0"
Chicago, Ill.	4'-0"
Jacksonville, Fla.	1'-0"
Milwaukee, Wis.	5'-0"
New York, N.Y.	4'-0"
Omaha, Neb.	3'-0"
St. Paul, Minn.	4'-0"
Seattle, Wash.	1'-6"

TECHNICAL INFORMATION ON SOIL TESTS

The type of soil test used depends on general information concerning water table, geographical location and topography, but especially on the size of the building and the loads, as well as information obtained about the conditions encountered when adjoining buildings were constructed.

Of all the methods listed, the test pit and the loading platform give immediate and sufficient answers to permit one to begin designing the footings for the building. All the other methods can be categorized as "test borings" in general terms.

OPEN TEST PIT FOR VISUAL INSPECTION OF SOIL

FIGURE 2-5   *Open test pit*

These are more complicated methods for unknown terrain and are described in detail, along with the required log of test borings, under the Supplementary Information section.

Test Pits

This method (Figure 2-5) is one of the simplest and probably the best for determining the nature of the soil because it makes possible the visual inspection of the soil layers, the actual conditions that will be met in building operation, and the compactness and the water content of the soil. It also provides access to the pit for inspection and for obtaining undisturbed samples for lab investigation.

Loading Platform

Loading platform tests are made to assist in determining the soil's safe bearing capacity. When it is not known to what extent the supporting power of a given soil varies with the area subjected to the unit load, and tests on small areas (test pits) are not a reliable guide for the safe load on large areas, loading platform tests are performed.

The loading platform (Figure 2-6) consists of a vertical timber or post which carries a platform to receive the test load, and which has four horizontal guys at the top to keep the post in a vertical position. The bottom of the post forming the loading area should be 24 in. × 24 in., making an area of 4 sq ft. The platform should be concentric with the post and as close to the bottom of the post as practicable; it may be loaded with pig iron, cement or sand in bags, or any other convenient material.

FIGURE 2-6 *Loading platform*

TESTING PROCEDURE: Apply sufficient load uniformly on platform as shown in Figure 2-7 to produce a center load of four times the proposed design load per square foot

$$\text{Center load} = \text{Load on platform} \times \frac{B}{A + B}$$

Read settlement every 24 hrs. until no settlement occurs in 24 hrs. Add 50% more load and read settlement every 24 hrs. until no settlement occurs in 24 hrs. Settlement under the proposed load should not show more than 3/4 in. Increment of settlement under 50% overload should not exceed 60% of settlement under proposed load. This is

15

FIGURE 2-7 *Overload added to platform*

shown in Figure 2-8. If the above limitations are not met, repeat the test with a reduced load.

Sample Problems

PROBLEM 1: Assume a 12,000-lb (6-ton) load on platform

  A = 5 ft

  B = 8 ft (see Figure 2-6)

Find center load:

$$\text{Center load} = \text{Load on platform} \times \left(\frac{B}{A + B}\right)$$

$$\text{Center load} = 12,000 \times \left(\frac{8}{5 + 8}\right)$$

$$= 12,000 \times 0.615$$

FIGURE 2-8 *Settlement with overload*

16

Simplify by using 0.6, thus

$$\text{Center load} = 12{,}000 \times 0.6$$
$$= 7200 \text{ lbs.}$$

If 7200 lbs. are carried by 4 sq. ft., logically then 1 sq. ft. carries 7200/4 = 1800 lbs. This 1800 lbs. is the design load of the structure per sq. ft., which means that the bearing capacity of soil tested is 1800 lbs. per sq. ft.

PROBLEM 2: Assume a soil-bearing test is to be made for a design load of 36,000 lbs.: find (a) the center load, (b) the load on platform, and (c) the dimensions of the platform.

(a) Find the center load:

Assume A = 5 ft., B = 8 ft.

$$\text{Center load} = 4 \times \text{design load}$$

$$\text{Center load} = 4 \times 36{,}000 = 144{,}000 \text{ lbs.}$$

(b) Find the load on platform:

$$\text{Load on platform} = \frac{\text{Center load}}{\dfrac{B}{A+B}}$$

$$\text{Load on platform} = \frac{144{,}000}{0.6}$$

$$= 240{,}000 \text{ lbs.}$$

(c) Find dimensions of platform:

Assume the platform is to be loaded with pig-iron blocks, 1 cu. ft., each weighing approximately 477 lbs. The total number of blocks on the platform will be:

$$\frac{240{,}000}{477} = 503 \text{ blocks}$$

For safe loading, the blocks on the platform should not be stacked higher than the length of the platform, including the overload.

EXAMPLE: Assume a platform of 15 ft. × 15 ft. The area is 225 sq. ft., which will take 225 blocks in one layer on the platform. Two layers will take 450 blocks, with a third partial layer of 53 blocks, making a total of 503 blocks, 3 ft. high. With a 50% overload, the blocks will not exceed a stacked height of 15 ft. This size platform can be satisfactory.

If a platform of 10 ft. × 10 ft. were considered, each layer would take 100 blocks. Total height would be 6 ft. A 50% overload would require another two layers, the total height at this point not exceeding a height of 10 ft., the dimension of the platform. The platform is, therefore, also considered satisfactory.

Log of Test Borings

Most urban areas require test borings as part of the building code requirements. When preliminary designs of the building have been finalized, the architect, through the structural engineers, will make a diagram showing where test borings are to be made (see Figure 2-9). The test boring report, known as the *log of test borings* (see Figures 2-10 and 2-11), gives the architect and structural engineer the necessary information to design footings, piers, foundations, etc., for the building and also to determine the depth of cellars or basements and whether the entire foundation has to be waterproofed or only dampproofed.

Test boring reports should give complete information regarding all holes that were made, including also those that were started and then abandoned. The report may be given in the form of a log, showing the location of the holes that were made on the plot plan, the starting elevation of each hole or boring, the depths at which the various strata of soils and rock are encountered, the depth of ground water, and the presence of fill or other materials. The borings should be made to a reasonable depth below the contemplated footings so that the true nature of the soil on which the footings are to rest is known.

Soil-bearing logs are often included on the contract drawings so that the contractor cannot ever claim that information was withheld.

FIGURE 2-9 *Plot plan showing location of test borings*

FIGURE 2-10 *Log of test borings*

FIGURE 2-11 *Log of test borings (cont.)*

18

REVIEW EXAMINATION

1. Undisturbed rock masses forming part of the original rock formation is the definition of what?

2. What is the definition of loose rock?

3. Detached rock particles 1/4 to 3 in., rounded and waterworn, is the definition of what?

4. Sand is defined as rock particles smaller than what size?

5. What is defined as sand, clays, and other materials resulting from the disintegration of rock masses?

6. A coherent mixture of clay with sand, gravel, and boulders is the definition of what?

7. One square foot of solid sound rock supports how many tons?

8. The bearing value of hardpan is how many tons?

9. The soil that supports 4 tons is what?

10. Name the soils that support from 10 to 80 tons per square foot.

11. What is the definition of gravel?

12. Name at least three methods by which soil can be tested for its bearing capacity.

13. What are cribbing blocks used in connection with?

14. The center load is equal to what?

15. The design load is the load of what in sq. ft.?

16. What is the center load when the load on the platform is 12,000 lbs.? (Distance A = 5 ft.; distance B = 8 ft.)

17. In the above problem, one cribbing block carries how many pounds?

18. If the load on the platform is 12,000 lbs., what is the load on the platform with the overload?

19. Apply a sufficient load on the platform to produce a center load of how many times the proposed design load; add 50% overload and read settlement every how many hours until no settlement occurs in how many hours.

20. Settlement under load on platform should not show more than a settlement of how many inches?

21. Settlement under 50% overload should not exceed what percent of settlement under proposed load?

22. If the above limitations are not met, the test should be repeated with what load?

23. When test borings are made, what is submitted to the architect?

24. If the soil is to be tested to safely withstand a design load of 10 tons, what load should be placed on the platform? (Assume A = 5 ft., B = 8 ft.)

ASSIGNMENT

1. Draw a sketch showing how reinforcing rods are used in footings.

2. Draw a sketch showing a pier in a foundation wall.

3. Prepare a sketch symbolizing the following: (a) hardpan, (b) gravel, (c) coarse wet sand, (d) soft clay.

4. Prepare a sketch, plan, and elevation of the loading box or platform.

5. Make a sketch of a building on a piece of property and locate by dimension where you want test borings to be made.

SUPPLEMENTARY INFORMATION

Sounding Rod

The sounding rod test is used not to bring up soil samples, but only to determine the elevation of sound rock and the approximate length of piles that may be required. A sounding rod is usually in the form of a solid steel rod or pipe, the pipe being driven in lengths of about 5 ft. and provided with a point at the lower end. Driving is often done by hand, occasionally with a hammer operated by a gasoline engine.

Provided that boulders or other obstacles are not mistaken for ledge rock, sounding rods may have a useful but limited application for the purpose of determining the depth to rock or other bearing, such as gravel. The results of such tests, however, should not be relied upon except in special cases where the character of the soil is already known and the only object of the investigation is to determine the depth to a firm stratum at various points upon the site. For example, sounding rods are used where land has been filled and only the depth to the firm bearing soil has to be determined.

Auger Boring

The auger boring test is designed to bring up soil samples from shallow foundations in sand and clay, or any other soil that will stick to the bit of the auger, for removal. Auger borings are made with a 2 or 2-1/2-in. auger fastened to a long pipe which is encased in a larger pipe. After a number of turns, the auger is removed, bringing up samples of the soil.

Such borings give a fairly good description of the types of soil, such as rock, boulders, or hardpan containing rock. Auger borings are most practical when used in sand or hard clay, but are difficult to use in coarse gravel and soft clay; they are not practical for depths exceeding 18 to 24 ft.

Wash Boring

This method is used to bring up both dry and wet samples. It is not as efficient as other methods, because the soil that is brought up is thoroughly mixed, one layer with another. It is useful, however, in locating bedrock and when the material is too compact for good results with an auger.

Wash borings are made with a pipe, 2 to 4 in. in diameter, driven into the soil and containing a smaller jet pipe through which water is forced. The flow of water washes the material at the bottom up to the surface, where it is collected and tabulated. The finer materials, such as clay, sometimes disappear in the washing and the heavier materials separate from each other, thus reducing the dependability of the samples. Wash borings may also be stopped by boulders which are then sometimes mistaken for bedrock. Wash borings can penetrate all other materials, however, and can be carried downward 100 ft. or more, and are often sufficiently reliable.

Dry Sample Boring

This method employs a pipe forced down into the soil. A smaller pipe, which is inserted into the larger pipe, has a sampling spoon at the bottom instead of a drill. The spoon is driven down and the pipe is lifted for the sample (see Figure 2-12). The contents of the 2-in. pipe are removed and placed in a jar or bag for laboratory testing. Samples of soil are usually taken every 5 in. by the dry boring method. Boring tests must show the nature of the soil in at least one location for every 2500 sq. ft. of building area (see Figure 2-9).

Rock Drilling

This method is necessary when rock is encountered in order to make certain that the boulder or thin layer of rock is not mistaken for bedrock. This means that the rock must be drilled for some distance until the core sample discloses bedrock. Core samples are placed in flat metal or wood containers (see Figure 2-13) and brought to the testing laboratory.

Core borings, also known as diamond drill borings, are more costly than other methods of testing but are the most dependable. They can penetrate to great depths, through all materials including rock, and bring up complete cores or cylinders of the material through which they pass. Books on soil mechanics or soil engineering may be

FIGURE 2-12   *Dry sample boring*

FIGURE 2-13　　*Rock core samples*

consulted for a more detailed description of how these tests are performed and the equipment that is used.

Ground Water

Below a certain level all soil is saturated with ground water. This level is often called the water table; it roughly follows surface contours but may be lowered by dry seasons, by pumping, or by covering the surface with buildings and pavements.

FIGURE 2-14　　*Waterproofing membrane*

Where there is any possibility of an actual hydrostatic head occurring at the level of the bottom of the floor slab, provisions must be made to relieve or resist the resulting pressure, and an appropriate type of waterproofing installed (see Figure 2-14).

3

UTILITIES AND SITE PREPARATION

This chapter deals with utilities and site excavation in that order, since planning to meet the utility needs of the project, be it large or small, must precede excavation. Public and private utilities for urban, suburban and rural areas are included. A typical plumbing drainage system is described with definitions of the various parts of the system. Site preparation entails the removal of old buildings, the installation of the utilities for the new structure, and excavation, which includes both the general excavation for cellars or basements with possible ground water conditions, as well as the trench excavations required for the utilities. The protection of adjoining structures that may require shoring and underpinning is also considered.

TECHNICAL INFORMATION ON UTILITIES

The phrase "public utilities" means the services that are supplied to the consumer by private utility companies, by the various departments of the city, town, and community, or, in some areas, by federal agencies for electrical power such as the Tennessee Valley Authority (TVA). Such services include (1) sewage disposal and storm-water drainage system, (2) supply of potable water, (3) gas for heating and cooking, (4) electricity for lighting, heating, and other uses, and (5) telephone service.

Figure 3-1 shows the typical utilities located within the street in an urban area. The house sewer lines from the various buildings connect to the main sewer within the center of the street. The water main is usually located 9 ft. from the curb and 4 ft. deep, while the gas main is usually 6 ft. from the curb and 3 ft. deep. Electrical conduits are also provided for electricity and telephone lines. There is a separate water system for fire hydrants.

Rainwater on sidewalks and on streets flows along the curb and is conducted into a catch basin which, in turn, may be connected to the public or main sewer. The main sewer then is known as a combination storm and sanitary sewer system. The storm sewer may, in certain areas, be independent of the sanitary sewer and therefore drains into its own piping system within the street.

Public Utilities in Suburban Areas

Telephone and electrical lines are carried either by poles above ground as shown in Figure 3-2 or by conduits in the street. Public main sewers may or may not be provided. If no main sewer exists, private sewer systems such as septic tanks with disposal fields or leaching pools are required for each home or other type of building.Gas and water supplies are usually located in the streets. A separate water system is provided for fire hydrants. Rainwater on sidewalks and streets flows along curbs and is conducted into a catch basin which,

FIGURE 3-1 *Typical urban (city) public utilities*

in turn, feeds into a storm drain which feeds to open drainage basins.

Rural Utilities

Utilities are usually limited to electricity and telephone lines carried by the electric or telephone poles (see Figure 3-3). In the rural home or other type of building, the owner must provide the sewer system—a septic tank with either one or more leaching pools or a subsoil disposal system.

WATER: The owner must also obtain an adequate supply of water. To obtain water in a rural area, as a rule a deep well must be driven, at a cost based on so many dollars per foot, to yield a required water capacity based on the nature of the project. In other words, a well must produce so many gallons per minute during continuous pumping for a minimum of 24 hours, and the water must meet tests for purity. Once these requirements are met, a water storage tank, either under air pressure or elevated sufficiently to obtain pressure by gravity, is installed. In either method (air pressure or gravity), the water from the deep well is pumped to the storage tank by electricity or wind power.

OTHER NEEDS: For cooking, bottled gas, wood, coal, electricity, or some combination of these methods is used. For heating, the occupants may use fuel oil, coal, wood, bottled gas and/or electricity, plus various types of solar and other energy collectors, depending upon local climate conditions and the availability of various systems.

The Typical Plumbing Drainage System

Figure 3-4 shows a typical plumbing drainage system within the building that conducts the sewage and the waste water to the public sewer or to a private sewage disposal system. This arrangement of the piping is typical for both large and small buildings whether urban, suburban, or rural. The system of pipes, fittings, and fixtures may be listed and defined as follows:

1. House sewer
2. House trap
3. Vent for house-trap fresh air inlet (abbreviated as F.A.I.)
4. House drain
5. Soil stack

FIGURE 3-2 *Typical suburban public utilities*

NO SEWER, WATER, GAS, STORM DRAINS, NOR FIRE HYDRANTS

FIGURE 3-3 *Typical rural utilities*

6. Waste stack
7. Branch line
8. Fixture trap
9. Fixtures
10. Vent lines

HOUSE SEWER: That portion of pipe leading from the house to the public sewer or private sewage disposal system (see Figure 3-5).

HOUSE TRAP: A device, fitting, or assembly of fittings installed in the building drain to prevent sewage gases from entering and circulating through the building drainage system inside the building (see Figure 3-6).

FRESH AIR INLET: Required on all plumbing drainage systems where a house trap is used (see Figure 3-6). The fresh air connection is made immediately behind the house trap; its other end

FIGURE 3-4   *Typical plumbing drainage system*

FIGURE 3-5   *The house sewer*

FIGURE 3-6   *The house trap*

is carried to the outside air. Its purpose is to prevent the breakage of the house-trap seal through a syphoning action.

HOUSE DRAIN: That part of the lowest piping of the drainage system which receives the discharge of soil, waste, and other drainage pipes inside the walls of the building and conveys such discharges to the house trap and thence to the public sewer or private sewage disposal system (see Figure 3-7).

SOIL STACK: The vertical pipe that receives the discharges from a water closet.

WASTE STACK: The vertical pipe that receives only liquid wastes as from a lavatory, tub, shower, or sink.

BRANCH LINE: A part of the piping system that connects to a fixture.

FIXTURE TRAP: A fitting or device designed and constructed so as to provide, when properly

vented, a liquid seal that will prevent the back-passage of air from the drainage system without materially affecting the flow of the sewage or waste water.

FIXTURES: Lavatories, sinks, water closets, bathtubs, shower stalls, urinals, etc.

VENT LINES: That part of the drainage system consisting of piping installed to permit adequate circulation of air in all parts of the sanitary drainage system and to prevent trap syphonage and back pressure.

House sewer connections for urban, suburban, and rural areas may be such as shown in Figure 3-8.

What Makes A Good Plumbing Drainage System?

The principal requirements of a good plumbing drainage system may be summarized as follows:

1. It must carry the spent and waste water rapidly away from the fixtures;

FIGURE 3-7   *The house drain*

FIGURE 3-8   *House sewer connections*

2. The passage of air, gas, odors, and vermin from the sewer into the building must be prevented;

3. The drainage pipes must be air-, gas-, and watertight.

4. The system must be so installed that slight movements or vibrations of the building, piping, or fixtures will not cause leakage.

The *septic tank disposal system*, shown in Figures 3-9 and 3-10, does not permit solid matter to enter the soil. Its primary function is to hold the sewage without leakage, to allow thorough digestion of the solid matter, and to retain suspended solids, letting only liquids (effluent) overflow into a disposal area.

The *disposal area* (see Figure 3-10) consists of field-type pipe, 4 in. in diameter, either solid pipe laid with open joints covered over with metal or tar paper to prevent fill-in by loose earth, or pipe with perforations (holes) in the bottom. The effluent liquid drains from each open joint or through the perforations and is purified by the microbes in the soil. Porous soil makes the best disposal area.

TECHNICAL INFORMATION ON SITE PREPARATION

The first step in the construction of a building is to prepare the site or property on which the building is to stand. Existing old buildings may need to be demolished and removed from the site, including their footings and foundation walls. Existing sewer, gas, and water lines are cut off and capped, and electric power lines disconnected or, if necessary, entirely removed. Existing trees and shrubs that are to remain on the site should be protected while construction work is in progress.

Figure 3-11 illustrates a plan and section of a site on which a proposed new building, outlined in dotted line, is to be erected. The smaller existing building must be removed because it now occupies the space of the proposed new building. Water, gas, sewer lines and electric power serving the existing building must be removed because the new building will require much larger pipes for water, gas, and sewer lines, and it will require greater electric service.

FIGURE 3-9 *Septic tank*

Shoring and Underpinning

A part of one wall of the new building, with footings lower than those of the adjacent building, is to be built directly against the adjacent building. Before any general excavation for the new building can be started, it becomes necessary to first lower the footings of the adjacent building to the level of the footings for the proposed new building (see Section A-A, Figure 3-11). This can be accomplished by using temporary supports such as posts, timbers, and beams, to carry the weight of the building until new and lower foundations are in place. The most frequently used types of temporary supports are shores, and for underpinning, needles or needle beams and pipe cylinders.

Shores consist of long wood posts placed in an inclined position against the wall to be supported (see Figure 3-12). The lower end of the shores rests on a wood platform with a face at right angles to the inclination of the shores. By introducing a jack, the posts or shores can be forced into close bearing against the wall. Shoring thus supports, braces, and stabilizes an existing wall while the construction of the footings and foundations of the new building are installed.

Needles for underpinning are wood or steel beams penetrating holes cut in an existing wall and supported on both sides of the wall on wood blocks or cribbing. Needle beams rest on heavy jacks (see Figure 3-13). The jacks are used to force the needle beams upward, thereby supporting the

FIGURE 3-10   *Septic tank disposal system*

wall. With such support, the old walls and footings are removed and new footings and walls at their proper levels are installed (see Figure 3-14). When this is done, the weight of the wall is then carried by the new foundation.

Pipe cylinders for underpinning are another method of support used in place of needle beams (see Figure 3-15). Hydraulic jacks, which react against the existing wall, press the sections of pipe cylinders into the ground to refusal and so transfer the weight of the wall to this new underpinning.

The final operation consists of transferring the loads of the old wall onto the new. This operation must be very carefully done in order to avoid any settlement. The usual procedure consists of bringing up the underpinning wall to within 2 or 3 in. of the bottom of the existing wall and filling the remaining space with dry-pack consisting of cement and sand with a minimum of water added. The pack is rammed into place until the gap is filled. The dry-pack has almost no shrinkage, due to the small amount of water. As soon as the entire weight of the wall has been transferred to the new sections of footings and foundations, the shoring and underpinning are removed and are replaced with new footings and foundations.

FIGURE 3-11   *Plan of building site*

FIGURE 3-12   *Method of shoring*

FIGURE 3-13   *The use of needle beams*

FIGURE 3-14   *Needle beams support wall while new foundations are installed*

Excavation

The work of excavation means the removal of all materials of every kind and description for the proper installation of the new foundation. Backfilling around the foundation walls, the spreading of additional fill to the levels indicated on the plans, and the final or finished grading and topping of the site are often included under the work of excavation. Figure 3-16 shows the work of excavation for a typical building. Excavation may be categorized and defined as follows:

REMOVAL OF TOPSOIL: After inspection of the site, if the top layer of the soil is good topsoil, it is removed by scraping the surface to the depth of the topsoil (usually about 6 in.) and depositing this material in a convenient corner of the site. When all backfilling and rough grading are completed, the topsoil is then spread over the area as a final topping for seeding, forming the finish grade. On sites where the topsoil is not worth saving, the builder is required to secure a good topsoil from suppliers of this material.

FIGURE 3-15   *The use of pipe cylinders*

FIGURE 3-16   *Excavation and backfilling*

EL. 0'-0" FINISHED
FIRST FLOOR

EL. -1'-6" FINISHED
GRADE

EL. -3'-0" EXISTING
GRADE

EL. -8'-0" FINISHED
CELLAR FLOOR

EL. -9'-4" FOOTING BASE

EL. -10'-0" FINISHED
BOILER ROOM FLOOR

UNDISTURBED EARTH

FIGURE 3-17   *Excavation levels as shown on section*

GENERAL EXCAVATION: This includes the excavation for cellars or basements, and floor levels below grade. General excavations may be made with power equipment such as clamshells, hoes,

Footings must rest on firm or undisturbed soil that will not settle under the imposed load. When general excavations are inadvertently carried to lower levels than those specified for the footings, it becomes the contractor's responsibility to fill in such excess excavation with a suitable layer of concrete (see Figure 3-18) the thickness of which is to be specified by the architect or engineer. Where soil is less cohesive or where space for excavation is limited, bracing is used to support the soil.

TRENCH EXCAVATIONS: Trenches for footings are generally excavated and trimmed by hand. This trimming is done just prior to pouring of the footings. Trenches for footings and foundations and any trenches required for the installation of sewer, water, gas and electric, and telephone conduits are dug with power equipment to the depths and widths specified.

Where the soil is not firm, trenches may require sheathing and bracing to prevent sliding or cave-in of the soil (see Figure 3-19). Planks may be

LOOSE TYPE SOIL SHALL BE SLOPED
OR MAY BE BRACED

CONCRETE FILL IF
EXCAVATION IS
CARRIED TOO
FAR

FIRM
SOIL

TRIMMING OF
FOOTING

FIGURE 3-18   *General excavation and bracing*

power shovels, or bulldozers. Specifications often state that the contractor is to excavate to the levels indicated on the plans, sections, and details, and to allow sufficient excavation around the foundation for the proper installation of the forms for the foundation walls.

The wall section in Figure 3-17 is typical of the excavation levels as they appear on the plans. The existing grade, or the level of the ground before building is begun, is shown as elevation minus three feet, written $EL - 3'-0''$. The finish or final grade is $EL - 1'-6''$ requiring a fill around the building. The minus elevations for the cellar floor and the finish boiler-room floor are indicated as $EL - 8'-0''$ and $EL - 10'-0''$ respectively. All minus dimensions are taken from a point marked $EL - 0'-0''$, which often is also the finish first-floor level.

BRACE

SHEATHING BOARDS
OR PLANKS

BRACE

PLANKS

PLANKS

METHOD OF
BRACING
TRENCH
EXCAVATIONS

METHOD OF
SHEATHING
AND BRACING
TRENCH
EXCAVATIONS

FIGURE 3-19   *Bracing or sheathing for trench excavations* installed against the excavated soil and braced. Where the soil is less cohesive, sheathing boards or planks are installed and braced on both sides of the walls for the entire length of the trench.

Where concrete columns and piers require deeper levels in order that their footings may be brought to the proper bearing soils, deep pits are excavated which may require lagging boards and bracing such as indicated in Figure 3-20. Because the lagging boards are driven into the ground similarly to piles, the process is called "sheet-piling." Sheet-piling may be of wood or steel, or a combination of both (see Figure 3-21).

FIGURE 3-20   *Method of sheet piling and bracing deep pits for columns or piers*

SHEET STEEL PILING

ARCHED-WEB STEEL PILING

DEEP ARCH STEEL PILING

FIGURE 3-21   *Types of steel sheet piling*

FIGURE 3-22   *Pumping water from excavation*

FIGURE 3-23   *The well-point system*

WATER PROBLEMS IN EXCAVATION: All excavations must be kept dry in order to make possible the installation of footings and foundation walls. After heavy rains, water collected in excavations must be pumped out (see Figure 3-22).

Wherever ground water is present and where excavations are carried below ground water and tide levels, it becomes necessary to maintain continuous pumping operations. This is accomplished by the use of well points driven into the ground around the excavation. These well points are piped together above the ground and connected to one or more pumps. By this method the water is pumped out of the ground to lower the ground water level below the depth of the excavation (see Figure 3-23).

BACKFILLING AROUND FOUNDATIONS: After the forms for the foundation are removed, the area around the walls is backfilled with a soil consisting of sand and gravel, and small rock or earth. It is deposited in layers 12 in. thick, thoroughly compacted to avoid settlement. A well-tamped backfill

exerts less pressure against the foundation walls than a loose fill (see Figure 3-24), which may cause failure of foundations, especially during heavy rains when surface water causes loose fill to become liquid and push against the walls.

EXCESS AND ADDITIONAL FILL: In preparation for the new building on the site, excess earth must be removed from the site or, when necessary, spread over areas that require fill. See the Supplementary Information for a method of computing cut and fill.

REVIEW EXAMINATION

1. Where are public utilities in an urban area usually located?

2. The water main in a typical urban area may be how many feet below the street level and how many feet from the curb?

CORRECT BACK FILL   INCORRECT BACK FILL

FIGURE 3-24   *Backfill around walls*

3. What are three other public utilities and by what agencies may they be supplied?

4. The house sewer is that portion of pipe running from the house drain and connecting to what in the street?

5. In order to prevent the back-up of gases the house trap is always filled with what?

6. The fresh air inlet protects the water seal in the house trap by not allowing what to happen?

7. What are the typical rural public utilities provided?

8. How does the soil stack differ from the waste stack?

9. The typical rural house plumbing system connects to what?

10. What does the typical suburban house plumbing system connect to?

11. When building foundations must be brought to a lower level because of adjacent excavation, what temporary supports may be used?

12. When an existing building is to be demolished, what is the first operation?

13. What is the first step taken when beginning to excavate a site?

14. The earth excavation from cellars and basements is used for what purpose?

15. The earth fill around foundations should be well-tamped to accomplish what?

16. When excavations are carried lower than called for on the plans, what must be done with the excess excavation under the footings?

17. Where the soil is not self-supporting in trench excavation, what are the trench requirements?

18. For what purpose are lagging boards used?

19. When is a well point system used?

20. What is the most suitable material for backfilling around a foundation?

ASSIGNMENT

1. Prepare a sketch of the typical plumbing system within a building. Label all pipe.

2. Prepare a sketch of a typical street in an urban area with all its utilities.

3. Sketch a typical septic tank with a disposal field.

4. Prepare a free-hand sketch illustrating the correct method of backfilling around a foundation wall.

5. Prepare a sketch illustrating a footing and foundation wall with a 4-in. concrete slab or 6-in. gravel fill. Show the finished grade 8 in. above the foundation wall. Locate the minus dimensions of the cellar slab.

6. Make a sketch illustrating bracing and sheet-piling a trench.

SUPPLEMENTARY INFORMATION

Problems of Private Sewage Disposal System

Pollution is a major concern today; private sewage disposal systems must be approved by the health and/or environmental departments having jurisdiction in the area where the building is to be constructed. The following indicates how a subsoil disposal drain system is calculated, but in general, the system must be approved before it can be installed (see Tables 3-1 and 3-2).

TEST FOR ABSORPTION RATE: Dig a test pit 12″ square by 1′-6″ deep within the future subsoil disposal drain area. Quickly fill the pit with 6 in. of water and establish time in seconds until water disappears.

$$\frac{\text{Time in sec.}}{6} = \text{Seconds required for water to drop 1 in.}$$

PROBLEM: A test pit shows 24 sec. elapsing before water disappears. What is the number of lin. ft. required for the subsoil disposal drainage field for a building having an occupancy of 16 people?

$$\frac{24 \text{ sec:}}{6} = 4 \text{ sec. required for water to drop 1 in.}$$

From Table 3-1 we can see that the soil rating is medium absorption, and from Table 3-2 we see that for 16 people the required number of lin. ft. of subsoil disposal drains is 650′-0″.

The Fixture Unit

To determine the capacity or size of a drainage and vent pipe plumbing system, a convenient commonly used method is based upon a unit called a *fixture unit*. A fixture unit has been set as a rate of discharge of 7-1/2 gal. per minute from a fixture. This is approximately the rate of discharge from one lavatory. Table 3-3 lists the equivalent fixture units of various fixtures.

TABLE 3-1   *Soil absorption ratings*

	Rapid Absorption	Medium Absorption	Slow Absorption
Seconds required for water to drop 1 in.	0 to 3	3 to 5	5 to 30

TABLE 3-2   *Length of subsoil disposal drains for number of people served**

No. of Persons Served	Linear Feet Required		
	Rapid Absorption	Medium Absorption	Slow Absorption
1–4	100	150	200
5–9	200	350	700
10–14	340	500	1000
15–20	475	650	1250

*Table based on 50 gal. of sewage per person in 24 hrs.

TABLE 3-3   *Equivalent fixture units*

Fixture	Fixture Units	Fixture	Fixture Units
Lavatory	1	Water closet	6
Kitchen sink	1½	Shower	3
Bathtub	2	Floor drain	3
Urinal	3	Slop sink	4
Laundry tray	3	Roof drainage (180 sq. ft.)	1

TABLE 3-4   *Relation of pipe sizes to fixture units*

No. of Units on Horizontal Branch	Pipe Diameter (in inches)
1	1¼
3	1½
6	2
12	2½
20	3

TABLE 3-5   *Slopes for various types of banked earth*

	Slope of Repose		
Type of Earth	Length (ft.)	Height (ft.)	Angle of Repose
Clean sand	1'–6"	1	33°–41'
Sand and clay	1'–4"	1	36°–53'
Rotten rock	1'–4"	1	36°–64'
Damp soft clay	3'–0"	1	26°–34'

Building codes give tables of maximum permissible loads for sanitary drainage piping also in terms of fixture units. For example, the size of piping in any horizontal fixture branch is controlled by the number of fixture units that drain into it. The required pipe diameter is indicated in Table 3-4.

Retaining Walls

Retaining walls are independent walls designed to hold back a bank or earth where the grade is sloped. The angle of the slope, known as the angle of repose, is largely controlled by the nature of the soil. Sand, for example, requires a slope angle ratio of 1 to 1-1/2; that is, for every 1-1/2 ft. of horizontal length, the soil rises 1 ft. of height. Other soils require different slopes, as indicated in Table 3-5.

The retaining wall in Figure 3-25 is provided with weep holes, 4 to 6 ft. apart, to drain off the water accumulated in the soil and thereby reduce the pressure against the retaining wall.

FIGURE 3-25   *The angle and slope of repose*

Banked earth slopes may also be contained by piling up stones or concrete blocks, as shown in Figure 3-26.

Examples of the various types of retaining walls used where large changes of grade occur are shown in Figure 3-27.

Computing Cut and Fill

In computing the earth excavation for a rectangular building, 12 × 22 ft., when the bottom of the excavation is to be 94.5 ft., refer to Fig. 3-28 and proceed as follows:

Find the difference in height (in feet) at each corner.

CONCRETE BLOCK RIP-RAP STONE RIP-RAP

18"

2'-6"

1'-0"

SANDY SOIL 25% PEAT MOSS

STONE

BATTER 3" PER FOOT IN COLD REGIONS, 1½" PER FOOT IN FROST FREE REGIONS. SPACES BETWEEN STONES MAY BE FILLED WITH TOP SOIL AND PLANTS, IF DESIRED.

FIGURE 3-26 *Banked earth slopes supported by concrete blocks or stone*

WOOD CRIBBING
(CONCRETE CRIBBING IS AVAILABLE)

FIGURE 3-27 *Types of retaining walls where large changes of grade occur*

FIGURE 3-28 *Computing earth excavation*

(A)	(B)	(C)	(D)
102.5 ft.	102.2 ft.	98.8 ft.	100.4 ft.
− 94.5 ft.	− 94.5 ft.	−94.5 ft.	− 94.5 ft.
8.0 ft.	7.7 ft.	4.3 ft.	5.9 ft.

Add these figures and find the average.

$$8.0 + 7.7 + 4.3 + 5.9 = 25.9 \div 4 = 6.48 \text{ ft.}$$

The volume equals the average height multiplied by the area of the excavation and divided by 27 to arrive at cubic yards.

$$V = \frac{6.48 \times 12 \times 22}{27} = 63.36 \text{ cu. yds.}$$

4

FOOTINGS AND FOUNDATIONS

INTRODUCTION

The weight of a building is transferred through foundations, piers, and columns onto footings which must be of sufficient size and type to meet the bearing capacity of the soil. This chapter covers the various types of footings and foundations frequently used in building construction, with particular attention to the details of reinforced concrete piers and to footings for supporting steel columns. The use of pilings with concrete footings where the soil has a low load-bearing capacity is also examined.

TECHNICAL INFORMATION

FOOTINGS: The fundamental supporting elements designed to carry the total weight of the building. They must be constructed upon undisturbed (virgin) soil and they must be calculated to support the load upon whatever type of soil is found on the site. They must always be below the frost line, otherwise the alternate expansion and contraction of the earth during freezing and thawing may heave the footing, the foundation wall, and the structure above.

FOUNDATION WALLS: That part of a building which is located between the footing at the bottom and the supports of the floor nearest the grade at the top. Foundation walls provide (a) protection against water and frost penetration, (b) lateral support for the enclosed building area against pressures exerted by the surrounding earth, and (c) the distribution of the vertical loads of the superstructure to the footings.

The loads carried by foundation walls are the *dead* loads and the *live* loads. The dead loads are those which act constantly on the foundation such as the weight of the superstructure and the foundation itself, and the live loads are those which are not constant, such as the weight of furniture and people and snow.

Dead loads are usually easily calculated by summing up the total weight of the materials used in the construction. Such loads are usually assumed to be uniformly distributed over the length and thickness of the foundation wall.

Loads that are variable, moving, or periodic such as wind, impact forces and earthquakes are the live loads. The kind and magnitude of live loads acting on a structure differ according to locality, occupancy, and other factors. Building codes specify minimum live loads which may be used in sizing foundation walls and footings.

PILES: Vertical supporting members driven into the ground to help bear the vertical load of any structure resting upon it. The basic principle is that any length of material driven into any substance other than water develops friction along its length. It is this friction that provides support. The total friction developed by the piles in the soil should always be greater than the load imposed upon the footings at the top of the pile. Piling therefore is one method of increasing the load-carrying capacity of any type of soil to the degree required for a structure.

Types of Footings

MAT FOOTING: This serves as a foundation for the entire building; i.e., it is both footing and foundation wall (see Figure 4-1). Made of reinforced concrete, it acts as one unit, distributing the building loads over its entire area. Because of its proximity to the ground surface, it is generally used in areas where there is no freezing.

RAFT OR BOAT FOOTING: This type (see Figure 4-2) is used in areas where quicksand, muck, or silt are the bearing soils. It is made of reinforced concrete and, most important, its construction must be watertight. Its size is dictated by the total building load in relation to displacement of the muck and silt upon which it rests.

REINFORCED CONCRETE SLAB ACTS AS ONE UNIT AND DISTRIBUTES BUILDING LOADS OVER THE ENTIRE SURFACE

FIGURE 4-1   *Mat footing*

FIGURE 4-2   *Raft or boat footing*

FIGURE 4-3   *Wall footings*

FIGURE 4-5   *Grillage footing*

WALL FOOTING: Usually made of concrete or reinforced concrete, it is designed to spread the imposed loads of a foundation wall over a larger ground area. The spread may be designed as a series of steps in a vertical or horizontal direction (see Figure 4-3).

COLUMN PIER FOOTING: This type is used under individual columns or piers. The columns may be of brick, concrete block, reinforced concrete, or steel. As in wall footings, the column footing is designed to spread the load of the column over a larger ground area. This can be done in a number of ways, as shown in Figure 4-4 for a simple and a stepped footing, and in Figure 4-5 for a grillage footing. The grillage is constructed of a series of steel beams placed adjacent and parallel to each other, with a second layer of similar steel placed at right angles. A bearing plate, which will receive the steel column, is anchored to the grillage. The entire grillage area is then encased in concrete. This type of footing is used for columns supporting very heavy loads.

FIGURE 4-4   *Column or pier footings*

STEEL COLUMN ON REINFORCED FOOTING: The concrete footing (see Figure 4-6) is reinforced with 14 @ #5 rods each way, or a total of 28 reinforcing rods. (*Note:* The #5 represents the rod diameter in eighths of an inch.) In the footing are two 3/4-inch anchors installed to receive the setting plate. The 1/4-inch setting plate is placed true and level on cement grout before the billet plate is set. Then the steel column with a billet plate welded to its base is placed on the setting plate and bolted down. Locations and sizes of reinforcings are given only for illustrative purposes. Steel column, billet plate, and footing sizes are calculated to meet the imposed loads and soil-bearing capacity.

STEEL COLUMN ON REINFORCED CONCRETE PIER OR COLUMN: The reinforced concrete column (see Figure 4-7) is shown resting on a reinforced concrete footing. Four vertical reinforcing rods in the concrete pier or column are bound with lateral ties, usually spaced 11 to 12 in. apart to keep the verticals rigid while the concrete is poured into the forms. To create a stronger bond between footing and pier or column, there are metal rods or dowels protruding from the footing that tie it to the column when it is poured. On top of the pier or column are the grout, the setting plate, and the steel column with the billet plate welded to the bottom. Reinforced concrete pier and column schedules on the steel plans give the minus dimensions; that is, the location of the top and bottom in relation to elevation 0'-0", which in most cases represents the level of the finished first floor.

CONCRETE PIER AND COLUMN REINFORCING: Reinforced concrete piers or columns may have 4, 6, 8, 10, or more vertical bars, depending on the size

NUTS AND WASHERS — — BILLET PLATE

SECTION LINE

PLAN

¼" SETTING PLATE

STEEL COLUMN

BILLET PLATE

CEMENT GROUT

3" CLEAR

14 @ #5 EACH WAY

3" CLEAR — — SECTION

2 @ ¾" ANCHORS

FIGURE 4-6   *Steel columns on reinforced concrete footing*

BOLTS AND WASHERS

FINISHED 1st FLOOR EL. ±0'-0"

STEEL COLUMN

BILLET PLATE

SETTING PLATE

CEMENT GROUT

ANCHORS

LATERAL TIES

VERTICAL BARS

PLAN OF REINFORCED CONCRETE COLUMN

-1-4"

REINFORCED CONCRETE COLUMN

DOWELS

PLAN OF FOOTING REINFORCINGS EACH WAY

-12'-8"

FOOTING

-14'-0"

REINFORCINGS IN FOOTING

FIGURE 4-7   *Steel column on reinforced concrete column on reinforced concrete footing*

42

FIGURE 4-8 *Typical arrangement of reinforcing steel in reinforced concrete columns*

FOUNDATION WALLS: The most commonly used types of foundation walls are shown in Figure 4-9. Poured stone concrete walls and concrete block walls are used for relatively light construction such as houses and smaller commercial or industrial buildings. The reinforced concrete wall, with both vertical and horizontal reinforcing rods to resist both vertical and lateral stresses, is designed for larger and heavier structures.

CORNER PIERS: Figure 4-10 illustrates two design variations for corner pier foundations that are to receive the structural steel columns. At (A) the reinforced concrete pier has its individual footing designed to carry the weights imposed. Such footings are often larger and deeper than the adjacent wall footings. At (B) the corner pier is an integral part of the foundation wall, and the footings for both wall and pier are of the same thickness. It can safely be assumed that the first type (A) can carry heavier loads than type (B).

of the column. Figure 4-8 indicates such columns with their vertical bars and lateral ties as required by the American Concrete Institute. The 4-bar column requires a single tie per set. A set occurs every 11 or 12 in. of column height.

FIGURE 4-9 *Typical foundation walls*

FIGURE 4-10 *Reinforced concrete columns at corners*

Types of Piles

WOOD PILES: Tree trunks of Douglas fir or Southern pine are driven with the small end down (see Figure 4-11, A). The diameter at the tip varies from 6 to 8 in., while the butt end is rarely less than 12 in. The pile is tapered uniformly and the wood is untreated if embedded below permanent ground-water level. Such untreated timber piles may be considered permanent if entirely embedded in soil and cut off below the lowest present or future ground-water level or if entirely submerged in fresh water. Where unfavorable conditions occur

spected and filled with concrete. Such piles are about 37 ft. in length.

METAL PIPE PILES: The piles are cylindrical shells 10 to 18 in. in diameter. The thickness of the steel shell varies from 1/4 to 1/2 in. (see Figure 4-12). Sections are sunk in 20-ft. lengths. This type of pile is usually driven to a point of refusal or to rock bottom. As it is driven down, the pipe fills with soil which is then blown out by means of compressed air. When point of refusal or rock is reached, the pipe is filled with concrete. Pipe lengths of up to 100 ft. have been used.

FIGURE 4-11   *Piles*

such as ground water containing alkali or acids, untreated piles cannot be used. Piles for these conditions are impregnated with coal tar or other preservative to stop them from rotting.

PRECAST CONCRETE PILES: These may be round, square, or octagonal, and are made up to 40 ft. in length (see Figure 4-11, B). The piles are reinforced internally to resist stresses caused by handling and driving.

CAST-IN-PLACE PILES: These are constructed by driving a steel shell into the ground by means of a heavy core called a mandrel (see Figure 4-11, C). When sufficient resistance has been obtained, the core is withdrawn. The driven shell is then in-

FIGURE 4-12   *Pipe piles*

FIGURE 4-13   *H-column pile*

FIGURE 4-14   *Pile cluster*

STRUCTURAL STEEL H-COLUMN PILES: The steel H-columns are usually driven to a point of refusal or rock bottom (see Figure 4-13). They can be driven through dense, hard earth and can support very heavy loads. The top of the steel H-column is encased in concrete and coated with a rust-inhibiting paint to about 8 in. above and 2 ft. below grade.

PILE CLUSTERS: Piles are generally driven in clusters (see Figure 4-14) specifically designed to support columns, piers, and walls. A cluster may include from 3 to 25 piles and more if necessary to meet load conditions.

STEP TAPER PILES: Two types are described here and illustrated in Figure 4-15. Pipe step taper piles (Figure 4-15, left) consist of a step taper shell upper section and a closed end steel pipe lower

FIGURE 4-15   *Step taper piles showing details of a pipe step taper pile (left) and a wood step taper pile (right)*

section. It is used where the required pile length is beyond the limits of available equipment to drive an all-shell pile.

The length of the shell and pipe sections can be varied to meet job requirements. Both pipe and shell are filled with concrete to complete the pile.

Wood step taper piles consist of a step taper shell, cast-in-place concrete upper section, and a timber pile lower section. The timber section is usually untreated and driven entirely below the permanent ground water table. The permanent concrete section extends through the zone of fluctuating water level. Several types of water-tight joints are used to connect the timber and concrete sections as shown in details B. These joints are designed to provide permanent action under the loading conditions for which they are used.

REVIEW EXAMINATION

1. What word means a structural unit used to distribute building loads to the bearing materials?

2. What are the different types of footings?

3. What are the dimensional variations of the diameter of the tips of wood piles?

4. Name two kinds of wood used for wood piles.

5. Name two types of concrete piles.

6. The steel casing for a shell pile is driven into the ground with the aid of what?

7. The diameter of metal pipe piles have what dimensional variation?

8. Sections of the metal pipe pile are sunk in lengths of how many feet?

9. After the metal pipe piles are in place and the soil inside the pipe is blown out by means of compressed air, the pile is filled with what?

10. What is the range in the number of piles in a pile cluster?

11. The setting plate receives what type of plate?

12. The setting plate is set into a bed of what?

13. What is the diameter of a #5 reinforcing bar?

14. The steel column stands plumb and true on what type of plate?

15. The base of a steel column and the billet plate are what?

16. Foundation walls may be constructed of what materials?

ASSIGNMENT

1. Prepare a sketch of a reinforced concrete column resting on a reinforced concrete footing. Place a steel column on top indicating the grout, setting plate, and billet plate. Show all reinforcing.

2. Sketch three types of piles.

3. Sketch three types of wall footings

SUPPLEMENTARY INFORMATION

Reinforcing

See Table 4-1 for standard sizes and weights and new bar designation numbers. Reinforcing rods or bars are designated by a symbol (#) and a number, for example: 4 – #2 @ 12″ OC, which means four 1/4-in. round rods at 12 in. on center.

TABLE 4-1   *Standard sizes and weights of reinforcing bars*

Former Bar Designation (in.)	New Bar Designation	Unit Weight (lb. ft.)	Diameter	Cross Section (sq. in.)
1/4 round	#2	0.167	0.250	0.05
3/8 round	#3	0.376	0.375	0.11
1/2 round	#4	0.668	0.500	0.20
5/8 round	#5	1.043	0.625	0.31
3/4 round	#6	1.502	0.750	0.44
7/8 round	#7	2.044	0.875	0.60
1 round	#8	2.67	1.000	0.79
1-1/8 round	#9	3.4	1.128	1.00
1-1/4 round	#10	4.303	1.127	1.27
1-3/8 round	#11	5.313	1.410	1.56

FIGURE 4-16   *Bar edge distance*

SPACING OF REINFORCINGS: The space between reinforcing rods must satisfy the conditions shown in Figure 4-16. When concrete is poured over the reinforcing rods within a footing, the larger particles of the aggregates must flow around and beneath the reinforcing rods so that no voids are created. Rods must be entirely surrounded by the concrete if their full efficiency is to be realized.

Edge distance of reinforcing rods is affected by aggregate size, size of bar or rod, and by moist or wet ground conditions (see Figure 4-16).

PURPOSE OF REINFORCING BARS: What is the exact function of the reinforcing in footings and foundations as shown in several illustrations in this unit? Reinforcing bars are placed near the bottom of footings and slabs and in walls near the edges of the wall. To understand the reason for the location of the bars, assume a board supported at both ends on two carpenter's horses. If a man were to stand on the board it would bend under his weight (see Figure 4-17). The bottom of the board would be in tension (pulling apart) while the top would be in compression. Similarly, a concrete footing supporting a foundation wall acts as the loaded board. The reinforcing bars, strong in tension, will not be

FIGURE 4-17   *Loaded board*

stretched, hence preventing (counteracting) the bending action of the footing. The same principle applies to a wall with vertical bars near its outside and inside surfaces—here the tensile strength of the bars prevents the loaded wall from buckling because of the downward pressures of the imposed weight of the building. A wall that would tend to buckle toward the inside because of the pressure of the earth on one side would have the vertical bars near the inside surface.

Loads imposed on concrete floor slabs require the reinforcings near the bottom of the slab. Slabs subjected to hydrostatic pressure (lifting of the slab) would require bars near the top of the slab.

Testing the Load-Bearing Capacity of a Concrete Pile

Where there is doubt as to the true carrying capacity of a driven pile, load tests must be performed on such piles. The method of testing and the equipment used is illustrated in Figure 4-18, A, B, C. The steps in erecting the equipment is outlined in the following:

LOAD TEST PROCEDURE:

1. Level and prepare subgrade in the vicinity of the test pile.

2. Position telltale extensometer, bearing plates, and hydraulic jacks concentrically over the pile head.

3. Carefully construct the load test box (see Figure 4-18, A) to provide a concentric load on the pile.

4. Load test box with sufficient soil to provide required reaction for testing.

5. Establish two reference bench marks for level readings.

6. Position reference beam on its own independent supports.

7. Attach all gages and scales as shown in Figure 4-18, B and C.

8. Give ample notification, prior to the start of the testing, to the designated representative of the building department.

9. Using the hydraulic pump, induce load onto pile through jack acting against the test box, making certain to maintain constant load at each increment (Table 4-2).

10. Record data and proceed as outlined in the Schedule of Loading.

11. A complete record of the load test shall be filed with the building department (the commissioner or other designated head).

STEEL SHELL FILLED WITH DRY MIX CONCRETE

6" x 8" TIMBERS

EARTH FILL

12" x 12" TIMBERS 20' LONG

24 WF 100 OR EQUIV. x 20'

JACKING BEAM

TIMBER CRIB (AS REQ.)

DRY MIX CONCRETE BULB

TOP OF FRANKI PILE

SEE DETAIL

BOTTOM BULB OF FRANKI PILE

(A)

TELLTALE EXTENSOMETER

EXTENSOMETER SUPPORT BEAM

JACK SCALE

JACK

PLATE

TELL-TALE SCALE

EXTENSOMETER (120° APART)

TELLTALE

(B)

THRUST PLATE

JACK RAM

JACK

VIEW "A"

JACK SCALE

TELLTALE EXTENSOMETER

EXTENSOMETER

TELLTALE SCALE

TELLTALE SLEEVE

GROUT

(C)

FIGURE 4-18   *Load test procedure*
(Courtesy of the Frankie Pile Corp.)

The test pile must be instrumented so that the movements of the base and butt can be independently determined. The extensometers must provide readings to the nearest 0.001 in. Additional settlement observations shall be taken using an engineer's level reading to 0.001 ft.

Other Typical Footings

The poured concrete footing (Figure 4-19) supports a concrete block foundation wall. The wall thickness W is equal to the thickness of the footing. The width of the footing is 2W, while the footing protrudes from the wall a distance of W/2.

The footing for a wood basement column (Figure 4-20) may be 12″ × 24″ which may support a tapered concrete pedestal. The wood, 4″ × 4″ or 5″ × 5″, is doweled to the pedestal.

Figure 4-21 shows a section of a continuous concrete footing for an exterior concrete wall. The footing is connected to the concrete slab on grade and to the concrete wall above grade by reinforcing dowels. The reinforcing dowels lap the wall vertical reinforcement 40 bar diameters or not less than 24″. The size and spacing of the reinforcing steel is determined by calculation. The depth and width of the footing depends on the soil conditions.

TABLE 4-2 *Schedule of loading*

Increment Numbers	Loading % Design Load	Actual Load	Notes
0	0	0 tons	Record initial reading of all dials, scales, and bench marks
1	50	65.0 tons	Apply first increment of load and record settlements*
2	75	97.5 tons	Apply second increment of load and record settlement*
3	100	130.0 tons	Apply third increment of load and record settlement* †
4	125	162.5 tons	Apply fourth increment of load and record settlement* †
5	150	195.0 tons	Apply fifth increment of load and record settlement* †
6	175	227.5 tons	Apply sixth increment of load and record settlement* †
7	200	260.0 tons	Apply seventh increment of load and record settlement* † ¶
5	150	195.0 tons	Reduce load to fifth increment and record readings—hold for 1 hr.
3	100	130.0 tons	Reduce load to third increment and record readings—hold for 1 hr.
1	50	65.0 tons	Reduce load to first increment and record readings—hold for 1 hr.
0	0	0 tons	Reduce load to zero and record readings; leave all dials and gages intact for 24 hrs.
0	0	0 tons	Record final readings and dismantle load test box and equipment

*Under each load increment, settlement observations shall be made and recorded at 1/2 min., 1 min., 2 min., 4 min., and each 4 min. thereafter after application of load increment, except in the instance of the total load where, after the 4-min. reading, the time interval shall be successively doubled until the final settlement limitation is reached and the load removed.

†After the proposed working load has been applied and for each increment thereafter, the test load shall remain in place until there is no measurable settlement (0.002 in. or less) in a 2-hr. period.

¶ The total test load shall remain in place at least 96 hrs., and until settlement does not exceed 0.00 in. in the last 48 hrs.

FIGURE 4-19   *Concrete footing for block wall*

FIGURE 4-20   *Footing for basement column*

FIGURE 4.21   *Reinforced concrete footing for warm climates*

Concrete Pile Caps

Figure 4-22 shows the method in which a round reinforced concrete column and footing is supported by concrete pile caps. Note that the pile caps penetrate the footing a distance of 6 in., and also note the footing dowels entering the concrete column a minimum of 2'-0".

FIGURE 4-22   *Concrete pile cap*

5

SITE AND BUILDING DRAINAGE

INTRODUCTION

This chapter deals with the drainage of water from roof areas and the ground areas surrounding the building, which includes yard and area drains, parking area drains, and subsoil drains.

TECHNICAL INFORMATION

Rainwater from roofs, ground surface water, and water from other areas must be collected and conducted to some point of discharge. In urban areas it is discharged into a storm sewer or a combination storm and sanitary sewer by means of the house drain and house sewer. In suburban areas it is discharged into storm sewers or combination storm and sanitary sewers if they are available, and if not, into underground basins which receive the rainwater and in turn slowly dissipate it into the earth. In rural areas it is either discharged directly to the ground or piped to underground basins, lakes, streams, and rivers.

Roof Drainage

There are two general methods of draining a roof: by interior ridges and valleys built into the roof, and by eave gutters under overhanging eaves. Eave gutters are used for gable roofs or other types having a steep slope and overhanging eaves such as are found on private dwellings, barns, and similar structures (see Figure 5-1). Interior ridges and

FIGURE 5-1 *Gutters for drainage of pitched roofs*

FIGURE 5-2 *Roof gutters or valleys*

valleys are used for structures with flat roofs (see Figure 5-2).

LEADERS: The water is conducted from the roof to the point of discharge by pipes called leaders which may run inside or outside the building. Inside leaders are of cast iron or wrought iron, bell-and-spigot type, and must be made gas and watertight by using hemp (oakum) and lead. Where leaders pass through the roof, the opening must be tightly flashed to prevent leakage around the opening (see Figure 5-3). Outside leaders may be any one of several types of sheet metal such as galvanized iron, copper, stainless steel, or aluminum. They are available in various standard and custom-designed shapes such as round, square, or rectangular.

SIZE OF GUTTERS AND LEADERS: The size of gutters and leaders required is governed by the area of roof to be drained and the intensity of rainfall. This of course varies in different parts of the country. Rainwater from roofs must be carried away as fast as the rain falls; therefore, the maximum rate of rainfall that occurs during heavy thunder showers must be the governing factor. In some instances a rate of fall of as much as 8 in. per hour has been recorded. Gutters and leaders large enough to carry away this amount of water must be installed.

The first step in designing a system of gutters and leaders is to locate the leaders. This may be dictated largely by architectural conditions. However, the maximum spacing recommended for leaders is 75 ft. The next step is to calculate the area drained per leader, and from this to determine the size of the leader. Authorities differ in their recommendations, which range from 75 to 250 sq. ft. of roof surface to each sq. in. of leader cross section. This difference is reflected in Tables 5-1 and 5-2. The Copper and Brass Research Association recommends that 150 sq. ft. of roof area be allowed for each sq. in. of leader area. Table 5-1 shows the relationship of size and shape (type) of leader to roof area drainage.

For semicircular sheet metal gutters under overhanging roofs, the top dimension (diameter) of the gutter is equal to the size of the leader. Other shapes should have the same cross-sectional area.

The sizes of gutters and leaders must also be correlated. Table 5-2 gives the size of each for various roof areas, as recommended in a United States Department of Commerce Report based on a rainfall rate of 4 in. per hour.

Yard and Area Drains

The purpose of yard and area drains (see Figure 5-4) is to convey the storm water as fast as it falls, thus preventing the formation of pools of water.

In paved yards such as courts, schoolyards, and other similar places, *drainage inlets* or *catch basins*, the more generally used term, are built below the surface (see Figure 5-5). The catch basin may be of brick, concrete block, concrete, or precast concrete. A screened opening in the top permits the rainwater to enter the catch basin from which it flows by drainpipe to the storm sewer, combination storm and sanitary sewer, or underground basins which disperse the water back into the

TABLE 5-1 *Roof area drained by various sizes and types of outside leaders*

Type of Leader	Size of Leader (in.)	Cross Sectional Area of Leader (sq. in.)	Roof Area Drained (sq. ft.)
Plain round	3 diameter	7.07	1060
	4 diameter	12.57	1885
	5 diameter	19.63	2945
	6 diameter	28.27	4240
Corrugated rectangular	1 3/4 × 2 1/4	3.9	585
	2 3/8 × 3 1/4	7.71	1156
	2 1/4 × 4 7/8	10.96	1644
	3 3/4 × 5	18.75	2812
	2 × 3	6	900
	2 × 4	8	1200
Plain rectangular	3 × 4	12	1800
	4 × 5	20	3000
	4 × 6	24	3600

TABLE 5-2 *Size of gutters and leaders (rate of 4" rainfall per hour)*

Area of Roof to be Drained (sq. ft.)	Size of Gutter (in.)	Diameter of Inside Leader * (in.)
up to 90	3	1 1/4
91 to 270	4	2
271 to 810	4	2 1/2
811 to 1800	5	3
1801 to 3600	6	4
3601 to 5500	8	5
5501 to 9800	10	6

*Outside leaders should be one pipe size larger.

ground. The opening must be screened in order to keep out material carried by the water such as paper, leaves, or sticks that might clog the drainpipe. All paved areas, yards, courts, etc. exceeding 15 sq. ft. should be drained into the storm or

FIGURE 5-3 *Roof drain detail*

AREA DRAIN

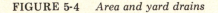

YARD DRAIN

FIGURE 5-4 *Area and yard drains*

CAST IRON FRAME

FIGURE 5-5 *Yard drainage inlet or catch basin*

combination storm and sanitary sewer, if such is available, or into the underground basins.

The capacity of yard and area drains depends on the rate of rainfall. This may be estimated at 4 in. per hr. Thus an area of 60 ft. × 100 ft. to be drained could yield the following quantity of water:

$$60 \times 100 = 6000 \text{ sq. ft.}$$

$$6000 \times 4/12 = 2000 \text{ cu. ft. per hr.}$$

$$= 33.3 \text{ cu. ft. per min.}$$

$$= 249.45 \text{ or } 250 \text{ gals. per min.}$$

Note:

$$1 \text{ cu. ft.} = 7.491 \text{ gals.}$$

Drainage within the Building

Where cellar floor drains are located below the level of the public storm or combination storm and sanitary sewers in the street, sump pumps are employed to lift the water to higher levels so that it can be drained off (see Figure 5-6). A detail of the sump pump is shown in Figure 5-7.

Floor drains in cellars must include a trap of the deep-seal type (see Figure 5-8). Such drains

FIGURE 5-6 *Sump pump installed in cellar floor*

FIGURE 5-7 *Detail of sump pump servicing floor drain or drains*

FIGURE 5-8   *Floor drain*

should be provided with a water supply by means of a faucet located not more than 3 ft. above the floor, except where other suitable means for maintaining the trap seal are provided.

Subsoil Drainage

UNDERGROUND BASINS: This type of basin is manufactured in three sections: drain ring, solid

ring, and dome (see Figure 5-9). These underground basins are used singly or in series to collect rainwater on paved areas. The water runs either into the opening at the top of the dome or is collected in a series of yard drainage inlets (catch basins) which are connected by pipes to the drainage basin (see Figure 5-10). The lower ring of the underground basin is provided with drain hole openings designed especially to let the water dissipate into the earth without allowing the holes to become clogged with earth. Drainage also takes place at the bottom of the basin.

SIZES: Drain rings and solid rings are obtainable in 4-, 6-, 8-, and 10-ft. diameters. The available heights of drain rings and solid rings are 2′–0″ and 4′–6″.

Foundation Drains

The foundations and cellar floors of buildings are frequently provided with exterior drainage systems (foundation drainage) designed to carry off ground water and surface water which pen-

FIGURE 5-9   *Underground basin*

FIGURE 5-10   *Parking area drainage*

etrate through backfill (see Figure 5-11). The simplest form of subsoil drainage for this condition consists of a line of open-joint clay tile laid along the outside perimeter of the building in gravel backfill at the level of the bottom of the footings (see Figure 5-12). The water collected by the pipes is carried into a dry well located at least 10'-0" away from the building. This system is primarily designed to drain off surface water which penetrates through backfill and would otherwise build up against the foundation walls and enter into the cellar. A dry well built of field stone, gravel, and sand is shown in Figure 5-13. This type is used in typical rural areas. Wherever one builds there are city, town, and state requirements governing building and site drainage, and plans must be submitted for official approval. The following requirements and sample problem are based upon the code requirements of a typical town in the United States.

FIGURE 5-11 *Foundation drainage*

FIGURE 5-12 *Details of foundation drain*

FIGURE 5-13 *Fieldstone dry well*

Drainage Requirements

The following standards must be used for establishing site drainage of projects submitted for approval to the planning board and town engineer:

1. All storm water shall be contained on the site.

2. Where soil conditions and all other requirements of the town engineer so justify, an underground basin shall be selected in accordance with the following formula:

   (A) *Water runoff factors:*

1.	Pavement (graded 5% or less)	0.90
2.	Pavement (graded in excess of 5%)	0.95
3.	Roof deck	1.00
4.	Seeded (graded 5% or less)	0.08
5.	Seeded (graded in excess of 5%)	0.17
6.	Other areas (minimum)	0.30

3. Computations for cu. ft. of rainfall shall be determined as follows:

   (A) Required capacity (cu. ft.) of area (sq. ft.) to be drained *times* runoff factor *times* 0.12 (1-1/2 in. of rainfall = 0.12 ft.).

4. Underground basins with drainage slots shall be designed allowing for ground absorption as follows:

   (A) Total capacity (cu. ft.) = area in sq. ft. *times* runoff factor *times* 0.12.

5. Determination for selection of underground basins may be guided as follows:

   (A) Standard $8'-0''$ diameter of basin contains 42 cu. ft. for each ft. of height. Standard $10'-0''$ diameter contains 67 cu. ft. for each ft. of height.

   (B) No credit for drainage shall be given for basin height above the level of inlet pipes.

Typical Problem

Find the equivalent drainage for the following developed land area and building.

Total capacity 12,740 sq. ft. times 0.12 ft. (rainfall) = 1528.8 sq. ft.

$$\frac{1528.8}{42 \text{ cu. ft.}} = 36.40 \text{ lin. ft.}$$

Using a $4'-6''$ high basin section, divide the linear feet by $4'-6''$, or 36.4/4.5 = 8.1, or 8 sections of $8'-0''$ diameter. Assuming a 10-ft. diameter basin which can hold 67 cu. ft. per foot of height, the linear footage of basin will be:

$$\frac{1528.8}{67} = 22.82 \text{ lin. ft.}$$

Using a $4'-0''$ high basin section, divide the linear feet by $4'-0''$, or 22.8/4 = 5.7, or 6 sections of 10-ft. diameter. The 6 sections can be installed as 2 basins of 3 sections each. This is determined by the water table.

REVIEW EXAMINATION

1. In urban areas, where may rainwater be discharged directly?

2. Eave gutters are used on what type of roofs?

3. Inside leaders must be made of what material?

4. What is the size of gutters and leaders governed by?

5. What is the recommended spacing of leaders?

6. The Copper and Brass Research Association recommends how many sq. ft. of roof area to be allowed for each 1 sq. in. of leader area?

7. What must floor drains in cellars have?

8. What is the water runoff factor for a roof deck?

9. For each 1 ft of height, an 8-ft. diameter underground basin contains how many cu. ft.?

10. For each 1 ft. of height, a 10-ft. diameter underground basin contains how many cu. ft.?

ASSIGNMENT

1. Determine the number of underground basins of 8-ft. diameter required for the following paved areas:

   12,500 sq. ft. for parking

Area (sq. ft.)	Use	Material	Runoff Factor	Drainage (sq. ft.)
6,500	Parking	Paving	0.90	5,850
6,500	Building	Roof deck	1.00	6,500
3,000	Landscaping	Seeded (graded 5% or less)	0.08	240
500	Undeveloped	Earth	0.30	150
16,500			Equivalent Drainage	12,740

7,200 sq. ft. for roof deck

2,000 sq. ft. for landscaping

SUPPLEMENTARY INFORMATION

Ground-Water Level

When the ground-water level is found to be considerably above the lowest floor of the building, it is necessary to waterproof the floor and walls and to design the structure to resist the pressure of the water (see Figure 5-14).

For each foot of height the pressure is 62-1/2 psf (pounds per sq. ft.). If the water rises 3 ft. above a basement floor, the upward pressure on the floor is 3 times 62-1/2, or 187-1/2 psf. This is far more than the weight of the usual 4-in.-thick concrete slab, which weighs approximately 45 psf—therefore the slab must be heavier and reinforced against this pressure. Correspondingly, lateral pressure is exerted wherever ground water collects against foundation walls, the pressure varying with the height of the water above the level under consideration. The foundation walls therefore must be reinforced in order to withstand this lateral pressure.

A proper method of foundation waterproofing is shown in Figure 5-15. The waterproof membrane should be protected by 1-in. cement or 1/2-in. wallboard or by 4-in. brick. The floor membrane should be placed on a leveling bed of concrete having a lightweight aggregate and of 1-in. minimum thickness.

FIGURE 5-14   *Membrane waterproofing*

FIGURE 5-15   *Detail "A" in Fig. 5-14*

Maintaining Ground-Water Level

To prevent the ground-water level from rising higher than desired, a sealed tank with a pipe gooseneck is employed as shown in Figure 5-16. The terra cotta drain tile adjacent to the footing of the building collects the ground water, which is conducted to a sealed concrete pit with a gooseneck pipe emptying into a sump pit where the water is pumped out. The location of the top of the gooseneck determines the level at which the ground water must rise no further.

Land or Site Drainage

The amount of storm water runoff is determined by the volume of water discharged from a watershed area and is measured in cubic feet of discharge per second.

The intensity and the duration of a rainfall has all to do with the time of the water runoff. Another factor is the shape of the land and its ability to absorb water plus the land's ground cover.

To compute runoff, the following formula is used:

$$Q = CIA$$

Q = Storm water in cu. ft./sec.

C = Coefficient of runoff (rainwater percentage— see Table 5-3)

I = Intensity of rainfall in inches per hour for a particular locality

A = Area in acres

TABLE 5-3   *Values of C in the formula Q = CIA*

Surface Type	Minimum	Optimum	Maximum
Roofs	0.90	0.95	1.00
Paving—concrete or asphalt	0.90	0.95	1.00
Macadam roads	0.70	0.80	0.90
Gravel	0.30	0.70	0.70
Unpaved streets	0.30	0.60	0.75
Cultivated land	0.30	0.60	0.82
Lawns and grass areas	0.10	0.35	0.60
Woodland	0.10	0.20	0.60
Pasture	0.10	0.16	0.60

FIGURE 5-16   *Method of controlling ground water level*

The value Q is the key to the sizing of pipe for the storm sewer system.

The pipes are sized in the following manner:

1. Find the capacity of the sewer pipe by computing runoff from different drainage areas, using the formula Q = CIA.

2. Select the sizes of pipe and slopes having adequate velocity for self cleaning, such as 2.5 ft./sec. minimum velocity.

3. Invert and rim elevations for pipe line must be known to determine pipe slope.

4. Determine a minimum depth for pipe lines below the frost level.

The following problem is an example of how to compute storm water runoff in cu. ft./sec. so that the pipe sizes may be determined from the Manning Formula chart (Fig. 5-17) for pipe lines numbers 1 through 5 in Fig. 5-18. Runoff is from lawns or grass areas. Pipe lines have a slope of 1%. The site is located in northeast Kansas.

LINE NO. 1:   Areas A and B = 7 acres.

$$Q = CIA$$
$$Q = 0.35 \times 2.5 \times 7$$
$$Q = 6.13 \text{ cu. ft./sec.}$$

From the Manning chart, 6.13 cu. ft./sec. @ pipe slope of 0.1% = 22″ pipe.

LINE NO. 2:   Area C = 4.5 acres.

$$Q = CIA$$
$$Q = 0.35 \times 2.5 \times 4.5$$
$$Q = 3.94 \text{ cu. ft./sec.}$$

Pipe lines numbers 1 and 2 = 10.07 cu. ft./sec.
From the Manning chart, 10.07 cu. ft./sec. @ pipe slope of 0.1% = 26″ pipe.

LINE NO. 3:   Areas D and E = 8 acres.

$$Q = CIA$$
$$Q = 0.35 \times 2.5 \times 8$$
$$Q = 7.0 \text{ cu. ft./sec.}$$

From the Manning chart, 7.0 cu. ft./sec. @ pipe slope of 0.1% = 22″ pipe.

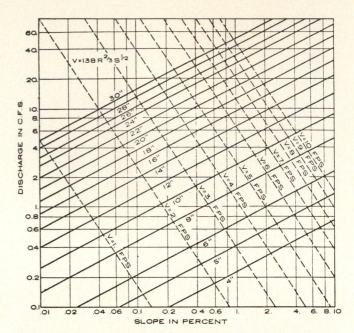

FIGURE 5-17   *The Manning Formula Chart. Size of tile drain pipes (Courtesy U.S. Dept. Agricultural Bull. 854)*

FIGURE 5-18   *Foundation or site drainage*

LINE NO. 4:   This includes pipe lines numbers 1 + 2 + 3.

$$Q = 17.07 \text{ cu. ft./sec.}$$

From the Manning chart, 17.07 cu. ft./sec. @ pipe slope of 0.1 = 30″ pipe.

LINE NO. 5:   This includes area F and lines 1 through 4.

$$Q = CIA$$
$$Q = 0.35 \times 2.5 \times 1$$
$$Q = 0.875 \text{ cu. ft./sec.}$$

Lines 1 through 5 = 17.94 cu. ft./sec.
From the Manning chart, 17.94 cu. ft./sec. @ pipe slope of 0.1% = 30″ pipe.

6

CEMENTITIOUS MATERIALS
AND CONCRETE

INTRODUCTION

This chapter deals with the study of various cementitious materials and with concrete, in which cement is a major component. Cementitious materials include lime, gypsum, cement, plastic, asphalt, and tar and their combination with other materials to form concretes, plasters, and mortars which are used for structure, finishing, paving, and bonding masonry materials and other construction units.

Concrete is composed of sand, gravel, and other aggregates held together by a hardened paste of cement and water. A study in depth of this major construction material is beyond the scope of this book. This unit deals only with the design of concrete mixtures, the effect of the quantity of water on the strength of concrete, recommended water-cement ratios, the selection of consistency, and the selection of aggregates and other materials. It should be noted here that all concrete is now mixed by weight instead of by volume, as was done formerly.

TECHNICAL INFORMATION
ON CEMENTITIOUS MATERIALS

Lime

Lime is the product resulting from the crushing of dolomite limestone, a rock consisting mainly of magnesium and calcium carbonate, and the burning of it in kilns to 2000°F., causing the limestone to break down into carbon dioxide (gas) and calcium oxide (solid). The solids are pulverized into a fine powder known as quicklime.

Quicklime can never be used as such for structural purposes; it must first be slaked in water to form a putty. During the slaking process, violent, almost explosive reactions occur in which very large quantities of heat are given off. The quicklime is marketed in paper bags, steel drums, and in bulk (see Figure 6-1).

Hydrated lime is lime that has gone through the slaking process; that is, enough water has been added to satisfy its chemical affinity for water, after which it is air-separated and the solids sifted to a fine dry powder so that 98% will pass through a 200-mesh screen. Today very little slaking of lime is done at construction sites; instead, manufacturers produce hydrated lime, which is marketed in various forms as shown in Figure 6-2. Hydrated

FIGURE 6-1 *Containers for marketing quicklime*

FIGURE 6-2 *Containers for marketing hydrated lime*

lime is used for plastering, as well as in cement mortars to increase their workability, plasticity, and water-holding capacity. The lime, further, reduces the separation or segregation of the sand and cement in mortars or plasters.

Gypsum

Gypsum is a hydrated sulfate of calcium occurring naturally in sedimentary rocks, which is used in making plaster of Paris. When heated from 325 to 340°F., it loses most of its water and is then finely ground into powder called plaster of Paris. The heating process is known as "calcining." This calcined product is used for plasters, plaster-type products and materials, fireproofers, and for slowing down the setting time of portland cement.

Cement

The materials necessary in the manufacture of cement are lime, silica, iron oxide, and alumina, which are obtained by mixing an impure clay-bearing limestone with pure limestone, or by mixing limestone with clay or shale. These ingredients are mixed in proper and closely controlled proportions. During the manufacturing process, the raw materials are ground and burned to form "clinkers." These are then cooled and pulverized to produce cement. The strength of the cement is increased with the fineness of grinding.

Portland cement finds its greatest use in building construction for making concrete and mortars. Concrete may be reinforced, cast, or prefabricated into numerous building units, while the mortars serve as the bonding agent in masonry work. When water is added to portland cement, a paste is formed which soon loses its plasticity and begins to harden. The initial set takes place within 45 min. and a final set in about 10 hrs. Portland cement continues to harden increasingly over a very long period of time.

There are eight important types of portland cement generally used in building construction:

I   Normal portland

IA   With air-entraining additive

II   Moderate portland

IIA   With air-entraining additive

III   High early strength portland

IIIA   With air-entraining additive

IV   Low-heat portland

V   Sulfate-resisting portland

Types I and IA are for general use.

Types II and IIA are characterized by slow setting and less heat generated.

Types III and IIIA are used where quick setting and early strength are required.

Type IV is characterized by very slow setting and very little heat generated.

Type V is used where ground water and soils will attack other types of portland cement.

Other important uses of portland cement are in the manufacture of asbestos-cement products, cement brick, terrazzo, and artificial stone; as a basis for paints for concrete and masonry materials; and as a plaster for exterior surfaces. Some minor uses are for grouting, pointing, floor finishes, fill for leveling, and numerous others. Portland cement is sold in bags weighing 94 lbs., and occupies 1 cu. ft. by volume. It is also sold in bulk.

Masonry cements are mixtures of portland cement with hydrated lime, silica, slag, and other additives. Because most masonry mortars are covered by patents, the exact make of the mixtures is not disclosed. There are two types of masonry mortars: Types I and II, which are available in white or gray color and in both waterproof and nonwaterproof.

Keene's cement is derived from gypsum. When gypsum is heated at a high temperature, between 1000 to 1400° F., all the water is driven off and the product, called hard-burned gypsum, is the result. By grinding and the addition of small quantities of alum, a tight, dense, water-resistant plaster is obtained.

Plastics—Synthetics

In the modern sense, plastics and synthetics can also be considered cementitious materials. They are used as adhesives, paints, and resilient flooring. When mixed with marble, cork, plastic, and other types of aggregate materials, they are used to produce seamless flooring and precast terrazzo-type flooring. Synthetics are also used with or without cement for a masonry-type high-strength mortar.

Asphalt

Asphalt is a cementitious material, dark in color, consisting of bitumens, either natural or the residue left after the distillation of crude oil. Asphalt liquifies with heat and in petroleum distillates, and it can be emulsified with water. In building construction there are many asphalt products used, such as dampproofing, asphalt shingles and siding, asphalt flooring, caulking, expansion and pressure joint material, and built-up roofing.

The most important use of asphalt as a cementitious material is when it is combined with aggregates to make asphaltic cement paving for roads, driveways, parking lots, etc., and asphalt blocks for sidewalks, paths, and terraces.

Tar

Tar is obtained from coal as a by-product from making coke for the steel industry or from the distillation of wood. Although both tar and asphalt are similarly used in building construction, tar can withstand sunlight, water, cold, and heat better than asphalt, but it does soften considerably in direct radiant heat from sunlight in summer.

TECHNICAL INFORMATION ON CONCRETE

Design of Concrete Mixtures

Two principal requirements of concrete are strength and durability—strength to perform the function of the structure and durability to resist exposure to the elements. These should be the governing considerations in the design of mixtures.

A third requirement is imposed by the fact that during placing, concrete must be workable. Still a fourth element in the design is economy. This is not in the same order of importance as strength and durability however. But a successfully designed concrete mix will achieve a proper balance between these four essentials.

BASIS FOR DESIGN OF MIXTURES: The design of concrete mixtures is based principally upon the relationship between the properties of the cement and the amount of mixing water used. A fundamental law—the *water-cement ratio*—has been established which may be stated as follows: For mixtures using sound and clean aggregates (sand and gravel or crushed rock), *the strength and other desirable properties of concrete under given job conditions are governed by the proportion of mixing water to the amount of cement.*

This principle may be more readily understood if the cement and water are thought of as forming a paste which, on hardening, binds the aggregate particles together. The strength of this paste is determined by the proportions of cement and water. Increasing the water content dilutes the paste and reduces the strength and durability of the concrete. A thin or watery paste, therefore, weakens binding power and does not form a strong or durable concrete.

The hardening of the cement-water paste results from the chemical reactions between the water and cement, called *hydration.* During this process, a certain amount of water chemically combines with the cement to become a part of the permanent solid structure of the concrete and also causes heat to be developed. In order to be complete, these reactions require time, the presence of moisture, and favorable temperatures. This total process is known as the *curing* of concrete.

To obtain plastic workable mixtures, more water is used than can be permanently (chemically) combined with the cement. There is a reason for this. During the curing process, if it is controlled correctly, the excess water will evaporate because of the generated heat, the sun, and air temperatures. Therefore, care should be taken that too much water is not lost, thereby stopping complete hydration. In order to counteract such excess loss of water, certain methods are used such as wetting down the concrete surfaces with water, covering the surface with straw, sand, or burlap, or covering with certain types of paper to keep water from evaporating too quickly. Thus, both factors—the quantities of water used and the extent and process of curing—directly affect the binding power (complete hydration) of the paste, and through it, the strength and durability of the concrete.

In view of the dependence of the properties of the concrete upon the quality of the paste, it will be seen that, as far as proportioning is concerned, the relative amounts of aggregate and cement are important only insofar as they affect workability, provided that the mixes are truly plastic and workable. Designing a concrete mix, therefore, consists of selecting the water-cement ratio that will produce concrete with the desired resistance to exposure and with the required strength, and finding the most suitable combination of aggregates that will give the necessary workability when mixed with cement and water in this ratio. Figure 6-3 illustrates the compressive strength of concrete in lbs. per sq. in. (psi) when the indicated water-cement ratios are used.

Selection of Consistency

The design of a concrete mix involves consideration of the requirements to be met in handling and placing the concrete, and the factors affecting economy. In describing the character of fresh concrete, three words are most often used: consistency, plasticity, and workability.

"Consistency" is a general term that describes the state of the fluidity of the mix: it includes the entire range of fluidity from the driest to the wettest possible mixtures. The word "plasticity" is used to describe a consistency of concrete which can be readily molded but which permits the fresh concrete to change form slowly if the mold is removed. "Workability" describes the specific concrete mix. For example, a fairly dry mix with larger aggregates can be used for a footing, and a more fluid mix can be used for a thin wall with reinforcings, yet each concrete mix has the correct workability to meet the requirements of its end use in the area in which it is to be placed in the construction of a building.

THE SLUMP TEST: This test measures the consistency of a concrete mix. It may be performed in the laboratory or in the field. The test specimen is formed in a mold made of #16-gauge galvanized metal, shaped like a cone, open at the top and bottom. The base of the cone is 8 in. in diameter, the top opening is 4 in. in diameter, and the height of the cone is 12 in. The top and bottom openings must be parallel and at right angles to the center line of the cone. The mold must be provided with foot pieces and handles as shown in Figure 6-4.

How the test must be performed: Samples of concrete for the test specimen should be taken at the mixer or, in the case of ready-mixed concrete, from the transportation vehicle during discharge. The sample of concrete from which test specimens are made must be representative of the entire batch. Such samples are obtained by repeatedly passing a scoop or pail through the discharging stream of concrete, starting the sampling operation at the beginning of discharge and repeating it until the entire batch is discharged. The sample thus obtained is transported to the place of molding of the specimen and, to counteract segregation, the concrete must be mixed with a shovel until it is uniform in appearance. The location in the construction of the batch of concrete thus sampled must be noted for future reference. As for the test itself, the mold is dampened and placed on a flat, moist, non-absorbent surface. From the sample of concrete obtained as described, the mold is filled in three layers, each approximately one-third the volume of the mold. Each layer is then rodded with 25 strokes of a 5/8-in. rod, 24 in. in length, bullet-pointed at the lower end. The strokes must be distributed in a uniform manner over the cross section of the mold and must penetrate into the underlying layer. The bottom layer is rodded throughout its depth. After the top layer has been rodded, the surface of the concrete is struck off with a trowel so that the mold is exactly filled; the mold is immediately removed from the concrete by being raised carefully in a vertical direction. The slump is measured immediately by determining the difference between the height of the mold and the height at the vertical axis of the specimen (see Figure 6-5).

The consistency is then recorded in terms of inches of subsidence of the specimen during the test, these values being known as the *slump*. After the slump measurement is completed, the side of the concrete frustum should be tapped gently with

FIGURE 6-3 *Effects of water on strength of concrete*

the tamping rod. The behavior of the concrete under this treatment is a valuable indication of the cohesiveness, workability, and placeability of the mix. A well-proportioned, workable mix will gradually slump to lower elevations as at A in Figure 6-5 and retain its original identity, whereas a poor mix will crumble, segregate, and fall apart as at B in Figure 6-5. Recommended slumps for various types of structures are shown in Table 6-1.

TABLE 6-1 *Recommended slumps for concrete*

Type of Structure	Slump in Inches	
	Maximum	Minimum
Massive sections; pavements and floors laid on ground	4	1
Heavy slabs; beams or walls	6	3
Thin walls and columns; ordinary slabs or beams	8	4

FIGURE 6-4 *Mold for slump test*

FIGURE 6-5 *Slump test*

Air-Entrained Concrete

Air-entrained concrete results when air-entraining agents are added either in the manufacturing of the cement or during the mixing of the concrete to cause millions of tiny air bubbles to develop within the entire mix.

This type of concrete was developed for road-building to counteract freezing and to withstand the salt used to melt ice. Today air-entrained concrete is used extensively in building construction because it has fine workability and cohesiveness and also because the entrained air keeps the aggregates from separating and the water from rising to the top of the concrete.

See Figure 6-6 for details on testing for air content in air-entrained concrete, and Figure 6-7 for comparative strengths of air-entrained and non-air-entrained concrete.

Selection of Aggregate Combinations

In determining the proportions of materials in a concrete mix, it is desirable to arrive at those proportions which will give the most economical results consistent with proper placement. These proportions are controlled not only by the water–cement ratio but also by the proportion of fine and coarse aggregates, type of cement, air-entraining additive and the various types of reinforcing (see Figures 6-8 and 6-9). A properly proportioned combination of well-graded fine and coarse aggre-

gate contains all sizes between the smallest and largest without an excessive amount of any one size.

Laboratory Report of a Concrete Design Mix

Shown on page 68 is a typical concrete design mix laboratory report by the director of a bureau of building design to the construction company assigned to do the job.

In the laboratory report for the 1500 psi lightweight fill, 500 lbs. of portland cement are used in 1 cu. yd. of concrete mix. Since a bag of cement weighs 94 lbs., we need 500/94 = 5.32 bags per cu. ft. of cement. To find the water–cement ratio, divide the gallons of water by the cu. ft. of cement, or

$$\frac{40.9}{5.32} = 7.7 \text{ W/C ratio}$$

Selection of Materials

CEMENT: All cement should conform to the standard specifications and test of the American Society for Testing Materials (ASTM).

FIGURE 6-6 *Instrument for testing air content in air-entrained concrete by the volumetric method*

FIGURE 6-7 *Compressive strength in 1, 5, 7, and 28 days for air-entrained and non-air-entrained concrete*

WATER: The water should be suitable for drinking unless it is known by test or experience that other waters are satisfactory. Sea water that contains salt should not be used for mixing concrete because it will corrode the steel reinforcements and chemically weaken the paste.

AGGREGATE: This word refers to an inert mineral filler used with the water-cement paste. All aggregates should consist of inert materials that are clean, hard, strong, and durable. The particles should not be covered with clay or dirt because this prevents proper bonding of the paste; it is

```
PO-105 New 30th Precinct
Station House
Contract No. 1 Gen. Const.
Concrete Design Mix
```

Gentlemen:

This is to acknowledge receipt of your letter of Feb. 23, 198- together with four (4) copies of laboratory reports No. 3534 dated Jan. 15 and Jan. 18, 198- and the water-cement ratio curves as prepared by Certified Laboratories, Inc.

This data is for the 1500 PSI lightweight concrete fill, 2500 PSI average concrete, 2500 PSI + 25% controlled, 2500 PSI + 25% pump concrete to be supplied by the concrete contractor [name of contractor] for use at the above project and will be filed with the Building Department as required by the Building Code.

	1500 PSI Ltw. Fill	2500 PSI Ave.	2500 PSI Controlled	2500 PSI Pump
One cu. yd. dryweights portland cement	500 lbs.	564 lbs.	495 lbs.	591 lbs.
Concrete sand	625 "	1205 "	1275 "	1445 "
Coarse aggregate	725 " nytrolite	1850 " (3/4" stone)	1850 " (3/4" stone)	1550 "
Water (gallons)	40.9	37.1	36.9	38.9
A.E. Agent (darex)	5.3 oz.	4.5 oz.	5.3 oz.	5.3 oz.
W/C ratio	7.7	6.18	7.01	6.19
Weight per cu. ft.	97.8	145.5	145.5	144.4
Lightweight fines	450 lbs.	-	-	-
Slump	5" ± 1"	5" ± 1"	5" ± 1"	5" ± 1"

```
Very truly yours,
Director
Bureau of Building Design
```

AGGREGATE SIZE 1.   AGGREGATE SIZE 2.   AGGREGATE SIZES 1 AND 2.

SAME AMOUNT OF WATER WHEN AGGREGATES 1 AND 2 ARE USED SEPARATELY

LESS WATER WHEN BOTH AGGREGATES ARE USED TOGETHER

FIGURE 6-8 *Aggregate size in relation to the amount of water*

important that only clean aggregates are used in concrete. The size and grading of aggregates are important from the standpoint of economy, because they have a very decided effect on the workability of the concrete and the amount of concrete that can be produced from a given volume of cement when used with a fixed proportion of water.

Aggregates passing through a No. 4 screen are known as fine aggregate, and since these comprise 20 to 40% of the volume of concrete, the fine aggregates should be tested for cleanliness, strength, hardness, and durability before they are used.

The maximum size of aggregate is governed by the nature of the work. In thin slabs or walls, the largest pieces of aggregate should not exceed

about one-fifth to one-fourth the thickness of the section of concrete being placed (see Figure 6-10).

In reinforced concrete, specifications usually limit the maximum size to three-fourths of the minimum clear spacing between reinforcing bars.

Sand and gravel suitable for concrete often are found as *bank-run gravel*—the natural mixture of sand, gravel, and stone as it comes from a gravel bank. Because bank-run gravel is rarely found in the proper mixture of sizes, it may therefore be necessary to screen it into various sizes (see Figure 6-11).

Gravel not larger than 1-1/2 in. in diameter is suitable for many types of construction. Where big stones occur in large numbers in bank-run gravel, it is necessary to screen the material first over a 1-1/2-in. screen. Material failing to pass this screen is discarded. Material passing through the 1-1/2-in. screen (8 openings to the foot) should then be passed over a No. 4 screen (4 openings to the inch). That part passing through the No. 4 screen is sand and fine aggregate, while the material remaining is 1/4 to 1-1/2 in. aggregate which is suitable for most constructions.

Crushed rock is generally used today as aggregate, because the strength of the crushed rock aggregate can be exactly controlled whereas bank-run gravel aggregates have a wide variety of strengths.

COURSE AGGREGATE (ECONOMICAL)   FINE AGGREGATE (LESS ECONOMICAL)   BIG, LITTLE AND FINE AGGREGATE (MOST ECONOMICAL)

FIGURE 6-9 *Aggregate combinations*

LARGEST AGGREGATE SIZE NOT TO EXCEED ONE QUARTER OF SLAB THICKNESS

AGGREGATE

THIN CONCRETE SLAB

AGGREGATE

SPACE BETWEEN BARS

AGGREGATE SIZE NOT TO EXCEED THREE QUARTERS OF SPACE BETWEEN BARS

#4 REINFORCING BARS 2½" O.C.

AGGREGATE SIZE BETWEEN REINFORCINGS IN FOOTING

FIGURE 6-10 *Aggregate size*

FIGURE 6-11   *Screening aggregate*

TABLE 6-2   *Types of lightweight aggregates*

Aggregate	Unit Weight lb./cu. ft.
Vermiculite	10
Perlite	9
Diatomite	31
Shale	60–76
Slag	30–60
Pumice	44–49

Lightweight concrete is characterized by lightweight aggregate, which is generally used as fill because it is light in weight, has insulating value, fire-resisting properties, and can be nailable (see Table 6-2). Depending on the type and quantity of aggregates used, lightweight concrete can develop structural characteristics, but in gaining strength it will lose its lightweight characteristics.

ADMIXTURES: Admixtures may be divided into two categories: those for mixing into concrete, and those for surface application or finish.

Concrete admixtures used for mixing into concrete include accelerators, retarders, finely divided powders, plasticizing agents, air-entraining agents, waterproofing compounds, and color pigments.

TABLE 6-3   *Types of admixtures*

Type of Admixture	Influence on Concrete or Mortar	Material Generally Used*	Major Use in Concrete and Mortar
Accelerators	Speeds up setting time	Calcium chloride	In cold weather to speed up setting time and strength.
Air-entraining agents	Produces millions of tiny air bubbles in the concrete	Rosin, stearates, beef tallow	Increases plasticity and resistance to freezing and thawing in concrete
Color pigments	Integral color	Metallic oxides	Colored floors, walks, terraces, and mortar
Inert powders	Improves workability	Powdered glass, stone, sand	Corrects deficiency in fines for coarse aggregates in concrete
Plasticizing agents	Lowers water–cement ratio, lubricates solid particles in mortar	Polyhydroxylated polymers	Makes mortar more plastic and workable
Pozzolanic powders	Controls alkali-aggregate reaction in concrete	Volcanic ashes, calcined shale and clay	Increases resistance to sulfate attack in concrete
Retarders	Slows setting of cement thereby reducing heat	Zinc oxide	In very hot weather and in massive concrete
Waterproofing	Decreases water absorption	Stearic acid	For concrete in contact with earth, such as basement slabs and foundation walls

*No attempt is made here to be all inclusive.

TABLE 6-4   *Admixtures for surface treatments*

Type of Material	Type of Surface	Major Application
Abrasive aggregate	Abrasive	Where a non-slip surface is necessary
Metallic oxides	Colored	Adds color to concrete
Zinc or magnesium fluosilicates	Hard and dustproof	Hardens and dustproofs surface
Metallic aggregates	Heavy wear	Where hardness, durability and wear resistance are necessary
Iron particles electrically grounded	Nonsparking	For areas where highly explosive or flammable materials are used or stored

Concrete admixtures used for surface applications or finishes for concrete are the following: hardeners, dustproofers, color pigments, special aggregates, sealers, abrasive materials, non-sparking materials, and fillers and patchers (see Tables 6-3 and 6-4).

The *finished* surface of concrete may be smooth, grooved, rough, polished, broomed, or given various types of pebble and stone chip finishes.

REVIEW EXAMINATION

1. What are the most commonly used cementitious materials?
2. Quicklime is the product resulting from the burning of what type of mineral?
3. What is lime that is slaked called?
4. In addition to its cementitious property, what other properties does lime contribute to mortar?
5. What is the material used to control the setting of portland cement?
6. Plaster and plaster-type products are made with what calcined mineral?
7. What is the cement that produces a hard, dense, water-resistant plaster?
8. Name the materials used in the manufacture of portland cement.
9. There are several types of portland cement. Name three.
10. The initial set of portland cement occurs in how many minutes and the final set in about how many hours?
11. Portland cement is distributed in bags containing how many cubic feet and weighing how many pounds?
12. Masonry cements are used to make what two types of mortar?
13. Plastic cementitious materials are used to produce what two types of flooring?
14. The most important use of asphalt as a cementitious material is to produce what two things?
15. What are the two principal requirements of concrete?
16. The strength of concrete is governed by what?
17. In describing the character of concrete, what three terms are most often used?
18. What does the slump test measure in a concrete mix?
19. In thin concrete slabs or walls, the largest pieces of aggregates should not exceed what fraction of the thickness of the section?
20. What do air-entraining agents add to concrete?
21. How is a concrete surface treated to make it a non-slip type?

ASSIGNMENT

1. Make sketches of six construction items that employ cementitious materials.
2. Prepare a plan and elevation scale drawing of the mold used for the slump test. Dimension the mold and label all parts.
3. In 50 words or less, describe how the slump test must be performed.

SUPPLEMENTARY INFORMATION

Special Types of Portland Cement

Portland cement is also manufactured in several other types, of which two are used extensively in building construction: *white portland cement*, waterproof or nonwaterproof, used in mortars for stonework and to produce very white concrete; and *portland pozzolanic cement*, used for hydraulic structures and in mortars to make more workable plastic mortars.

White portland cement is made by careful selection of suitable raw materials and by special manufacturing processes. Except for color, it has the same characteristics as gray portland cement and should be used in the same way. Because it is usually used where appearance is important, the forms should not be treated with grease, oil, or other materials that may cause stains.

Portland pozzolanic cement is made with portland cement and a pozzolana, a siliceous material. Various natural or artificial materials contain active silica, among them pozzola (volcanic ash), granulated slag, and pumice. Portland pozzolanic cement is produced by grinding together the portland cement clinker with the active silica until they are completely intermixed.

There are four types of portland-pozzolanic cement: type IP, type IP-A with air-entraining additive, type P, and type PA with air-entraining additive.

Portland blast-furnace slag cement has characteristics similar to portland cement types. Types IS and IS-A are similar to I and IA, Types IS (MH) and IS-A (MH) are similar to II and IIA, and Types IS (MS) and IS-A (MS) are similar to Type V.

Aluminous cement is made using bauxite, the ore from which aluminum is obtained, as the main raw material. This cement is quick setting. After 24 hrs. it has obtained the strength of normal portland which has set for 28 days. It also is resistant to salt action. Its major use is for roads, highways, driveways and parking lots exposed to severe freezing and the usage of salt in winter.

Oxychloric cement is a zinc or copper oxychloride and is used as the cementitious material to produce a very resilient, durable, seamless type of flooring.

Asphalt Pavement

When asphalt-type pavement is to be installed, the type of soil (well-drained, slightly drained, or impervious to drainage) affects the subbase course which can vary from 0 to 8 in. thick depending on the type of drainage. Subbase courses are of crushed stone or gravel, maximum size 2-1/2 in., well-rolled and tamped. Upon this subbase is placed a base course, 4 to 5 in. thick of crushed stone or gravel of 1 in. maximum size, with fine aggregate applied on the surface to fill voids. This course should also be rolled and tamped. The final finish surface is of either hot or cold asphalt, 1 to 3 in. thick, depending on the type of wear by car or truck.

Mixing Concrete

Concrete may be mixed by the following three methods:

1. Mixing completely in a stationary mixer, and transporting the mixed concrete to the point of delivery in a truck agitator or in a truck mixer operating at agitator speed in which the mix is agitated until its final deposit into the forms. This is known as ready-mixed concrete.

2. Mixing partially in a stationary mixer and completing the mixing in a truck mixer. This is called "shrink-mixed" concrete.

3. Dry-mixing (dry-batching) all the materials at the central concrete plant and continuing the mixing en route to the job in a truck mixer. (Water is added at the site before the concrete is deposited into the forms.) This is called transit-mixed concrete.

The modern transport mixing trucks are provided with water tanks and measuring devices; mixer capacities range from 1 to 10 cu. yd. maximum capacity.

The amount of mixing can increase or decrease the strength of the concrete. The greatest gain in strength is during the mixing time from 0 to 2 min.; from 6 to 10 min., there is little increase in the strength of the concrete. Figure 6-12 indicates how the compressive strength of concrete can be affected through the mixing time, as well as how the concrete strength increases after 7 and 20 days, after 3 months, and after 1 year.

CONCRETE FOR SMALL CONSTRUCTION: Table 6-5 summarizes mixtures suitable for small projects. Ready-mixed concrete for small work, packaged in

TABLE 6-5 *Suitable mixtures for various small concrete construction projects*

Type of Construction	Cement by Volume	Sand by Volume	Aggregate by Volume
Foundations and footings	1	3	5
Driveways, sidewalks, steps	1	2-1/4	3
Small floor slabs laid on earth	1	2-1/2	3

FIGURE 6-12   *Effect of mixing time on compressive strength*

paper bags, is available from building materials suppliers.

MID-TERM OR END-TERM
REVIEW EXAMINATION—CHAPTERS 1–6

1. In order to determine the bearing capacity of the soil and subgrade conditions, what must be done?

2. Who makes the feasibility study for a large building or groups of buildings?

3. The Clerk-of-the-Works is generally employed by whom?

4. Does the Clerk-of-the-Works check all the materials to be used in the construction?

5. Undisturbed rock masses that are part of the original rock formation is the definition of what material?

6. What are detached rock particles 1/4 to 3 in. in size, rounded and waterworn?

7. What are noncoherent rock particles smaller than 1/4 in.?

8. The National Building Code requires that footings be placed at least how many feet below the frost line?

9. What is compressed and partially carbonized vegetable matter?

10. What is the bearing capacity in tons per square foot for hardpan?

11. What is the bearing capacity of soft clay?

12. The depth of footings is controlled by what?

13. What is the center load for the loading platform?

14. When the 50% overload is applied to the load on the platform, the settlement must not exceed what percentage of settlement under the proposed load?

15. A platform load of 6 tons in which dimension A = 5 ft. and dimension B = 8 ft., the center load is equal to how many lbs.?

16. What is the design load equal to in problem 15?

17. Why are sounding-rod tests made?

18. Rock drilling is necessary when rock is encountered in order to make certain that the boulder or thin layer of rock is not mistaken for what?

19. What are services such as sewage disposal and drainage systems, water, gas, electricity, and telephone called?

20. Where are sewage disposal and drainage systems least likely to be found?

21. What is the portion of plumbing pipe leading from the building to the street sewer called?

22. What is the name of the vertical sewer pipe within the building that receives the discharge of a water closet?

23. A "fixture unit" has been set as a rate of discharge from a fixture at how many gallons per minute?

24. What is the rate of discharge of one water closet in terms of fixture units?

25. What are rural utilities usually limited to?

26. What is the purpose of the fresh air inlet immediately behind the house trap?

27. What is the purpose of vent lines in a plumbing drainage system?

28. In performing an absorption rate test, what must the measurements of the test pit be?

29. What is the length of a sub-soil sewage disposal drainage field serving 5 to 9 persons for a soil having a medium absorption rate?

30. When existing old buildings are to be removed for the construction of a new building, what is one of the first necessary steps?

31. What are the most frequently used types of temporary supports when the excavation of a new building is adjacent to an existing building?

32. In what position should shores be placed?

33. When bringing up the underpinning wall to within 2 or 3 in. of the bottom of the existing wall, what is the remaining space filled with?

34. What is the excavation required for the footing of a brick garden wall called?

35. When lagging boards and bracings are driven into the ground for deep excavations, what is the process called?

36. For what purpose are wellpoints driven into the ground?

37. Backfill around walls after the forms are removed must consist of what material(s)?

38. The angle of slope, known as the angle of repose, for a retaining wall, is largely controlled by what factor?

39. What angle of repose is required for a soil composed of sand and clay?

40. The retaining wall is provided with weep holes how many feet apart?

41. What is the type of footing most likely to be used where quicksand, muck, or silt are the bearing soils?

42. What is the pile that requires a steel shell known as?

43. What governs the size of gutters and leaders?

44. The capacity of yard and area drains depends on the rate of rainfall. How can this estimate be reached?

45. All paved areas should be drained into the storm or combination storm and sanitary sewer when such areas exceed how many square feet?

46. The crushing of what material produces lime?

47. Where is the slaking process of hydrated lime accomplished?

48. How much time does it take for the initial set of portland cement?

49. Where quick setting and early strength is necessary, what type of portland cement should be used?

50. What material is tar obtained from?

51. What is one of the principle requirements of concrete?

52. By what is the strength of concrete largely controlled?

53. The slump test measures what in concrete?

54. The largest piece of aggregate should not exceed what fractional part of the concrete slab thickness?

55. A greater strength for concrete can be achieved when its mixing time in minutes is _____.

56. Air-entraining concrete results when what ingredient is added to the mix?

57. Lightweight concrete is most desirable when used as _____.

58. The initial set for portland cement is how many minutes?

59. Name five important types of portland cement.

60. What is the most important use of asphalt?

7

PLACING AND POURING CONCRETE

INTRODUCTION

This chapter discusses the various kinds of forms used in concrete work, the care and supervision that must be exercised in placing concrete into forms to prevent "segregation" and "laitance," the precautions that must be taken during the curing of concrete, and the problems of expansion and contraction, including the provisions of construction joints to prevent the cracking of concrete work.

TECHNICAL INFORMATION

Forms for Concrete

The wood or metal construction that holds the concrete in place until it has hardened is called a form. Forms must be carefully put together to conform to the shape and dimensions of the concrete as shown on the plans, and are required to be substantial and sufficiently tight to prevent the leakage of water from the wet concrete. Consideration should be given to the cost of the formwork, because it constitutes a large part of the expense of concrete construction. Forms should be constructed with economy and simplicity whenever possible, with special attention given to ease of erection and stripping down after the concrete has hardened. Carefully dismantled forms can be reused numerous times.

Today, in most areas, building codes require that forms be designed by the structural engineer.

TYPICAL WOOD FORMS: Spruce and pine lumber are well-suited for wood forms, because they do not stain the exposed concrete surface. Green or partially seasoned lumber is preferable, because dry lumber swells when wet; but whether the wood form lumber is dry or seasoned it must be thoroughly wetted before the concrete is poured. Frequently wood forms are oiled or treated to fill the pores of the wood to prevent the absorption of water from the concrete and further provide for a smoother surface, thus preventing the concrete from sticking to the forms when they are removed.

The typical wood form for a footing (see Figure 7-1) may be constructed with 2 × 12-in. planks held in place by 2 × 2-in. stakes, 2 ft. long, driven halfway into the ground. The stakes are held together by 1 × 3-in. spacer ties, 4 ft.

FIGURE 7-1   *Form for footing*

FIGURE 7-2   *Tongue-and-groove form boards and ties*

FIGURE 7-3   *Plywood forms with drive wedge ties*

apart. Tongue-and-groove form boards, properly supported by ties, spreaders, stakes, and braces as shown in Figure 7-2 and Figure 7-3, are forms used for concrete foundation walls.

76

MAJOR REQUIREMENTS OF FORMWORK: In building and installing forms, one important factor must be kept in mind—they must be made strong enough to support the weight of the wet concrete and to overcome any sideward forces or pressures exerted by the concrete. Concrete weighs approximately 150 lbs. per cubic foot. This mass can be better visualized by referring to Figure 7-4 (a) which shows a sectional view of a concrete foundation and the formwork necessary to hold the wet con-

crete. The wall is 6 ft. high and 1 ft. wide. If a 1-ft. length of this wall, as shown in Figure 7-4(b) were to be considered, it would contain 6 cu. ft. of concrete, which has a total weight of 900 lbs. This weight causes a considerable sideward force against the forms, as indicated by A, B, C, and D. This force is overcome by proper bracing and by the use of form ties, which extend through the concrete and are fastened to the outer sides of the studs of the formwork (see Figure 7-5).

FIGURE 7-4   *Cross section of concrete foundation showing form work*

FIGURE 7-5   *Tongue-and-groove form boards and ties*

PLYWOOD FORMS: Plywoods have been developed that are suitable for concrete forms. The use of a special bonding agent, surface oiling, and edge sealing combine to make it a material that can be reused many times. Large smooth panels (see Figure 7-6) minimize the number of joints and tend to simplify construction. The material is strong and rigid and therefore requires fewer supports. It is identified by a special grade mark and is available in sizes up to 4 × 12 ft. and in thicknesses ranging from 1/2 to 3/4 in. It makes a smooth surface on the concrete and can be bent to form curved surfaces. Further advantages are that it can be sawed easily and nailed close to the edge without previous drilling and without splitting.

FORMWORK AROUND BEAMS: Steel beams that are to be encased in concrete are known as fireproofed steel beams. Figure 7-7 illustrates two methods of constructing formwork of this type that will receive the wet concrete. Snap-tie hangers in U-shaped form hold the tongue-and-groove beam sides and bottoms, studs, stringers, and joists. After the concrete is poured and hardened, the forms can easily be removed. Plywood forms for concrete columns, as shown in Figure 7-8(A), are held together with special metal locking squares which can be quickly installed and dismantled. For concrete slabs and reinforced concrete beams, as shown in Figure 7-8(B), plywood or 1-in. tongue-and-groove form boards are used for beam sides and bottom of slab, and thick plywood or 2-in. stock for beam bottoms.

METAL FORMS: Steel makes excellent forms for concrete and is used extensively where forms can be reused many times. These may be units such as wall panels, which can be assembled in a variety of shapes or special forms for units such as blocks,

FIGURE 7-6   *Plywood forms*

ornamental forms, etc. Because such metal forms are practically indestructible, the cost per unit may become quite small as the usage factor increases. Steel forms for making regular spaced concrete joists are shown in Figure 7-9. After the slab and concrete joists become self-supporting, the forms are removed. Steel domes may be used for two-way ribbed (waffle-type) slab construction (see Figure 7-10). They are rigid deepdrawn, one-piece units which can easily be removed when the concrete has hardened. The small hole in the center of the dome is used for the removal of the forms by applying compressed air at the hole. Permanent metal forms such as those shown in Figure 7-11 serve as the structural subfloor for concrete roofs and floor slabs.

SYNTHETIC FORMS: Glass fiber, reinforced polyester plastic, and paper pulp are used as formwork for roof and floor panels, for domes, and for two-way ribbed (waffle-type) slab construction in conjunction with flat-plate design. These forms are

FIGURE 7-7   *Formwork for beam concrete fireproofing*

METAL CLAMPS FOR
SQUARE COLUMNS

SLAB

T&G 1" PINE
OR PLYWOOD

2" STOCK OR
THICK PLYWOOD

BEAM

(A)
PLYWOOD FORMS FOR
CONCRETE COLUMNS
WITH LOCKING SQUARES

(B)
FORM FOR SLABS, BEAM
SIDES AND BOTTOMS

FIGURE 7-8   *Forms for columns and beams*

STEEL FORMS FOR FORMING
REGULAR SPACED CONCRETE
JOISTS

SLOPE = 1" IN 12"

STIFFNER ANGLES ON
20" & 30" FORMS

DEPTH

7/8"   WIDTH   7/8"

FIGURE 7-9   *Metal forms*

STEEL DOME FOR FORMING
WAFFLE PATTERN CEILING

2½"   19"   2½"

12"

ELEVATION

19"

19"

PLAN

19" x 19" SYSTEM

30" x 30" SYSTEM

3"   30"   3"

ELEVATION

30"

30"

PLAN

FIGURE 7-10   *Steel domes*

light in weight, flexible, and easily removed and rehandled. They require no oiling and are not subject to corrosion.

Reinforced paper tubes are used as forms for round columns and in tube-slab type of construction.

Removal of Forms

Forms should be removed in such a manner as to insure the complete safety of the structure. Where the structure as a whole is supported on shores, the removable floor forms, beams and girder sides, column and similar vertical forms may be removed, provided the concrete has achieved sufficient strength. In no case should the supporting forms or shoring be removed until the concrete members have acquired sufficient strength to support safely their weight and the loads for which they were designed.

Placing Concrete

No element in the entire cycle of concrete production requires more care than the final operation of placing concrete at the ultimate point of deposit.

Before placing concrete, all debris and foreign matter should be removed from places to be occupied by the concrete. The forms that receive the concrete should be thoroughly wetted or oiled or otherwise treated as required. Temporary openings should be provided where necessary to facilitate cleaning and inspection immediately before depositing concrete; these should be placed in such a way that excess water used in flushing the forms may be drained out.

PREVENTION OF SEGREGATION: With a well-designed mixture delivered with proper consistency and without segregation, placing of concrete is greatly simplified, but even in this case care must be exercised to continue to prevent segregation and to see that the material flows properly into the corners and angles of forms and around the reinforcements. Constant supervision is essential to insure such complete filling of the form and to prevent the rather common mistake of depositing continuously at one point (see Figure 7-12) and allowing the material to flow to distant points. Flowing over long distances will cause segregation, especially the separation of water and fine particles from the rest of the mass. Excessive amounts of tamping or shoveling in the forms will also cause the materials to separate. When the concrete is properly proportioned, the mass will be thoroughly consolidated with very little shoveling. Light spading of the concrete next to the forms will prevent honeycombing and will be conducive to

PERMANENT FORM

REINFORCING MESH

PERMANENT METAL FORM FOR CONCRETE ROOF AND FLOOR SLABS

FIGURE 7-11 *Rib form*

POOR PRACTICE GOOD PRACTICE

DEPOSIT CONCRETE AT VARIOUS POINTS IN ORDER TO PREVENT SEGREGATION

FIGURE 7-12 *Depositing concrete into forms*

better surface finishes. In placing concrete in deep layers, a gradual increase in the water content of the upper portion is quite certain to result from the increased pressure on the lower portions. The excess water should be worked to a low point, without actually causing flow, and removed. It should be remembered that excess water in the upper layer is just as objectionable as excess water in a mix.

LAITANCE: The whitish, chalklike substance of very little strength that forms on the upper surface of the concrete is called *laitance*; this laitance layer can be seen at the top of each day's work. Two preventive measures are necessary: (1) the concrete mixture should be of such consistency that laitance will be minimized; and (2) before each day's pouring, the laitance must be washed off and completely removed so that proper bonding between the pours is accomplished. If the laitance is not removed, bonding is not accomplished, the structure is weakened, and water can penetrate through this weakened joint (see Figure 7-13).

Construction Joints

Construction joints have no permanent function in a building and are only a method used to mark off divisions, both vertically and horizontally, in concrete work done on different days. Before starting the next pour, the surfaces previously poured are cleaned, roughened, and drenched with water, and it is general practice to bond the new and previously poured concrete by grooves and reinforcing rods (see Figure 7-14).

Curing of Concrete

The chemical reactions that take place as cement hardens continue for a very long period

LAITANCE CAN ONLY FORM FROM THE PRESSENCE OF EXCESS WATER AT THE TOP OF POURED CONCRETE

FIGURE 7-13 *Laitance formed by interrupted pours*

FIGURE 7-14 *Vertical construction joint with forms removed*

and result in a gradual increase in the strength of the concrete. In order for these reactions which constitute "curing" to continue, moisture must be present and the temperature must be favorable. A layer of water is always present on the surface when the concrete is placed, but if the evaporation of the water is not controlled and too much evaporation occurs, the chemical reactions required to achieve the full strength of the concrete will not be accomplished. Water evaporation should be controlled for 5 days or longer in one of the following ways:

1. By wetting down the concrete surface periodically with water;

2. By covering the surface with straw, sand, or burlap which is kept moist;

3. By covering the surfaces with certain types of paper to keep the water from evaporating.

When poured in winter concrete must be protected against freezing for at least 72 hrs. after being placed. The heat generated by the chemical reactions of the concrete is an important factor in maintaining the required temperatures during this period of time. If more heat is required, the mixing water and even the aggregate may be heated. Specifications often require that concrete be maintained above 70°F. for the first 3 days after placing, and above 50°F. for the first 5 days, but the materials should not be heated enough to raise the temperature of the concrete above 100°F.

After concrete has been placed, it can be protected by enclosing in some manner and maintaining heat in the enclosed space. Covering a temporary framework with canvas tarpaulins or reinforced plastic sheets is a common method. The heat also may be supplied by steam which is allowed to escape into the enclosed space to provide moisture for curing, or by heating units that burn gas, oil, or kerosene, or that depend on electricity.

Shrinkage of Concrete

Concrete changes somewhat in volume with different conditions of exposure. Shrinkage takes place from the time of installation and continues for a period of several months upon exposure to dry air conditions.

The fundamental cause of shrinkage is the loss of water resulting from evaporation and from absorption by the aggregate particles, earth, or the forms. Shrinkage during the first stage of setting is quite rapid, the rate depending upon the rate of evaporation. In small thin sections of concrete exposed to rapid drying conditions, a great deal of shrinkage will result in cracking. This can be avoided by preventing the loss of water from the mass by some of the methods already described.

Volume changes are also caused by temperature changes: higher temperatures cause expansion and lower temperatures cause contraction.

Expansion Joints

Buildings over 300 ft. in length should be separated by a transverse joint providing a plane of separation so that free movement of the two adjacent parts may take place. Reinforcement should never extend across the expansion joint; the break between the two sections should be complete; and exposed joints should be filled with an elastic joint filler. Figure 7-15 illustrates an expansion joint through a floor and one through a roof. Note the expansion joint filler and the provisions that are made in protecting the joint from water seepage.

HOW TO CALCULATE EXPANSION FOR A 300-FT. CONCRETE BUILDING: The coefficient of expansion for concrete is:

0.0000065 in. per change in $1°$F., assuming a temperature difference from $0°$ in winter to $90°$ in summer where the building is to be located.

The formula is:

Length (ft.) $\times$ 12 $\times$ coefficient of expansion $\times$ temperature difference

or   300 ft. $\times$ 12 $\times$ 0.0000065 $\times$ $90°$ = Expansion in inches

= 2.1 in.

Therefore the expansion joint at the center of the building is a minimum of 1.05 in.

REVIEW EXAMINATION

1. Name the four types of forms that can be used in concrete work.

2. Give the thickness of the wood form material used for concrete beam sides; for concrete beam bottoms.

3. For plywood forms, what is the range of thickness of the plywood?

4. What type of form material may be used for two-way ribbed (waffle-type) slab construction?

5. In depositing concrete into the forms, name two ways in which segregation may occur.

6. What should be done with the laitance that forms on

EXPANSION JOINT THRU ROOF   EXPANSION JOINT THRU FLOOR

FIGURE 7-15 *Expansion joints through floor and roof*

top of a concrete pour before the next pour can be made?

7. Name three methods in which water evaporation of freshly poured concrete can be reduced.

8. Freshly poured concrete must be protected against freezing for how long a period?

9. What is the fundamental cause of shrinkage in concrete?

10. A transverse expansion joint must be used in buildings that exceed a length of how many feet?

ASSIGNMENT

1. Sketch a waffle-type floor construction illustrating the form that is used.

2. Sketch a construction system illustrating the use of permanent forms.

3. Sketch a detail indicating a wood form used for a concrete footing.

SUPPLEMENTARY INFORMATION

Concrete Test Specimens

When concrete is placed, a sample of the concrete is taken to the testing laboratory to determine its compressive strength and to check that the requirements for which it is intended are met. This is done by depositing the concrete in 6 × 12-in. cast iron molds in general use by the testing laboratory. The depositing of the concrete into the mold must be done under strict supervision and according to specific, controlled controlled conditions. The specimen should be marked, weighed, and stored. Standard cured test specimens should be tested for compressive strength as soon as practicable. Details of testing can be found in any comprehensive text on concrete.

Placing Concrete under Water by the Tremie Method

Concrete should not be deposited under water if it is possible to deposit in air, because there is always some uncertainty about the results obtained from placing it under water. The additional expense and delay of avoiding this method are nearly

FIGURE 7-16 *Tremie method of placing concrete under water*

always warranted. Where conditions are such that concrete must be placed under water, expert supervision is necessary and every precaution must be taken to prevent the cement from being washed out of the mix. A fairly rich mix, containing at least seven sacks of cement per cubic yard of concrete should be used.

One successful method of placing concrete under water is by use of a *tremie* (see Figure 7-16), a steel pipe or tube with funnel-shaped upper end long enough so that the lower end will reach the bottom of the work when the upper end is above the water level. When placing operations are to start, the lower end of the tremie has a special operable closure cover to prevent the entrance of water or the escape of concrete. The tremie is filled with concrete and lowered into position. When the lower end reaches the bottom of the work, the cover opens and the concrete is allowed to flow out slowly. As concreting proceeds, the lower end is kept submerged in the concrete for several feet and the tremie kept constantly full of concrete.

Vibrating Concrete

Vibrators are used when concrete has been poured into the form. They ensure that the concrete completely surrounds the reinforcing, they eliminate air pockets and, most important, they permit the mixes to be made with less water. The time allowed for vibrating and the spacing of the insertion points for the vibrator(s) must be carefully controlled because too much vibration causes a separation of the aggregates, with the larger aggregates falling to the bottom of the form.

Pumping Concrete

The transporting of concrete from the area of mixing (be it job mix or transit mix) to the area where it is to be poured has been a difficult, time-consuming, and costly operation, particularly for multistoried buildings. Methods have now been developed whereby concrete can be pumped directly from place of delivery to areas of placement.

When the pumping method has been selected for a job, then the mix, the cement–water ratio, the aggregate composition, air-entraining additives, and the height to be pumped all have to be tested and found satisfactory before any concrete can actually be installed.

8

BUILDING WITH CONCRETE

INTRODUCTION

This chapter reviews the major uses of concrete in the building industry. Reinforced concrete floor and roof systems, concrete planks and decking, prestressed concrete, precast reinforced concrete panels used as curtain walls, thin shell construction, and concrete rigid frames are considered in detail.

TECHNICAL INFORMATION

Concrete is used in residential and small construction work for footings, foundations, slabs on grade, steps, walks, and innumerable other areas where the loads and forces imposed are great enough to require that the concrete be reinforced with steel rods or mesh. Concrete is called "reinforced concrete" when such steel rods or reinforcing mesh are installed.

Reinforced Concrete

When steel and concrete are combined, the compressive strength of concrete and the tensile strength of steel are used to their best advantage. Concrete can develop a compressive strength of 10,000 psi, whereas steel can be manufactured to develop a tensile strength of over 150,000 psi.

One of the many advantages of reinforced concrete is that supporting beam shapes can be controlled in size and contour, as shown in Figure 8-1.

There are four reinforced beam, column, and slab systems commonly used in building construction: one-way, two-way, flat slab two-way, and flat slab four-way. These are illustrated in Figure 8-2.

The *grid* or *pan floor system* is achieved by placing steel, plastic, or paper pans or domes on temporary forms and filling the voids with concrete and reinforcing steel. Steel, plastic, or paper pans are available in widths of 10 to 30 in., depths of 8 to 16 in., and in lengths of 1'-0" to 3'-0", and with end closures tapered or straight for all the various pan sizes. Steel, plastic, or paper domes are available in sizes 18 × 18 in. to 30 × 30 in. with depths of 8 to 14 in. The width of the rib, controlled by the depth of the pans or domes is

BEAM & SLAB DESIGNED FOR PARTICULAR LOADING

BEAM ELONGATED AND 6" LESS DEEP DESIGNED FOR SAME PARTICULAR LOAD

FIGURE 8-1 *Supporting beam shapes*

generally 5 in. for the deeper type and 4 in. for the shallower type (see Figures 8-3 and 8-4).

The *tube-slab system* employs uniformly spaced metal or paper tubes as fillers, around which is poured the concrete with reinforcings (see Figure 8-5). The tubes are placed within a slab near the center so that the concrete can form around the tubes. The thicknesses of slab and the tube diameter and spacing vary as required for span loading conditions. Tube slabs range from 10 to 30 in. in thickness, with a span range from 18 to 80 ft. The tube-slab system is a practical system for many types of structural framing, because it results in a flat ceiling (see Figure 8-6).

Concrete planks and decking can be defined as prefabricated reinforced concrete slabs or panel units that will span between supporting beams, walls, or partitions to form floors or roofs. Planks and decking are available in sizes ranging from 15 to 32 in. in width, 4 to 10 ft. in length, and 1 to 4 in. in thickness. Some such planks are made of lightweight concrete, integrally cast into galvanized edgings of tongue-and-groove contour that form the tongue-and-groove edges on all four sides of the finished plank (see Figure 8-7). Special clips are provided to anchor the planks to the supporting members. Another type is the channel plank illustrated in Figure 8-8. It is 24 in. wide and 3-3/4 in. thick at its ends and 1 to 1-1/2 in. thick through its center.

The planks are fastened to the steel beams by means of metal clips. Where planks are used for floors around stairwell openings or openings for ducts and shafts, the plank ends must be properly supported and correctly detailed.

FIGURE 8-2 *Reinforced concrete beam, column, and slab systems*

DOMES

SECTION A-A

PANS

REFLECTED CEILING PLAN

19" OR 30"

19" OR 30"

PLAN

3" 19" OR 30" 3"

10"

ELEVATION

19"×19" AND 30"×30" DOME SYSTEM

TAPERED END PAN

2½" VARIES 2½"

8"

ELEVATION

STRAIGHT RUN PAN

FIGURE 8-3   *Steel domes and pans*

DOME
2 WAY REINFORCING

PAN
I WAY REINFORCING

FIGURE 8-4   *Reinforced slab and beams with domes and pan type forms*

REINFORCED
CONCRETE BEAM

PAPER TUBE
FILLERS

FIGURE 8-6   *Tube-slab with 3'-0" reinforced concrete beam*

TYPICAL WEB
REINFORCING
BETWEEN TUBES

DUCT
SPACE

TUBE FILLER

REINFORCING

MESH

FIGURE 8-5   *The tube-slab system of construction*

15" TO 32" W x 4'-0" TO 10'-0" L

LIGHTWEIGHT CONCRETE PLANK

BUILT-UP ROOF ON INSULATION

18"

CONCRETE PLANK ON
ROOF OVERHANG

PARAPET WALL

CANT STRIP

PROVIDE CONTINUOUS
SUPPORT WHEN METAL
EDGING IS REMOVED

PURLIN

CONCRETE PLANK IN
PARAPET WALL

CONCRETE PLANK ON FLAT ROOF

1 3/4"

1 3/4"

NO. 10 CLIP
NAIL HOLE 1/8" ∅

THRUST ANGLE
(WELDED)

NO. 10 CLIP

TRUSS

LIGHT TRUSSES TO 8'-0" O.C.

NO 10 CLIP

SAG ROD

PURLIN

TRUSS

TRUSSES WITH PURLIN

CONCRETE PLANK ON PITCHED ROOF

FIGURE 8-7   *Concrete planks and decking*

REINFORCING ROD

1' MIN. FOR ROOFS
1 1/2" MIN. FOR FLOORS

REINFORCING MESH

3 3/4"

2"

24"

TYPICAL CHANNEL PLANK

1 1/4"

18 GA. GALV. CLIP AT
AT DIAGONAL CORNERS

BEAM

PLANKS CLIPPED TO BEAM

2'-0"

3 3/4"

1" MIN.

STEEL BEAM

CHANNEL PLANKS FOR FLOOR AND ROOFS

FIGURE 8-8   *Channel planks*

89

Prestressed Concrete

When a reinforced concrete beam is designed, the steel reinforcing is calculated to overcome the bending within the beam. By prestressing the steel, the cross-sectional area of the beam can be reduced because the concrete is compressed as explained below, and therefore any future bending of the beam has been overcome by the prestressing of the steel.

Prestressed concrete may be either pre-tensioned or post-tensioned. Pre-tensioning is accomplished by placing the reinforcing rods or wire cables in an empty form and pulling them to their required tensile stress by means of hydraulic jacks. The concrete is then poured into the form and allowed to cure. The jacks are released and the stress in the wires is transferred by the bond between the materials. That is, as the steel attempts to shorten and return to its original length, it compresses the beam by transferring the prestressing force by bond to the concrete.

In post-tensioning, the steel is stretched after the concrete has hardened. To achieve this, pipe conduits are placed in the concrete through which wire cables are stretched against the ends of the member. Final transfer of prestress from steel to concrete can be achieved by mechanical devices at the end anchorage.

Prestressed concrete is two to three times stronger than reinforced concrete. It allows for larger spans and the support of heavier loads.

Figure 8-9 illustrates two prestressed concrete beams of slightly different design. One is notched to receive a wood nailing strip or a dovetail anchor, while the other is provided with notched-out shelves for seating the prefabricated deck. Figure 8-10 shows how the decking is installed in each type of beam.

Double-tee floor and roof units have advantages insofar as they are precast, prestressed, and ready for installation, their light weight and long span resulting in economy of framing (see Figure 8-11). Here the double-tee unit can be cambered to compensate for deflection. The concrete forming the beam weighs about 105 lbs. per cu. ft. and attains a minimum strength of 3750 psi after 28 days. The weight of the double-tee is 28 lbs. per sq. ft. The usual minimum bearing required is 4 in. on steel, and 6 in. on masonry. The top surfaces are purposely rough to increase the bond between the slab and the concrete topping. A typical single prestressed tee section is shown in Figure 8-12, and some typical construction details are shown in Figure 8-13.

LOADS PER LINEAR FOOT FOR CONCRETE TEE JOISTS			
SPAN IN FT.	20	45	64
LB'S./LIN.FT. 16"	584	128	—
LB'S./LIN.FT. 20"	873	293	82

PRESTRESSED REINFORCED CONCRETE BEAMS- SPANS FROM 16'-0" TO 32'-0" IN INCREMENTS OF 2'-0"

FIGURE 8-9 *Prestressed concrete beams for floor and roof construction*

FIGURE 8-10 *Application of decking on prestressed beams*

SPANS RANGE FROM 20' TO 32'

1½"

12"

1'-0" 2'-0" 1'-0"

SPANS RANGE FROM 15' TO 32'

2"

12½"

1'-0" 2'-0" 1'-0"

FIGURE 8-11 *Double-tee floor and roof units*

NOMINAL 6'-0" OR 8'-0"

3½"

2"

PRESTRESSING STRANDS

STIRRUPS

VARIES

8¾"

FIGURE 8-12 *Typical prestressed tee section*

FLASHING
CANT STRIP
BUILT-UP ROOFING
DOUBLE TEE
MASONRY FILLER
CONCRETE BLOCK FILLED SOLID

PARAPET WALL DETAIL

GRAVEL STOP
MASONRY FILLER
BUILT-UP ROOFING
DOUBLE TEE
CONCRETE BLOCK FILLED SOLID

FASCIA DETAIL

CANT STRIP
FASCIA
MASONY FILLER
CONCRETE BLOCK WALL

CANTILEVERED FASCIA DETAIL

DOME
FLASHING
BUILT-UP ROOF
2"x6" FRAME
DOUBLE TEE

SKYDOME DETAIL

FIGURE 8-13 *Typical construction details using double-tee units*

91

8" CORE PLANK

12" CORE PLANK

FIGURE 8-14 *Core planks and applications*

Precast, prestressed, hollow-core sections are usually 4 or 8 ft. wide and may be 4, 6, 8, 10 and 12 in. in thickness. Spans range from 15 to 50 ft., capable of supporting superimposed loads of over 200 psi. Figure 8-14 illustrates the core plank, together with some typical installation details. This type of floor may be used with reinforced concrete and masonry structures as well as with steel frame.

The cores may serve as a passage for utility lines and can also be utilized for warm air heating systems. The smooth undersurface of the slab formed by the planks may be painted directly when smooth or serve as an acoustical surface when textured.

Figure 8-15 shows another type of precast, prestressed hollow-core unit.

Reinforced Concrete Used as Curtain Walls

Prefabricated panels of reinforced concrete are extensively used as curtain walls for buildings with steel or concrete framing. The panels of numerous designs may extend from floor to floor and are provided with quick anchoring devices that allow for ease of erection and installation.

FIGURE 8-15 *Prestressed tongue-and-groove concrete flooring and roof decking units*

A typical such panel is shown in Figure 8-16, including a partial elevation and a fastening detail of the panel. Figure 8-17 shows a variation of the panel over a window head and sill. A fastening detail is also shown.

SECTION 1-1

FIGURE 8-16   *Concrete panel as curtain wall*

FIGURE 8-17   *Concrete panel as curtain wall (cont.)*

94

REVIEW EXAMINATION

1. Concrete is called "reinforced concrete" when either of what two materials are installed?

2. Concrete can develop a compressive strength of what psi?

3. Steel can be manufactured to develop a tensile strength of over what psi?

4. What are the four reinforced beam, column, and slab systems commonly used in building construction?

5. The tube-slab system employs what type of tubes as fillers, around which concrete is poured?

6. What are the various widths and lengths available for concrete planks and decking?

7. Prestressed concrete is how many times stronger than reinforced concrete?

8. Spans for precast, prestressed, hollow-core sections may range from how many to how many feet?

9. What are prefabricated panels of reinforced concrete extensively used as?

10. The double-tee unit is cambered to compensate for what?

ASSIGNMENT

1. By sketch or illustration show other applications of concrete in building.

2. Sketch a channel and a core plank and give nominal dimensions.

3. Illustrate the difference between one-way and two-way ribbed construction.

SUPPLEMENTARY INFORMATION

Other Systems of Concrete Construction

THIN SHELL CONSTRUCTION: This is a structural system in which concrete is used economically as a roof, wall, or a combination of both. The system permits a freedom of design shapes in both plan and section. It is strong and has a great capacity to carry unbalanced loads. Shells derive their strength from their ability to transfer loads by membrane stresses. These are direct stresses, such as compression, tension, and shear, acting over the entire thickness of the shell at any point. There is no bending of an element of the shell such as exists in a flat slab, except of minor magnitude caused by edge and end conditions. The thin-shell system of construction lends itself to many forms of building shapes, of which the barrel shell is most common. Other shapes, such as the multiple barrel shell, the "north light" shell, the butterfly shell, and the typical flat corrugated shell are some of the better-known types currently used (see Figure 8-18).

Placement of bars in shells may be in the form of reinforcing bars or a combination of bars and mesh. There are usually three layers of bars or mesh in a shell section (see Figure 8-19). The *diagonal bars* placed at the bottom of the shell resist diagonal tension, the *longitudinal bars* at the center resist the main tensile forces below the neutral axis, and the *transverse bars* at the top of the section resist some moment and shrinkage stresses.

RIGID FRAME: Concrete rigid frames may be combined with shell construction, particularly in the long-type barrel form. The more common types of concrete rigid frames have the appearance of a rather flat arch and are most suitable for gymnasiums, auditoriums, hangars, markets, and armories (see Figure 8-20). Economical spans are generally between 60 and 100 ft., and the frames may be 20 ft. or more on center. As in most arches, the lower ends of the legs are usually connected with a tie or they are restrained from outward movement by buttresses. The frames may be provided with roof purlins, struts, or any of a number of precast concrete roof deckings.

LIFT-SLAB SYSTEM: The floor slabs are poured on grade, one on top of the other with all electrical conduits, chases, and shafts for plumbing, heating, and air-conditioning installed on grade. When the slabs are cured, they are raised to the various floor heights by jacks. This system requires special equipment and special designs for column supports, floor slabs, and connections of slabs to vertical supports (see Figure 8-21).

TILT-UP SYSTEM: The tilt-up system consists of casting reinforced concrete slabs on the previously poured concrete floor. When these slabs are cured they are tilted-up to a vertical position. The slabs may be load-bearing or non-load-bearing. The design of the reinforcing, pick-up points for lifting, joining, and columns should be done by a structural engineer (see Figure 8-22).

BARREL

MULTIPLE BARREL

NORTH LIGHT SHELLS

BUTTERFLY SHELL

BEAM

SECTION

BEAM

BEAM

END ELEVATION

FLAT CORRUGATED SHELL

TIES

ELEVATION

TENSION RING

SECTION

SUPPORTS
TIES

HALF PLAN

TENSION RING

SUPPORTS

PLAN

THIN SHELL DOMES

FIGURE 8-18   *Concrete thin shell structural forms*

TRANSVERSE BARS AT TOP

DIAGONAL BARS AT BOTTOM

LONGITUDINAL BARS AT CENTER

FIGURE 8-19   *Placement of reinforcing bars in thin shell*

TIE IN SLAB

BUTTRESS

FLAT ARCH TYPE

FIGURE 8-20   *Rigid concrete frames*

FIGURE 8-21   *Tilt-up system*

PLANK SYSTEM: In the plank system, precast concrete planks are easily fastened to steel, wood, or concrete beams. The longitudinal edges of the planks are tongue-and-grooved (see Figure 8-23) with bevels forming V-joints. Plank ends are square-cut and must be placed over beams.

BULB-TEE: The bulb-tee system (see Figure 8-24) is used for spanning between bulb-tee purlins. The sides of the tile (or plank) are chamfered for grout application and the ends may be tongue-and-grooved, or they may be square-cut.

DUAL-TEE: The dual-tee system (see Figure 8-25) for roof decks incorporates the panel with a specially designed corrosion-resistant sub-purlin of cold rolled 18-gauge steel, which is inserted on the job into a pre-cut kerf in the panel.

END BEARING

STEP 1

INTERLOCKING CLIP DETAIL

STEP 2

CONCRETE JOIST CONSTRUCTION

STEP 3

FIGURE 8-22   *Lift-slab system*

FIGURE 8-23   *The plank system*

DECKING
USED AS TILE

GROUT

CONCRETE
WOOD FIBER

PURLIN

BULB TEE APPLICATION

BULB TEE

BULB TEE ANCHORING
IN TILE SYSTEM

GROUT

TILE

BULB TEE

TONGUE & GROOVE ENDS

FIGURE 8-24   *The bulb-tee system*

DUAL TEE
SUB-PURLIN

DECKING

DUAL TEE
SUB-PURLIN

WELDS

MAIN PURLIN

FIGURE 8-25   *Dual tee fastening details*

9

BRICK

INTRODUCTION

This chapter covers the manufacturing processes of clay and shale brick, the standard and special shapes generally used, physical characteristics, brick wall patterns, bonding and joints, and types of brick wall construction.

TECHNICAL INFORMATION

Manufacturing Methods

Clay and shale brick are manufactured by the soft-mud process, the stiff-mud process, and the dry-press process. In all these processes the bricks are formed to the desired shape, dried, and then burned in kilns. The chief difference in the finished brick is the method of molding.

The soft-mud process requires that the clays be mixed with sufficient water (20 to 30% moisture) so that they can be easily molded (see Figure 9-1). In order to stop the wet clay from sticking to the mold, either water or sand is used. When water is used, the finished brick is known as water-struck brick, and when sand is used, the brick is known as sand-struck brick.

The stiff-mud process requires that the clays be mixed with only sufficient water (12 to 15% moisture) so that they can be extruded through a die (see Figure 9-2). The brick sizes are cut by using tightly stretched wires. If the ends are cut the brick is known as end-cut and if the sides are cut, the brick is known as side-cut. Both types are called wire-cut brick.

In the dry-press process the clays are mixed with only enough water (7 to 10% moisture) so that they are almost in a dry state. Then they are molded into shapes with high pressure (see Figure 9-3).

Brick that is first pressed into oversize molds and then re-pressed in molds of the current size of brick is called a re-pressed brick.

MOLD FOR BRICK

FIGURE 9-1 *Soft mud process*

SIDE CUT

END CUT

FIGURE 9-2 *Brick produced by the extrusion method*

FIGURE 9-3 *Dry press process*

By varying the types of clays and introducing various metal oxides, various colors are produced.

Types and Grades of Brick

The types of brick generally used in building construction are common and face brick. Common brick is available in three grades:

Grade SW is used where heavy rain and freezing are encountered. Its compressive strength is about 2000 psi in flat position. It has a high resistance to frost. Its water absorption percentage is about 18% and a maximum saturation coefficient of 0.80, and a maximum water absorption of about 20%.

Grade MW is used where rain and freezing are not extreme; in relatively dry locations. Its minimum compressive strength is about 2500 psi. It has a maximum water absorption percentage of about 22% and a maximum saturation coefficient of about 0.90, and a maximum water absorption of 25%.

Grade NW is used where there is minimum rain and freezing. Mostly used for interior or backup brick. Its compressive strength is about 1500 psi. Its maximum water absorption percentage and maximum saturation coefficient of water absorption have no limit.

The Saturation Coefficient

The saturation coefficient is determined by submerging a dry brick in boiling water for 5 hrs. and allowing both water and brick to cool to room temperature. The hot water percentage absorption is:

$$Ah = \frac{Wh - Wd}{Wd} \times 100$$

where

Wh = hot saturated weight

Wd = dry weight

Ah = hot percent absorption

The formula for calculating the percent of absorption is:

$$Ac = \frac{Wc - Wd}{Wd} \times 100$$

where

Wc = cold saturated weight

Wd = dry weight

Ac = cold percent absorption

The coefficient of saturation is the ratio of the cold saturation to the hot saturation percentages, thus:

$$Cs = \frac{Ac}{Ah}$$

where

Ac = cold water coefficient

Ah = hot water coefficient

Cs = saturation coefficient

TYPICAL EXAMPLE: A common brick weighs 4 lbs. 12 oz. If after 24 hrs. submerged in cold water it weighs 5 lbs. 8 oz., and after 5 hrs. submerged in boiling water the brick weighs 5 lbs. 10 oz., calculate:

(a) cold water percentage of absorption

(b) hot water percentage of absorption

(c) coefficient of saturation.

SOLUTION:

(a) The cold water percentage of absorption:

$$Ac = \frac{Wc - Wd}{Wd} \times 100 = \frac{5\text{-}1/2 - 4\text{-}3/4}{4\text{-}3/4} \times 100$$
$$= 15.8\%$$

(b) The hot water percentage of absorption:

$$Ah = \frac{Wh - Wd}{Wd} \times 100 = \frac{5\text{-}5/8 - 4\text{-}3/4}{4\text{-}3/4} \times 100$$
$$= 18.4\%$$

(c) The coefficient of absorption:

$$Cs = \frac{Ac}{Ah} = \frac{15.8}{18.4} = 0.86$$

Face brick is available in SW and MW grades similar to common brick and three other grades based upon factors affecting the appearance:

Grade FBX: high degree of mechanical perfection and narrow color range.

Grade FBS: variations in mechanical perfection and wide color range.

Grade FBA: nonuniformity in size, color, and texture of brick units.

Size of Brick

Most common and face brick are manufactured in standard sizes with minor variations in dimension. The United States Bureau of Standards recommends that brick sizes should be as shown in Table 9-1 and Figure 9-4. All bricks vary slightly in their dimensions because of the shrinkage of the clays in burning.

Physical Requirements

The various grades of common and face brick (including FBX, FBS, and FBA) are required to meet exact physical requirements (see Table 9-2).

Most brick today is made with round or rectangular holes instead of being solid because these

TABLE 9-1 *Size of common, face, and modular brick*

Type of Brick	Depth	Width	Length
Common and face brick*	$2\frac{1}{4}''$ not including mortar joint	$3\frac{3}{4}''$ not including mortar joint	$8''$ not including mortar joint
Modular common and face brick	$2''$, $2\frac{2}{3}''$, $4''$, and $5\frac{1}{3}''$ including mortar joint	$4''$ including mortar joint	$8''$ and $12''$ including mortar joint

*Permissible variables are: plus or minus $\frac{1}{16}''$ in depth, $\frac{1}{8}''$ in width, and $\frac{1}{4}''$ in length

TABLE 9-2 *Physical requirements of brick*

Grade of Brick	Building Brick (common brick) Solid or Cored	Maximum Saturation Coefficient	Face Brick, Solid or Cored, and Hollow Brick	Maximum Saturation Coefficient
SW	3000 psi	0.78	3000 psi	0.78
MW	2500 psi	0.88	2500 psi	0.88
NW	1500 psi	no limit		

COMMON AND FACE BRICK- DIMENSIONS DO NOT INCLUDE MORTAR JOINTS

MODULAR COMMON AND FACE BRICK DIMENSIONS INCLUDE ONE MORTAR JOINT OR TWO HALF JOINTS

FIGURE 9-4 *Brick*

voids allow the brick to be more evenly burned throughout in the kiln.

In order to meet the physical requirements for the various grades of brick as established by the American Society for Testing Materials (ASTM), the definition of a brick is a unit whose net cross-sectional area in every plane parallel to the bearing surface is 75% or more of its gross cross-sectional area measured in the same plane. A solid brick measuring 3-3/4 × 7-3/4 in. = 29.06 sq. in. of bearing surface. With holes or voids, the cross-sectional area of the brick should be 75% of the total area, or 21.79 sq. in. The difference of 7.27 sq. in. is that of the holes or voids (see Figure 9-5).

Brick may be named or identified by a particular placement within a wall. Ordinarily, as one views a brick wall, the horizontal brick are called *stretchers*. When the brick-lengths are placed at right angles to the length of the wall, the brick are called *headers*. Similarly, others placed standing on end are known as *soldiers*. Figure 9-6 illustrates the various methods of placing brick.

Most brick manufacturers make a limited number of special-shaped brick such as bullnose, bullnose stretcher and header, bullnose starter (left or right), and internal bullnose return (see Figure 9-7).

Brick Bonds

Brick bonds are used primarily to assist in the strengthening of the brick wall. By bonding brick, various patterns or designs are created, of which some of the more common and better known are shown in Figure 9-8. These are the *common header bond*, where a header course is placed every 5th,

6th, or 7th course, the *common stretcher-header bond*, the *all-stretcher bond*, which is reinforced every sixth course with metal ties placed between the joints, and the *stacked bond*, with similar metal reinforcings every sixth course.

Brick hardness depends on the degree of burning received in the kiln. After burning, brick is sorted into the three following categories:

1. Brick nearest the fire—these are overburned, usually warped and discolored, and used where a decorative type brick is desired. They are known as *clinker brick*.

2. Brick with the right amount of burning—known as *hard-burned brick* and used for general brick work.

3. Under-burned brick—known as *soft brick* and used for back-up or in areas where strength is not of prime importance.

In building construction today most brick is used as a veneer with a masonry type backup, usually concrete block, and therefore many brick sizes are dimensioned so that the coursing of brick coordinates with the coursing of the backup material (see Figure 9-9).

FIGURE 9-5 *Hollow brick (showing names of the six surfaces of brick)*

FIGURE 9-6 *Placement of brick*

FIGURE 9-7 *Special shapes*

FIGURE 9-8   *Types of brick bonds generally used today in building construction*

FIGURE 9-9   *Brick veneer*

There are other types of brick used to create decorative walls where the horizontal coursing is the dominant design factor. Two of such types are the *Roman*, 1-1/2 × 11-3/4 in., and the *Norman*, 3-3/4 × 11-5/8 in. (See Figure 9-10).

The standard brick, 2-1/4 × 7-3/4 × 3-3/4 in., with 3/8 or 1/2-in. mortar joints, is generally used in the four common types of wall constructions shown in Figure 9-11. These are the plain 4-in. brick veneer wall; the 10-in. cavity wall; the 8-in. solid wall; and the 12-in. solid wall.

MODULAR BRICK: Table 9-3 gives data for modular brick construction, including the modular grid system, types and dimensions of modular brick, and modular brick height.

REVIEW EXAMINATION

1. Name the three processes used in manufacturing brick.
2. If the molds are made wet in order to stop the wet clay from sticking, what are the bricks called?
3. If the molds are sanded, what are the bricks called?
4. Give the dimensions of common and face brick.
5. At what courses may header bonds be located?
6. The hardness of brick depends upon what?
7. What are the three grades of brick that meet exact physical requirements?
8. The compressive strength in psi of an MW brick is greater than that of an SW brick—true or false?

ROMAN – WITH 1/2" HORIZONTAL JOINTS AND 1/4" VERTICAL JOINTS

NORMAN– WITH 3/4" HORIZONTAL JOINTS AND 3/8" VERTICAL JOINTS

ROMAN   NORMAN

FIGURE 9-10   *Decorative brick*

ANCHORS

HEADER COURSE (CAN BE ELIMINATED IF TIES ARE INSTALLED)

HEADER COURSE (CAN BE ELIMINATED IF TIES ARE INSTALLED)

4" VENEER	10" CAVITY WALL	8" SOLID WALL	12" SOLID WALL
615 BRICKS	1230 BRICKS	1232 BRICKS	1848 BRICKS
7.2 CU. FT.	14.4 CU. FT.	18.6 CU. FT.	27.8 CU. FT.

QUANTITIES OF BRICK AND MORTAR (1/2" JOINT) PER 100 SQ. FT. OF WALL – BRICK SIZE 2 1/4" x 3 3/4" x 8"

FIGURE 9-11   *Types of brick wall construction*

TABLE 9-3   *Brick height table for modular brick: height from center line to center line of mortar joints*

THE MODULAR BRICK SYSTEM

THE GRID LINES MAKE THE MODULAR SYSTEM WORK BOTH HORIZONTALLY AND VERTICALLY.

MODULAR BRICKS

ROMAN   STANDARD   ENGINEER   ECONOMY-8   ECONOMY-12

BRICK HEIGHT TABLE FOR MODULAR BRICK: HEIGHT FROM CENTER LINE TO CENTER LINE OF MORTAR JOINTS

BRICK FLAT – NOMINAL SIZES SHOWN
(NOMINAL DIMENSIONS INCLUDE BRICK PLUS MORTAR JOINT)

NO. OF COURSES	ROMAN 2" x 4" x 12	STANDARD 2⅔" x 4" x 8"	ENGINEER 3.2" x 4" x 8"	ECONOMY-8 4" x 4" x 8"	ECONOMY-12 4" x 4" x 12"
1	0'-2"	0'-2⅔"	0'-3.2"	0'-4"	0'-4"
2	0'-4"	0'-5⅓"	0'-6.4"	0'-8"	0'-8"
3	0'-6"	0'-8"	0'-9.6"	1'-0"	1'-0"
4	0'-8"	0'-10⅔"	1'-0.8"	1'-4"	1'-4"
5	0'-10"	1'-1⅓"	1'-4"	1'-8"	1'-8"
6	1'-0"	1'-4"	1'-7.2"	2'-0"	2'-0"
7	1'-2"	1'-6⅔"	1'-10.4"	2'-4"	2'-4"
8	1'-4"	1'-9⅓"	2'-1.6"	2'-8"	2'-8"
9	1'-6"	2'-0"	2'-4.8"	3'-0"	3'-0"
10	1'-8"	2'-2⅔"	2'-8"	3'-4"	3'-4"
11	1'-10"	2'-5⅓"	2'-11.2"	3'-8"	3'-8"
12	2'-0"	2'-8"	3'-2.4"	4'-0"	4'-0"
13	2'-2"	2'-10⅔"	3'-5.6"	4'-4"	4'-4"
14	2'-4"	3'-1⅓"	3'-8.8"	4'-8"	4'-8"
15	2'-6"	3'-4"	4'-0"	5'-0"	5'-0"
16	2'-8"	3'-6⅔"	4'-3.2"	5'-4"	5'-4"
17	2'-10"	3'-9⅓"	4'-6.4"	5'-8"	5'-8"
18	3'-0"	4'-0"	4'-9.6"	6'-0"	6'-0"
19	3'-2"	4'-2⅔"	5'-0.8"	6'-4"	6'-4"
20	3'-4"	4'-5⅓"	5'-4"	6'-8"	6'-8"
21	3'-6"	4'-8"	5'-7.2"	7'-0"	7'-0"
22	3'-8"	4'-10⅔"	5'-10.4"	7'-4"	7'-4"
23	3'-10"	5'-1⅓"	6'-1.6"	7'-8"	7'-8"
24	4'-0"	5'-4"	6'-4.8"	8'-0"	8'-0"
25	4'-2"	5'-6⅔"	6'-8"	8'-4"	8'-4"
26	4'-4"	5'-9⅓"	6'-11.2"	8'-8"	8'-8"
27	4'-6"	6'-0"	7'-2.4"	9'-0"	9'-0"
28	4'-8"	6'-2⅔"	7'-5.6"	9'-4"	9'-4"
29	4'-10"	6'-5⅓"	7'-8.8"	9'-8"	9'-8"
30	5'-0"	6'-8"	8'-0"	10'-0"	10'-0"
31	5'-2"	6'-10⅔"	8'-3.2"	10'-4"	10'-4"
32	5'-4"	7'-1⅓"	8'-6.4"	10'-8"	10'-8"
33	5'-6"	7'-4"	8'-9.6"	11'-0"	11'-0"
34	5'-8"	7'-6⅔"	9'-0.8"	11'-4"	11'-4"
35	5'-10"	7'-9⅓"	9'-4"	11'-8"	11'-8"
36	6'-0"	8'-0"	9'-7.2"	12'-0"	12'-0"
37	6'-2"	8'-2⅔"	9'-10.4"	12'-4"	12'-4"
38	6'-4"	8'-5⅓"	10'-1.6"	12'-8"	12'-8"
39	6'-6"	8'-8"	10'-4.8"	13'-0"	13'-0"
40	6'-8"	8'-10⅔"	10'-8"	13'-4"	13'-4"
41	6'-10"	9'-1⅓"	10'-11.2"	13'-8"	13'-8"
42	7'-0"	9'-4"	11'-2.4"	14'-0"	14'-0"
43	7'-2"	9'-6⅔"	11'-5.6"	14'-4"	14'-4"
44	7'-4"	9'-9⅓"	11'-8.8"	14'-8"	14'-8"
45	7'-6"	10'-0"	12'-0"	15'-0"	15'-0"
46	7'-8"	10'-2⅔"	12'-3.2"	15'-4"	15'-4"
47	7'-10"	10'-5⅓"	12'-6.4"	15'-8"	15'-8"
48	8'-0"	10'-8"	12'-9.6"	16'-0"	16'-0"
49	8'-2"	10'-10⅔"	13'-0.8"	16'-4"	16'-4"
50	8'-4"	11'-1⅓"	13'-4"	16'-8"	16'-8"
60	10'-0"	13'-4"	16'-0"	20'-0"	20'-0"
70	11'-8"	15'-6⅔"	18'-8"	23'-4"	23'-4"
80	13'-4"	17'-9⅓"	21'-4"	26'-8"	26'-8"
90	15'-0"	20'-0"	24'-0"	30'-0"	30'-0"
100	16'-8"	22'-2⅔"	26'-8"	33'-4"	33'-4"

9. Name the six sides of a brick.

10. In reference to hollow brick, what must the net cross-sectional area in every plane parallel to the bearing surface be?

ASSIGNMENT

1. Make a freehand sketch to scale showing four brick wall types.

2. Make a freehand sketch to scale showing six various placements of brick.

3. Make a freehand sketch showing a hollow brick and the names of six sides of brick.

SUPPLEMENTARY INFORMATION

Water Absorption of Brick

The rate of absorption plays an important role in the bonding of the brick to the mortar in the joint. If the brick absorbs water from the mortar too quickly a poor bond will result, causing leaks and other damage. Tests have indicated that brick with absorption rates in excess of 0.7 oz. per min. must be wetted sufficiently to prevent the rapid absorption of the water from the mortar and thereby allowing the time required for the proper setting of the mortar.

All brick should be laid in temperatures above 40°F., and in very high temperatures such as 90°F and over, caution should be taken that the brick is sufficiently wetted so that the mortar does not set too fast.

In all building construction brick work, the horizontal and vertical brick coursing should be checked for window openings, door openings, floor-to-floor heights, etc.

Other Types of Brick

GLAZED FACING BRICK: Bricks that receive a glaze on one face are known as "glazed facing brick." The glaze is applied directly after the brick is removed from the kiln, and is again burned until the glaze is fused to the brick. Because different color glazes may be applied, a large variety of colored facing brick can be made. Glazes may have a mat or gloss finish.

TABLE 9-4   *Cement brick strength requirements*

Grade	Compressive Strength (PSI)		Modulus of Rupture (PSI)	
	5 Tests Mean	Minimum Individual	5 Tests Mean	Minimum Individual
B	2250	1500	450	300
C	1250	1000	300	200

CEMENT BRICK: This type is manufactured in the same sizes as common and face brick and there are two grades, B and C (see Table 9-4). Cement brick is manufactured from a controlled mixture of portland cement and aggregates (sand, crushed rock, gravel, blast-furnace slag, or burned clay or shale). Grade B is frost-resistant and Grade C is used for backup and interior work. Various colors and textures are available.

SAND-LIME BRICK: Manufactured by the semi-dry method in presses and cured in autoclaves for 24 hrs. with steam, this brick is made from 5 to 10% hydrated lime and sand.

Sand-lime brick is graded the same as common and face brick and has good frost resistance and better fire resistance than common or face brick. Its natural color is a pearl-gray, but other colors are available.

ADOBE BRICK: Made from natural clays to which straw is added to prevent shrinkage and cracks. Both are mixed to a consistency for molding and then placed in the sun for 2 weeks to dry. Adobe brick should always be protected from moisture by large roof overhangs and concrete foundations to prevent capillary action.

SHAPES AND NAMES OF CUT BRICK: Figure 9-12 illustrates brick that are cut or split into other shapes and are used to fulfill a definite need in brick construction.

Pointing and Cleaning

All holes left by nails in a brick wall should be filled with mortar using a chisel or putty knife. Holes left in mortar joints should be filled or pointed with additional mortar.

Brick work can be cleaned with soap powder or other mild solutions. This should not be done until the joints have sufficiently hardened so that the mortar in the joint does not wash away. The earliest time for cleaning a masonry wall is 48 hrs. after construction.

The cleaning of brick is often done with the use of muriatic (or hydrochloric) acid mixed in

KING CLOSURE   QUEEN CLOSURE   BAT (HALF BRICK)

SPLIT BRICK (SOAP)   THREE QUARTER BRICK   ONE QUARTER BRICK

BRICK CORNER OR PIER   CORNER OF SOLDIER COURSE   CORNER OF SOLID BRICK WALL

FIGURE 9-12   *Shapes, names, and placement of brick*

proportions of one part acid to nine parts water. In place of the acid the brick can be cleaned by scrubbing with soap and warm water.

Parging

In a wall consisting of more than one thickness, parging is the back plastering of the face brick to provide additional insurance against any leakage. Parging should be done as the wall is laid up. Extreme care must be taken because the pressure applied when parging the wall of the newly laid units often can break the bond between the units and their mortar joints, causing cracks that may contribute to leaks.

10

BUILDING WITH BRICK

INTRODUCTION

This chapter provides information on brick mortars and joints, strength of brick walls, isolated piers and piers within a wall, expansion joints and expansion joint materials, brick coursing, accessories for brickwork, and illustrations of wall sections showing various methods of building with brick.

TECHNICAL INFORMATION

Mortars

The mortars used for brickwork are divided into five categories:

1. *Type M* — rigorous exposure, load-bearing, and below grade.
2. *Type S* — severe exposure, load-bearing, and below grade.
3. *Type N* — light loads, mild exposure, above grade.
4. *Type O* — light loads, interior work.
5. *Type K* — nonbearing, bearing where compressive strength does not exceed 75 psi.

Mortars are available ready-mixed (in bags), premixed (mixed at plant and transported to site), and job-mixed (ingredients are mixed by hand or in a cement mixer at site). Mortars for large construction are controlled by laboratory testing to meet the requirements known as *property specifications* as shown in Table 10-1, or by predetermined proportions by volume, known as *proportion specification*, as shown in Table 10-2.

Sand for mortar is generally white and is graded by size of joint (see Table 10-3).

For small jobs there exist premixed mortars that can be obtained usually from any local building supply store. For the small portable mixer the following mortar is used: 1–2–4; namely, one part portland cement to 2 parts lime putty to 4 parts fine sand.

TABLE 10-1   *Property specifications for mortars*

Type of Mortar	Compressive Strength in psi
M	2500
S	1800
N	750
O	350
K	75

TABLE 10-2   *Mortar proportion specification by volume and weight*

Type of Mortar	Portland Cement 94 lbs. = 1 cu. ft.	Masonry Cement	Lime Putty 40 lbs. = 1 cu. ft.	Sand 80 lbs. = 1 cu. ft.
M	1 94 lbs.	1 94 lbs.	—	
	1 94 lbs.	—	1/4 10 lbs.	
S	1/2 47 lbs.	1 94 lbs.	—	**FOR ALL TYPES:**
	1 94 lbs.	—	Greater than 1/4 to 1/2 + 10 lbs. to 20 lbs.	Not less than 2-1/4, 180 lbs. and not more than 3 times the sum of the volumes of the cement and lime putty
N	—	1 94 lbs.	—	
	1	—	Greater than 1/2 to 1-1/4 + 20 lbs. to 30 lbs.	
O	—	1 94 lbs.	—	
	1	—	Greater than 1-1/2 to 2-1/2 + 60 lbs. to 100 lbs.	
K	1	—	Greater than 2-1/2 to 4 + 100 lbs. to 160 lbs.	

TABLE 10-3   *Sand graded for mortar joints over 1/4"*

Screen No.	Size of Opening (in inches)	Percentage of Sand Retained (by weight)	
		Maximum	Minimum
8	0.097	10	0
16	0.049	40	15
30	0.0232	65	35
50	0.0117	85	75
100	0.0059	98	95

Mortar Joints

Mortar joints for brickwork are generally 3/8 and 1/2 in. Exterior joints should be of such a type that will easily shed water, whereas on the interior or in climates with little rainfall the joints do not have to shed water. The difference is illustrated in Figure 10-1.

Strength of Brick Walls

The strength of brick walls is often influenced by workmanship. Walls categorized as "inspected," type A workmanship, using SW brick and type M mortar, will have a strength of one-half the compressive strength of the brick. Walls categorized as "ordinary," type B workmanship, have a strength of two-thirds that of type A workmanship according to standard tests.

Piers

Brick piers are used to laterally support walls [see Figure 10-2 (a)]. Where brick piers are used to support girders or roof trusses, their dimensions should be sufficient so that the allowable compressive working stress of the brick masonry is not exceeded [see Figure 10-2 (b)]. The formula used is:

$$A = P/f_c$$

where   A = required area in sq. in.

P = load

f_c = allowable compressive working stress in psi

WEATHER STRUCK   FLUSH   ROUND RODDED   V-SHAPED   RAKED   STRIPPED (WOODEN STRIPS PLACED AT EACH JOINT)   TROWELED   BEADED

BRICK JOINTS WHICH SHED WATER

BRICK JOINTS WHICH DO NOT SHED WATER

FIGURE 10-1   *Mortar joints*

12"

PILASTER

BY MOST CODES THIS DISTANCE SHOULD BE 18 TO 24 TIMES THE WALL THICKNESS 18'-0" TO 24'-0"

(a) BRICK PILASTERS USED FOR LATERAL SUPPORT

BRICK PIER   CONTROL JOINTS

24"   20"   12"   VARIES   24"   12"   GIRDER

(b) BRICK PIERS USED TO SUPPORT BEAMS OR GIRDERS

FIGURE 10-2   *Brick piers and pilasters*

EXAMPLE: A roof load on a roof truss is 480,000 lbs., or 480 kips (a kip is 1000 lbs.). This load is supported by brick masonry which when inspected was classed as type A workmanship. The compressive strength of brick is 2500 psi. Because the allowable working stress is taken as one-half of the compressive strength of the material, the allowable working stress is therefore 1250 psi.

Therefore,

$$A = \frac{P}{fc}$$

$$A = \frac{480,000}{1250} = 384 \text{ sq. in.}$$

This would provide for a pier dimension of 16 × 24 in. For safety factor reasons, a somewhat larger pier can be selected, such as 20 × 24 in., or 16 × 28 in. (see Figure 10-2, B).

Isolated brick piers are calculated by using the same formula, but their heights are limited by codes to six to ten times their least dimensions.

Expansion Joints

All large buildings over 200'-0" long or buildings with one or more wings require at least one expansion joint whether they are of masonry, concrete, or steel frame construction. When new additions are added to existing buildings, they must be separated by expansion joints (see Figure 10-3).

EXAMPLE: A brick masonry building is 400'-0" long. The coefficient of linear expansion of brick is 0.0000031 in. per degree Fahrenheit. Using the formula:

Length in in. × temperature range × coefficient of expansion

or:

Expansion = 400 × 12 × 100 × 0.0000031

where:

400 = length in ft. × 12 in. (conversion of ft. to in.)

100 = average temperature range (e.g., 0° to 100°) winter and summer extremes

Total expansion of building is 1.488 in. or 1-1/2 in. On the basis of this information, an expansion joint of 1 in. would be necessary at the center of the building as shown in Figure 10-4. These expansion joints completely isolate one part of the building from the other, including foundations, exterior walls, partitions, floor slabs, ceilings, parapets, and roof construction, and roofing (see Figure 10-5).

NEW WING OR BUILDING ADJACENT TO EXISTING BUILDING

LONG BUILDING

LONG BUILDING WITH WINGS

FIGURE 10-3 *Expansion joints*

FIGURE 10-4 *Expansion of a building*

EXPANSION JOINT BETWEEN NEW AND EXISTING BUILDING

EXPANSION JOINT IN LENGTH OF LONG BUILDING

FIGURE 10-5   *Expansion joints*

FILLERS AND WATERSTOPS FOR EXPANSION JOINTS: Fillers are manufactured in three types: premolded, mastic, and metal.

Pre-molded type:

1. Vinyl, neoprene, and other resilient-type plastics
2. Cork
3. Rubber and synthetic rubbers
4. Asphalt-impregnated materials

Mastic type:

1. Epoxy
2. Asphalt

3. Synthetic rubbers
4. Silicones

Metal type: Bellows (soft copper or stainless steel)

Coursing

In brick construction work, both vertical and horizontal coursing of the brick is of utmost importance. In vertical coursing, window and door openings must be carefully calculated by brick coursing because most windows and doors are manufactured in stock sizes, both in height and width, as shown in Figure 10-6 and Table 10-4.

ALL VERTICAL DIMENSIONS MUST BE IN BRICK COURSING (BRICK HEIGHT PLUS JOINT)

ALL HORIZONTAL DIMENSIONS MUST BE IN BRICK COURSING (BRICK LENGTH PLUS JOINTS)

FIGURE 10-6   *Openings in brick*

TABLE 10-4　*Vertical coursing of standard and modular brick*

$2\frac{1}{4}$" + $\frac{3}{8}$" joint		$2\frac{1}{4}$" + $\frac{1}{2}$" joint		$2\frac{2}{3}$" Modular (includes joint)		4" Modular (includes joint)	
Course	Height	Course	Height	Course	Height	Course	Height
1	$2\frac{5}{8}$"	1	$2\frac{3}{4}$"	1	$2\frac{2}{3}$"	1	4"
2	$5\frac{1}{4}$"	2	$5\frac{1}{2}$"	2	$5\frac{1}{3}$"	2	8"
3	$7\frac{7}{8}$"	3	$8\frac{1}{4}$"	3	8"	3	12"
4	$10\frac{1}{2}$"	4	11"	4	$10\frac{2}{3}$"	4	1'-4"
5	$1'-1\frac{1}{8}$"	5	$1'-1\frac{3}{4}$"	5	$1'-1\frac{1}{3}$"	5	1'-8"
6	$1'-3\frac{3}{4}$"	6	$1'-4\frac{1}{2}$"	6	1'-4"	6	2'-0"
7	$1'-6\frac{3}{8}$"	7	$1'-7\frac{1}{4}$"	7	$1'-6\frac{2}{3}$"	7	2'-4"
8	1'-9"	8	1'-10"	8	$1'-9\frac{1}{3}$"	8	2'-8"
9	$1'-11\frac{5}{8}$"	9	$2'-0\frac{3}{4}$"	9	2'-0"	9	3'-0"
10	$2'-2\frac{1}{4}$"	10	$2'-3\frac{1}{2}$"				

Examples of Wall Sections

BRICK VENEER WITH FRAME BACKING: This section (see Figure 10-7) illustrates how the brick veneer is started on a concrete ledge somewhat below grade. The veneer wall is bonded to the sheathing by corrugated metal ties spaced 16 in. o.c. horizontally and vertically, and is carried up to or beyond the soffit line, or as high as the overhanging rafters will permit. The brick veneer in this construction is non-load-bearing and is therefore used only for appearance.

BRICK VENEER WITH METAL STUD BACKING: A "new" exterior brick masonry wall system has come on the market and is widely used. This system is both an innovation and an adaptation of the conventional brick veneer over wood studs system that has been used successfully for one- and two-family houses for decades. The wall system is brick veneer over metal stud-backup with gypsum sheathing (see Figure 10-8).

A veneered wall is, by definition, "a wall having a facing of masonry units or other weather-resisting noncombustible materials securely attached to the backing, but not so bonded as to intentionally exert common action under load." A brick veneered wall consists of an exterior layer of brick, isolated from the backup by a minimum 1-in. airspace, and attached to the backup with corrosion resistant metal ties.

BRICK CAVITY WALL WITH STEEL FRAME AND OPEN WEB STEEL JOISTS: This wall section (see Figure 10-9) illustrates how the brick veneer wall is anchored to concrete block by means of cavity wall ties and by dovetail cavity wall anchors. The spandrel steel sections support open-web steel floor and roof joists, which are covered by corrugated steel sheets acting as permanent forms for the 2-1/2-in. reinforced concrete slab. Note the spandrel flashing and the weep-holes for the elimination of condensation from the cavity.

REVIEW EXAMINATION

1. Name the three types of mortars used in brickwork.

2. For large construction, mortars are controlled by what two methods?

3. What are the generally used sizes of mortar joints?

4. In the formula A = P/fc, what is A? P? fc?

5. When you add an addition or a new wing to a building, what do you install at their connection?

6. Name the three types of fillers and waterstops that are used in expansion joints.

7. In a building using face brick on the exterior, what is of utmost importance in the way of calculations that must be made?

8. Name two types of brick joints that shed water.

9. Name two types of brick joints that do not shed water.

10. Over what length should a building have an expansion joint?

ASSIGNMENT

1. Draw a freehand sketch showing where expansion joints are required in buildings.

Labels (left side, top to bottom):
½" PLYWOOD SHEATHING
240 LBS. PER 100 SQ. FT. ASPHALT STRIP SHINGLES
15 # FELT
2"x6" ROOF RAFTER
WOOD FASCIA
WOOD SOFFIT
FACE BRICK
1" AIR SPACE
½" PLYWOOD SHEATHING
15# FELT BUILDING PAPER
WEATHER STRUCK JOINT
CORRUGATED ANCHORS
2"x8" HEADER
METAL FLASHING
WEEP HOLES IN VERTICAL JOINTS, 8" O.C.
DAMPROOFING
FINISH GRADE
CONCRETE LEDGE
DAMPROOFING
CONCRETE FOOTING

Labels (right side, top to bottom):
2"x6" CEILING BEAM
INSULATION
SHEET ROCK
TWO 2"x4's
INSULATION
2"x4"
25/32" WOOD STRIP FLOORING
2"x8" FLOOR JOIST
5/8" PLYWOOD SUB FLOORING
SHEETROCK
TWO 2"x4's
WOOD BASE
25/32" WOOD STRIP FLOORING
2"x8" FLOOR JOIST
5/8" PLYWOOD SUB FLOORING
INSULATION
4"x6" SILL
ANCHORS 4'-0" O.C.
CONCRETE FOUNDATION
EXPANSION JOINT
CONCRETE SLAB

FIGURE 10-7 *Brick veneer on wood frame*

Labels:
1" MINIMUM AIR SPACE
METAL STUD
WEEP HOLE
FOUNDATION
FLASHING

FIGURE 10-8 *Brick veneer with metal stud backing*

2. Draw a freehand sketch to scale showing eight types of brick joints.

SUPPLEMENTARY INFORMATION

Efflorescence

This is a white stain that appears on brickwork and is caused by soluble salts which are in the material and brought to the surface of the brick by moisture. In order to overcome efflorescence, it is necessary to check the type of brick (most brick now produced do not have soluble salts),

FIGURE 10-9 *Brick cavity wall with steel frame and open-web steel joists*

the type of mortar and, most important, the correct installation of the flashing.

Accessories

Accessories for brickwork are of utmost importance in building construction. They consist of cavity wall ties, reinforcing, nailing plugs, anchors and ties, nails, and various control and expansion joint materials. These are illustrated in Figures 10-10 and 10-11.

Special Mortars and Mortar Admixtures

PLASTIC MORTAR: There is an epoxy cement mortar which is now being used for brickwork. This mortar is applied in a ribbon with a type of caulking gun—it sets in 24 hrs. and reaches full

CAVITY WALL TIES
10", 12" & 1'-2" WALLS

CORRUGATED TIES
8", 12", 1'-4" & 1'-8" WALLS

CASE-HARDENED
CUT NAILS

8", 12" & 1'-4"
SOLID MASONRY
WALL

10", 12" & 1'-2"
CAVITY
WALL

8", 12" & 1'-4"
SOLID MASONRY
WALL

NAILING PLUG

BRICK JOINT

NAIL FOLLOWS BENDS

REINFORCINGS

CORRUGATED DOVE-TAIL ANCHOR
(FOR CONCRETE & BRICK)

WIRE DOVETAIL ANCHOR
(FOR CONCRETE & BRICK)

5"

8" & 12"

WIRE MESH WALL TIES
(AVAILABLE IN ALL SIZES)

1'-4"

5"

STOCK BRICK VENTS
(AVAILABLE IN VARIOUS
DEPTHS 8", 12" ETC.)

FIGURE 10-10   *Brick work accessories*

MASONRY BACK-UP

BRICK

MASONRY BACK-UP

BRICK

VERTICAL PLASTIC STRESS
RELIEVING JOINT

SYNTHETIC RUBBER STRESS
RELIEVING JOINT

VINYL TYPE
EXPANSION JOINT
WATER STOP

DUMBELL VINYL TYPE
EXPANSION JOINT
WATER STOP

CENTER BULB VINYL
COMPRESSION TYPE
EXPANSION JOINT
WATER STOP

FIGURE 10-11   *Control and expansion joint materials*

117

strength in 72 hrs. It not only is equal to conventional mortars in compressive strength but also has the advantage of great tensile strength, whereas conventional mortar has very small tensile strength. With this type of mortar, prefabricated brick and concrete panels 12'-0" long by 8'-0" high can be made and then lifted into place in the building.

MORTAR ADMIXTURES: These consist of accelerators, plasticizing agents, waterproofing agents, and color pigments. Admixtures come in powders, paste, and liquid form and are usually patented and sold under trade names.

GROUT: This refers to mortars containing finely ground iron particles and hardening elements mixed with cement. Grout sets rapidly, does not shrink or expand, and forms a hard, strong, durable material. It is used for setting steel columns, etc., onto concrete or masonry walls, and also for heavy machinery installations.

Fire Brick

This type is made of fire clay that contains 50% alumina and is used for fireplaces where intense heat is present. Fire brick is installed with a fire clay-type of mortar. There are other kinds of special brick such as refractory brick (used where very high temperatures are present), flooring and paving brick (see Figure 10-12), acid brick (used where acids are present), and brick for reinforced brick walls (see Figure 10-13).

More Examples of Wall Sections

BRICK WITH CONCRETE BLOCK BACKUP: This is shown in Figure 10-14. The brick veneer and the concrete block backing in this wall section are tied by corrugated flat wall ties. The ends of the wood floor joists are fire-cut and bear a minimum of 4 in. on filled-in solid blocks. The wall is provided on its inside surface with 1 × 2-in. furring strips and 1-in. insulation. The finish is wire lath and plaster. The relatively flat roof is covered with white marble chips (to reflect radiant sun heat) on a built-up roof on tongue-and-groove wood roofing boards.

A BRICK WALL WITH REINFORCED CONCRETE: This is illustrated in Figure 10-15. The brick wall with concrete block backing is integrated with the concrete floor and roof slabs. The roof slab, for example, is cast to form part of the wall lintel and cap over a window opening. The roof is insulated with 1-1/2-in. rigid insulation and a pitched fill provides for proper roof drainage. Note the corrugated wall anchors, the spandrel flashing, the base and cap flashing, and the expansion joints where the concrete sidewalk and the cellar slab meets the wall.

Mortars for Small Construction

For small construction work, the materials used for mortars are usually in the following proportions:

1.0 part cement

3.0 parts sand

0.25 part of hydrated lime

Ready-mixed mortars for small work, furnished in paper bags, are available from building materials suppliers.

Reinforced Brick Wall

Brick used for reinforced brick masonry is the same as that used for ordinary brick masonry. The brick, however, should have a compressive strength of at least 2500 psi. The reinforcing steel is the same as that used for concrete. Hard grade steel should not be used for this type of construction type M mortar should be used because of its high strength. Wire for tying reinforcing steel should be 18-gauge soft annealed iron wire. All reinforcing steel (see Figure 10-16) must be firmly embedded in mortar. Horizontal bars are laid in a bed of mortar. More mortar is spread on top of the rods and smoothed out for the bed joint of the next layer of bricks.

Vertical bars are placed in the vertical mortar joints. They are held in position by wood templates in which holes have been drilled at the proper bar spacing. The brick is laid up around bars.

Horizontal and vertical bars in brick masonry need not be wired together as recommended for reinforcing steel in concrete walls. The minimum spacing (center to center) between parallel bars is 1-1/2 times the bar diameter.

FLOORING AND PAVING BRICKS   FIRE AND KEFRACTORY BRICK

FIGURE 10-12   *Special types of brick*

STRETCHER   ANGLE

GROUTLOCK   LINTEL

PLAN   PLAN

REINFORCED
BRICK

FIGURE 10-13   *Special brick for reinforced concrete walls*

ALUMINUM GRAVEL STOP

WHITE MARBLE CHIPS (TO REFLECT RADIANT SUN HEAT) ON BUILT-UP ROOF ON T&G WOOD SHEATHING

INSULATION

WOOD FASCIA

1" ROUND VENT WITH SCREEN

½" WEATHER PROOF PLYWOOD SOFFIT

CORRUGATED FLAT WALL TIES

FLUSH TYPE JOINTS

CONCRETE BLOCK FILLED IN SOLID

FACE BRICK

5"x8" BRICK VENT

FINISH GRADE

DEPTH CONTROLLED BY FROST LINE

2"x8" PLATE

ANCHOR (TOP BLOCK SOLID)

WIRE LATH & PLASTER

1" INSULATION BETWEEN 1"x2" FURRING STRIPS

PLASTER GROUND

WOOD BASE

2"x8" FLOOR JOIST (FIRE CUT)

WIRE LATH & PLASTER

VINYL ASBESTOS TILE ON 3/16" UNDERLAYMENT BOARDS ON T&G WOOD SUB-FLOOR

2" RIGID FOAM INSULATION

2"x8" FLOOR JOIST (FIRE CUT)

CRAWL SPACE

2" CONCRETE SLAB

SHEET PLASTIC MOISTURE BARRIER

CONCRETE BLOCK FOUNDATION WALL

CONCRETE FOOTING

FIGURE 10-14 *Brick with concrete block back-up*

120

DOWELS
CONTINUOUS FLASHING
CORRUGATED WALL TIES
SPANDREL FLASHING
DOVETAIL SLOT
DOVETAIL CORRUGATED WALL ANCHORS
ALUMINUM SILL
CORRUGATED WALL ANCHORS
FACE BRICK
DAMPPROOFING
DOVETAIL CORRUGATED WALL ANCHORS
EXPANSION JOINT
SIDEWALK
DAMPPROOFING
FOOTING

PRECAST CONCRETE COPING
DRIP
BASE & CAP FLASHING
BUILT-UP ROOFING
1½" RIGID INSULATION
FILL FOR ROOF DRAINAGE
REINFORCED CONCRETE BEAMS & SLABS
ALUMINUM CLOSURE AT HEAD ONLY
WINDOW ANCHORS
ALUMINUM WINDOW
WINDOW ANCHORS
ALUMINUM STOOL
SILL ANCHOR STRAPS
CONCRETE BLOCK WITH SPECIAL GLAZED SURFACE
¼" POLYESTER TERRAZZO
REINFORCED CONCRETE BEAMS & SLABS
EXPANSION JOINT
REINFORCED CONCRETE SLAB
GRAVEL FILL

FIGURE 10-15 *Brick wall with reinforced concrete*

FIGURE 10-16 *Brick wall with reinforcings*

Brick Wall Supporting Floor Joists

A section of a brick wall is shown in Figure 10-17, supporting floor joists and lightweight concrete over the wood floor. The floor joists are connected to a 2″ × 8″ wood ledger by standard joist hangers. The ledger is bolted to the wall. The wood flooring is nailed to the ledger to transfer floor diaphragm stress into the wall. The horizontal reinforcing bars act as a bond beam in the masonry wall.

Brick Wall and Poured Concrete Slab

A poured concrete slab (see Figure 10-18) is cast into a section of brick wall. The slab is cast into the wall for vertical support. The slab diaphragm stress is transferred to the wall by the reinforcing dowels.

Quantity Take-offs for Brick Wall Construction

Tables 10-5 and 10-6 are useful in that they show quantities of brick, concrete block, and mortar needed for 100 sq. ft. of composite wall of various thicknesses and for 100 sq. ft. of solid brick wall of various thicknesses.

FIGURE 10-17 *Method of supporting floor joists in a brick wall*

FIGURE 10-18 *Brick wall combined with a poured concrete slab*

TABLE 10-5 *Quantities for 100 sq. ft. of composite wall*

QUANTITIES FOR 100 SQ. FT. COMPOSITE WALL

BLOCK BRICK MORTAR	7TH COURSE BONDING	7TH COURSE BONDING	6TH COURSE BONDING	7TH COURSE BONDING
NUMBER OF STRETCHER BLOCK	97 BLOCKS 4″x 8″x 16″	97 BLOCKS 8″x 8″x 16″	57 BLOCKS 8″x 8″x 16″	193 BLOCKS 4″x 5″x 12″
NUMBER OF HEADER BLOCK			57 BLOCKS 8″x 8″x 16″	
NUMBER OF BRICK	772	868	788	770
MORTAR * CU. FT.	11.2	12.2	12.2	11.8
CU. YDS.	.407	.452	.452	.438

* NOTE. MORTAR QUANTITIES BASED ON 3/8″ JOINTS WITH FACE-SHELL BEDDING FOR THE BLOCK. QUANTITIES ARE NET. ALLOW FOR WASTE.

123

TABLE 10-6 *Brick and mortar for 100 square feet of solid brick wall*

Joint Thickness	1/4″	3/8″	1/2″	5/8″
4-in. wall				
Bricks—no.	698	655	616	581
Mortar—cu. ft.	4.0	5.7	7.2	8.6
cu. yd.	.148	.211	.267	.318
*Wt.—1 sq. ft. wall—lb.	33.6	34.0	34.2	34.6
8-in. wall				
Bricks—no.	1396	1310	1232	1161
Mortar—cu. ft.	12.2	15.5	18.6	21.3
cu. yd.	.452	.574	.689	.788
*Wt.—1 sq. ft. wall—lb.	72.6	73.2	73.9	74.3
12-in. wall				
Bricks—no.	2095	1965	1848	1742
Mortar—cu. ft.	20.3	25.3	29.9	34.0
cu. yd.	.752	.937	1.11	1.26
*Wt.—1 sq. ft. wall—lb.	111.4	112.4	113.4	114.1
16-in. wall				
Bricks—no.	2793	2620	2464	2322
Mortar—cu. ft.	28.5	35.1	41.4	46.7
cu. yd.	1.06	1.30	1.53	1.73
*Wt.—1 sq. ft. wall—lb.	150.1	151.0	152.9	153.9

Common brick 2-1/4″ × 8″. All joints filled.

Quantities are net—Allow for waste.

*Approximate wt. wall = No. bricks × 4.1 lb. + cu. ft. mortar × 125 lb.

11

OTHER MASONRY UNITS

INTRODUCTION

This chapter covers the various masonry-type units other than brick, such as structural load-bearing and non-load-bearing clay wall tile, facing tile, concrete block, concrete block with special surface finish, terra cotta, and gypsum block. These materials are discussed with regard to their sizes and uses, including information on their load-bearing capacities, fire ratings, and their general material composition.

TECHNICAL INFORMATION

By definition, a masonry unit is a rectangular-shaped block whose net cross-sectional area in any plane parallel to the bearing surface is less than 75% of its gross cross-sectional area measured in the same plane. For example: The masonry unit shown in Figure 11-1 measures 3-3/4 × 7-3/4 in. Therefore, its area is:

$$3.75 \times 7.75 = 29.06 \text{ sq. in.}$$

The area of two holes is:

$$2.25 \times 2.75 \times 2 = 12.38 \text{ sq. in.}$$

Net bearing cross-sectional area
$$= 16.68 \text{ sq. in.}$$
$$75\% \text{ of } 29.06 = 21.8 \text{ sq. in.}$$

Because the net bearing area of the block is less than 75% of total area, the block by definition is a masonry unit.

Structural Clay Tile

This type of tile is a hollow masonry unit used in building construction for load-bearing and non-load-bearing walls, fireproofing, backup, and furring, but not for exterior or interior surface finish (see Figure 11-2).

Load-bearing structural tile is manufactured in two grades: LBX for general masonry work, and LB for masonry where there is a 3-in. or more exterior facing. Non-load-bearing, fireproofing, and furring tile are manufactured in one grade only. In the building construction field, these structural tiles are still used extensively but are not as important as they formerly were because of new methods of fireproofing steel, the widespread use of pre-fabricated partitions, and the development of various types of concrete block and new methods of finishing surfaces.

Load-Bearing Structural Facing Tile

This type of tile is very extensively used in building construction for interior partitions, for backup for exterior walls and, in combination with only masonry units, for partitions. Load-bearing structural facing tiles are manufactured in two classes, *standard* and *special duty* (see Table 11-1).

TABLE 11-1 *Compressive strength of load-bearing structural facing tile*

Class	Minimum Compressive Strength of Single Uni (PSI gross area)	
	End Construction	*Side Construction*
Standard	1000	500
Special duty	2000	1000

FIGURE 11-1 *Definition of a masonry unit*

126

STRUCTURAL CLAY WALL TILE — LOAD BEARING

STRUCTURAL CLAY WALL TILE — LOAD BEARING — END CONSTRUCTION

STRUCTURAL CLAY WALL TILE — NON LOAD BEARING
PARTITION AND FURRING TILE

2 HOUR AND 4 HOUR
RATING FIREPROOFED
COLUMN

2 HOUR RATING
SOFFIT
FIREPROOFED
BEAM

STRUCTURAL CLAY TILE FIREPROOFING

FIGURE 11-2   *Structural clay tile*

They are available in a wide range of colors, either bright or matte finish, and in various textures including an acoustical type. The sizes have been standardized. These tiles are manufactured for both end and side construction. Also, special shapes for cove bases, sills, caps, lintels, miters, internal and external corners, jambs, and starters are standardized and readily available (see Figure 11-3). This type of tile has a most important additional feature in that it is available with finish surfaces on both sides.

Load-bearing structural facing tile is generally called *structural facing tile*, or *SFT*, and is graded in two categories: FTX, with a high degree of mechanical perfection and narrow range in color variation—these are used where low water absorption, easy maintenance, and resistance to stain are required; and FTS, with good mechanical perfection and wide range in color variation.

Concrete Block

Concrete block is perhaps the most widely used masonry unit material in building construction today, other than brick. Because of the ease in manufacture and its light weight, strength, and fireproofing qualities, it has supplanted many other types of masonry units. It is used for foundations, backup, fireproofing, load-bearing and non-load-bearing walls and partitions and, with special surface finishes, for exterior and interior areas where easy maintenance and stain resistance are required (see Figure 11-4).

Concrete block units made in two-core design instead of three offer several advantages. One is the face shell thickness at the center web which increases the tensile strength of the unit and reduces the tendency of cracking due to drying, shrinkage, and temperature changes. Two-core block has three webs, reducing heat conduction 3% to 4%, is about 4 lbs. lighter in weight, and allows more space for placing conduit or other utilities.

Grades of Concrete Masonry Units

Load-bearing concrete units are classified in the American Society for Testing and Materials (ASTM) specifications as Grade N and Grade S, with grade N units suitable for general use, such as for exterior walls below and above grade, interior walls, and backup. Grade S units are limited to use above grade in exterior walls with weather protective coatings and in walls not exposed to the weather.

4" STRETCHER FINISHED ONE SIDE OR BOTH SIDES

SOAP FINISHED ONE SIDE ONLY

6" STRETCHER FINISHED ONE SIDE OR BOTH SIDES

8" STRETCHER FINISHED ONE SIDE OR BOTH SIDES

STRUCTURAL CLAY FACING TILE—LOAD BEARING—SIDE CONSTRUCTION
(DIFFERENT MANUFACTURERS SUPPLY BOTH SIDE AND END CONSTRUCTION TYPES)

ACOUSTICAL TYPE   INTERNAL CORNER   EXTERNAL CORNER

FIGURE 11-3   *Structural clay facing tile—load bearing*

3 CORE
STRETCHER

2 OR 3 CORE
STRETCHER

2 OR 3 CORE
STRETCHER

2 OR 3 CORE
CORNER BLOCK

2 OR 3 CORE
WINDOW JAMB BLOCK

JAMB
BLOCK

LOAD-BEARING AND NON-LOAD-BEARING CONCRETE BLOCK

FIREPROOFING AND PARTITION CONCRETE BLOCK

HEADER BLOCK

LINTEL BLOCK

FIGURE 11-4 *Concrete block*

129

Concrete block is manufactured not only in 7-3/4-in. heights but also in 3-1/2-in. and 5-in. heights in order to meet the heights of brick and structural facing tile. Load-bearing concrete block is manufactured either solid or cored, and all non-load-bearing block is cored. Load-bearing concrete block is graded in two categories, for compressive strength, *grade A* and *grade B* (see Table 11-2).

Concrete Block with Surface Finish (Glazed Masonry Units)

Concrete block with colored, durable, and easily maintained surface is used for backup, load-bearing and non-load-bearing walls and partitions, and where a hard, durable, easily maintained finish surface is required (see Figure 11-5). It is available with both faces of the block having a colored, durable finish.

Special shapes are available such as caps, lintel blocks, bull noses, header blocks, and thin caps and bases.

This type of concrete block is manufactured so that the durable surface is slightly larger than the block to which it is applied so that all joints are 1/4 in. (see Figure 11-6).

Terra Cotta (Ceramic Veneer)

This type of masonry unit was very widely used in building construction in the past. Recently has it again become popular, its name having been changed to ceramic veneer. This material has the advantage of being a burned clay product and, more important, it is available in larger sizes, the maximum size being 2 ft.-8-3/4 in. long × 4 ft.-3 in. high and only 0'-2-5/8 in. thick (see Figure 11-7). It is available in a limited range of colors but can be obtained in a wide range of colors with glazed finishes.

TABLE 11-2   *Load-bearing concrete block*

Type of Block	Thickness of Shell (minimum)	Grade	Compressive Strength of Average Gross Area (PSI)	
			5 blocks average	1 block
Hollow load-bearing	1 1/2" or over	A	1000	800
	1 1/4" or over	B	700	600
Hollow non-load-bearing	not less than 1/2"		350	300
Solid load-bearing		A	1800	1600
		B	1200	1000

FIGURE 11-5   *Concrete block with surface finish (glazed masonry unit)*

CROSS SECTION   LONGITUDINAL SECTION A-A

FIGURE 11-6 *Concrete block and surface finish*

FACE PANEL   CORNER PANEL

FIGURE 11-7 *Ceramic veneer (terra cotta)*

Gypsum Block

Gypsum blocks are manufactured from gypsum plaster (plaster of Paris) into solid and cored blocks which are used for fireproofing and non-load-bearing partitions where finish plaster will be applied. Gypsum, because of its chemical and physical make-up, has good fireproofing characteristics. For example, 2 in. of gypsum block has the same fire rating as 4 in. of concrete block (see Figure 11-8 and Table 11-3).

SPLIT   SOLID   CORED

FIGURE 11-8 *Types of gypsum block*

TABLE 11-3 *Fire ratings of gypsum block*

Type of Gypsum Block	With Plaster One or Both Sides	Fire Resistance (hours)
2" solid for fireproofing steel	one side	4
3" hollow for fireproofing steel	one side	4
3" hollow partition	one side both sides	1 1/2 3
4" hollow partition	one side both sides	3 4
6" hollow partition	one side both sides	4 5

REVIEW EXAMINATION

1. A masonry unit's net cross-sectional area in any plane parallel to the bearing surface is less than what percentage of its gross cross-sectional area measured in the same plane?

2. Structural clay tile is used in building construction for what purposes?

3. Structural clay tile is installed in building construction by what two construction methods?

4. What are the two grades for load-bearing structural tile?

5. Load-bearing structural facing tile is graded in what two categories?

6. The load-bearing structural facing tile FTS grade has a high degree of mechanical perfection and a narrow range of color variation—true or false?

7. Structural facing tile cannot be manufactured with finish surfaces on both sides—true or false?

8. What are the advantages of using terra cotta (ceramic facings)?

9. Name four uses of concrete block in building construction.

10. In what two ways is load-bearing concrete block manufactured?

11. What are the two grades of load-bearing concrete block?

12. In what circumstances is concrete block with colored, durable, and easily maintained surface used in building construction?

13. What is gypsum block used for?

ASSIGNMENT

1. Draw a freehand sketch to scale showing a masonry unit.
2. Draw a freehand sketch to scale showing the various types of load-bearing structural facing tile (side construction).

SUPPLEMENTARY INFORMATION

WATER ABSORPTION OF CONCRETE BLOCK: All concrete block is manufactured with a maximum water absorption of 1 lb. per cu. ft. of concrete, based on the average of five blocks per cu. ft. of concrete, each block weighing 15 lbs.

SPECIAL TYPES OF CONCRETE BLOCK: With the development of concrete block with special surfaces, a new group of special concrete blocks is now manufactured, including concrete block with high acoustical value and a durable surface, block with a highly dense and polished surface, and block with a wide variety of surface textures incorporating marble chips, pebbles, and the like, and molded textures.

12

BUILDING WITH MASONRY MATERIALS

INTRODUCTION

This chapter covers building with other masonry materials—their limitations in height, strength, and load-bearing capacities, and methods of installation in building construction.

The masonry units other than brick include structural clay tile and facing tile, concrete block, special finished concrete block, terra cotta and gypsum block, and various types of mortar and joints used with these units.

TECHNICAL INFORMATION

Structural Clay Tile

Structural clay tile is manufactured in natural finish—that is, the color of the clay, which may be red, brownish, or yellowish. It is produced in two grades; namely, LBX and LB, each with different compressive strengths measured in psi (see Table 12-1).

LOAD REQUIREMENTS: Structural clay tile is used for fireproofing such as that around steel columns, for wall furring, as a backup in walls where a plaster or ceramic tile is applied as a finish surface, but most of all as a load-bearing or non-load-bearing wall. Figure 12-1 illustrates structural clay tile for partition walls, one with a plaster finish on both sides and the other with a plaster finish on one side and a ceramic tile finish on the other. Height and length limitations of structural clay tile walls as imposed by most building codes are shown in Figure 12-2. The limitations apply to both side and end construction methods.

MORTARS: (See also Chapter 10, Building with Brick.) Mortars for structural clay tile are type M, used where fireproofing is required, type S, for load-bearing, and type N, for non-load bearing exterior and partition walls. Mortar joints are generally 1/4-in., struck flush. Figure 12-3 shows typical sections and a plan of structural clay tile, bearing and non-bearing walls.

WATER ABSORPTION: The water absorption rate of structural clay tile is very important because if it is too great, the water in the mortar will be absorbed by the tile, causing the mortar to set too quickly and thereby weakening the adhesion.

FIGURE 12-1 *Structural clay tile used for load bearing and non-load bearing partitions*

The two grades of structural clay tile, therefore, are controlled as to their water absorption rates in percentages. The LBX tile will absorb 19% and the LB tile 28%. A permissible variation in the rate of absorption of the tile delivered to a construction site should not be more than 12%.

FIRE RESISTANCE: The fire-resistance rating for structural clay tile is based on the number of cells and the wall thickness (see Table 12-2).

Structural Facing Tile

Structural facing tile is used for load-bearing and non-load-bearing walls and partitions and backup areas where easy maintenance is required and a hard, colored, finish surface is of importance. The two classes of structural facing tile, FTX and FTS, are manufactured with a maximum water absorption rate as indicated in Table 12-3.

The same mortars are used for structural facing tile as are used for structural clay tile except that the joints are generally 1/4 in. The sand used in the mortars should pass a No. 16 screen. The wall sections in Figure 12-4 show application of structural facing tile.

When structural facing tile is used in construction, such as around a door opening, it is necessary to calculate both horizontal and vertical joints so that there will be a minimum of cutting of the structural facing tile (see Figure 12-5). This is also true for window sills and at door bases where special shapes have to meet both vertical and horizontal dimensions.

**2" HOLLOW TILE HAS A HEIGHT LIMITATION OF 9'-0"
AND A LENGTH LIMITATION OF 6'-0"**

FIGURE 12-2 *Height and length limitations of hollow structural clay tile, both side and end construction*

FIGURE 12-3 *Application of structural clay tile*

TABLE 12-1 *Load requirements for load-bearing structural clay tile*

Grade	Minimum Compressive Strength (PSI) for Single Unit	
	End Construction	Side Construction
LBX	1000	500
LB	700	500

TABLE 12-2 *Fire resistance rating for load-bearing structural clay wall tile for wall thicknesses as shown*

Type of Wall Construction	Combustible Material Framed into Wall (wood joists)				Noncombustible Materials Framed into Wall (steel joists)			
	4 hr.	3 hr.	2 hr.	1 hr.	4 hr.	3 hr.	2 hr.	1 hr.
Unplastered	16" 4 cells	16" 4 cells	12" 3 cells	12" 3 cells	12" 4 cells	12" 3 cells	12" 3 cells	8" 2 cells
Plastered (gypsum) one side	same as above	12" 3 cells	12" 2 cells	8" 2 cells	12" 3 cells	same as above	8" 2 cells	same as above
Plastered (gypsum) both sides	same as above	same as above	same as above	same as above	same as above	8" 3 cells	same as above	same as above

TABLE 12-3 *Maximum water absorption (percent) average for structural facing tile*

Class	After Submersion in Cold Water for 24 hrs.	After Submersion in Boiling Water for 1 hr.
FTX	7	9
FTS	13	16

TABLE 12-4 *Effects of different aggregates in concrete block*

Aggregate type	Weight lbs. per unit	Color	Texture	"U" factor
Sand and gravel	38 to 43	Light gray	Fine	8" = 0.59 and 12" = 0.49
Cinder	26 to 33	Dark gray	Coarse to medium	8" = 0.37 and 12" = 0.35
Shale, clay, or slag	26 to 33	Light gray	Fine, medium	8" = 0.33 and 12" = 0.32

Concrete Block

Concrete block varies in weight, color, texture, and coefficients of heat transmission with the type of aggregate used (see Table 12-4).

EFFECT OF DIFFERENT AGGREGATES: The different aggregates in concrete block also greatly affect its strength and denseness but can impart other characteristics which may be desirable. For example, sand and gravel give the concrete block high compressive strength and low water absorption but also denseness and durable strength; cinders decrease compressive strength but increase fire-resistance and insulating properties and also make the blocks nailable; shale, clay, and slag give high strength but also increase fire-resistance and insulating value, besides making the block nailable.

DIMENSIONAL LIMITATIONS: In general, building codes specify height limitations for various thicknesses of concrete block used as supporting walls

SECTION THRU EXTERIOR CAVITY WALL

FACE BRICK
CAVITY WALL ANCHOR
WEEP HOLES
DAMPROOFING
STRUCTURAL FACING TILE
STRUCTURAL FACING TILE COVE BASE
PRE-CAST EPOXY TERRAZZO

SECTION THRU PARTITION

COVE BASE
CERAMIC TILE
STRUCTURAL FACING TILE
FEATHER EDGE BASE
VINYL ASBESTOS TILE

PARTITION WALL WITH ONE SIDE ACOUSTICAL TYPE STRUCTURAL FACING TILE

ACOUSTICAL STRUCTURAL FACING TILE
VINYL TILE
STRUCTURAL FACING TILE
COVE BASE
QUARRY TILE

LOAD BEARING PARTITION

FEATHER EDGE BASE
SHEET VINYL
STRUCTURAL FACING TILE
FEATHER EDGE BASE
SHEET VINYL

STRUCTURAL FACING TILE ON ONE SIDE OF A PARTITION

CERAMIC TILE
STRUCTURAL FACING TILE
CONCRETE BLOCK
FEATHER EDGE BASE
RUBBER TILE

FIGURE 12-4   *Application of structural facing tile*

HEAD OF DOOR BUCK REINFORCED
BUCK ANCHORS

HEAD

BULLNOSE

ELEVATION

BASE COURSE 5 3/16"
10 COURSES OF 7 3/4"

PLAN

STEEL BUCKS
ANCHORS
2"   2'-8'   2"

MITER

BULL NOSE BASE

FIGURE 12-5   *Details of door in structural facing tile partition*

137

(load-bearing) such as in residences or single or multistoried buildings (see Figure 12-6).

Height limitations are restricted to 12'-0" for 8-in. block and 35'-0" for 12-in. block, and the block must increase in size by 4 in. for every 35'-0" additional height. Horizontally and vertically, the maximum distance between lateral supports for concrete block walls is 12'-0" for 8-in. block and 18'-0" for 12-in. block. Cavity walls are restricted to three-story buildings and have the same restrictions on lateral supports, both vertically and horizontally, as 8-in. block.

MORTARS AND SPECIAL SHAPES: The most frequently used concrete block shapes other than standard (for which see Chapter 11) are shown in Figure 12-7. However, manufacturers make other sizes and shapes to meet various special conditions and requirements that occur in construction. The mortars used for concrete block construction are summarized in Table 12-5.

CONTROL JOINTS: In all concrete block construction control joints must be installed to eliminate cracking due to thermal expansion and contrac-

FIGURE 12-6   *General size restrictions of concrete block when used as load-bearing walls*

TABLE 12-5   *Classes of mortar for concrete block*

Type of Mortar	Cementitious Materials cu. ft.	Masonry Cement cu. ft.	Lime Putty cu. ft.	Sand cu. ft.	Type of Support	Exterior or Interior Location
M	1	1	—		Heavy loads and below grade	Interior and exterior
	1	—	1/4			
				FOR ALL TYPES:		
S	1/2	1	Greater than 1/4 to 1/2	Not less than 2-1/4 and not more than 3 times the volumes of cement and lime used	Heavy loads and below grade	Interior and exterior
	1	—				
N	—	1	Greater than 1/2 to 1-1/4		Light loads	Interior
	1	—				
O	—	1	Greater than 1-1/2 to 2-1/2		Light loads	Interior
	1	—				
K	1	—	Greater than 2-1/2 to 4		Partitions Nonbearing	Interior

PARTITION   STARTER OR FILLER   SOLID

FIGURE 12-7   *Concrete block shapes available other than standard shapes*

tion. In long horizontal walls and partitions, control joints should be installed approximately every 20'-0". Other areas where they should be installed are generally at pilasters, columns, intersections, and openings (see Figures 12-8 and 12-9).

EXTERIOR AND INTERIOR USES OF CONCRETE BLOCK: When concrete block is used on exterior walls (except in very dry climates), either the denseness and water resistance of the block or the surface treatment must be considered in order to stop penetration of water into the interior of the building. This can be accomplished by applying a stucco with a waterproof cement, by painting the surface with a waterproof paint, or by using a special dense-surface block (see Figure 12-10, A and B), Figure 12-10, C, shows a load-bearing

concrete block partition with open-web steel joists.

Load-bearing and non-load-bearing concrete block interior partitions with various types of surface treatments such as ceramic tile, wood panels, structural facing tile, etc., are shown in Figure 12-11.

CONCRETE BLOCK WITH SPECIAL SURFACE FINISHES: Manufacturers are researching and producing concrete block with special surface treatments making possible durable, colored, and easily maintained surfaces. These blocks can replace brick, structural facing tile, acoustical materials, etc. At present the generally accepted special surface finished concrete blocks for building construction are acoustical type surfaces and durable

FIGURE 12-8   *Control joints in concrete block construction*

FIGURE 12-9   *Control joint at opening*

surfaces, for interior treatments and also for very dense water-resistant surfaces for exterior walls. The exterior types are identical in size and shape to standard type concrete blocks. The acoustical and special colored, durable types vary in construction details because of the increased dimensions of the surface finishes (see Figures 12-12 and 12-13). The mortars used for these types of concrete block are the same as for standard concrete block. With durable, colored surface finish block, the joints are 1/4-in. flush joints.

Terra Cotta (Ceramic Veneer)

When using this material in building construction (see Figure 12-14), it is important to control the possible warpage of the surfaces, because a piece of material this size, when burned in a kiln, can warp to a considerable degree. Necessary restrictions have therefore been established on the acceptable limitations of warpage in a surface. For example, a piece of terra cotta 2-5/8 in. thick, 4 ft., 3 in. high, and 2 ft., 8-1/2 in. wide could

FIGURE 12-10   *Concrete block construction with waterproof surface treatments*

CONCRETE BLOCK NON LOAD BEARING PARTITION

CONCRETE BLOCK NON LOAD BEARING PARTITION

FIGURE 12-11 *Non-load bearing interior partitions*

INTERIOR PARTITION

INTERIOR PARTITION

FIGURE 12-12 *Concrete block with durable colored surface*

INTERIOR WALL

EXTERIOR WALL

FIGURE 12-13 *Concrete block for interior and exterior walls*

ADHESION TYPE CERAMIC VENEER ON MASONRY

ADHESION TYPE CERAMIC VENEER ON WOOD

ANCHOR TYPE CERAMIC VENEER ON CONCRETE OR MASONRY WALL

FIGURE 12-14 *Ceramic veneer*

141

warp in burning as much as 2 in. (see Table 12-6). Note that for anchor-type ceramic veneer the minimum number of anchors has also been specified.

Gypsum Block

Gypsum block is used extensively in building construction for interior partitions because of its light weight and good fire-resistant rating. It should never be used in areas where water or heavy moisture are present because it will absorb moisture, become less strong, and will eventually disintegrate. Most building codes limit the height of gypsum block partitions (see Figure 12-15). The faces of gypsum block cannot be used as a finish wall surface and must receive a protecting finish coat, generally of gypsum plaster. When installing a gypsum block partition it is always advisable to install a starter course of concrete block or structural clay tile at the floor.

REVIEW EXAMINATION

1. What are the two grades of structural clay tile?

2. The maximum height that a 6-in. structural clay tile wall or partition can be built is what?

3. Non-load-bearing structural clay tile is installed with type A mortar—true or false?

4. Is the water absorption rate of structural clay tile important?

5. What are the two classes of structural facing tile?

6. The joints for structural facing tile are how big?

7. Can structural facing tile be obtained with both faces having a hard, colored, and easily maintained finish surface?

8. The horizontal and vertical courses should be what, when structural facing tile is to be installed in a building?

9. The type of aggregate used in manufacturing concrete block affects what factors of the concrete block?

10. Do building codes specify height restrictions for thickness of concrete block walls?

11. Do building codes specify height restrictions by the number of stories in a building for thickness of concrete block walls?

12. Control joints are installed in concrete block walls and partitions to stop what?

13. When concrete block is used on exterior walls, what must be done to prevent moisture and water from penetrating into the interior?

TABLE 12-6   *Maximum face distortions per size of terra cotta*

Area (in sq. ft.)	Maximum distortion of warpage in inches	Minimum number of anchors
1 sq. ft. or less	$\frac{1}{16}''$	0
1 sq. ft. to 2 sq. ft.	$\frac{1}{8}''$	2
2 sq. ft. to 4 sq. ft.	$\frac{1}{8}''$	3
4 sq. ft. to 12 sq. ft.	$\frac{3}{16}''$	4
12 sq. ft. to 20 sq. ft.	$\frac{3}{16}''$ and over	6
Greater than 20 sq. ft.	$\frac{3}{16}''$ and over	one for each 35 sq. ft.

STARTER COURSES TO BE CONCRETE BLOCK OR STRUCTURAL CLAY TILE

FIGURE 12-15   *Height limitations of gypsum block partitions*

14. Concrete block with durable, colored, and easily maintained surfaces are manufactured with this surface on one side only—true or false?

15. Ceramic veneer is manufactured in what two types?

ASSIGNMENT

1. Draw a freehand sketch to scale of a door in a structural facing tile and a concrete block partition, both in plan and elevation.

2. Draw a freehand sketch to scale of control joints in concrete block walls and partitions.

SUPPLEMENTARY INFORMATION

More About Concrete Block

DECORATIVE SHAPES OF CONCRETE BLOCK: Concrete block manufactured in shapes with various voids is used to construct pierced decorative walls, partitions, screens, etc. Heights and lengths of the block vary according to the penetrations (see Figure 12-16).

JOINTS: The joints used for concrete block are shown in Figure 12-17.

ACCESSORIES: The various accessories used with other masonry units in order to strengthen, reinforce, anchor, relieve pressure, etc., are shown in Figure 12-18.

FIGURE 12-16   *Examples of pierced concrete block*

"V" TYPE   FLUSH   WEATHER STRUCK

RAKED   BEADED

FIGURE 12-17   *Mortar joints used for concrete block*

PRE-MOLDED CONTROL JOINT FILLER   PRE-MOLDED CONTROL JOINT FILLER WITH VINYL TIP   VINYL FILLED ROPE

CONTROL JOINT ACCESSORIES FOR CONCRETE BLOCK

REINFORCING   REINFORCING BLOCK & BRICK   MESH

REINFORCING FOR CONCRETE BLOCK, STRUCTURAL CLAY & FACING TILE

FIGURE 12-18   *Masonry accessories*

13

STONE; FLOOR AND WALL TILE

INTRODUCTION
TECHNICAL INFORMATION
    Stone
        Dimension stone (cut stone, ashlar)
        Rubble stone (ashlar)
        Flagstone
        Crushed stone
        Stone dust
        Monumental stone
    Floor and Wall Tile
        Quarry tile
        Pavers
        Vitrification
REVIEW EXAMINATION
ASSIGNMENT
SUPPLEMENTARY INFORMATION
    Ceramic Mosaic Tile
    Color in Stone
MID-TERM OR END-TERM
    REVIEW EXAMINATION—CHAPTERS 7–13

INTRODUCTION

Stone and tile are two materials that have been used in building construction from the earliest times. This chapter discusses the kinds of stone and the types of floor and wall tile that are used in present day building construction.

TECHNICAL INFORMATION

Stone

There are three groups of stone used in building construction: *igneous stone*, formed by solidification from a molten state (for example, granite); *sedimentary stone*, formed by the breaking down of stone into small particles which are cemented together by chemical or organic action, for example, limestone; and *metamorphic stone*, the ultimate product from both igneous and sedimentary stone, formed either by pressure, heat, or moisture or by various combinations of these forces (for example, marble). Table 13-1 summarizes these three groups, giving basic data on the weight and strength of each.

Stone is available for building construction in four categories: (1) dimension (cut stone, ashlar); (2) rubble stone; (3) flagstone; and (4) crushed stone. Stone dust and monumental stone are categories of lesser importance, not related to building constructions.

The various types of stonework are identified by the shape and the surface or finish treatment of the stone (see Figure 13-1).

DIMENSION STONE (CUT STONE, ASHLAR): This type of stone is pre-cut to a specific size, squared to dimensions each way, to a specific thickness, and with specific finishes. It is used for exterior veneers, interior wall finishes, prefabricated panels,

preassembled systems, toilet partitions, stair treads, flooring, sills, copings (see Figure 13-2).

Dimension (cut) stone is available in rough, smooth, textured, and polished finishes and in a very wide variety of colors, including numerous variations of veining and color combinations. Stone veneers vary from 7/8 in. thick (minimum) up to 2-1/6 in. thick or more. Generally, the maximum practical size is 8 ft. high and 12 ft. wide; however, larger sizes are now available. All dimension stone veneers are set at a minimum of 1 in. from the backup material; shop drawings are required to show sizes, joints, anchoring methods, and special shapes. Generally both vertical and horizontal joints are made 1/4 in. The types of stone used for dimension (cut) stone are granite, marble, limestone, slate, and soapstone.

RUBBLE STONE (ASHLAR): This type of stone is delivered from the quarries in irregular shapes, with one good face, and with certain size limits, usually 12 in. high and 2 ft. long. The stone mills cut this rubble stone into blocks and pieces for veneers, copings, sills, curbing, etc. Rubble stone veneers vary in shape, size and finish with the type of stone used. For granite and soapstone, see Figure 13-3 and for limestone, sandstone and brownstone, see Figure 13-4.

FLAGSTONE: Flagstones are thin slabs of stone, from 7/8 to 2 in. thick, either irregular or squared, with the finished surface available smooth, slightly rough, or polished. They are used for terraces, walks, floors, stair treads, flooring, blackboards, sills, and counter tops (see Figure 13-5). The stones used for flagstones are bluestone, limestone, sandstone, slate, and soapstone.

CRUSHED STONE: Crushed stone consists of granules, chips, or irregular shapes that have been graded and sized. It differs from gravel in that it is generally composed of one type of stone. Sizes

TABLE 13-1 *Type of stone, name of stone, weight, and compressive strength*

Type of Stone	Name of Stone	Weight (lbs. per cu. ft.)	Compressive Strength (lbs. per sq. in.)
Igneous	Granite	162.7 to 184.6	13,000 to 32,000
Sedimentary	Limestone	131 to 170	2,600 to 21,320
	Sandstone	135 to 170	7,700 to 12,000
	Marble	131 to 177.1	12,156 to 22,900
Metamorphic	Slate	175	10,000 to 15,000
	Soapstone	170	9,000 to 14,000

FIELD STONE   COURSED FIELD STONE

ONLY BROKEN
WITH A STONE
HAMMER

BROKEN ASHLAR
RECTANGULAR   BROKEN ASHLAR
NARROW

STONES OF RANDOM
HEIGHT WITH NO
HORIZONTAL COURSES
(BROKEN WITH STONE
HAMMER OR PRE-CUT
BY STONE SUPPLIERS)

COURSED ASHLAR
HORIZONTAL   BROKEN ASHLAR
RECTANGULAR

STONE OF SAME
HEIGHT USED TO
MAKE HORIZONTAL
COURSES (PRE-CUT
BY STONE SUPPLIERS)

CUT STONE ASHLAR
STACKED JOINTS   CUT STONE ASHLAR
BROKEN JOINTS

ANY STONE WORK
PRE-DIMENSIONED
BY STONE SUPPLIERS

FIGURE 13-1   *Stonework*

CUT-STONE COPING   CUT-STONE SILL

STONE VENEER   PREFABRICATED UNIT   PREASSEMBLED UNIT

FIGURE 13-2   *Use of cut stone*

FIGURE 13-3 *Granite and soapstone*

FIGURE 13-4 *Limestone and sandstone*

FIGURE 13-5 *Flagstone*

start at 1/4 in. and can be obtained in fixed sizes up to 2-1/2 in.

Crushed granite is used for terrazzo-type flooring, artificial stone, precast concrete panels, and surfacing treatments for buildings.

Crushed limestone is used as aggregate for concrete and asphaltic concrete, and as sand for mortar, plaster, and concrete. Screened limestone chips are used for surfacing built-up roofs and in terrazzo, artificial stone, precast concrete panels, and surfacing treatment for buildings.

Crushed marble is used in terrazzo-type flooring, artificial stone, precast concrete panels, surfacing treatment for buildings, and for surfacing built-up roofs.

STONE DUST: Waste stone from the quarries, stone mills, and stone suppliers which cannot be used as crushed stone is pulverized into stone dust, which is used as a filler in asphalt-type resilient flooring, shingles, siding, rubber products, paints, paper, linoleum, and textiles.

MONUMENTAL STONE: Monumental stone is available rough or finished and is used for sculpture, monuments, and the like.

Floor and Wall Tile

Floor and wall tile may be defined as small thin solid slabs, either glazed or unglazed, made from clay or a mixture of clay and other ceramic materials and fired (burned) in kilns to produce a strong, durable material. They differ, as shown in Table 13-2, principally in composition of tile body, surface finish (glazed or unglazed), process of manufacture (dust-press or plastic method), and degree of vitrification (extent to which the tile absorbs water).

148

There are two methods of manufacturing floor and wall tile: the *dust-press process*, in which the damp mix is shaped with steel dies under heavy pressure, and the *plastic process*, in which the mix has sufficient water added so it is plastic and can then be extruded and cut or molded by hand. The dust-press process gives mechanical dimension precision to the tiles, whereas the plastic process yields tile with a hand-made appearance.

All floor and wall tile less than 36 sq. in. are based on the 6-in. square (see Figure 13-6). Through this method all sizes and shapes of floor and wall tile can be combined into almost unlimited patterns and designs.

There are designated grades of tile: glazed wall tile and ceramic mosaics are graded as *standards* and *seconds*; all other types of tile do not have any designated grades. The difference in grades covers warpage and surface defects only, because both grades have the same wear, strength, and sanitary qualities.

FIGURE 13-6   *Floor and wall tile*

QUARRY TILE: Three grades are available: *select*, *standard*, and *seconds*. Standard grade is controlled as follows: warpage of a maximum of 0.024 in. in the 6-in. length and 0.017 in. in the 4-1/4-in. length; no surface defects visible at a distance of 3'–0". Seconds cannot have a fracture of the body.

TABLE 13-2   *Basic information for wall and floor tile*

Type	Grades	Sizes	Mfg. Process	Surface	Vitrification	Use
Glazed wall tile (interior) White or colored	Standard and seconds	From a minimum of $2\frac{1}{8}''$ by $2\frac{1}{8}''$ to a maximum of 72 sq. in.	Dust-press process	Glazed surface impervious to moisture	Nonvitreous	Interior wall surfaces
Ceramic mosaic tile White or colored	Standard and seconds	From a minimum of $\frac{1}{4}''$ by $\frac{1}{4}''$ to a maximum of 6 sq. in.	Dust-press and plastic processes	Unglazed	Semivitreous, vitreous, and impervious	Interior and exterior floors and walls
Glazed weatherproof tile White or colored	Standard	From a minimum of $\frac{1}{4}''$ by $\frac{1}{4}''$ to a maximum of 6 sq. in.	Dust-press and plastic processes	Glazed surface impervious to moisture	Semivitreous and vitreous	Interior and exterior floors and walls
Quarry tile	Select, standard, and seconds	From a minimum of $2\frac{3}{4}''$ by $2\frac{3}{4}''$ to a maximum of 81 sq. in.	Plastic process	Unglazed	Vitreous and impervious	Interior and exterior floors, walks, and terraces
Pavers	Standard and seconds	From a minimum of $3''$ by $3''$ to a maximum of 36 sq. in.	Dust-press and plastic processes	Unglazed	Vitreous and impervious	Interior and exterior floors, walks, and terraces

Quarry tile is available in 1/2-in., 3/4-in., and 3/8-in. thicknesses. Sizes range from 2-1/4 to 9 in. in widths, and from 2-3/4 to 9 in. in length.

PAVERS: These are unglazed tile having 6 sq. in. or more of facial area, and they are used for floors where heavy traffic is anticipated.

VITRIFICATION: All floor and wall tile are classified into four degrees of vitrification: *non-vitreous*, which can have a moisture absorption of more than 7% of the weight of the tile; *semi-vitreous* in which the limits of moisture absorption are restricted to 3 to 7% of the weight of the tile; *vitreous*, which limits moisture absorption to less than 3% of the weight of the tile; *impervious*, in which moisture absorption is negligible or none. All the different types of floor and wall tile have special trim pieces for bases, caps, corners, moldings, angles, and the like (see Figure 13-7).

REVIEW EXAMINATION

1. Name the three groups of stone used in building construction.
2. Name the six types of stone available for building construction.
3. Name two types of metamorphic stone.
4. Name an igenous type of stone.
5. What is the minimum thickness of dimension (cut) stone?
6. Give three uses of crushed stone.
7. The thickness of vertical and horizontal joints for dimension (cut) stone is what?

8. Name the two manufacturing processes used to make wall and floor tile.
9. Floor and wall tile less than 36 sq. in. is based upon what?
10. What are the two grades of glazed wall tile and ceramic mosaic tiles?
11. What are the four degrees of vitrification?
12. What are bases, caps, moldings for wall, and floor tile known as?

ASSIGNMENT

1. Draw a freehand sketch showing the various types of stonework.
2. Draw a freehand sketch showing the various floor layouts for the various shapes of flagstones.

SUPPLEMENTARY INFORMATION

Ceramic Mosaic Tile

Ceramic mosaic tiles are mounted on sheets of paper about 2 sq. ft. in area by the manufacturer. The tiles are spaced to allow for grouting and pointing. After the tiles are installed, the paper is wetted and removed and the tile is ready for pointing. By this method, any design can be factory-mounted on paper so that the design or pattern repeats accurately when the mounted tile on the paper is installed.

Today many glazed wall tiles are made with nibs so that when installed, the joints are all of similar widths (see Figure 13-8).

FIGURE 13-7 *Trim pieces for floor and wall tile*

FIGURE 13-8   *Wall tile*

There are two methods of installing wall and floor tiles: with *cement mortar*, and with *adhesive* (thinset). With the cement mortar method all trim pieces have to have sufficient radius to take care of the thickness of the mortar (see Figure 13-9), whereas with the adhesive method, the trim pieces are equal in thickness to the tile (Figure 13-10).

Color in Stone

Feldspar, hornblende, and mica are responsible for the colors of granite. Feldspar makes granite pink, red, brown, buff, gray, and white. Hornblende and mica make granite dark green and black.

Iron oxides give limestone reddish and yellowish colors and organic materials give limestone gray to black colors. Most limestone for building construction are gray and buff or combinations of these colors.

Marble is available in colors varying from white to black and also with wide variations of veining and color combinations.

Bluestone is available only in a blue-gray color.

Sandstone, which is similar to limestone, is available in white, gray, yellow, brown, and red.

Soapstone is available in gray, green, and blue.

Iron sulfides produce in slate the black, blue, and gray colors, iron oxide the red and purple colors, and chlorite the green color.

FIGURE 13-9   *Cement mortar setting method*

FIGURE 13-10   *Adhesive setting method*

**MID-TERM OR END-TERM
REVIEW EXAMINATION—CHAPTERS 7–13**

1. Name seven types of concrete form ties.

2. By whom are concrete forms designed?

3. What are reinforced paper tubes used for in concrete construction?

4. What is the lift-slab system?

5. What are the directions of the reinforcing in flat slabs?

6. Name the two different types of reinforced concrete beams and slab systems.

7. What is the tilt-up system?

8. What are the sizes of concrete test specimens?

9. What lumber is well-suited for the building of forms for concrete?

10. What type of form material may be used for two-way ribbed (waffle-type) construction?

11. When depositing concrete into forms, what may cause segregation?

12. The presence of laitance in concrete indicates what fault?

13. In curing, what is the evaporation of water reduced by?

14. What causes volume changes in cured concrete?

15. What is the fundamental cause of shrinkage of concrete at the time of curing?

16. What should exposed construction joints in concrete slabs be filled with?

17. What is necessary when conditions demand the placing of concrete under water?

18. Concrete test specimens should be removed from the molds not sooner than ——————————— hrs.

19. Concrete is called "reinforced concrete" when what is added?

20. What are prefabricated panels of reinforced concrete extensively used as?

21. What are the soft-mud process, the stiff-mud process, and the dry-press process used to manufacture?

22. The type FBX brick has what distinct quality?

23. Of the grades of brick identified as SW, MW, and NW, what is the minimum compressive strength of MW?

24. What is an important factor in the bonding of brick to the mortar joint?

25. What is adobe brick made of?

26. What is type A mortar intended for?

27. Give the two sizes of mortar joints generally used in brick work.

28. When a new wing is added to an existing building, what must the point of connection be provided with?

29. Name the brick joint that sheds water best?

30. The building that requires an expansion joint must be at least ——————————— ft. long.

31. What is the coefficient of linear expansion of brick?

32. The filler used in expansion joints is known as a ——————————— type.

33. Efflorescence, a white stain that appears on brick, is caused by what?

34. A masonry unit's cross-sectional area in any plane parallel to the bearing surface is less than which of the following percentage of its cross-sectional area measured in the same plane: 50%, 65%, or 75%?

35. Name three uses of structural clay tile.

36. What is the most widely used masonry unit other than brick?

37. What are the masonry units that are graded LBX and LB?

38. What is the mortar used for structural clay tile where fireproofing is required?

39. What is the maximum height that a 6-in. structural clay tile wall or partition can be built?

40. What is the measurement recommended for structural tile mortar joints?

41. Control joints are installed in concrete block walls and partitions to stop ———————————.

42. What is the stone formed by solidification from a molten state?

43. What is the compressive strength of soapstone?

44. How is stone dust used in paints?

45. What does soapstone weigh?

46. What is crushed granite used for?

47. What color does hornblende make granite?

48. Iron oxides give limestone what color?

49. In what colors is soapstone available?

50. Most limestone for buildings is what color?

14

STONE AND FLOOR AND WALL TILE IN CONSTRUCTION

INTRODUCTION

This chapter covers two topics: types and uses of stone in construction, and the installation of ceramic floor and wall tile. Both were highly developed crafts in former times, and both have been affected by new construction methods, so that here only the basic types and the simple essentials of installation will be presented.

TECHNICAL INFORMATION

Stone

The most generally used categories of stone for building construction are: dimension (cut) stone, rubble stone, and flagstone.

Dimension (cut) stone veneers or thin slabs of granite, limestone, and marble are generally used for exterior veneers, interior wall finishes, flooring, toilet partitions, and stair treads and risers. Moldings, copings, sills, bases, and special trim or shapes that are used with veneers or thin slabs are usually manufactured from the same type of stone as the veneers or thin slabs. Usually all joints are 1/4 in. and the various methods of joining are shown in Figure 14-1.

MORTARS: The mortars used for setting stone, pointing, and grouting are made with nonstaining portland cement or nonstaining waterproof portland cement, sand with no impurities or salt, clean fresh water, and hydrated lime or quicklime putty (see Table 14-1).

In most veneer stonework, the backup material should be dampproofed and the space behind the veneer must be open so that no moisture can develop. The veneer is set with spot attachments of mortar. In cases where solid grouting is necessary, nonstaining waterproof portland cement should be used.

ACCESSORIES: There are many types of anchors, ties, etc., used in installing veneers that are designed for use with masonry, concrete, and steel (see Figure 14-2).

FIGURE 14-1   *Methods of joining stone veneer*

ANCHORS FOR JOINING VENEERS TO MASONRY BACK-UP

STRAP ANCHOR · 2-WAY STRAP ANCHOR · ANCHOR STRAP WITH PIN · TWISTED STRAP ANCHOR

ANCHORS FOR JOINING VENEERS

CRAMP ANCHOR · WIRE CRAMP ANCHOR · PIN · THREADED DOWELS

ANCHORS FOR JOINING VENEERS TO CONCRETE BACK-UP

DOVETAIL STRAP ANCHOR · 2-WAY DOVETAIL STRAP ANCHOR · DOVETAIL STRAP WITH PIN · CORRUGATED DOVETAIL STRAP

THREADED HOOK ANCHOR WITH DOWEL · THREADED EYE BOLT ANCHOR WITH DOWEL · STRAP ANCHOR WITH SLOT · 2-WAY STRAP ANCHOR WITH SLOT

HANGER WITH DOWEL · 2-WAY HANGER · THREADED BOLT WITH RECTANGULAR WASHER · WEDGE TYPE ANCHOR

ANCHORS USED IN INSTALLING VENEERS TO STEEL AND FOR HUNG CEILINGS

FIGURE 14-2   *Anchors used in installing veneers*

TABLE 14-1   *Mortars for setting stone by volume*

Mortar	Nonstaining Portland Cement or Nonstaining Waterproof Portland Cement	Sand	Lime
Setting	1	6	1
Pointing	1	2	Sufficient to make a very stiff mortar
Grouting	1	$1\frac{1}{2}$	

TABLE 14-2   *Numbers of anchors in relation to size of stone veneer 7/8" thick*

Size of Stone in Square Feet	Number of Anchors
2	2
2 to 4	3
4 to 12	4
12 to 20	6
20 and greater	1 extra anchor for each additional 3 sq. ft.

The number of anchors necessary to support the veneer is controlled by the thickness and the size in square feet (see Table 14-2).

STONE VENEER SECTIONS: Figures 14-3 and 14-4 show stone veneers with masonry backup and concrete backup, including stone wainscot on the interior. Stone veneers are often used for vestibule and entrance ceilings, soffits, and toilet partitions. For methods for supporting stone ceilings and soffits, see Figure 14-5. The installation of stone toilet partitions is shown in Figure 14-6.

RUBBLE STONE: Granite and limestone are used for exterior and interior veneers. Granite is manufactured in rectangular pieces 3-1/2 to 4-1/2 in. thick, 6 to 24 in. long by 2 to 16 in. high. The edges are sawed, tooled, or split, and squared or angular. The exposed surface is available in various textures, such as sawed, tooled, split, and seamed. When installed, the joints vary from 1/2 to 1-1/2 in.

155

FIGURE 14-3 *Section through stone veneer with steel construction and masonry back-up*

FIGURE 14-4 *Section through stone veneer with reinforced concrete back-up*

FIGURE 14-5   *Typical details of stone ceilings and soffits*

FIGURE 14-6   *Typical details of stone toilet partitions*

Limestone, on the other hand is manufactured in two types: (1) sawed on four sides to any specific size, exposed surface available in various finishes; when installed the joints are 1/4 in. for larger sizes and 1/2 in. for smaller sizes; (2) split face ashlar, sawed top and bottom, 3-1/2 to 4-1/2 in. thick, 2-1/4, 5, and 7-3/4 in. high, and random lengths (see Figures 14-7 and 14-8).

PROTECTION OF STONE: All types of stonework, when installed, should be protected from damage from construction traffic and also from possible staining by other materials during construction.

FLAGSTONES: These are available in bluestone, granite, limestone, sandstone, slate, and soapstone. Flagstone is 7/8 to 2 in. thick, and is generally used for terraces, floors, walks, stair treads, sills, blackboards, etc.

GRANITE ASHLAR

LIMESTONE ASHLAR

LIMESTONE ASHLAR

FIGURE 14-7   *Rubble stone*

157

FIGURE 14-8 *Ashlar veneer on masonry back-up*

Bluestone flagstones have square edges, 1 in. thick in 1'-0" and 2'-0" squares. Granite flagstones have square edges, 7/8 to 1 in. thick, in 2'-0" and 3'-0" squares. Limestone and sandstone flagstones are 1 to 2 in. thick and are available in 2'-0" up to 4'-0" squares. Slate flagstones are 7/8 in. thick and are available in three types: four edges sawed and squared; irregular, with two edges sawed; and random, with no edges sawed. Soapstone flagstones are 7/8 to 1 in. thick, squared edges, and 1'-0" up to 3'-0" squares.

All flagstones for terraces, walks, and floors, are generally installed on a concrete slab base with a mortar bed of 7/8 in. on the interior and 1-1/4 in. on the exterior. The mortar should be a relatively dry mix of 1 part portland cement and 3 parts fine sand. Pointing mortar is 1 part portland cement, 1-1/2 parts fine sand, with enough clean water to make a workable paste (see Figure 14-9). On the exterior, flagstones may be laid in a bed of sand without a concrete slab so that grass can grow in the joints (see Figure 14-10).

Floor and Wall Tile

TERMINOLOGY: Ceramic tile is a general term used for all types of floor and wall tile. *Glazed tile* is any tile with a glaze on it. *Ceramic mosaic* is small glazed or unglazed tile, mounted on paper. *Mosaic* indicates designs created by artists for floors and walls.

INSTALLATION: Floor and wall tile are installed by the cement mortar setting method and the adhesive setting method. For either, the size of joints is controlled to a minimum and a maximum (see Table 14-3). When floor and wall tile are installed with cement mortar, the mixes are controlled by volume for the different coats (see Table

FIGURE 14-9 *Flagstone in mortar*

FIGURE 14-10 *Flagstone in sand*

TABLE 14-3 *Widths of joints for floor and wall tile*

Size	Type of Tile	Joints Minimum	Maximum
$2\frac{3}{16}$" square or smaller	Ceramic mosaic glazed or unglazed	$\frac{1}{16}$"	$\frac{1}{8}$"
$2\frac{3}{16}$" to $4\frac{1}{4}$"	Unglazed tile	$\frac{1}{8}$"	$\frac{1}{4}$"
6" × 6" and	Unglazed tile	$\frac{1}{4}$"	$\frac{3}{4}$"
3" × 3" and larger	Glazed tile	$\frac{1}{16}$"	$\frac{1}{4}$"
All sizes	Quarry	$\frac{3}{8}$"	$\frac{3}{4}$"

TABLE 14-4 *Mortar mixes by volume for floor and wall tile*

| Mortar | Vertical Surfaces | | | Horizontal Surfaces |
	Scratch	Leveling	Setting	Setting
Portland cement	1 part	1 part	1 part	1 part
Hydrated lime	20%	1½ parts	½ to 1 part	10% (maximum)
Sand	4 parts	4 to 7 parts	4 to 7 parts	4 to 7 parts

14-4). The sand used for these mortars must be very carefully graded (see Table 14-5 and Figure 14-11).

The installation of floor tile in bathrooms and showers requires that the area be carefully waterproofed (see Figure 14-12). Where excessive water is not present, no waterproofing is necessary. For countertops, particularly in kitchens and bathrooms, the installation of tile at walls, sinks and lavatories, and countertop cooking range require careful detailing (see Figures 14-13 and 14-14).

MORTARS: Mortars for adhesive setting (thin-set) consist of portland cement and a resinous or latex additive, epoxy mortar, and organic adhesives. Sheets of floor and wall tile using high-bond-strength grout are available in prefabricated squares. Wall tiles in 17-1/4 in. and 24 in. squares and in sheets to fit various tube sizes, including strips for internal corners and tube sides, are readily available. Floor tiles in 24-in. squares are available with pressure-sensitive adhesive to be applied directly to the substrate.

FIGURE 14-11   *Types of floor, wall and quarry tile*

FLOOR TILE WITH WATERPROOFING CEMENT MORTAR METHOD

FLOOR TILE WITH WATERPROOFING ADHESIVE METHOD

FIGURE 14-12   *Bathroom and shower floor tile*

REVIEW EXAMINATION

1. What are the three categories of stone generally used in building construction?

2. Which types of stone are most used for dimension (cut) stone veneers?

3. What types of portland cement are used for setting, pointing, and grouting of dimension (cut) stone veneers?

TABLE 14-5   *Percentages of sand passing sieve sizes*

Types of Mortar	No. 4	No. 8	No. 16	No. 30	No. 50	No. 100
Setting beds	100%	95% to 100%	60% to 85%	35% to 60%	15% to 30%	0% to 5%
Pointing				100%		0% to 5%

SINK OR LAVATORY ON
UNDERSIDE OF COUNTER

COUNTER TOP EDGE

SINK OR LAVATORY ON
TOP OF COUNTER

COUNTER TOP INTERSECTING WALL

FIGURE 14-13   *Cement mortar method*

SINK OR LAVATORY ON
UNDERSIDE OF COUNTER

COUNTER TOP EDGE

SINK OR LAVATORY ON
TOP OF COUNTER

COUNTER TOP INTERSECTING WALL

FIGURE 14-14   *Adhesive method*

4. What is the minimum thickness of dimension (cut) stone veneer?

5. Name the four basic types of anchors.

6. What type of stone is used for ashlar type?

7. Name four types of stone from which flagstones are made.

8. What is the general term used to describe all types of floor and wall tile?

9. What are small glazed and unglazed tiles called?

10. What are the two methods used for installing floor and wall tile?

ASSIGNMENT

1. Make a freehand sketch section to scale showing the use of dimension (cut) stone veneer with masonry back-up through exterior wall of a one-story building.

2. Make freehand sketches showing installation by adhesive method of ceramic mosaic tile on a kitchen countertop with sink.

SUPPLEMENTARY INFORMATION

Limestone Surface Textures

The surface texture or fineness of grain of limestone for building construction is graded thus: A—statuary, B—select, C—standard, D—rustic, E—variegated, and F—Old Gothic. Grades A, B, C, and D vary only in fineness of grain from fine to coarse and are buff or gray in color. Grade E is unselected grain size and the color is a mixture of gray and buff. Grade F is a mixture of grades D and E but includes stone with seams and markings.

Marble Classifications

Marbles are classified on the basis of their natural qualities. Grade A is for sound marbles with uniform and good working qualities. Grade B is similar to A except that they have fewer good working properties. Grade C marbles have uncertain working qualities and contain flaws, voids, veins, and lines of separation. Grade D is similar to C but has poor working qualities and larger proportion of flaws, voids, etc.

Tile Accessories

Manufacturers supply tile and matching colors of bathroom accessories such as soap dishes, towel bars, toilet paper holders, etc. The accessories are made in tile sizes so they can be easily installed. Recessed types should be located on plans and details so that openings and rough boxes can be installed in the backup material to receive them.

Tile Cleavage Plane

When installing large floor areas with tile, it is necessary to install a cleavage plane because the expansion and contraction of the structural slab may cause cracks in the setting bed and tile joints. A layer of bitumen-saturated felt building paper, 13.9 lbs. per 100 sq. ft., is laid directly on the concrete slab, then wire mesh and the setting bed are installed. By this method this cleavage plane separates the slab from the tile and any movement of the slab is independent of the tile.

Epoxies for Exterior Stone Veneers

Because of the epoxy adhesives and new anchoring systems, marble, granite, and limestone veneers and precast panels with stone veneers are finding greater application in exterior facing for buildings. The veneers 7/8 in. thick and greater are applied with a grid system (see Figure 14-15).

With epoxies, stainless steel U-shaped clips are bonded with epoxy adhesives to the stone veneer and then bolted with clip angles to the structural building frame (see Figure 14-16).

Veneers with small angles plus epoxy bonding are able to form entire column covers of almost any shape or form (see Figure 14-17).

FIGURE 14-15   *Application of veneer with grid system*

FIGURE 14-16   *Method for anchoring stone veneer*

FIGURE 14-17   *Vertical column cover*

STONE VENEER

CAST IN THREADED STUD AND ANGLE WITH SLOT FOR ALIGNMENT

CONCRETE FILL

STRUCTURAL SLAB

PRECAST CONCRETE OR OTHER TYPE OF BACK-UP

FIGURE 14-18   *Precast concrete panel with supporting clips*

The precast concrete panels with stone veneers have the advantage that the backup material onto which they are installed can have any type of clip, anchor, or other fastening device cast into or applied onto the backup material to support the panels (see Figure 14-18).

15

WOOD

INTRODUCTION

Wood, one of our earliest building materials, may still be called a contemporary material because of the many new uses to which it has been put in recent years. Through improved methods of cutting and milling, thin veneers can be produced which, when glued together in layers, form a stronger board than that which is cut from the tree. Wood chips and wood pulp bonded with adhesives into panels and acoustical tile, and small pieces of solid wood laminated to make structural beams, girders, columns, and arches are some of the contemporary uses of wood. Also, a whole new group of surfacing woods and wood products with transparent plastics which give permanent finished surfaces has been developed and greatly improved in recent years. These are some of the items that will be further dealt with in the following chapters. But in this chapter, some of the fundamental facts about wood will be reviewed. Types of wood, seasoning, grading, sizes, quality standards, and classifications will be emphasized.

TECHNICAL INFORMATION

Softwoods and Hardwoods

It is generally known that all lumber is divided into two major groups; the softwoods and the hardwoods. The softwoods, in general, are from coniferous (evergreen) trees, while the hardwoods are from deciduous leaf-bearing trees (those which drop their leaves at the end of the season).

The words "softwoods" and "hardwoods" are used mainly as a matter of custom, for not all so-called softwoods are soft, nor are all so-called hardwoods necessarily hard. For example, longleaf Southern yellow pine and Douglas fir, both belonging to the softwood family, are harder than poplar and basswood, which belong to the hardwood family (see Figure 15-1 and Table 15-1).

SEASONING: All lumber when first cut from trees is called "green" wood. Before it can be used, it should be seasoned either by air-drying or kiln-drying, which will reduce the moisture content. Seasoning of lumber will reduce its weight, reduce shrinkage and warping, and increase the strength of the lumber, its nail-holding power, and its ability to hold paint.

Shrinkage, distortion, and warping in lumber are caused by the location of the annual growth rings of a tree. Therefore, how lumber is cut from a tree is of utmost importance, as Figure 15-2 clearly shows. Some boards, such as A, will warp, and others, such as B, will remain flat; post C will remain square, but post D will be distorted in shape.

GRADING OF LUMBER FOR USE: The grade of a piece of lumber is established by the number, character, and location of imperfections that will lower the strength, weaken the durability, and affect the use of the lumber. The most common imperfections are knots, checks, and pitch pockets.

American Lumber Standards Association specifies that lumber be classified according to its principal uses.

1. *Yard lumber*—primarily that which is used in light frame construction.
2. *Structural lumber*—that which is 5 in. or more in thickness and width, and is graded on the basis of strength.
3. *Factory* or *shop lumber*—that which is intended for further manufacture and is graded on a basis of the proportion of area of a piece of lumber for the production of a limited number of cuttings of specified minimum size and quality.

SIZES OF LUMBER: Commonly used softwood boards and dimension lumber established by the American Lumber Standards are given in Table 15-2.

TABLE 15-1   *Hardness to softness of deciduous and coniferous trees*

Type of Wood	Soft	Relatively Soft	Hard
Hardwoods (deciduous) leaf-bearing	Alder, Basswood, and Poplar	Magnolia and Sweetgum	Walnut, Birch, Cherry, Oak, and Maple
Softwoods (coniferous) evergreens	White Pine, Ponderosa Pine, and Cedar	Cypress, Redwood, Spruce, Fir, and Hemlock	Douglas Fir and Longleaf Southern Yellow Pine

FIGURE 15-1 *Hardness to softness of deciduous and coniferous trees*

TABLE 15-2 *Softwood lumber sizes: Government's acceptance of new lumber standards*

Nominal Size (inches)	Size when Dry or Seasoned, 19% Moisture Content or Under (inches)	Size when Green or Unseasoned, Over 19% Moisture Content (inches)
1 × 4	$\frac{3}{4}$ × $3\frac{1}{2}$	$\frac{25}{32}$ × $3\frac{9}{16}$
1 × 6	$\frac{3}{4}$ × $5\frac{1}{2}$	$\frac{25}{32}$ × $5\frac{5}{8}$
1 × 8	$\frac{3}{4}$ × $7\frac{1}{4}$	$\frac{25}{32}$ × $7\frac{1}{2}$
1 × 10	$\frac{3}{4}$ × $9\frac{1}{4}$	$\frac{25}{32}$ × $9\frac{1}{2}$
1 × 12	$\frac{3}{4}$ × $11\frac{1}{4}$	$\frac{25}{32}$ × $11\frac{1}{2}$
2 × 4	$1\frac{1}{2}$ × $3\frac{1}{2}$	$1\frac{9}{16}$ × $3\frac{9}{16}$
2 × 6	$1\frac{1}{2}$ × $5\frac{1}{2}$	$1\frac{9}{16}$ × $5\frac{5}{8}$
2 × 8	$1\frac{1}{2}$ × $7\frac{1}{4}$	$1\frac{9}{16}$ × $7\frac{1}{2}$
2 × 10	$1\frac{1}{2}$ × $9\frac{1}{4}$	$1\frac{9}{16}$ × $9\frac{1}{2}$
2 × 12	$1\frac{1}{2}$ × $11\frac{1}{4}$	$1\frac{9}{16}$ × $11\frac{1}{2}$
4 × 4	$3\frac{1}{2}$ × $3\frac{1}{2}$	$3\frac{9}{16}$ × $3\frac{9}{16}$
4 × 6	$3\frac{1}{2}$ × $5\frac{1}{2}$	$3\frac{9}{16}$ × $5\frac{5}{8}$
4 × 8	$3\frac{1}{2}$ × $7\frac{1}{4}$	$3\frac{9}{16}$ × $7\frac{1}{2}$
4 × 10	$3\frac{1}{2}$ × $9\frac{1}{4}$	$3\frac{9}{16}$ × $9\frac{1}{2}$
4 × 12	$3\frac{1}{2}$ × $11\frac{1}{4}$	$3\frac{9}{16}$ × $11\frac{1}{2}$

Yard Lumber

This is lumber for general building purposes, including house construction (see Figure 15-3). It is less than 5 in. in thickness and is sold in classifications by dimensions as follows:

1. *Strips*—less than 2 in. thick, not over 8 in. wide.

2. *Boards*—less than 2 in. thick and 8 in. or more in width.

3. *Dimension lumber*—all yard lumber with the exception of boards, strips, and timbers. Specifically, it is yard lumber between 2 and 5 in. thick and 2 in. or more in width.

4. *Planks*—yard lumber that is 2 in. to less than 4 in. in thickness and 8 in. or over in width.

5. *Scantlings*—yard lumber that is 2 in. to under 5 in. in thickness and less than 8 in. in width.

6. *Heavy joists*—yard lumber 4 in. to less than 6 in. in thickness and 8 in. or over in width.

QUALITY STANDARDS OF YARD LUMBER: Yard lumber is classified into two main divisions on the basis of quality, namely:

FIGURE 15-2 *Shrinkage, distortion, and warpage caused by annual growth rings*

1. *Select lumber*—that which is generally clear, contains no defects or only a limited number with respect to both size and type, and is smoothly finished and suitable for use as a whole for finishing purposes or where large clear pieces are required. It is further classified by grades A, B, C, and D. Grades A and B are suitable for natural finish; Grades C and D have defects and blemishes of somewhat greater extent than A and B, which can be covered by paint.

2. *Common lumber*—this is classified by the American Lumber Standards Association as lumber having defects and blemishes not suitable for finishing purposes, but quite satisfactory for general utility and construction purposes. Lumber under this heading is also further classified into Numbers 1, 2, 3, 4, and 5 common. In Numbers 1 and 2 common, all defects and blemishes must be sound. Such lumber is used for purposes in which surface covering or strength is required. Numbers 3, 4, and 5 common contain very coarse defects that will cause some waste within a piece. Such lumber is used where strength is not required.

Structural Lumber

Structural timbers are primarily classified according to size and use as follows (see also Figure 15-4).

Beams and *Stringers*—lumber 5 in. or more in thickness and 8 in. or more in width, graded with respect to its strength in bending when loaded on the narrow face.

Joists and *Planks*—lumber 2 in. to slightly less than 5 in. thick, and 4 or more in. in width, graded with respect to

FIGURE 15-3   *Yard lumber for general building purposes*

FIGURE 15-4   *Structural lumber*

its strength in bending when loaded either on the narrow face or on the wide face as a plank.

Posts and *Timbers*—lumber that is square or approximately square in cross section, 4 in. and larger, graded for use as posts or columns carrying longitudinal load, but adopted for uses in which strength in bending is not important.

GRADING BY STRENGTH: All structural lumber is graded according to its strength in bending. The different species of softwood structural lumber are further tabulated by allowable unit stresses. For example, 2-in. thick Southern pine (dense, structural, 86% kiln-dried) has a fiber stress in bending (F) and a tensile strength parallel to the grain (T) of 3000 psi, whereas 2-in. thick Redwood (dense structure) has only 1700 psi in fiber stress in bending and in tensile strength parallel to the grain.

Factory or Shop Lumber

This is a special-purpose lumber machined from common boards. It is milled in various patterns, the most common of which are those used as sub-flooring, siding, wall and roof sheathing, finished flooring, and car-siding (see Figure 15-5).

Ship-lap—this lumber is used for sub-flooring, wall and roof sheathing and siding; it has lapped edge and makes a fairly tight joint between boards, but not as tight as dressed and matched lumber.

Dressed and Matched (D & M) Lumber—this is primarily used for sub-flooring, wall and roof sheathing, or where a tight joint is needed between boards. Edges are of tongue-and-groove design.

Flooring—this refers to lumber used for finished flooring. It is of hardwood and the harder species of softwoods, cut in thicknesses of 5/16 and 25/32 in.

Siding—several profiles of siding are available in softwoods, varying according to local popularity and design requirements.

Car-siding—this has, in addition to tongue-and-groove design, edges that are beveled and a beveled groove on one surface. This is also called V-joint siding. It is used for roof sheathing where the interior face is left exposed, and for vertical siding.

Drop-siding—used primarily for the exterior of buildings, this is provided with tongue-and-groove edges and may also have ship-lap edges.

Wedged Siding—this is a plain tapered piece of wood.

REVIEW EXAMINATION

1. Name four of the hardwood trees.
2. Name four of the softwood trees.

DROP SIDING
EXTERIOR OF BUILDING

BEVEL SIDING
FOR SIDING ONLY

FLOORING
FINISH FLOORING OF HARD WOOD

CAR SIDING
ROOF SHEATHING WHERE INTERIOR SIDE IS LEFT EXPOSED

SHIPLAP SIDING
SUB-FLOORING, WALL AND ROOF SHEATHING AND SIDING

DRESSED & MATCHED
(OR D&M LUMBER)
SUB-FLOORING, WALL AND ROOF SHEATHING

FIGURE 15-5 *Factory or shop lumber (pattern)*

3. Yard lumber is primarily used for what purpose?

4. Name the three lumber classifications specified by the American Lumber Standards Association.

5. What is factory or shop lumber? Give an example.

6. Give the definition of a board. What are its dimensional limitations?

7. What is the actual size of a 2 × 8?

8. Is a 2 × 8 a plank, a board, or is it dimension lumber?

9. What are the two divisions of yard lumber in respect to quality standards?

10. Select lumber has how many grade classifications?

11. Common lumber has how many grade classifications?

12. Structural lumber is classified according to what two factors?

ASSIGNMENT

1. Sketch four types of factory or shop lumber.

2. Sketch four types of yard lumber.

3. Sketch two types of structural lumber.

SUPPLEMENTARY INFORMATION

Moisture Content

Wood swells as it absorbs moisture and shrinks as it loses moisture. In wood there are two types of water: *free water* in the cell cavities and intercellular spaces, and *absorbed water* held in the fibers and rays. When all free water is removed but the absorbed water remains, the fiber saturation point is reached. This is approximately 30% of total moisture content for all species of trees. Shrinkage occurs below the fiber saturation point, and at 15% moisture content about one-half of the total possible shrinkage is attained. For each following 1% loss or increase in moisture below or above the fiber saturation point, the wood shrinks or swells 1/30 of the total shrinkage or swelling. Wood should therefore be seasoned, and air-dried or kiln-dried to a specified moisture content adaptable to the various regions of the United States. The map shown in Figure 15-6 indicates the areas in the United States where wood is specified for its moisture content.

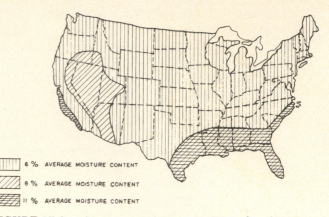

FIGURE 15-6 *Average moisture content for interior finish woodwork in the United States*

Wood Preservatives

Wood is attacked by fungi, insects, and marine borers. Decay in wood is caused by fungi; most decay occurs where the moisture content is above the fiber saturation point. Insects, most commonly termites, both subterranean and nonsubterranean, attack wood because it is their food. Carpenter ants and powder-pest beetles also attack wood, but to find shelter, not food. Marine organisms attack wood placed in salt water or brackish water.

There are two types of wood preservatives that will protect wood from fungi, insects, and marine organisms: *oil-type*, such as creosote, and *water-borne salts*, such as chromated zinc chloride.

Types of Lumber Sawing

A log of wood is sawed by two methods: *plain-sawing* and *quarter-sawing*, as shown in Figure 15-7 and Table 15-3.

TABLE 15-3 *Advantages of plain-sawed and quarter-sawed lumber*

Plain-Sawed	Quarter-Sawed
Less waste	Ray and grain patterns
Affects strength less	pronounced
Shrinks and swells less	Less raised grain, surface checks,
in thickness	and splits
Costs less	Shrinks and swells less in width
	Wears evenly

Wood Grade Markings

Typical grade stamp markings that may be found on boards in local lumber yards are indicated in Figure 15-8.

PLAIN SAWED   QUARTER SAWED

FIGURE 15-7   *Types of lumber sawing*

(W WP)	THIS IS THE MARKING OF A LARGE LUMBER TRADE ASSOCIATION. WESTERN WOOD PRODUCTS ASSOCIATION
12	THE NUMBER OF THE MILL THAT PROCESSED THE BOARD
3 COM	DESIGNATES THE GRADE. IN THIS CASE NO. 3 COMMON
PSP	INDICATES THE SPECIES OF WOOD. IN THIS CASE PONDEROSA PINE AND SUGAR PINE
S-DRY	INDICATES THE MOISTURE CONTENT. IN THIS CASE "S-DRY" MEANS THE BOARD HAS LESS THAN 19% MOISTURE

FIGURE 15-8   *Some typical wood grade markings*

16

WOOD AND WOOD PRODUCTS

INTRODUCTION

This chapter deals with building products that are made from wood. Although there is an endless variety of wood products, some of the more important are considered in this unit. Plywood and its many uses, particle board, wood fiber, and pulp products and their numerous applications are discussed, together with information on jointing and edge treatments.

TECHNICAL INFORMATION

Wood may be sliced into thin veneers; it may also be processed mechanically and chemically into pulp, chips, and fibers, and the waste from wood such as sawdust, shavings, and chips may be and are used to manufacture a great variety of wood products.

Plywood

Plywood is made of softwood used in building construction and hardwood used for cabinet work and furniture. It is made of an odd number of layers or plies of thin wood veneer bonded together so that the direction of the grain of adjacent plies is at right angles. The outside plies are called "faces" and "backs" while the center ply is called the "core." In the case of five or more plies, the inner plies that are bonded directly and at right angle to the face and core are called the "cross-bands" (see Figure 16-1).

Plywood panels are made with cores of a wood veneer, particle board, solid wood, wood fiber and pulp products, and other types of materials. In the veneer core panel, all plies are veneer less than 1/4 in. thick. Panel thicknesses generally range from 1/8 to 1-1/8 in., consisting of an odd number of plies ranging from 3 to 11 or more. Almost all softwood panels have veneer cores.

FACE VENEER
CROSS BAND
CORE
CROSS BAND
BACK VENEER

5-PLY VENEER CORE

FACE VENEER
PARTICLE BOARD CORE
FACE VENEER

3-PLY PARTICLE BOARD CORE

FACE VENEER
CROSS BAND
LUMBER CORE
CROSS BAND
BACK VENEER

5-PLY LUMBER CORE

FACE VENEER
CROSS BAND
HOLLOW EGGCRATE CORE OF FIBER BOARD OR WOOD

5-PLY HOLLOW CORE

FACE VENEER
CROSS BAND
CORRUGATED HEAVY PAPER

5-PLY CORRUGATED CORE

FACE VENEER
FOAM TYPE PLASTIC CORE

3-PLY FOAM PLASTIC CORE

FIGURE 16-1 *Plywood*

Particle board cores are medium-density board made from wood particles. They are being used more and more, replacing the lumber core panel and the veneer core in plywood because of their dimensional stability.

The solid lumber core is composed of strips of lumber edge-glued into a solid slab. This type is usually 5-ply, 3/4 in. thick; for special uses, thicknesses from 1/2 to 1-1/8 in. are manufactured (see Figure 16-1).

PLYWOOD VENEER CUTS: The manner in which veneers are cut determines the various visual effects obtained. Two woods of the same species with their veneers cut differently will have entirely different visual characters, even though their colors are similar.

Six different methods of cutting plywood veneers are used depending on the type of veneer required. For example, the log is placed centrally in a lathe and turned against a razor-sharp blade (like unwinding a roll of paper) to produce what is known as the "rotary" cut. Other methods of cutting and slicing (see Figure 16-2) are plain slicing, quarter slicing, half-round slicing, back cut, and rift cut. The different cuts produce different grain characteristics.

BASIC TYPES OF PLYWOOD: Plywood is manufactured in two basic types; *exterior* and *interior*. Adhesives for bonding exterior-type panels are waterproof. Glues used for interior plywood are lightly moisture-resistant but not waterproof.

GRADES OF FACE TREATMENTS: Plywood panels are generally available in five different face or outer veneer treatments (see Table 16-1).

AVAILABLE SIZES OF PLYWOOD PANELS: Standard-size plywood panels are 4 by 8 ft., but they can also be furnished in widths of 2-1/2, 3, and 3-1/2 ft., and in lengths of 5, 6, 7, 9, 10, and 12 ft. Larger sizes such as 16 by 24 ft., or even 50 ft. in length are manufactured for specific uses.

PLYWOOD SIZES FOR EXTERIOR USES: When plywood is used as outside siding, a minimum thickness of 3/8 in. is required. When used as wall sheathing (see Figure 16-3), a thickness of not less than 5/16 in. is acceptable when the stud spacing is 16-in. o.c., and 3/8 in. is permissible when the stud spacing is 24-in. o.c. For roof

TYPE OF CUTTING	METHOD OF CUTTING	GRAIN CHARACTERISTICS
ROTARY	LOG / KNIFE	GRAIN MATCHING IS DIFFICULT
PLAIN SLICING	KNIFE	
QUARTER SLICING	KNIFE	NARROW PIECES
HALF-ROUND SLICING / OFTEN USED ON RED OAK	CENTER POINT OF ROTATION / KNIFE	RESEMBLES ROTARY CUT
BACK-CUT	CENTER POINT OF ROTATION / KNIFE	GRAIN CHARACTERISTICS SMALLER THAN PLAIN SLICING
RIFT-CUT / NORMALLY LIMITED TO OAK	CENTER POINT OF ROTATION / KNIFE	FAIRLY UNIFORM GRAIN NARROW PIECES

FIGURE 16-2 *The six principal methods of cutting veneers*

TABLE 16-1 *Grades of face treatment*

Grade	Face or Outer Treatment
A	Smooth surface suitable for fine finish or painting
B	Somewhat lower in appearance quality than A
C and D	Have some defects — used where appearance is not important
N	Natural finish, free of all open defects

sheathing, a 5/16-in. thickness may be used with rafters 16-in. o.c., and 3/8-in. for rafters 24-in. o.c.

Generally, when plywood is used for wall or roof sheathing, it is not necessarily the strength of the plywood that controls the thickness, but the holding power of the nails required for the type of roofing or siding selected.

JOINTING OF EXTERIOR PLYWOOD PANELS: Jointing of plywood panels must be carefully considered if water is to be prevented from entering the building. Horizontal joints may be shiplapped by fitting the ends of two panels or by introducing a molding that may also serve as a design treatment. Shiplapping may be used on all four edges of the panel to form a weathertight joint. With adjacent panels, Figure 16-4 illustrates some of the horizontal and vertical jointing of plywood panels used for exterior sheathing and siding.

JOINTING OF INTERIOR PLYWOOD PANELS: The jointing of plywood when used for interior finishes and cabinets and built-in furniture depends on design considerations and the handling of the edges of the plywood (see Figure 16-5).

Fiber and Wood Pulp Products

Logs of wood are converted into wood pulp, chips, and fibers by mechanical or chemical processes. These converted materials are then processed into various types of papers, boards, and insulating materials (see Table 16-2).

FIBERBOARD: Most fiberboards are manufactured from wood pulp, waste paper, and fibers. They are lightweight, noncombustible, strong, and possess good acoustical and insulating values. They are available with various surface treatments and find a variety of uses in the construction field for

WOOD FRAME BOX-SILL
CONSTRUCTION WITH
PLYWOOD SHEATHING
AND SUB-FLOORING

WOOD FRAME ROOF CONSTRUCTION
WITH PLYWOOD ROOF SHEATHING
AND WOOD SHINGLES

FIGURE 16-3 *Plywood wall and roof sheathing with board and batten siding and wood roof shingles*

BUTT JOINT FOR
SHEATHING
HORIZONTAL
AND VERTICAL

SHIPLAP FOR
PLYWOOD SIDING
HORIZONTAL
AND VERTICAL

BUT-JOINT WITH
METAL FLASHING
HORIZONTAL

SHIPLAP WITH
WOOD WATER
DRIP OR
MOULDING
HORIZONTAL

BUTT JOINT WITH
WOOD BATTEN
VERTICAL

TONGUE & GROOVE
WITH VERTICAL CUT

CORNER WITH WOOD
COVER VERTICAL

FIGURE 16-4 *Exterior vertical and horizontal joining of plywood sheathing and siding*

FIGURE 16-5 *Interior plywood joining and end grain treatments*

TABLE 16-2 *Commonly used fiber and wood pulp products*

Material	Shape	Use
1. Acoustical	1/2″ to 2″ thick, in squares or rectangles, in 12″ modules, maximum 24″ × 48″	Acoustical treatment for walls and ceilings
2. Building paper (sheathing paper)	In rolls, asphalt-impregnated or coated, weighing from 3 to 10 lbs. per 100 sq. ft.	Sheathing paper, vapor barriers, deafening paper under wood floors, and temporary protective covering of finish materials
3. Fiberboards	Boards 3/8″ to 1-7/8″ in thickness, 4′-0″ wide and 8′-0″ long; in 1/2″ thickness it is available in panels 8′-0″ in width and 16′-0″ in length	Interior walls and ceilings, exterior sheathing, and finish exterior walls in residential work
4. Flashing	In rolls, laminated with 1-, 2-, or 3-oz. copper foil	Concealed flashing, waterproofing, and vapor barrier
5. Hardboards	Tempered or standard, 1/8″ to 5/16″ in thickness, 4′-0″ wide, and 4′-0″ to 12′-0″ in 2′-0″ increments and 16′-0″ in length	*Standard* is used for interior work such as underlayment, cabinet, and millwork; *tempered* is used for both interior and exterior work such as siding, cabinet and millwork, and panelling where one surface has been given a special surface finish
6. Particle board (chip board)	Boards 1/4″ to 3/4″ and thicker, 4′-0″ wide and 8′-0″ to 16′-0″ long	Cores for wood and plastic laminate veneers, cabinet and millwork
7. Roofing felt	In rolls weighing from 12 to 30 lbs. per 100 sq. ft.	Built-up roofing, dampproofing, and waterproofing

sheathing, insulation, and as interior and exterior finishes for residential buildings.

HARDBOARD: Wood chips of controlled size are placed in a vat under high-pressure steam. When this pressure is released, the chips blow apart and the fibers and the wood lignin are separated from the unusable materials. This mixture is formed into boards, which are finally compressed with heat to form hard, dense boards.

There are three types of hardboard: *standard*, *tempered*, and *low-density*.

Standard and low-density boards are used only in the interior of buildings, whereas tempered boards are used on the exterior and interior of buildings and in interior areas where moisture and water are present.

Tempered boards are standard hardboard impregnated with oils and resins and subjected to high heat; it is available with a variety of special surface finishes such as grooves, textures, and black color.

PARTICLE BOARD: Particle board (chip board) is a product which is dry-formed of particles of wood bonded together with a synthetic resin or other binders. It might be considered a three-ply board because its outer layers are made of finely cut flakes to provide a smooth, hard surface, and the inner layer is made of more coarsely cut material. In addition to its many uses, the particle or chip board is primarily used as a core stock for high-pressure plastic laminate veneers and hardwood

veneers. As core stock, it is used by manufacturers of furniture, cabinets, countertops, wall paneling, partitions, and doors of all types. Figure 16-6 illustrates some of the details in the use of the particle board for cabinet doors, millwork, and sliding closet doors.

REVIEW EXAMINATION

1. What are the outside plies of a plywood panel called?

2. What are the plies to which the face and back are glued in a five-ply panel called?

3. Name the three types of plywood cores.

4. What are the two basic types in which plywood is manufactured?

5. What is the common size of plywood panel?

6. When plywood is used as wall sheathing on a stud spacing of 16-in. o.c., the thickness of the plywood must be at least how thick?

7. What is a simple type of horizontal joint in joining exterior panels?

8. In addition to its many other uses, the particle or chip board when used with high-pressure plastic laminates is primarily used as what?

9. Name the three types of hardboard.

10. By mechanical or chemical processes, wood logs are converted into what three things?

11. When using plywood for roof or wall sheathing, what controls the thickness?

FIGURE 16-6 *Details of particle board used as cabinet doors, millwork, and sliding doors*

12. Name two properties wood fiberboards offer.

ASSIGNMENT

1. Sketch a five-ply plywood panel and label or name all the laminations.
2. Make a sketch showing a use of plywood other than those illustrated in this unit.

SUPPLEMENTARY INFORMATION

Laminated Fiberboard Decking

This decking is manufactured by laminating two or more fiberboards together. It is available in 5/8 to 3-in. thicknesses, 2'-0" and 3'-0" widths, and 4'-0" to 12'-0" lengths, with a tongue-and-groove finish on all four edges.

The thicker the decking, the greater the insulation value and the spanning between supports, and also the nail-holding power. When wood rafters are exposed, this material is the sheathing, insulating, and finish surface between the rafters (see Figure 16-7).

FIGURE 16-7 *Laminated fiberboard decking with exposed roof rafters.*

Insulating Board

Fiber insulating boards are manufactured in 1/2-in., 5/8-in., 3/4-in., and 1-in. thicknesses, 4'-0" wide, and from 4'-0" to 16'-0" in length. This type of board is also used for manufacturing fiber-type acoustical tile, and is used in building construction for sheathing in residential buildings and as roof insulation for types of buildings with flat roofs or slightly pitched roofs.

Concrete Forms

Heavy paper in spiral form is manufactured in almost any diameter for use as forms for reinforced concrete columns and slabs. It is also made into dome-type and egg crate-type forms (see Figure 16-8).

Wallpaper

Wallpaper is generally used for decorative or plain interior wall covering. It is manufactured in rolls and sheets of various widths and lengths, and is available with a wide variety of special finishes such as water-resistant, waterproof, and mark-resistant.

Com-Ply Wall Studs and Floor Joists

The U.S. Department of Housing and Urban Development and the USDA Forest Service have performed cooperative research that has led to the development of new composite lumber products called Com-Ply.

Com-Ply lumber such as studs and joists are structural sandwich-type constructions with a particle board core placed between layers of solid

FIGURE 16-8 *Paper forms*

TABLE 16-3   *Minimum plywood bending radii*

Panel Thickness (in.)	Across Grain (in.)	Parallel to Grain (ft.)
1/4	24	5
5/16	24	6
3/8	36	8
1/2	72	12
5/8	96	16
3/4	144	20

wood veneer. The studs are intended to be used interchangeably with 2″ × 4″ wall studs of sawed lumber and at the same spacings, but are not intended as general substitutes for 2″ × 4″ sawed lumber.

The Com-Ply floor joists, on the other hand, are intended to be used as substitutes for those of sawed lumber and as a complete framing system.

Composite lumber such as Com-Ply requires fewer trees to produce the same amount of lumber than does conventional sawing practice.

The particle board which makes up a large portion of Com-Ply studs and joists is made from chipped-up wood that comes from forest residues, mill residues, or low quality timber.

Bending Plywood

When plywood is used for circular forms and shapes, it is necessary to find the minimum bending radius for the thickness of plywood being used. Table 16-3 gives the minimum radii for various thicknesses of plywood bent both across and parallel to the grain.

17

LAMINATED WOOD AND
SOLID WOOD STRUCTURAL MEMBERS

INTRODUCTION

In this chapter, the laminated wood structural members reviewed include beams, girders, timbers, decking, arches, trusses, and stressed-skin plywood panels. Solid wood structural members reviewed include the different types of trusses and timber connectors, as well as details of a nail-glued roof truss.

TECHNICAL INFORMATION

Laminated Wood Structural Members

Glue-laminated lumber is the product resulting from the joining together by glue of two or more smaller pieces of lumber to form a larger, stronger member. Generally, 1- or 2-in. thick stock is bonded to form beams, columns, arches, and various other structural members. The major advantage of such glued members lies in the fact that they are one-third stronger than a sawed member of equal size, as shown graphically in Figure 17-1. This permits a slenderizing of design without sacrificing strength. Tests prove that the glued joint (the bond) is stronger than the wood itself, and time does not affect the bonding qualities of the glue. Another important advantage of laminated lumber is that larger pieces of lumber in both length and cross section may be obtained than is possible in single sawed pieces of solid wood. Furthermore, beams of varying cross section can be built to have a greater shear resistance at points where it is most desired.

Laminated Beams and Girders

Because laminated beams are manufactured in a plant where they are assembled, glued, planed, sawed, treated with preservatives, and finished with the natural wood grains showing, no plas-

FIGURE 17-1 *Sawed and glue-laminated members of equal strength*

FIGURE 17-2 *Glue-laminated beams*

tering or painting or other decorative treatments are necessary unless they are specified to conform to the requirements of the architectural design. These beams are economically practical when used as a finished product and exposed as a part of the architectural design, but when used merely as concealed structural units, they are generally uneconomical. For spans up to 24 ft., solid timbers are usually cheaper than laminated sections except where extremely heavy loads are to be supported. Beyond that limit, glue-laminated beams or wood trusses are generally used. Figure 17-2 illustrates a wide variety in shapes of glue-laminated beams.

Laminated Timbers

Such timbers are superior to solid wood structural members. First, they have greater strength and rigidity than solid beams because they are vertically laminated to resist twisting, and second, there is uniform moisture control because the members are kiln-dried before laminating to a 12 to 15% moisture content (see Figure 17-3). Laminated timbers are manufactured in lengths from 12 to 60 ft. in increments of 1 ft. All timbers are given protective treatment with a water-repellent sealer.

FIGURE 17-3   *Uniform moisture control*

Laminated Beam Support Connections

Laminated beams may be supported at their ends by masonry walls, laminated columns, simple frame wall construction, or steel columns. Figure 17-4 illustrates such supports together with the connection rough hardware for fastening the beams.

Laminated Decking

The decking here is part of a structural concept that utilizes post and beam or arch construction with exposed roof decking (see Figure 17-5). This system contributes to simplified building through the use of fewer supporting elements than required in conventional frame construction. Laminated decking provides a V-grooved paneled ceiling with natural wood finish for spans between beams of up to 8′-0″. Before the lumber used for decking is bonded, it is kiln-dried to a completely uniform moisture content, thus assuring dimensional stability. Decking is available in laminated

FIGURE 17-4   *Laminated beam support connections*

FIGURE 17-5   *Laminated beams supporting laminated decking*

thicknesses of 2-1/4 in., 2-3/4 in., 3 in., 3-3/4 in., and 4 in. (see Figure 17-6).

Two-Hinged and Three-Hinged Arches

Laminated two- and three-hinged arches are manufactured similarly to wood laminated beams and girders. They are curved and glued together under high pressure to make a solid and rigid member. Control of moisture content and the use of structural glues with a high water resistance insure a stable and permanently bonded structural member.

Laminated arches provide a means of roofing large areas without obstructions from floor to ceiling. Arch units may be spaced as much as 15 to 20 ft. apart, in which case purlins are used, which in turn support the roof deck material.

The two-hinged arches are particularly adaptable for wide spans. They have been used for spans up to 250 ft., and are practical for even larger spans. However, the most common spans range from 30 to 100 ft.

These structural units are installed by various methods, as shown in Figure 17-7, including foundation-anchored, tied, buttressed, or combinations of these methods. With foundation buttresses, the horizontal thrust is contained by the foundations. With tie rods below grade, to counteract the horizontal thrust, simple vertical foundations can be used. Tied arches are supported by columns or bearing walls, with headroom being obtained by having the tie rods located at the top of the columns or walls. Buttressed arches are contained by concrete or masonry buttresses of sufficient size to counteract the horizontal thrust of the arches.

STANDARD V-PATTERN WITH 5 15/32" FACE

FIGURE 17-6 *Laminated decking*

FIGURE 17-7 *Two-hinged arches*

FIGURE 17-8 *Three-hinged arches*

Three-hinged arches, as shown in Figure 17-8, are widely used in churches, gymnasiums, auditoriums, and other types of buildings where large clear open areas are required. Specific types include the Tudor, the Gothic, and the parabolic. They are composed of two laminated units, fastened at the top or ridge of the arch and at its two foundation ends. Functionally, they provide clear span framing for both sidewalls and roof. Generally the horizontal thrust is counteracted by installing the rods below the finished floor.

Arches of this type are generally left exposed, because the natural wood form and grained surface can become a design feature of the interior or the exterior.

Laminated Wood Trusses

A wood truss is a complete structural unit with laminated wood top and bottom chords. Web members are solidly bolted between the laminated members with heavy steel bolts and straps. Trusses have an advantage over the arches in that they do not require ties, special foundations, or buttresses. Commonly used spans range from 40 to 150 ft., and some manufacturers are equipped to produce spans greater than 150 ft. Of the numerous types of wood trusses available, the bow-string type (see Figure 17-9) is perhaps the most common. Wood trusses may be supported by steel, concrete, or wood columns, or by masonry walls or piers. Typical examples of support and connection are shown in Figure 17-10).

FIGURE 17-9 *A typical bow string truss*

Stressed Skin Plywood Panels

Plywood panels are nailed and glued to thin stringers to form an integral member capable of resisting stresses (see Figure 17-11). Such panels are used extensively in prefabricated building construction for floors and roofs because they permit thinner and shallower framing members than does conventional frame construction. All panels are standard 4-ft. wide plywood with the face grain parallel to the length. The lengths vary depending on their loading. Normally spans range up to 12 ft., but can be used for larger spans of 16 to 18 ft. When used as roof panels, the top and bottom plywood skins are 3/8 in. in thickness of exterior plywood. In panels used as floors, the top skin is 5/8 in. in thickness, while the lower skin is 3/8 in. in thickness; both skins are of interior plywood. The structural action of the stressed-skin panel is similar to the steel beam. The top flange of the beam when loaded tends to bend and set up a compressive stress while its bottom face is in tension.

MASONRY WALL   LAMINATED COLUMN

TYPICAL HEEL CONNECTIONS   BRACE CONNECTION

FIGURE 17-10   *Laminated wood truss connections and supports*

FIGURE 17-11   *Stressed skin plywood panels*

These actions tend to cause the plywood to slip from the beams; therefore, because nails alone cannot prevent such movement, the panels are glued to the tops and bottoms of beams under a pressure of 150 lbs. per sq. in. The type of glue used is very important—when panels are exposed to moisture, a highly moisture-resistant type of glue must be used.

Solid Wood Trusses

The type of built-up wood roof trusses used in a building is determined by the length of the required span, the material of which the truss is constructed, and the manner in which the truss is loaded. Several designs, all of which provide a method of roofing clear space, are shown in

Figure 17-12. They are suitable for residential construction, housing, and industrial and commercial construction.

Typical lightweight trusses such as is used in residences are shown in Figure 17-13. These trusses can be prefabricated in a shop, as the larger ones usually are, or can be built on the site. In the latter case, they are fabricated on the ground, using lightweight material, usually 2 × 4s and 2 × 6s, generally placed 2'-0" on centers on the exterior frame walls. The parts of trusses can be joined with either plywood connectors or suitable metal timber connectors at critical points. The roof sheathing is nailed directly to the trusses. Figure 17-13 shows a solid wood truss joined with split-ring connectors. Such trusses are used for spans from 20 to 35 ft. in length. Figure 17-14 shows the construction details of a nail-glued roof truss.

184

HOWE TRUSS
PARALLEL CHORDS

BOW-STRING TRUSS

PITCHED HOWE TRUSS

FAN TRUSS

FIGURE 17-12 *Types of timber trusses*

3-2½" SPLIT RINGS
1-¼" BOLT

1"x4" SCAB

1-2"x6"

1-2"x4"

1-2"x4"

6" 12" 6"

1-2"x6"

1-2½" SPLIT RING
1-½" BOLT

2-2½" SPLIT RINGS
1-½" BOLT

2-2½" SPLIT RINGS
2-½" BOLTS

FIGURE 17-13 *Solid wood truss*

TOP CHORD
PEAK GUSSET
INTERMEDIATE GUSSET
LONG DIAGONAL
½" PLYSCORD SCAB
SHORT DIAGONAL

16"

LARGE HEEL
GUSSET

24"

8'-0"

3'-10"

12'-0"

12'-0"

3'-9¾"

SPAN = 24'-0"

2/12 NAIL-GLUED ROOF TRUSS 2'-0" O.C.

4 d NAILS

2"x4"

10"

12"

½" PLYSCORD

INTERMEDIATE GUSSET

⅜"

2"x4"

2"x4"

2"x4"

2"x4"

16"

4 d NAILS

½" PLYSCORD

PEAK GUSSET

2"x4's

4 d NAILS

½" 3"

6¾"

36"

½" PLYSCORD

LARGE HEEL GUSSET

6 d NAILS

2"x4"

24"

BOTTOM CHORD SPLICE

FIGURE 17-14 *2/12 pitch nail-glued roof truss*
(Courtesy of Small Homes Council, Urbana, Ill.)

185

REVIEW EXAMINATION

1. What is the advantage of a glue-laminated beam over a sawed member?

2. What is the thickness of the boards used in fabricating a laminated beam?

3. Laminated timbers are manufactured in lengths ranging from 12 ft. to 60 ft. in what increments?

4. Laminated decking is available in what thicknesses?

5. Practical and most common spans of laminated two-hinged arches range from what span to what span in feet?

6. What are two-hinged arches particularly adaptable for?

7. What is the advantage of laminated wood trusses over arches?

8. What is the structural action of the stressed-skin panel similar to?

9. What is the purpose of trusses?

10. Name the roof truss considered to be one of the most efficient for spans exceeding 80 ft.

ASSIGNMENT

1. Sketch three laminated beam support connections.

2. Sketch a two-hinged and a three-hinged laminated arch, showing methods of counteracting horizontal thrust.

SUPPLEMENTARY INFORMATION

Design Considerations

Glue-laminated structural members are available in widths of 3-1/4, 5-1/4, 7, 9, 11, and 12-1/2 in. and in beam depths ranging from 3-1/8 to 92-1/2 in.

Following is an example of how sectional dimensions are calculated, together with the section properties of a 5-1/4-in.-wide glue-laminated member of various beam depths and number of laminations (see Table 17-1).

Timber Connectors

When bolts are used in solid timber framing, the stresses are concentrated on the relatively small areas on which the bolts bear. Use of timber connectors affords a comparatively large area of wood against which the connector exerts pressure, and thus the stresses are distributed over almost the entire cross-sectional area of the timbers that are connected. The connectors transmit loads from one member to another with a minimum reduction of the cross-sectional area of the joined members, and they permit the use of small pieces of lumber in the construction of solid wood trusses.

The various types of connectors in common use are the split ring, the toothed ring, the claw plate, and the shear plate (see Figure 17-15).

Nail-Glued Headers over Openings

These consist of two upper flanges, 2 × 4-in., and a single 2 × 4-in. lower flange separated by vertical 2 × 4-in. spacers 2′-0″ on centers (see Figure 17-16). A skin of plywood is glued and nailed to the framing members on one or both sides of the framing members. The nail-glued header serves as a lintel over larger openings which is capable of supporting roof loads greater than lintels of solid framing lumber.

Figure 17-17 illustrates the header spans attainable under various design loads for type A and B headers when the overall truss lengths are known.

The Rigid Plywood Frame

Figure 17-18 is composed of two vertical members and two rafters of 2 × 8-in. nominal size lumber. The rafters have a 5 to 12 pitch and are fastened at their crown by plywood gusset plates on two sides (see Detail A) and to the frame leg at haunch (see Detail B). The frame is attached to a

SPLIT   TOOTHED   CLAW   SHEAR
RING   RING   PLATE   PLATE

FIGURE 17-15   *Timber connectors*

TABLE 17-1 *How to calculate sectional dimensions*

$$\text{Area} = A = H \times W$$

$$\text{Section Modulus} = S = \frac{H^2 \times W}{6}$$

$$\text{Moment of Inertia} = I = \frac{H^3 \times W}{12}$$

Section Properties of 5 1/4-in. Glue-laminated Member

No. of Lams	W Beam Width (in.)	H Beam Depth (in.)	A Area (in.²)	S Section Modulus (in.³)	I Moment of Inertia (in.⁴)	Weight per Lin. Ft. (lbs.)
13	5-1/4	21	110.3	385.9	4,052	26.03
14	5-1/4	22-5/8	118.3	447.9	5,067	28.04
15	5-1/4	24-1/4	127.3	514.6	6,239	30.06
16	5-1/4	25-7/8	135.8	585.8	7,579	32.07
17	5-1/4	27-1/2	144.4	661.7	9,099	34.08
18	5-1/4	29-1/8	152.9	742.2	10,809	36.10
19	5-1/4	30-3/4	161.4	827.4	12,720	38.11
20	5-1/4	32-3/8	170	917.1	14,850	40.10

GENERAL DIMENSIONS FOR ALL HEADERS

TYPE A – PLYWOOD ON ONE SIDE

TYPE B– PLYWOOD ON TWO SIDES

FIGURE 17-16   *Nail-glued header*

FIGURE 17-17   *Header spans*

sill plate, which is the same size as the vertical or leg member (see Detail C).

The number of nails used at the connections, the size of the nails, and their spacing is important, because this patented frame is engineered to precise specifications. For center-to-center distances between frames, consult the Douglas Fir Plywood Association, Tacoma, Washington.

Wood Dome Construction

This type of roof construction is adaptable for wide spans and economy of construction. Horizontal thrust is contained by a tension ring at the periphery of the structure so that all members are in compression. Glulam (glued laminated) segments of the dome are of small, economical section dimensions, and the walls need not be buttressed. Ratio of rise to span is low, minimizing the amount of decking required. Dome patterns are radial rib, triangular, and triax; the latter two are assembled on the ground, then raised into position and connected to the tension ring, thus saving the cost of scaffolding. Dome patterns in plan are shown in Figure 17-19.

FIGURE 17-18 *Plywood rigid frame*

(Courtesy of Douglas Fir Plywood Assoc., Tacoma, Washington)

RADAX*
PATTERN

VERAX*
PATTERN

TRIAX*
PATTERN

* TRADEMARK OF TIMBER STRUCTURES INC.

FIGURE 17-19 *Laminated wood domes*

18

BUILDING WITH WOOD

INTRODUCTION

This chapter deals with some of the major details used in contemporary wood frame construction based on laminated wood bents and a unique system in which two milled members are employed to form the major part of the construction. Also included are light frame conventional sections and details, and post and beam construction.

TECHNICAL INFORMATION

The Contemporary House

A contemporary house (see Figure 18-1) employs a system of framing and construction consisting of five laminated wood bents in hollow rectangular shape from which the roof plane hangs and upon which the floor structure rests.

CEILING BEAMS: The ceiling beams are suspended from the laminated bents by means of joist hangers which are attached to a channel iron, bolted to the top cord of the laminated wood bents (see Figure 18-2, Section 1-1). The top and bottom cords of the wood bents are composed of nineteen wood members, glued and laminated together under high

pressure, forming a 9 × 30-3/4-in. beam. The floor joists are resting on and span the lower cords of the wood bents (see Figure 18-3).

ROOF CONSTRUCTION: Roof purlins running at right angles to the ceiling beams provide the nailing for the roof sheathing and roofing material. The roof cornice (see Figure 18-4) is of a beveled wood blocking, finished with copper fascia. The roof is a built-up roofing.

WALL CONSTRUCTION: Instead of the usual stud wall, there are a number of milled sections (see Figure 18-5) which, when in place, will receive all doors, windows, glass, and other wall panels. When the floor or platform is in place, strip A is placed around the outside edges of the floor instead of the usual shoe or sole plate. This immediately provides the exterior bottom trim with a drip or shadow line under the striated plywood panels used on the outside faces of the walls.

Figures 18-6 and 18-7 show sections and isometric drawings illustrating how strip A can take the place of the usual 2 × 4 sole plate on both frame and masonry sills. Strip A, because it projects above the finish floor when it is laid in place, acts as the baseboard. The walls can be insulated as usual, and the exterior and interior panels and finish can be applied.

FRONT ELEVATION

SIDE VIEW OF WOOD BENT

GLUE-LAM
19 LAMS

FRONT VIEW OF WOOD BENTS

FIGURE 18-1   *Contemporary house, architect John M. Johansen*

FIGURE 18-2   *Ceiling beams supported from top chord of laminated bents, section 1-1 (see Fig. 18-1)*

FIGURE 18-3   *Floor joists resting on bottom chord of laminated bents, section 2-2 (see Fig. 18-1)*

FIGURE 18-4   *Cornice at roof, detail 3 (see Fig. 18-1)*

FIGURE 18-5   *Milled section*

191

FIGURE 18-6   *Strip (A) in frame construction*

FIGURE 18-7   *Strip (A) in concrete slab on grade construction*

EXTERIOR CORNER   INTERMEDIATE POST

DOOR OPENING

FIGURE 18-8   *Details illustrating the use of strip (B)*

Vertical 4 × 4s are capped by another strip A, nailed directly on top of the posts. This strip also can act as a head trim for all doors and windows. All vertical members, strip B, serve as vertical mullions and post casings, because the building on which these milled sections are used are ideally suited to post and beam construction. Around all door openings, double vertical strip Bs are used for additional stability. Filler pieces are provided for closing in where two B strips are used (see Figure 18-8).

The wall section (see Figure 18-9) illustrates the use of strip A and strip B from foundation to roof.

Figure 18-10 illustrates the extension of the house beyond the laminated wood bents (see Figure 18-1, Section 4-4). The protruding area serves as a porch with roof overhead and two side walls. Note the B strips, the vertical members providing for exterior and interior finish. Panels of glass are fixed at the two side walls, and there are sliding glass doors in the middle leading to the cantilevered porch.

Conventional Wood Frame Construction

Frame structures for houses may be constructed by four different methods known as balloon framing, braced framing, western or platform framing, and the modern braced framing. Although these methods are essentially the same, the western or platform framing is the most commonly used of the four methods (see Figure 18-11). In this method, after placing of the sill header and floor joists, the subflooring is installed, forming the platform. On this platform, all exterior and interior bearing walls are installed, using 2 × 4-in. studs spaced usually 16-in. o.c., and set on a sole plate and capped with a girt of two 2 × 4-in. members. The second floor joists are next placed in the girts of the bearing walls. The subflooring forms the second-floor platform. In like manner, all exterior and interior bearing walls are installed to receive the ceiling beams and roof rafters.

Light wood framing details are shown in Figures 18-12 and 18-13.

REVIEW EXAMINATION

1. When two wood floor joists are supported on a wood girder, what is the minimum dimension for bearing?

2. When framing around openings, what is used to support the header beam?

3. In the contemporary house the entire construction system is supported by what?

4. The advantage of a milled section as illustrated is that it can serve multiple purposes. Name three.

5. Frame structures for houses may be constructed in what four different methods?

6. What is the most common and often-used of the above methods?

ASSIGNMENT

1. Sketch a detail showing how the top bent of the contemporary house supports the ceiling beams.

2. Sketch the western or platform frame wall section.

SUPPLEMENTARY INFORMATION

Post and Beam Construction

In post and beam construction (see Figure 18-14), the roof beams may be placed transversely where the top end of the beam is fastened against a ridge and the lower end of the beam is resting on a post 4 × 4-in. minimum size. The rafters may be spaced from 2'-0" to 4'-0" on centers depending on their spans. Roof planks which span the rafters serve as the roof sheathing and, in many cases, as the inside finished ceiling. Post and beam construction may also be accomplished when the roof beams are placed longitudinally and supported intermittently or at their ends by posts.

Advantages of post and beam construction are that it provides a greater flexibility in interior room planning and allows the use of large panel wall coverings between the structural post supports.

Nails

Figure 18-15 gives the size, diameter, length, and number of nails per pound for wood frame construction. Figure 18-16 shows nails used for specific purposes.

All-Weather Wood Foundation

An all-weather wood foundation is basically a below-grade stud wall built of pressure-preservative-

Labels in Figure 18-9:

LEAD COATED GRAVEL STOP

3 PLY BUILT-UP ROOFING
SLAG GRAVEL
RIGID INSULATION

FASCIA

STRIP (A)

EXTERIOR PANEL

WOOD DECKING

INSULATION

BEAMS AT POSTS ONLY

HORIZONTAL STOP

STRIP (A)

GLASS

VERTICAL STOP

STRIP (B)

STRIP (A)

GLASS

GLASS

HORIZONTAL STOP

INTERIOR PANEL

CEILING BEAMS

STRIP (A)

DOUBLE JOISTS AT POSTS

DISTANCE VARIES

PLAN SHOWING USE OF STRIP (B) AND POSTS

FIGURE 18-9 *Post and beam construction using strips (A) and (B)*

PORCH

FIXED GLASS

STRIP (B)

STRIP (B)

¾" STUCCO ON ⅜" PLYWOOD

STRIP (B)

LAMINATED WOOD BENT

FIGURE 18-10 *Section 4-4 (see Fig. 18-1)*

194

Labels on left diagram (top to bottom):
ROOF SHEATHING
ROOF RAFTERS
RAFTER NOTCHED
CEILING BEAMS
PLATE 2-2"x4"
2"x4" STUDS
2"x4" SOLE
2ND FLOOR SUB-FLOOR
FLOOR JOISTS
2" BLOCKING CUT IN BETWEEN JOISTS
GIRT 2-2"x4"
WALL SHEATHING
2"x4" SOLE PLATE
1ST FLOOR SUB-FLOOR
FLOOR JOIST
HEADER
2"x6" SILL
FOOTING

JOISTS AT RIGHT ANGLES TO EXTERIOR WALL

Labels on right diagram (top to bottom):
GABLE END
ATTIC FLOOR AT HEAD ROOM HEIGHT ONLY
CEILING BEAMS
PLATE 2-2"x4"
FLOOR JOIST
CROSS BRIDGING
STUD
FLOOR JOIST
CROSS BRIDGING

JOISTS PARALLEL TO EXTERIOR WALL

FIGURE 18-11   *Western or platform framing*

treated lumber and plywood. It is used on luxury as well as low cost houses, apartments, schools, and office buildings and the system can even be adapted for such uses as retaining walls. A typical detail for a crawl space for an all-weather wood foundation (AWWF) and an AWWF stem wall, concrete slab, is shown in Fig. 18-17. For more information write to: American Plywood Association, 7011 South 19th Street, P.O. Box 11700, Tacoma, Wash. 98411; ask for All Weather Wood Foundation Systems.

JOISTS BEARING ON STEEL GIRDER, MINIMUM LAP 4"

10 d = 10 PENNY NAIL = 3" LONG
20d = 20 PENNY NAIL = 3" LONG

JOISTS BEARING ON WOOD GIRDER, MINIMUM LAP 4"

JOIST NOTCHED OVER LEDGER STRIP

GIRDER IN GIRDER BOX
TWO 20d AT END OF EACH PIECE, EACH SIDE; OTHERS STAGGERED 32" APART

1"x3" CROSS BRACING

TYPES OF SILL ANCHORS

DOUBLE 2"x6" SILL

FIGURE 18-12   *Light wood framing details*

RAFTERS WITH OUTRIGGERS

RAFTERS AND CEILING JOISTS RESTING ON WALL PLATES

WINDOW OPENING

FRAMING AROUND FLOOR OPENING

FIGURE 18-13   *Light wood framing details (cont.)*

4"x10" ROOF BEAM

T&G ROOF PLANKS

DETAIL 2

DETAIL 1

POSTS AT EACH
EACH END OF
RIDGE BEAM

4"x12" RIDGE BEAM

4"x4" POSTS 4'-0" O.C.

STUD

ROOF
PLANK

PLATE
BETWEEN
POSTS AND
BEAMS

METAL TIE PLATE

POST

ROOF BEAM

FILLER PANEL

DETAIL 1

METAL TIE STRAP

ROOF
BEAM

METAL TIE
PLATE

RIDGE BEAM

ROOF PLANK

DETAIL 2

POST AND BEAM CONSTRUCTION-TRANSVERSE BEAM

T&G PLANKS

DETAIL 2

DETAIL 1

CEILING
BEAMS,
THREE 4"x10"

PLATE
TWO 2"x4"

POST
4"x 4"

ROOF PLANKS

TOP
PLATE

STUD

DETAIL 1

METAL TIE STRAP

ROOF PLANKS

RIDGE
BEAM

POST

DETAIL 2

POST AND BEAM CONSTRUCTION-LONGITUDINAL BEAMS

FIGURE 18-14   Post and beam construction

197

DIA. OF HEAD

FLAT HEAD WITH DIAMOND POINT
FLAT-HEADED NAILS MEASURED HERE
CEMENT-COATED NAILS MEASURED HERE

17/32″
1/2″
15/32″
7/16″
13/32″
11/32″
5/16″
5/16″
9/32″
9/32″
17/64″
17/64″
1/4″
1/4″
13/64″
11/64″

DOUBLE-HEADED NAILS

STRONG HOLD NAILS

DIAMOND BARGE SPIKES   HEADLESS DOWELS   HOOK   OFF SET

F   LF   LFR

FLAT (COMMON)   LARGE FLAT   LARGE REINFORCED   BRAD HEAD   CUT NAIL

TYPES OF NAIL HEADS

B   D   L D   N   C   FRONT SIDE   SIDE   FRONT

BLUNT   DIAMOND   LONG DIAMOND   NEEDLE   CHISEL   DUCK BILL   CUT NAIL

TYPES OF NAIL POINTS

HEAD →   ← SHANK   → POINT

DIA. OF HEAD	17/32″	1/2″	15/32″	7/16″	13/32″	11/32″	5/16″	5/16″	9/32″	9/32″	17/64″	17/64″	1/4″	1/4″	13/64″	11/64″
PENNY	60	50	40	30	20	16	12	10	9	8	7	6	5	4	3	2
INCHES	6″	5½″	5″	4½″	4″	3½″	3¼″	3″	2¾″	2½″	2¼″	2″	1¾″	1½″	1¼″	1″
GAUGE	#2	#3	#4	#5	#6	#8	#9	#9	10¾	10¼	11½	11½	12½	12½	14	15
NO. OF NAILS PER LB.	10.7	13.5	17.3	22.7	29.7	47.4	66.1	66	92.1	101	150	167	254	296	543	847

CEMENT-COATED NAILS HAVE APPROX. TWICE NAIL HOLDING POWER OF PLAIN NAILS AND ACID-ETCHED NAILS HAVE STILL GREATER POWER.

COATINGS: NICKEL, CHROME, CADMIUM, ETCHED ACID AND PARKERIZED.
MATERIALS: ZINC, ALUMINUM, STAINLESS STEEL, TIN, CEMENT, BRASS, IRON OR STEEL, COPPER (GALV.), MONEL.

FIGURE 18-15 *Common nails*

1. Spike for gutter.
2. Purlin nail.
3. Construction nail—pole type.
4. Nail for roof decking application.
5. Trussed rafter nail.
6. Hardboard nail—no drilling required.
7. Nail for fastening materials to concrete, brick, etc.
8-9. Nails for built-up roofing.
    Annular thread for wood and plywood (9).
    Spiral thread for gypsum decking (8).
10. Hardened concrete stub nail for plywood and metal fixtures to plywood.
11. Masonry nail for sills and partition plates.

FIGURE 18-16 *Nails for specific uses (Courtesy of Independent Nail and Packaging Co.)*

FIGURE 18-17 *All-weather foundations*

19

METALS

INTRODUCTION

This chapter deals with the metals that are extensively used in construction: iron, steel, stainless steel, aluminum, brass, bronze, lead, copper, and zinc. These metals are divided into two major groups, ferrous and nonferrous.

TECHNICAL INFORMATION

Characteristics of Metals

The ferrous metals include iron, cast iron, wrought iron, and iron-based metals such as the various carbon steels, stainless steel, and weathering steel.

Aluminum, brass, bronze, copper, lead and zinc are nonferrous metals. There are others in this group such as tin, which at one time was widely used for roofing and siding; gold and silver, which have decorative uses; and chromium, titanium, and others, which are ingredients in alloys. Here the emphasis is on metal used in construction.

As a group, metals are substances that have a hardness, can conduct heat and electricity, and possess certain mechanical properties. The most important characteristic is their power to resist change in shape. Almost all metals used in construction are alloys and not the pure metals. Pure iron, for example, is as soft and bendable as copper.

Most metals deteriorate as a result of the slow action of substances in the air, soil and water, or of chemical agents to which they are exposed. This is called *corrosion*. The rusting of iron and steel are examples of corrosion. Another type of deterioration is galvanic action.

GALVANIC ACTION: When different metals or alloys are joined or brought into contact with each other and moisture is present, a galvanic action starts—an electrical current starts to flow from one metal to the other and in time one of the metals is eaten away while the other remains intact. How long this takes depends on the amount of moisture present, even if it is only the humidity in the air. In or near the ocean or in the presence of water containing minerals, galvanic action can become much more intense.

For example, if aluminum siding is applied with steel nails, the aluminum around the steel will gradually be eaten away and the siding will eventually fall off. In order to overcome this galvanic

TABLE 19-1 *Galvanic table with detail showing method of isolation of interacting metals*

Aluminum
Zinc
Iron and Steel
Stainless steel
Lead
Brasses
Copper
Bronze
Gold

action, different metals must be isolated or applied with metals that are compatible and will not start this electrical action. The galvanic table (Table 19-1) shows the metals listed in a sequence in which each metal is attacked through galvanic action by all the metals that follow it in the table. Thus, aluminum is attacked by all metals listed, whereas gold is not attacked by any of the metals. Steel nails cannot be used to secure stainless steel; the stainless steel will, through galvanic action, disintegrate the steel nails.

Uses of Metal in Buildings

Metals are used in six major categories in the construction of buildings, as outlined in Table 19-2.

Weights of Metals

Metals vary considerably in their weight, as can be seen in Table 19-3. In the construction field, however, the weight of the metals or building materials becomes important only in the multistoried building. Consideration of relative weights then becomes the problem of the structural engineer and also must be considered by the professional estimator, who calculates the quantities of materials required from the working drawings for a building.

TABLE 19-2 *Uses of metals in buildings*

Category	Metal	Where Used
1. Structure	Steel, weathering steel	Structural steel, reinforcing of concrete
2. Hollow metalwork (including curtain walls)	Steel, stainless steel, weathering steel, aluminum, brass, bronze	Doors, bucks, partitions panels, windows, mullions, curtain walls
3. Miscellaneous metalwork	Steel, stainless steel, weathering steel, aluminum wrought iron, cast iron, brass, zinc, bronze	Railings, fencing, stairs, lintels, gratings, ladders, hardware
4. Ornamental metalwork	Stainless steel, weathering steel, aluminum, brass, bronze	Plaques, letters, grilles, railings, screens, sculpture, hardware
5. Flashing	Stainless steel, zinc, lead, copper, aluminum	Cap and base flashing, spandrel flashing, coping, caps, thru-wall flashing, leaders and gutters
6. Miscellaneous	Steel, stainless steel, weathering steel, aluminum, copper, brass, lead, zinc, bronze	Nuts, bolts, rivets, screws, nails, wire, cable, washers, hangers, inserts

TABLE 19-3 *Weights of metals*

Metal	Specific Gravity	Weight Pounds per 10 Cubic Inches	Weight Conversion Factor
Iron, steel, and stainless steel	7.80 to 7.90	2.82 to 2.85	2.9
Aluminum	2.70	0.975	1.0
Copper	8.89	3.210	3.28
Brass	8.20 to 8.60	2.961 to 3.105	3.17
Bronze	8.78	3.171	3.27
Zinc	7.04 to 7.16	2.54 to 2.59	2.64

An article that weighs 6 lbs. in aluminum will weight 6 times 3.17, or 19.02 lbs. in brass. The weight of an article in the other metal must be divided by the conversion factor to find out what it would weigh in aluminum—a copper article weighing 25 lbs. would weigh 25 divided by 3.28, or 7.62 lbs. in aluminum.

Ferrous Metals

IRON, STEEL, STAINLESS STEEL, AND WEATHERING STEEL: The element *iron* is used to make wrought and cast iron, steel, stainless steel, and weathering steel. The characteristics of these irons and steels depend upon the iron–carbon percentages and the addition of small quantities of other elements such as nickel, chromium, manganese, boron, aluminum, copper, and silicon (see Tables 19-4 and 19-5).

CAST AND WROUGHT IRON: Cast iron is a hard and brittle material which can be cast into almost any shape and can be welded by any of the generally used methods. In the field of construction it is used for dampers, manhole covers, gratings, circular stairs, pipe, plumbing fixtures, hardware, etc.

Wrought iron is a soft, tough material which is resistant to corrosion. It can be bent, rolled, machined, and spun, and it can be welded by any of the generally used methods. In the field of construction it is used for railings, ornamental ironwork, grilles, pipe, and furniture. It is manufactured in pipe, rod, bar, plate, sheet, and bent shapes.

STEEL: Steel is a hard, strong material which can be rolled, drawn, bent, and cast; it can be welded

TABLE 19-4   *Percentages of carbon*

Wrought Iron	Cast Iron	Carbon Steel	Stainless Steel
Less than 0.1% carbon	More than 2.0% carbon	Less than 2.0% carbon	Less than 0.2% carbon

TABLE 19-5   *Percentages of alloying elements in steel, stainless steel and weathering steel*

Alloying Element	Carbon Steel	Stainless Steel	Weathering Steel
Nickel		3.5% to 14.0%	0.25% to 1.10%
Chromium	With aluminum and boron, less than 3.99%	14.0% to 19.0%	0.30% to 1.25%
Manganese	Less than 1.65%	1.0% to 10.0%	0.20% to 0.35% (maximum)
Copper	Less than 0.60%		0.20% to 0.30%
Silicon	Less than 0.60%	1.0% maximum	0.10% to 0.90%
Vanadium			0.01% to 0.10%

by any of the generally used methods. In the construction field it is extensively used for structural framing, as reinforcing and forms for concrete, and in hollow metal work, miscellaneous metal work, and ornamental metal work, etc.

Structural framing consists of various rolled sections, bent shapes, tubular shapes and open-web joists as shown in Figure 19-1, 19-2, 19-3, and 19-4.

Reinforcing and forms for concrete. Steel reinforcing bars and wire mesh are used for reinforced concrete and steel wire rope is used for prestressed concrete (see Tables 19-6 and 19-7 and Figures 19-5 and 19-6).

There are many types of forms for concrete and reinforced concrete, such as forms for foun-

CHANNEL   ZEE   DOUBLE "C" CHANNEL

DOUBLE "C" LIP TO LIP   DOUBLE "C" BACK TO BACK

HAT   STRUT

FIGURE 19-2   *Bent shapes*

SQUARE   RECTANGULAR   ROUND

FIGURE 19-3   *Tube shapes*

BEAMS   CHANNEL   ANGLE   TEE
COLUMNS
GIRDERS

FIGURE 19-1   *Rolled sections*

BENT ROD

ANGLES

SECTION   ELEVATION

FIGURE 19-4   *Open web steel joist*

TABLE 19-6   *Plain and deformed reinforcing bars*

Number	Weight lb./ft.	Diameter in.
3	0.38	0.375 or 3/8"
4	0.67	0.500 or 1/2"
5	1.04	0.675 or 5/8"
6	1.50	0.750 or 3/4"
7	2.04	0.875 or 7/8"
8	2.67	1.000 or 1"
9	3.40	1.128 or 1-1/8"
10	4.30	1.270 or 1-1/4"
11	5.31	1.410 or 1-3/8"
14	7.65	1.693 or 1-11/16"
18	13.60	2.257 or 2-1/4"

TABLE 19-7   *Commonly used wire mesh for reinforcing concrete*

Size of Mesh	Gauge of Wire	Weight in Pounds per 100 sq. ft.
WWF 6 × 6	W1.4 × W1.4	21
WWF 6 × 6	W2.1 × W2.1	30
WWF 6 × 6	W2.9 × W2.9	42

1/4" TO 1/2" Ø

6 x 7 MEANS
6 STRANDS OF WIRE, EACH
STRAND CONTAINING 7 WIRES
STANDARD WIRE ROPE:
6x7, 6x9, 6x37, 8x19

FIGURE 19-5   *Wire rope*

STEEL DECKING
REINFORCING

WIRE MESH
CORRUGATED STEEL
WIRE MESH SPOT WELDED

WIRE MESH
REINFORCING ROD
STEEL PAN OR DOME

FIGURE 19-6   *Concrete forms*

dation walls, steel decking, corrugated steel, steel pans, and domes (see Figure 19-6).

STAINLESS STEEL: This is a very hard, stiff, strong, and corrosion-resistant material that can be machined, cast, rolled, drawn, bent, formed and welded, and soldered. Stainless steel is manufactured in sheet, strip, plate, bar, tubing, castings, and structural shapes. It is widely used in the construction field for doors, windows, curtain walls, signs, grilles, louvres, railings, flashing, and structures in which it is exposed to the atmosphere. There is a wide variety of finishes from a mirror-like finish to a rough hammered finish.

Nonferrous Metals

ALUMINUM: All aluminums used in building construction are alloys and vary from soft to almost as strong as steel; all are very corrosion-resistant. Aluminum is a lightweight metal and therefore has many advantages over other metals such as copper, brass, and steel. Its comparative lighter weight reduces shipping, handling, and installation costs (see Table 19-3).

Aluminum alloys are divided into two main categories: those for casting and those for wrought aluminum products. Wrought aluminum can be extruded, bent, formed, rolled, spun, machined, and welded and soldered by special methods. It is manufactured in sheet, strip, plate, rod, bar, pipe, tube, wire, foil, and numerous extruded shapes both standard and specially designed (see Figure 19-7). Aluminum is used for windows, doors, curtain walls, railings, screens, louvres, signs, plaques, copings, and flashings.

CORROSION OF ALUMINUM: Aluminum in contact with other metals that create galvanic action or with materials that create a chemical action can corrode when a moisture condition is present. To

FIGURE 19-7   *Extruded window sash and frame jamb section*

offset this possibility, proper protective measures must be taken. The aluminum should be isolated from these metals and materials by being coated with asphalt or by plastic (neoprene) washers or by a combination of both. When aluminum is used near the seacoast or in heavy industrial sections of the country, a noticeable amount of oxidation takes place. The rate of oxidation decreases substantially after about two years of weathering and then proceeds at a very slow rate. The penetration depth of this oxidation does not occur evenly all over the surface but develops in isolated spots (pitting). It spreads to new areas slowly, yet is not much deeper after twenty years than after one or two years.

COPPER: Copper is a soft, corrosion-resistant, reddish metal used extensively in the building construction field for flashing, roofing, screens, and tubing. Because it is one of the best conductors of electricity, it is also used extensively in the electrical field. When exposed to the elements, copper develops a bright green coating which will then stop any further corrosion. Unfortunately, this coating can permanently stain adjoining materials, and care should always be taken to prevent such staining when copper is used.

BRASS: When copper and zinc are combined, the result is an alloy called brass. Brass can vary in color, strength, and corrosion resistance depending on the percentage of copper and zinc (see Table 19-8).

Brasses with 36 to 45% zinc are stronger but less corrosion-resistant, whereas the brasses with from 5 to 36% zinc are softer and more corrosion-resistant. Lead is added in small quantities to brasses to make them more workable.

TABLE 19-8   *Color variations of brasses*

Color	Copper	Zinc
Bronze color	90%	10%
Golden color	85%	15%
Yellow color	80%–62%	20%–38%
Silvery white	55%	45%

BRONZE: When copper and tin are combined, the resulting alloy is bronze. As originally developed, bronze was an alloy of 90% copper and 10% tin. This bronze is golden-brown in color, corrosion-resistant, strong and hard, but difficult to work. It was used primarily for casting. Now, most "bronzes" are alloys of copper, zinc, and small percentages of tin so that, in effect, there is little difference between "bronze" and "brass," and in today's terminology the words have almost become interchangeable if not synonymous. Brasses with the color of bronze are now known as architectural bronze, commercial bronze, and naval bronze. With these types of bronze, care should be taken in checking their specific characteristics in relation to where they are used in buildings.

LEAD: Lead is a soft, heavy, corrosion resistant, blue-gray metal used in building construction for flashing, vibration control, shields against x-rays and gamma rays, and hot-dipped protective coatings. It also finds great use combined with tin for coatings in the manufacture of terne metal.

ZINC: This is a medium-hard, low-strength, corrosion-resistant metal used in building construction for flashings, copings, roofing, hardware, and bathroom accessories. It also finds great use as a protective coating for iron and steel, called "galvanizing." When zinc is alloyed with copper it produces brass, and when alloyed with copper and nickel, it produces nickel silvers.

REVIEW EXAMINATION

1. What are the two major groups of metals?

2. Do metals resist change in shape?

3. When metals are exposed to the air, soil, water, or chemical agents, what happens?

4. When two different metals are in contact and moisture is present, what happens?

5. Cast iron, wrought iron, steel, and stainless steel depend upon what percentages of what two things for their characteristics?

6. What are the most important characteristics of stainless steel?

7. Name three areas where steel is used in the construction field.

8. What similar characteristics do aluminum and stainless steel share?

9. What is copper used for in the construction field?

10. Bronze is an alloy of copper and what?

11. Brass is an alloy of copper and what?

12. Name two areas in the construction field where zinc is used.

ASSIGNMENT

1. Make a sketch at 1/2-in. = 1'-0" of several steel-rolled sections and tubular shapes.

2. In 50 words or less, describe where the different metals are used in the construction of buildings.

SUPPLEMENTARY INFORMATION

Carbon Steels

Carbon steels not only vary greatly by the percentages of iron and carbon but are also controlled by heat treatment and mechanical work during manufacture. The strength varies depending on whether it is slowly or rapidly cooled and whether it is hot- or cold-rolled. Thus carbon steels may be specified either by chemical composition, by method of manufacture and mechanical properties, or by a system of numerical designations. Table 19-9 lists the carbon steels according to use in the construction field and in relation to carbon percentages.

TABLE 19-9 *Carbon steels used in building construction*

Use	Carbon Percentages
Steel castings	limited to 0.12 to 0.50
Reinforcing for concrete	limited to 0.40 to 0.70
Structural shapes and small structural shapes	0.22
Cold-rolled steel (sheet)	not over 0.35
Wire for mesh and wire cloth	low
Wire for pre-stressed concrete	limited to 0.90 to 1.10
Rivets	limited to 0.05 to 0.20
Screws, nails, etc.	limited to 0.08 to 0.16

Weathering Steel

Weathering steel is a high-strength, low-alloy steel which, when exposed to the atmosphere, develops a highly protective coating of a dark brown to a warm purple-black color. These steels are used exposed for roofing, siding, windows, trim, structures, and ornamental designs. The minimum thickness for exposed weathering steels is 18-gauge (0.0478 in.).

When these steels are incorporated in an architectural design, care should be taken that the adjacent materials used are of such a type and character that resist staining, because as the colored protective coating develops on the weathering steel, some of it washes off and can cause staining.

Designations for Metal Products

Wire is designated by gauge number for ferrous and nonferrous types; it is also designated by diameter in decimals of an inch, as shown in Table 19-10. Note that the smaller the gauge number, the larger the diameter.

Sheet and strip metals have different methods of designation depending on the metal. For example, steel and zinc are designated by gauges, copper by weight per square foot in ounces, and aluminum by alloy (see Tables 19-11, 19-12, 19-13, and 19-14).

Steel wire mesh reinforcing for concrete is indicated in this way:

$$\text{WWF } 6 \times 6 - \text{W1.4} \times \text{W1.4}$$

These symbols are used on both structural and architectural drawings as shown in Figure 19-8.

To explain these symbols, let us take first WWF 6 × 6. The WWF refers to woven wire fabric, the first 6 represents the longitudinal wire spacing and the second 6 represents the transverse wire spacing. Next, W1.4 × W1.4: the first W1.4 represents the longitudinal wire size and the second W1.4 represents the transverse wire size, both are 10 gauge (see Figure 19-9).

Similarly, WWF 8 × 12—W7 × W4 indicates that longitudinal wires are 8-in. on center and transverse wires are 12 in. on center. Likewise, longitudinal wires are 0-gauge with the transverse wires 4-gauge (see Figure 19-10).

FIGURE 19-8 *Steel woven wire fabric reinforcing*

TABLE 19-10 *Wire gauges of ferrous and nonferrous wire*

Gauge No.	Ferrous American Steel Wire Gauge (decimals of an inch)	Nonferrous American Wire Gauge (decimals of an inch)	Woven Wire Fabric Symbols
00	0.3310	0.3648	W 8.5, W 8, W 7.5
0	0.3065	0.3249	W 7, W 6.5
1	0.2830	0.2893	W 6, W 5.5
2	0.2625	0.2576	W 5
3	0.2437	0.2294	W 4.5
4	0.2253	0.2043	W 4, W 3.5
5	0.2070	0.1819	W 4, W 3
6	0.1920	0.1620	W 2.9
7	0.1770	0.1443	W 2.5
8	0.1620	0.1285	W 2.1, W 2
9	0.1483	0.1144	W 1.5
10	0.1350	0.1019	W 1.4
11	0.1205	0.0907	
12	0.1055	0.0808	
13	0.0915	0.0720	
14	9.0800	0.0641	
15	0.0720	0.0571	
16	0.0625	0.0508	
17	0.0540	0.0453	
18	0.0475	0.0403	
19	0.0410	0.0359	
20	0.0348	0.0320	

TABLE 19-11 *Zinc designations*

Gauge	Thickness (in inches)
9	0.018
10	0.020
11	0.024
12	0.028

TABLE 19-12 *Copper designations*

Weight per Sq. Ft. (ounces)	Thickness (in inches)
16	0.0190
20	0.0245
24	0.0300
32	0.0405

LONGITUDINAL WIRES ARE W 1.4 (No 10 GAUGE

TRANSVERSE WIRES ARE W 1.4 (No 10 GAUGE) AND EXTEND BEYOND THE OUTSIDE LONGITUDINAL WIRES ON BOTH SIDES

FIGURE 19-9 *Woven wire fabric 6 × 6-W 1.4 × W 1.4*

LONGITUDINAL WIRES ARE W 7 (No O GAUGE)

TRANSVERSE WIRES ARE W 4 (No 4 GAUGE AND EXTEN BEYOND THE OUTSIDE LONGITUDINAL WIRES ON BOTH SIDES

FIGURE 19-10 *Woven wire fabric 8 × 12-W 7 × W 4*

TABLE 19-13 *Aluminum designations*

Alloy	Thickness Available (inches)
1100-0	0.02, 0.025, 0.032
1100-H14	0.04, 0.051, 0.064
3003-H14	0.02, 0.025, 0.032

TABLE 19-14 *Steel and stainless steel designations*

Gauge	Steel Thickness (in inches)	Stainless Steel Thickness (in inches)
8	0.1644	0.171875
9	0.1495	0.15625
10	0.1345	0.140625

20

USING METALS IN BUILDING

INTRODUCTION

When ferrous and nonferrous metals are used in the construction of buildings there are many important conditions which must be considered such as strength, fire protection, resistance to corrosion, galvanic action with other metals, staining, and most important, where and why they are used. This chapter will cover the uses of iron, steel, stainless steel, aluminum, brass, bronze, copper, zinc, and lead in building construction under the following categories: structural steel, hollow metal, miscellaneous metal, ornamental metal, curtain walls, metal partitions, windows, doors, and flashing.

TECHNICAL INFORMATION

Structural Steel Framing

The structural system of a building may be defined as the method used to support the building both vertically and horizontally. When masonry walls or piers are used for the vertical support, the method is known as wall bearing (see Figure 20-1).

When a building is supported entirely by steel, this is known as structural steel framing (see Figure 20-2). When very large areas are to be framed, steel trusses are used either with masonry walls with piers or steel columns (see Figure 20-3).

WALL BEARING WITH STRUCTURAL STEEL

WALL BEARING WITH OPEN WEB STEEL JOISTS

WALL BEARING WITH STEEL DECKING

FIGURE 20-1 *Wall bearing*

A TYPICAL PANEL OF STEEL FRAMING

FIGURE 20-2   *Structural steel framing*

FINK TRUSS

HOWE TRUSS

WARREN TRUSS

PRATT TRUSS

FIGURE 20-3   *Trusses*

2" MINIMUM

WIRE MESH REINFORCING

2"

2"

FIGURE 20-4   *Structural steel framing with reinforced concrete slab*

STEEL FRAMING WITH STEEL DECKING FLOORING
(THIS IS NOT A FIREPROOF SYSTEM)

STEEL DECKING

STEEL DECKING WELDED TO STRUCTURAL STEEL

STRUCTURAL STEEL

WIRE MESH REINFORCING

REINFORCING RODS

SUPPORTS FOR METAL PAN FORMS WITH POSTS

METAL PANS (STEEL)

STRUCTURAL STEEL

FORMS

STEEL FRAMING WITH METAL PAN TYPE FLOOR CONSTRUCTION

REINFORCED CONCRETE SLAB ON TOP OF STRUCTURAL STEEL

REINFORCING RODS 12" O.C.

REINFORCING RODS 18" O.C.

METAL STOP WELDED TO TOP OF STEEL

REINFORCING RODS WELDED TO METAL STOP

SPRAY-ON FIREPROOFING

STRUCTURAL STEEL

COMPOSITE STEEL FLOOR FRAMING (REINFORCED CONCRETE SLAB SET ON TOP OF STRUCTURAL STEEL)

REINFORCED CONCRETE SLAB

2½" MINIMUM

WIRE MESH REINFORCING

OPEN-WEB STEEL JOISTS

CORRUGATED METAL

STRUCTURAL STEEL

STRUCTURAL STEEL FRAMING WITH OPEN-WEB STEEL JOISTS WITH REINFORCED CONCRETE SLAB FLOOR

FIGURE 20-5   *Steel framing with roof and floor construction*

There are many combinations of steel framing with systems of floor or roof construction—for example, structural steel framing with reinforced concrete slabs, shown in Figure 20-4. Some of the generally used combinations are shown in Figure 20-5.

211

Hollow Metal

Hollow metal in building construction covers the light gauge ferrous and nonferrous metals which are bent, extruded, and welded into shapes to form doors, bucks, louvres, partitions, windows, etc. This type of metal work covers such a wide variety of types, shapes, and details that it is impossible to cover them all and therefore only the most typical are illustrated. Interior door bucks and frames are usually made of steel (see Figure 20-6), whereas exterior door bucks and frames are made of steel, stainless steel, aluminum and, in special cases, bronze (see Figures 20-7 and 20-8).

Louvres for interior doors and louvres in exterior walls for heating, ventilation, and air-conditioning are generally made of steel or aluminum and, in special conditions, of stainless steel and bronze (see Figure 20-9).

The metals most used in manufacturing windows are steel and aluminum. In special conditions, stainless steel and bronze are used. When using metal windows in building construction it is necessary to consider the type, category, surrounding materials, climate, type of glass, orientation, security, insect screens, and most important, type of heating and air-conditioning (see Figures 20-10 and 20-11).

Miscellaneous Metal

The ferrous metals—steel, iron and cast iron—are generally used in miscellaneous metal work in building construction and include loose lintels, railings, fences, gratings, ladders, stairs, etc. Some nonferrous metals are also used in this type of work (see Figures 20-12 through 20-17).

Ornamental Metal

Aluminum, bronze, brass, and stainless steel are the metals used for ornamental metal work in building construction, and include grilles, screens, railings, letters, hardware, plaques, etc. (see Figures 20-18 through 20-21).

FIGURE 20-7 _Exterior steel, stainless steel, and aluminum door bucks and frames_

FIGURE 20-6 _Interior steel door bucks and frames_

FIGURE 20-8   *Details of steel and stainless steel doors*

FIGURE 20-9   *Louvers*

FIGURE 20-10   *Steel window detail*

FIGURE 20-11   *Aluminum window detail*

6" MINIMUM BEARING

MASONRY WALL
2"∅ STEEL PIPE
STEEL WALL BRACKET

MASONRY WALL
WELDED OR FASTENED WITH MACHINE SCREWS
ANCHOR BOLTS

SECTION OF WALL RAILING

ELEVATION OF WALL RAILING

8"
CONCRETE BLOCK
TWO 3½"×4"×⅜" ANGLES
DOOR BUCK

SECTION A-A

FIGURE 20-12   *Detail of loose lintel*

2"∅ STEEL PIPE
STEEL CHANNEL
½"×½" SQUARE STEEL ROD
½"×2" FLAT STEEL BAR
STEEL STRINGER

ELEVATION OF STAIRS

CONCRETE TREAD POURED IN PLACE IN STEEL PAN
MESH REINFORCING
METAL RISER
STRINGER
BENT METAL OR CHANNEL STRINGER
ANGLES

STEEL PAN

FIGURE 20-13   *Typical steel pan stairs*

2"∅ PIPE WELDED OR FASTENED WITH MACHINE SCREWS TO CHANNEL
½"×1" CHANNEL WELDED TO BALUSTERS
½"×2" BAR WELDED TO BALUSTERS
SLOT IN STRINGER FOR BALUSTER
½"×½ SQUARE ROD WELDED TO STRINGER
SEE ENLARGED VIEW BELOW

SECTION A-A
STEEL PAN
ANGLE SUPPORT

FIGURE 20-14   *Hand rails*

CROSS BARS

BEARING BARS

FIGURE 20-15 *Gratings*

FIGURE 20-18 *Ornamental grills*

RUNGS – 5/8" OR 3/4" ROUND STEEL BARS OR 1" STEEL PIPE

SUPPORTS TO WALL STEEL ANGLES

8" TO 12"

STRINGERS OF FLAT STEEL BARS, ANGLES, CHANNELS OR PIPES

USUALLY 18"

FIGURE 20-16 *Typical ladder*

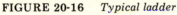

FIGURE 20-19 *Ornamental screens and grills*

TOP & BOTTOM RAILS 1 5/8" Ø GALVANIZED OR VINYL COATED STEEL PIPE OR ALUMINUM

2 1/2" Ø GALVANIZED OR VINYL COATED STEEL PIPE OR ALUMINUM

5'-0"–12'-0"

22" 30"

MESH SIZE – 2", NO. 9 GAUGE WIRE, GALVANIZED OR VINYL COATED STEEL OR ALUMINUM

FIGURE 20-17 *Typical chain link fence*

B
A
A
B
ELEVATION

SECTION A-A

SECTION B-B

B
A
A
B
ELEVATION

SECTION A-A

SECTION B-B

B
A
A
B
ELEVATION

SECTION A-A

SECTION B-B

FIGURE 20-20 *Letters*

FIGURE 20-21   *Ornamental railings*

FIGURE 20-22   *Porcelain enamel metal facing panels*

Curtain Walls

There are four basic types of curtain walls: facing type, prefabricated facing type, grid type, and structural type.

FACING: The facing type consists of a protective finish surface applied to a masonry wall. This surface can be steel with a baked enamel finish (porcelain enamel metal), aluminum, or stainless steel (see Figure 20-22 and 20-23).

PREFABRICATED: The prefabricated panels consist of an exterior face and a finished interior face with insulation placed between. This type of panel may be as thin as 1-1/2 in. and have insulating characteristics better than a wall consisting of 4-in. brick, 6-in. concrete block, and 5/8 to 3/4-in. plaster finish on the interior (see Figures 20-24 through 20-27).

GRID: The grid system is most often used for stone veneers. See Figure 14-15 in Chapter 14 on Stone and Floor and Wall Tile in Construction for a typical detail.

STRUCTURAL: This type of curtain wall is generally used for buildings of two to four floors, because the supporting grid becomes too complicated structurally for greater heights (see Figure 20-28).

FIGURE 20-23   *Aluminum or stainless steel facing panels*

ADVANTAGES OF CURTAIN WALL TYPE OF CONSTRUCTION: These can be a source of savings in building costs and energy, as the following list shows:

1. Less thickness of exterior walls;
2. Lightweight, saves steel tonnage of structural steel;
3. Saves time in construction;
4. Because of thinness, valuable rentable floor area is added;
5. When foam insulation is used, heating and air conditioning losses are minimized.

FINISHED METAL
INTERIOR SURFACE

INSULATION

1 1/2
1 1/2

FINISHED METAL
EXTERIOR
SURFACE

INTERIOR SUPPORTING
CONTINUOUS L CLIPS

PLAN

FIGURE 20-24   *Prefabricated panels*

COMPLETE UNIT
INCLUDING,
SUPPORTING GRID,
PANELS, WINDOWS
ETC. WHICH IS
ATTACHED TO
STRUCTURAL FRAME

GRID

WINDOW

PANEL

FIGURE 20-26   *Prefabricated panels*
(*continued*)

FINISHED METAL
INTERIOR SURFACE

INSULATION

CAST METAL
EXTERIOR
SURFACE

PLAN

FIGURE 20-25   *Prefabricated panels*
(*continued*)

GRID FRAME
ATTACHED TO
STRUCTURE

PREFABRICATED
PANELS

ALUMINUM
WINDOW

FIGURE 20-27   *Grid system with panels*

217

FIGURE 20-28 *Structural curtain wall*

Flashing

Flashing may be defined as both the method and the material used to weatherproof and waterproof the joints wherever different parts of a building or different materials are brought together. Thus, flashing stops the penetrations of water into the interior of the building.

There are two methods of installing flashing: exposed flashing, and concealed flashing. For exposed flashing, the nonferrous metals—aluminum, zinc, and lead—are generally used, as is the ferrous metal stainless steel.

For concealed flashing, not only are the nonferrous metals—aluminum, copper, zinc, and lead—and the ferrous metal—stainless steel—used, but also coated fabrics, plastics, and coated paper pulp products (see Figure 20-29).

When pipes, ducts, sky domes, railing supports, chimneys, or any other penetration of the roofing material occur, flashing is required (see Figures 20-30 through 20-34).

The edge of roof overhangs require special flashing details in order to terminate the roofing and protect the edge of the overhang (see Figure 20-35).

FIGURE 20-29 *Typical section showing both exposed and concealed flashing*

218

FIGURE 20-30   *Detail of pipe through roof*

FIGURE 20-31   *Detail of pipe rail supports*

FIGURE 20-32   *Duct through roof*

FIGURE 20-33   *Detail of chimney*

FIGURE 20-34   *Detail of skydome*

FIGURE 20-35   *Aluminum gravel stops and fasciae*

219

REVIEW EXAMINATION

1. Name four categories of uses of metals in building construction.

2. A wall bearing structural system of a building has what kind of vertical supporting walls?

3. Structural steel framing uses what for all supporting members?

4. Name three combinations of steel framing.

5. Hollow metalwork consists of bent, extruded, and welded metals of what sorts?

6. Miscellaneous metalwork includes what four things?

7. Aluminum or stainless steel letters used in building construction are included in what category of uses of metals?

8. Name three types of curtain walls.

9. Three advantages of curtain wall type of construction are what?

10. What are two major types of flashing?

11. What three metals are generally used for exposed flashing?

12. Which ferrous metal is used for flashing?

13. What are the metals generally used for windows?

ASSIGNMENT

1. Make a sketch showing both concealed and exposed flashing.

2. In 50 words or less, describe the important conditions that must be considered in using metals in building construction.

SUPPLEMENTARY INFORMATION

Finish Hardware

A minor use of metals in building construction is for finish hardware, which constitutes one of the important problems to be solved in constructing buildings. Finish hardware requires schedules, keying and master keying, correct indication of the swing of doors, and types of finish on hardware. Finish hardware includes hinges (known as butts), locks, push plates, door pulls, kick plates, closers, door stops, etc.

Space Frames

The space frame is a truss-type structural system that spans in many directions, not only one (see Figure 20-36).

Extruded Steel and Stainless Steel

These materials are now available in a limited number of extruded shapes due to certain limitations based on a minimum of 1/8 in. in web thickness and 0.280 sq. in. in cross-sectional area.

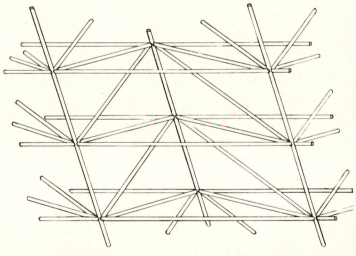

FIGURE 20-36   *Typical pipe space frame*

21

GLASS

INTRODUCTION

This chapter deals with the various types of glass in sheet form including *transparent* glass such as window and heavy sheet, plate, insulating, and tempered; and *translucent* glass such as patterned, corrugated, and glass block. Other types of glass materials are also discussed.

The invention of a new method of manufacturing glass has caused some difficulty in terminology because the glass produced is called *float glass*. In this process molten glass is actually floated onto a surface of molten tin and the result is a glass with a completely flat surface and a superior, bright finish. Furthermore, this glass is immediately ready for sizing and cutting, and is produced as window, heavy sheet, plate, tempered, reflective, patterned, and all other types of glass. It is expected that as more glass manufacturers change over to the molten tin process, all of the various types of glass used in the construction field will be produced by this process.

TECHNICAL INFORMATION

Originally glass was used for tableware and art objects and in small-sized sheets for windows. Today it has been developed not only into a very wide range of transparent, translucent, and opaque types but also into a wide variety of materials varying from glass fibers to aggregates for concrete and asphalt. Most transparent types of glass transmit 85 to 95% of visible light and are impervious to ultraviolet light.

Definition

Glass is a ceramic material made from inorganic materials—sand (silicon dioxide), soda (sodium oxide), and lime (calcium oxide), with small amounts of aluminum, iron, magnesium, and potassium oxides. Glass can be blown, cast, pressed, rolled, extruded, spun, and ground.

WINDOW AND HEAVY SHEET GLASS

The manufacturing process for window and heavy sheet glass causes distortions that run in one direction through the glass. The degree of these distortions controls the grading of the glass. All window and heavy sheet glass is graded into three qualities:

AA—Specially selected quality

A—Select quality

B—General quality

Window glass is further subdivided by thickness: *single strength*, 0.085 to 0.10 in. thick, with a maximum size of 12 sq. ft., and *double strength*, 0.115 to 0.133 in. thick, with a maximum size of 33.33 sq. ft.

There are two other types of window glass: double strength *greenhouse* quality, which has a slight greenish cast and is available up to a maximum size of 1'-8" × 1'-8", and *picture*, a thin glass used for framing, made in 3/64 and 5/64-in. thicknesses and available in AA, A, and B qualities.

Plate Glass

Plate glass generally has both sides ground and polished so that 90% of total visible light and 77.4% of total radiant energy are transmitted. See Table 21-1 for available thicknesses, maximum sizes, and weights.

Plate glass is used in the manufacture of insulating, heat-absorbing and glare-reducing, and tempered glass; it also is used for mirrors and chalkboards.

When installing plate glass it is important to allow clearances between the glass and the frame in which it is installed (see Table 21-2).

Patterned Glass

Patterned glass (see Figure 21-1) is manufactured in a wide variety of patterns, textures, and designs either on one or on both sides; also, it is

TABLE 21-1   *Types of plate glass*

Types of Plate Glass	Thickness	Maximum Sizes	Weight
Silvering, mirror glazing	1/8" to 5/16"	10'-0" × 20'-0"	1.65 to 3.29 lbs. per sq. ft.
Commercial quality	5/16" to 1-1/4"	10'-0" × 25'-0"	4.06 to 16.45 lbs. per sq. ft.

TABLE 21-2   *Minimum clearances for installing plate glass*

Type of Plate Glass	Thickness	Around Edges	Between Glass and Back of Rabbet	Depth of Rabbet
Plate	1/8″ 1/4″	1/8″ 1/4″	1/16″ 1/8″	3/8″ 5/8″
Heavy plate	5/16″ and over	1/4″	1/8″	5/8″

FLUTED   RIBBED

HAMMERED

FIGURE 21-1   *Some types of patterned glass*

METAL TO GLASS SEAL

GLASS TO GLASS SEAL

FIGURE 21-2   *Glass seals*

TABLE 21-3   *Methods of manufacturing patterned glass*

Finish	Method	How Applied
Fire	Rolling	Both sides
Frosted	Etched with acid	Both sides
Sand-blasted	Compressed air	One side
Textured	Special type roller	One side

available in various degrees of transparency (see Table 21-3).

Patterned glass is manufactured in thicknesses of 1/8, 7/32, and 3/8 in.; in widths of 4′-0″, 4′-6″, and 5′-0″; and lengths of 8′-4″, 11′-0″, 11′-4″, and 12′-0″.

Insulating Glass

Type consists of two or more sheets of plate glass, or double-strength window glass separated by an air space or spaces. The sheets of glass are joined by a metal-to-glass seal or by the glass itself (see Figure 21-2). It is made in exact sizes and cannot be cut or changed once it is manufactured. When installed, insulating glass should never be in direct contact with the frame and no part of the glass should be covered with paint.

HEAT TRANSMISSION COEFFICIENTS: Insulating glass has a heat transmission coefficient (U-factor) ranging from 0.47 to 0.67, whereas an ordinary piece of window glass has a U-factor of 1.12. By multiplying the U-factor by the area of the glass by the inside-outside design temperature difference, the heat loss through the glass is found in BTUs per hour.

EXAMPLE: An outside design temperature of 0°F and an inside design temperature of 70°F (winter range). A 100°F outside temperature and an inside temperature of 70°F equals a design temperature of 30°F (common range).

A BTU (British Thermal Unit) is an amount of heat that can raise the temperature of 1 lb. of water 1°F at sea level. Therefore a sheet of ordinary window glass of 12 sq. ft. (assumed temp. diff. 70°F) has a heat loss of

$$12 \times 1.12 \times 70° = 940.8 \text{ BTU/hr.}$$

Similarly, a sheet of insulating glass of 12 sq. ft. has a heat loss of

$$12 \times 0.47 \times 70° = 394.8 \text{ BTU/hr.}$$

Heat loss through insulating glass is approximately 42% that of heat transmission through a piece of ordinary window glass of the same size. Insulating glass is available in various thicknesses and air space widths between the glass sheets. Their relative heat transmission coefficients are given in Table 21-4.

Tempered Glass

This type of glass is manufactured from plate glass and some types of patterned glass. The glass is heated to just below melting point and then the outside surfaces are immediately cooled by jets of air. The result is that the exterior surface is in compression and the interior is in tension and these stresses are in balance.

Tempered glass is three to five times stronger to impact forces than plate glass of the same thickness; therefore it is used in areas where impact and shock are present, such as in doors, sidelights to doors, windows at grade, store fronts, etc. Tempered glass cannot be cut, drilled, or sand-blasted after it is manufactured (see Table 21-5).

When tempered glass is used as a door, all hardware, holes and sand-blasting become an integral part of the door in the process of manufacture (see Figure 21-3).

TABLE 21-4   *Heat transmission coefficient (U-factor)* for various types of insulating glass*

Insulating Glass	Thickness of Glass	Air Space			U-factor
Metal seal	1/8"	1/4"			0.64
and one			1/2"		0.57
air space	1/4"		1/4"		0.62
				1/2"	0.52
Metal seal and two air spaces	1/4"		1/4"		0.47
Glass seal and one air space	1/8"	5/16"			0.67

Note: The U-factor can be converted to an R-factor by using the formula $U = \frac{1}{R}$; similarly, $R = \frac{1}{U}$. The current use of R-factors instead of U-factors is explained in Chapter 29.

TABLE 21-5   *Types of tempered glass*

Type of Glass	Thickness	Maximum Sizes	Weight
Plate	1/4" to 1 1/4"	6'-5" × 9'-2"	3.29 to 16.45 lbs. per sq. ft.
Patterned	7/32" to 3/8"	6'-0" × 12'-0"	2.75 to 5.00 lbs. per sq. ft.

Glare-Reducing and Heat-Absorbing Glass

These types of glass absorb high percentages of the total radiant heat of the sun and therefore the edges of the glass that are covered by the frame should be of a minimum depth. The reason is that the main area of the glass heats up quickly while the edges of the glass remain cold, and cracking will occur if the frame covers too much of the glass.

The glare-reducing and heat-absorbing qualities are developed by the chemical composition of the glass. These types of glass are made in plate, heavy sheet, patterned, and tempered; in the plate-type

FIGURE 21-3   *Tempered glass door showing hardware holes and sandblasting*

TABLE 21-6 *Solar radiation transmission*

Type of Glass	% of Ultraviolet	% of Daylight	% of Solar Radiation
1/4″ plate	67.8	89.1	79.9
1/4″ heat-absorbing	44.9	74.7	46.3
1/4″ glare-reducing	39.0	40.0	45.0

federal specifications require that not more than 50% of total solar radiation be transmitted (see Table 21-6).

Wire Glass

Vertical wires or hexagonal or diamond-shaped wire mesh are embedded in the middle of plate, patterned, or corrugated glass in the manufacturing process. Wire glass is 1/4 in. or thicker, with the wire mesh not larger than 7/8 in., and the gauge of the wire not less than No. 24.

Wire glass is used (1) where fire resistance is required (size limited to 5 sq. ft. with a maximum length of 4′-0″ or a maximum width of 4′-0″), and (2) in areas where impact and abuse are present and where flying broken glass would be dangerous, such as skylights, overhead lighting, etc.

Corrugated Glass

This is 3/8-in. thick rolled glass with a pattern on both sides, translucent, wired or unwired, with a standard length of 10′-0″ and a maximum length of 12′-0″ (see Figure 21-4).

Unwired corrugated glass is generally used for decorative partitions, both exterior and interior, where light and privacy are desired.

Wired corrugated glass is used for roofs, skylights, partitions, etc., where breakage must be avoided.

Glass Block

Glass blocks are manufactured in two types, solid and hollow. Hollow glass blocks have a dehydrated, partial-vacuum air space (see Figure 21-5) which serves an insulating function. The difference in the heat transmission coefficient (U-factor) and in light transmission between window glass and glass block is shown in Table 21-7. Solid glass blocks generally are used for decorative panels and in sidewalks for cellar or basement lights.

Glass block should never be used for load-bearing. When installed in a frame, the maximum area is 144 sq. ft. with a maximum height of 20′-0″ or a maximum length of 25′-0″. When installed without a frame, the maximum area is

FIGURE 21-4 *Corrugated glass*

FIGURE 21-5 *Glass block*

TABLE 21-7   *U-factor and light transmission*

Type of Glass	U-factor*	Light Transmission
Window glass	1.12	85% to 95%
Glass block, hollow	0.44 to 0.60	0% to 85%

*Using the formula $U = \frac{1}{R}$; similarly, $R = \frac{1}{U}$. The current use of R-factors instead of U-factors is explained in Chapter 29.

100 sq. ft. with a maximum height of 10′-0″ or a maximum length of 10′-0″.

The minimum clearances for hollow glass blocks in an opening without a frame are: head—1/2 in., jamb—3/8 in., and sill—1/4 in. The minimum clearance in an opening with a frame are: head, jamb, and sill—1/4 in.

Other Types of Glass Materials

There are numerous other types of glass material with architectural uses and characteristics (see Table 21-8).

1. What is glass made from?
2. What are the three qualities of window and heavy sheet glass?
3. Is plate glass ground and polished on one side or both sides?
4. Name three methods by which patterned glass is made.
5. How much stronger is tempered glass than plate glass?
6. How is insulating glass sealed?
7. A piece of insulating glass has approximately what percent of the heat loss per hour that window glass of the same size has.
8. Glare-reducing and heat-absorbing glass absorb a high percentage of what?
9. In wire glass, the mesh size should not be larger than what and the gauge of the wire should not be less than what?
10. Does corrugated glass have a pattern on one side or both sides?
11. Where is solid glass block used?
12. When glass block is installed in a frame, what should its maximum area be?

TABLE 21-8   *Glass materials used in architecture*

Material	Characteristics	Architectural Use
Cellular glass	Black, solid with tiny trapped air bubbles, with a U-factor of 0.13 to 0.09	Roof and wall insulation; industrial-type insulation
Chalkboards	Tempered plate glass with a colored vitreous glaze on one side	Chalkboards in schools, colleges, and universities
Glass fibers	5 to 16 microns thick	Insulating materials; reinforcing for plastics, papers, and textiles
Granular glass	Broken glass or waste glass, heated and made into aggregates	Aggregates for concrete
Heat-strengthened glass	Black to white in color and with ceramic glazes	Spandrels and curtain wall construction
Mirrors	Plate, window, and picture glass with one surface treated with a reflecting, thin coat of metal	Mirrors and one-way mirrors
Powdered glass	Finely ground glass powder	Filler for resilient flooring, paint, asphalt roofing and siding
Structural glass	Black, white, and various colors	Exterior and interior facing for buildings; toilet partitions
Laminated glass and safety glass	Sheets of window or plate glass with clear plastic laminated	Bulletproof glass; areas where severe shock may be encountered

226

TABLE 21-9   *Maximum range of glass sizes in sq. ft. for a given wind velocity*

Wind Velocity	Window Glass Thickness		Plate Glass Thickness			
	0.085"	0.133"	1.8"	1/4"	1/2"	1 1/4"
30 mph	35 sq. ft.	64.5 sq. ft.	72 sq. ft.	288 sq. ft.		
40 mph	17.5 sq. ft.	32.25 sq. ft.	36 sq. ft.	144 sq. ft.		
65 mph	8.7 sq. ft.	16.1 sq. ft.	18 sq. ft.	72 sq. ft.	244 sq. ft.	
120 mph	2.5 sq. ft.	4.6 sq. ft.	5 sq. ft.	20 sq. ft.	82 sq. ft.	81 sq. ft.

ASSIGNMENT

1. Make an elevation scale drawing of a tempered glass door showing all the hardware, holes, and sand blasting which become an integral part of manufacturing the door.

2. In 50 words or less explain how to obtain the BTU/hr. heat loss of a sheet of insulating glass, 24 sq. ft. with a U-factor of 0.67 with an outside temperature of 0°F and an interior temperature of 70°F.

Limiting Factors

EFFECT OF WIND VELOCITY: The size of glass used in glazing windows, doors, and store fronts is controlled by the velocity of the wind (see Table 21-9).

BENDING: Glass may be bent within definite limitations, but the maximum rise is 3'-0" and maximum width is 12'-0" (see Figure 21-6).

Colored Glass

Glass is manufactured in a variety of colors (see Table 21-10).

Insulating Glass as Heating Unit

Insulating glass (see Figure 21-7) is now manufactured using the inner sheet of glass as an electrical heating element. The outside sheet of glass is transparent with a reflective coating, but the inside sheet has a transparent electrical-resistant metallic coating on the air-space side, with electrical connections. The metallic oxide coating heats the glass and thus eliminates condensation and cold drafts, and there is no BTU loss through the window.

TABLE 21-10   *Materials used for coloring glass*

Material	Color
Copper	Blue-green, ruby
Cadmium	Ruby, orange, yellow
Iron	Yellow-green, blue-green, amber
Gold	Ruby
Manganese	Pink
Nickel	Brown, purple
Cobalt	Blue

FIGURE 21-6   *Bent glass*

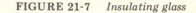

FIGURE 21-7   *Insulating glass*

Glass Used on Curtain Wall Panels

Tempered glass with insulation or with insulation and an interior facing are prefabricated for use in curtain wall panel construction (see Figure 21-8).

FIGURE 21-8 *Prefabricated glass curtain wall panels*

Reflective Glass

This type of glass consists of a flat glass (clear or tinted) coated on the outside with a transparent metallic oxide coating. This provides the glass with a permanent, durable, light- and heat-reflective exterior surface that has mirrorlike qualities. The outdoor reflectance is 35% and visible transmittance varies from 18% to 39%.

MID-TERM OR END-TERM
REVIEW EXAMINATION—CHAPTERS 14–21

1. What is the cut stone or dimension stone most likely to be used for stair treads and risers?

2. The mortars used for setting stone, pointing and grouting are made with what kind of portland cement?

3. In most veneer stonework the backup material should be what? Why must the space behind the veneer be open?

4. A stone measuring 6 sq. ft. and 7/8 in. thick requires how many anchors when used as a veneer?

5. What are the two materials used in setting floor and wall tile?

6. When installing large floor areas with tile, what must be installed to avoid expansion and contraction of the structural slab that may cause cracks in the setting bed and tile joints?

7. Wood from the evergreens, or coniferous cone-bearing trees, belong to what family of trees?

8. What is all lumber called when first cut from trees?

9. Lumber may be seasoned by what two drying methods?

10. The American Lumber Standards Association specifies that lumber be classified according to what principal uses?

11. What is the actual size of a 2 X 4-in. piece of lumber?

12. Yard lumber is used for what building purposes?

13. What two main divisions are there in yard lumber on the basis of quality?

14. What is D & M lumber?

15. What causes decay in wood?

16. What is an oil-type preservative for wood?

17. What is plywood made of softwood used for?

18. What is plywood made of hardwood used for?

19. What are the two main types of plywood that are manufactured?

20. What is the common and basic size of the plywood panel?

21. When plywood is used for exterior siding, what is the minimum thickness required?

22. What is the acceptable thickness of plywood used as exterior wall sheathing when the studs are 16″ o.c.?

23. For what purpose is particle or chip board used with high-pressure plastic laminate veneers and hardwood veneers?

24. In what thicknesses is laminated fiber board decking available?

25. What is the thickness of the smaller pieces of lumber that are laminated together to form a larger and stronger member?

26. Solid timbers are usually cheaper than laminated sections, except where extremely heavy loads are to be supported, for spans up to what dimension?

27. Laminated timbers are generally manufactured to what maximum and in what increments?

28. What are the three specific types of three-hinged arches?

228

29. What is another name for the conventional wood frame Western construction?

30. The studs of what two kinds of framing rest on the sill?

31. What advantage does post and beam construction provide in interior room planning?

32. What is the diameter of an 8d and 9d nail?

33. What kind of action begins when different metals or alloys are joined together with the presence of moisture?

34. What is the specific gravity of aluminum?

35. What is the specific gravity of copper?

36. Metals are either ferrous or nonferrous—which is zinc?

37. In the field of construction, dampers, manhole covers, gratings, pipe, plumbing fixtures are made of what material?

38. In building construction, what is the framing that consists of various rolled sections?

39. What is copper combined with to make bronze?

40. What bronze-colored metal is now known as architectural bronze?

41. How are ferrous and nonferrous wires designated?

42. What is the type of construction called when the entire method of supporting a building is in steel?

43. What are the two types of flashing?

44. What percentages of visible light are transmitted by most types of transparent glass?

45. What are the basic materials from which glass is made?

46. What is the glass consisting of two sheets of glass separated by an air-space?

47. What is the heat transmission coefficient (U-factor) of insulating glass consisting of three sheets of glass with two air-spaces?

48. A BTU is an amount of heat that can raise the temperature of how much water $1°F$ at sea level?

49. What type of glass is used where fire resistance is required?

50. What is the U-factor of window glass?

22

INSTALLATION OF GLASS AND GLASS MATERIALS

INTRODUCTION

This chapter deals with the installation of the various types of glass including transparent, translucent and opaque; with the preparations necessary to the materials and openings that will receive the glass; and with the various glazing materials.

TECHNICAL INFORMATION

Installation of Glass

The installation of transparent and translucent glass into a frame is called "glazing," whereas other types of glass materials require their own special methods of installation. The thickness and type of transparent or translucent glass for any type of installation should be checked for size of opening and wind loads.

GLAZING: Glazing includes preparing the frame to receive the glass, allowing clearances between the glass and the frame (glass must never be in tension), making a watertight seal between the glass and the frame with glazing materials, and installing setting blocks, spacers, and glazing points to keep glass completely separated from frame.

CLEARANCE BETWEEN GLASS AND FRAME: The various types of glass require different minimum clearances between glass and frame: around edges of glass, faces of glass to back and front of frame, and depth of the slot (rabbet) to hold the glass (see Table 22-1 and Figure 22-1).

When glass is installed in frames, setting blocks and spacers are used to keep the clearances required of glass to frame (see Figures 22-2 and 22-3).

PREPARATION FOR GLAZING: Preparation of the materials into which the various types of glass are to be installed include the following steps:

1. All surfaces should be thoroughly dry and rough projections removed; installation should not be done when the temperatures are below 40°F.

2. Wood should always be painted with a prime coat of paint.

3. Steel should be treated with a rust-inhibiting type of prime paint.

4. Aluminum should have any shop protective coating removed. Steel frames do not have to be prime painted if they have received a shop-applied bonderized paint or a zinc coating. Aluminum should be prime painted if an oil-based glazing compound is used.

Hardwoods (absorbent) may be prime painted with varnish when an elastic glazing compound is

TABLE 22-1   *Clearances between glass and frame (in inches)*

Type of Glass	Thickness	Minimum Clearance: Edges of Glass to Frame	Back and Front Faces of Glass to Frame	Depth of Slot (rabbet)
Window; single- and double-strength	0.087 0.113 1/8	1/8	1/16	3/8
Heavy sheet	3/16 7/32	1/8 1/4	1/8	1/2 3/4
Plate	1/8 1/4 and	1/8 1/4	1/16 1/8	3/8 5/8
Patterned	1/8 3/16 7/32	1/8 1/4	1/8	3/8 1/2 5/8
Insulating	1/2 3/4 1	1/8 1/4	1/8	1/2 3/4
Heat-absorbing and glare-reducing	0.125 1/8 3/16 7/32 1/4 3/8	1/4 min.	1/8	3/4

used; hardwoods (nonabsorbent) do not have to be prime painted if a metal sash putty is used.

GLAZING MATERIALS: There are many types of glazing materials available for making the joint between the glass and frame watertight:

1. *Putty*—white paint solid, linseed oil and with or without drying oils.

2. *Metal sash putty*—made of materials that will adhere to nonporous materials such as metals and nonabsorbent hardwoods.

3. *Elastic glazing compound*—made from processed oils and white paint solids that will remain plastic and resilient over a long period of time.

4. *Compression-type*—extruded or molded shapes of vinyl, neoprene, or other synthetics. In order to achieve a watertight joint the material must be compressed not less than 15%.

5. *Zipper types*—extruded or molded shapes of vinyl, neoprene, or other synthetics which can be compressed or squashed in order to install the glass and then made into a watertight joint by being stabilized by the insertion of a zipper strip (see Figure 22-3).

FIGURE 22-1 *Clearance between glass and frame*

FIGURE 22-2 *Window and door frames*

FIGURE 22-3   *Typical methods of installing glass in metal or wood frames*

Corrugated Glass

In installing corrugated glass for roofs and sky-lights, special care should be taken in lapping, attaching, insuring watertightness, and answering the problems of condensation (see Figure 22-4).

Glass Block

Glass block walls or partitions cannot be used for load-bearing, therefore the frame or opening must fit the dimension of the glass block and the top (head) of the frame or opening must take the load-bearing from the glass block. Glass block installed within an opening of masonry or steel frame is limited in size to 144 sq. ft., with a maximum height dimension of 20'-0" and a maximum width dimension of 25'-0". Glass block partitions or walls without support are limited in size to 100 sq. ft. with a maximum height of 10'-0" and a maximum length of 10'-0". In order to allow for

clearances, expansion, and possible deflection, it is necessary to use expansion strips, nonhardening caulking compound, oakum, and asphalt strips to break bond as shown in Figure 22-5.

REVIEW EXAMINATION

1. The installation of glass is called what?
2. What is used to keep the glass face free from the frame?
3. To make a watertight seal between glass and frame what material is used?
4. In installing glass, where are the setting blocks located?
5. How should the frame be prepared for glazing?
6. Glass should be installed above what temperature?
7. When an oil-based glazing compound is used, what should be done to the aluminum frame?
8. Can glass block be used for load-bearing?

FIGURE 22-4 *Corrugated glass skylights and roofs*

FIGURE 22-5 *Details showing installation of glass blocks*

9. What is used when glass block is installed to allow for clearance, expansion, and deflection?

10. When installing corrugated glass for roofs and skylights, name three areas where special care should be taken.

ASSIGNMENT

1. Sketch at least four details showing the installation of glass in wood and metal frames.

SUPPLEMENTARY INFORMATION

Other Types of Glazing Materials

For special type of glass materials there are available two other types of glazing materials:

1. *Polybutene tape*, a nondrying mastic made in extruded ribbon shapes of various widths and thicknesses, which must be applied with pressure. It has the in-built quality to remain plastic over a long period of time.

2. *Polysulfide elastomer*, a two-part synthetic rubber mixed on the job. This material requires the surrounding surfaces to be carefully protected because when it sets it is almost impossible to remove.

Heat-Strengthened Glass Installation

Heat-strengthened glass is manufactured from plate or patterned glass by applying a ceramic glaze to one side and heating until it is fused with the glass. It is opaque, similar to tempered glass, and is generally used in curtain wall construction. This glass has specific minimum clearances, as shown in Figure 22-6.

Structural Glass Installation

Structural glass is a ground and polished colored glass, either tempered or heat-strengthened. It cannot be cut or drilled, therefore shop drawings of the exact sizes of the units must be made before it can be manufactured. Generally it is used for interior and exterior wall surfaces, toilet partitions (see Figure 22-7), and counter tops. In installing, the back-up material must be plaster or a masonry material which has been sealed and made waterproof (see Figure 22-8).

⅛″ MIN.   ⅛″ MIN.

ELASTIC GLAZING COMPOUND
POLYBUTANE TAPE OR
POLYSULFIDE ELASTOMER

RESILIENT
SPACERS AT
EACH EDGE
WITH A MAXIMUM
SPACING OF 4'-0"

¾ MIN.
¼ MIN.

CURTAIN WALL FRAME

RESILIENT SETTING BLOCKS
LOCATED AT QUARTER POINTS
FROM EACH CORNER

FIGURE 22-6   *Installing heat-strengthened glass*

MASTIC TYPE ADHESIVE

PLASTER OF PARIS

WIRE ANCHORS

¼″

PLAN AT WALL

JOINT COMPOUND
WHITE OR COLORED

1¼″

1¼″

CORNER ANGLES

PLAN AT STYLE

BOLTS

PLAN AT CORNER

1¼″

FIGURE 22-7   *Toilet partition details*

¼″

MASONRY OR
PLASTER
SEALED AND
WATER-
PROOFED

CORK GASKET OR
POLYBUTANE TAPE

1/16″

JOINT
COMPOUND

MASTIC TYPE
ADHESIVE

HORIZONTAL INTERMEDIATE
JOINT

¼″

JOINT
COMPOUND

MASONRY OR
PLASTER SEALED
AND WATERPROOFED

1/16″

MASTIC TYPE
ADHESIVE

VERTICAL JOINT

¼″

MASONRY OR PLASTER
SEALED AND
WATERPROOFED

CORK GASKET OR POLYBUTANE TAPE

1/16″

JOINT COMPOUND

METAL "L" SUPPORT
FOR HORIZONTAL JOINT

MASTIC TYPE ADHESIVE

HORIZONTAL SUPPORTING JOINT

FIGURE 22-8   *Structural glass exterior walls*

23

PLASTICS

INTRODUCTION

This chapter covers the synthetic materials used in construction that are grouped under the general term "plastics." They include resins, adhesives, flooring, sheets, fibers, insulation, siding, plastic laminates, gaskets, sealants, foam, film, synthetic rubbers, carpets, and fabrics.

TECHNICAL INFORMATION

The word "plastic" means a synthetic material which is not rubber, glass, wood, natural resin, or metal. The word now covers such a large diversified group of materials that it can only be used in a very broad sense and cannot be used specifically to describe any one particular synthetic material.

Table 23-1 shows the main types of plastics and their uses. A wide variety of plastics is used in construction as well as for thousands of small items such as electrical devices, pipe, rough and finish hardware, bathroom accessories, etc.

Types of Plastics

Synthetic materials can be broadly divided into the following types: (1) those derived from cellulose, (2) synthetics resins, (3) those derived from proteins and natural resins, and (4) synthetic rubbers.

Synthetic resins can be divided into two types: *thermosetting*, which are formed (shaped) by heat but cannot be reformed by heat and whose molecules are linked in a three-dimensional arrangement; and *thermoplastic*, which can be softened by heat and upon cooling regain their original properties and whose molecules are linear or threadlike in form.

Plastic Flooring

Plastic flooring materials include sheet, tile, seamless, paint, interior and exterior sport and utility surfaces, and carpet. Plastic sheet flooring is solid vinyl plastic in rolls 6, 9, and 12 ft. wide, up to 50 ft. in length and in 0.069, 0.080, 0.100,

TABLE 23-1 *Types of plastic*

Plastic	Typical Name*	Major Use	Derivation
1. ABS	ABS	Shower stalls, bathtub enclosures, building panels	Acrylonitrile-butadiene-styrene copolymer
2. Acrylic	Lucite, Plexiglas	Skydomes, glazing, light fixtures	Polymer or copolymer of acrylic acid
3. Alkyd	Alkyd	Vehicles in paints, lacquers and enamels	Polyester resin, oil-modified
4. Allyl	Contact adhesives	Applying plastic laminates and other sheet material to walls and surfaces	Polyester resin derived from allyl alcohol and dibasic acids
5. Casein	Elmer's Glue	Interior wood lamination adhesives	Casein from milk acidified with dilute sulfuric acid
6. Cellulose	Cellophane, Lumerith	Transparent thin sheets, artificial leather	Reaction of cellulose with acetic acid, acetic anhydride and sulfuric acid as a catalyst
7. Chloroprene**	Neoprene	Gaskets, sealants, and joint fillers	Derived from acetylene and chlorine. Its polymers yield compounds similar to rubber
8. Epoxy	Epoxy	Seamless flooring, tough waterproof paints for walls and floors, adhesives	Derived from the reactivity of the epoxides
9. Ethyl cellulose	Duco cement	Household glues, hot-melt adhesives	Alkali cellulose and ethyl chloride

TABLE 23-1   *Types of plastic (continued)*

Plastic	Typical Name*	Major Use	Derivation
10. Fluorocarbon	Teflon, Aclar	Tent, cable, and air structures	Compounds of carbon and fluorine
11. Latex**	Latex	Water-base paints	Natural or synthetic rubber
12. Melamines	Melamines	Plastic laminates	Derived from melamine and formaldehyde
13. Phenol-formaldehyde	Phenolics, Bakelite	Baked enamels, finish hardware, electrical devices, plastic laminates	Condensation of phenol with formaldehyde
14. Polyamides	Nylon, Fiberthin	Tent, cable, and air structures, pulleys, rollers, fabrics	Polymerization of a diamine and a dibasic acid
15. Polybutene	Vistanex	Pressure-sensitive tapes, caulking and sealing compounds	Isotactic polymers of isobutene
16. Polycarbonate	Lexan, Rowlex	Glazing when an unbreakable material is required	Resin derived from a phenol compound and a polyester of carbolic acid
17. Polyester	Dacron, Mylar	Seamless flooring, textiles, adhesives	Polycondensation of dicarboxylic acids with hydroxyl alcohol
18. Polyethylene	Polyethylene	Damproofing and waterproofing sheets and films, pipe	Polymerizing of ethylene with peroxide catalyst
19. Polystyrene**	Styrofoam, styron	Foam insulation	Polymerized styrene
20. Polysulfide**	Thiokol	Sealants, glazing compounds	A sulfide compound with two sulfur atoms per molecule
21. Polyurethane	Polyurethane, Perlon, Igamid	Foam insulation, insulating materials, adhesives, vehicle in paints, baked coatings, fibers	Condensation reaction of a drying oil and polyisocyanate
22. Polyvinyl	Vinyls, PVC, Gcon	Paints, flooring, adhesives, pipe, siding, gutters; tent, cable and air structures	Resins derived by polymerization or copolymerization of vinyl monomers
23. Silicone**	Silicones	Water resistant and protective coatings, adhesives, sealants, gaskets	Silicon is heated in methychloride to yield methychlorosilanes which by distillation are separated and purified
24. Urea-formaldehyde	Ureas	Baked enamels, adhesives, protective coatings	Urea and formaldehyde are united in a two-stage process
25. Zien	Zien	Adhesives, imitation shellac, grease resistant coatings	Derived from corn processing

*Many of these are trade names and are offered as examples. No attempt is made to be all-inclusive.

**Synthetic rubbers.

TABLE 23-2   *Types of plastic floor tiles*

	Vinyl	Vinyl Asbestos	Vinyl Surfaced
Squares	9″, 12″, 18″, 36″	9″, 12″	9″, 12″, 36″
Rectangles	18″ × 36″		12″ × 24″
Thickness	3/32″, 1/8″	1/16″, 3/32″, 1/8″	1/8″, 3/16″

0.110, 0.180 and 0.224 in. thicknesses. Plastic flooring tiles include vinyl, vinyl asbestos, and various resilient materials with a vinyl surface. They are available in various sizes and thicknesses (see Table 23-2). Both plastic sheet and tile flooring is available in a wide variety of colors, textures and patterns. Feature strips, inserts and inlays are available for both sheet and tile flooring. Bases are of solid vinyl and in a limited range of colors.

Transparent, Colored, and Opaque Sheets

Transparent, colored, or opaque sheets are used for skydomes and decorative screens and for glazing. They do not have the toughness of polycarbonate sheet but will not break. In general, all these materials are not as hard as glass and their surfaces can be damaged. See Table 23-3 for thicknesses, dimensions, and glazing information.

Polycarbonate sheets are extremely tough, almost unbreakable, and remain stable from 60 to 300°F. Because of these characteristics, polycarbonate sheets have become a substitute for glass in areas where vandalism, thermal shock, and impact are present, and where safety from breakage is required. It also is used in areas where protective mesh, screens, and railings are usually installed. Polycarbonate sheet has a light transmission of 82 to 89%, depending on thickness; it has self-fire-extinguishing characteristics, and it is manufactured in a variety of colors.

Transparent, transparent bronze and gray, and obscure polycarbonate sheets are available. There are also laminated types for use where bullet resistance and security are required (see Tables 23-4 and 23-5). Gray sheets have a light transmission

TABLE 23-3   *Sizes of plastic sheets*

Thickness	1/16″, 5/16″, 1/8″, 3/16″ and 1/4″
Width	2′-0″ to 10′-0″, in 1′-0″ and 2′-0″ modules
Length	3′-0″ to 12′-0″, in 1′-0″ and 2′-0″ modules
Glazing	All standard window glass sizes

TABLE 23-4   *Type and sizes of polycarbonate sheets*

Thickness	1/16″, 5/16″, 1/8″, 3/16″, 1/4″, 3/8″ and 1/2″
Width	2′-0″ to 6′-0″, in 1′-0″ modules
Length	4′-0″ to 8′-0″, in 2′-0″ modules

of 50%. They are also available patterned, colored, translucent, transparent, semi-opaque and reflective.

Corrugated, Shiplap, and V-Crimp Plastic Sheet

This material is manufactured with glass fibers used as reinforcing. Translucent and available in limited colors, it finds use in the construction of buildings for porch roofs, shades, screen walls, and clerestory windows. The corrugations and the V-crimp as well as the glass fibers give these types of plastic sheet the strength to span from 2′-8″ to 4′-6″ for a 100-lb. load (see Table 23-6).

Plastic Laminates

This type of thin, hard plastic sheet with decorative, colorful designs, patterns, finishes and a variety of surface treatments is used in the con-

TABLE 23-5   *Types and sizes of polycarbonate laminated sheets*

	Security	Bullet-Resistant
Thickness	3/8″, 1/2″ and 5/8″	1-3/16″, 1-9/16″ and 1-3/4″
Width	3′-0″	2′-0″ and 4′-0″
Length	4′-0″	3′-0″, 5′-0″ and 7′-0″

TABLE 23-6   *Data for corrugated plastic sheets*

Corrugation Spacing	Thickness	Length	Width	Maximum Span for 100-lb. Load
1/4″	1/16″	8′-0″, 10′-0″, 12′-0″	2′-2″, 3′-0″	2′-8″
2 1/2″	1/16″	4′-0″, 5′-0″, 6′-0″, 8′-0″, 10′-0″, 12′-0″	2′-2″, 2′-10″, 3′-4″, 4′-2″	4′-0″
2.67″	1/16″	8′-0″, 10′-0″, 12′-0″	2′-11″	4′-6″
3″	3/32″	8′-0″, 10′-0″, 12′-0″	2′-6″	4′-6″
4.2″	3/32″	8′-0″, 10′-0″, 12′-0″	3′-6″	4′-6″

TABLE 23-7   *Types and sizes of plastic laminates*

Type	Thickness	Width	Length
General-purpose	1/16″	2′-0″, 2′-6″, 3′-0″, 4′-0″	5′-0″, 6′-0″, 7′-0″, 8′-0″, 10′-0″
Cigarette-proof Vertical	1/32″	2′-0″, 4′-0″	6′-0″, 8′-0″ 10′-0″
Postforming	3/64″	2′-6″, 3′-0″, 4′-0″	6′-0″, 8′-0″ 10′-0″

struction field as finish surface for walls, partitions, doors, countertops, kitchen cabinets, and furniture. It can be applied either in the shop or at the site. It is available in four types: general-purpose, cigarette-proof, vertical, and postforming for forming curves (see Table 23-7).

Gaskets and Sealants

Plastics were adopted very early in the construction field for glazing. With the development of curtain wall type of construction, plastics were used as sealants. Today, we find a tremendous variety of plastic gaskets, tapes, sealants, fillers, etc. Figure 23-1 shows some of these newer methods.

Plastic sealants are available in a form to be applied by a caulking gun as two compounds which are mixed and then applied, and also as various types of sealing tapes. These plastic sealants all have the following characteristics: they remain adhesive, flexible, and elastic for 10 to 20 years; they are used for glazing, caulking, and as fillers for all types of joints between different materials. Plastics have answered the problem of construction joints in masonry and in expansion joints in large buildings (see Figure 23-2).

Plastic Foams

Foams are produced from glass, polyurethane, polystyrene, cellulose, polyisocyanurate, etc. Of these the polyurethane and polystyrene were the first to be used. Table 23-8 lists available sizes.

Foam manufacturers produce four types of foam insulation: (1) preformed board and flexible and rigid sheet, (2) foamed-at-site of construction, (3) block form, and (4) spray-on. Plastic foam is

TABLE 23-8   *Plastic foam sheet and board*

	Width	Length	Thickness
Polyurethane	3′-0″, 4′-0″	4′-0″ to 12′-0″	11/16″ to 2′-0″
Polystyrene	2′-0″ to 4′-0″	3′-0″, 8′-0″, 9′-0″, 12′-0″	1/2″, 3/4″, 1″, 1-1/2″, 2″, 3″, 4″

FIGURE 23-1 *Installation of glass using plastics*

FIGURE 23-2 *Construction joints in masonry*

244

used as an integral part of plastic carpet and plastic roofing materials to which it imparts both resilient qualities and insulation. Plastic foam, which consists of thousands of sealed air bubbles, has exceptional R-factors (1 in. has an R-factor of 7.15 to 9.09). It is used for all types of insulation and has the added advantage of serving as a moisture and vapor barrier.

Plastic foamed at the site of construction answers the problem of insulation of areas that in the past could never be adequately insulated with other types of insulation. When the ingredients are mixed and injected into these areas, their foaming action completely fills the voids.

Another by-product of this foam action is that with heat, certain of the polyurethane plastics become adhesive. Through this method, sandwich panels can be manufactured (see Figure 23-3). With other types of foam plastic the finish surfaces can be bonded to the foam with special types of adhesives. Any combination of materials can thus be used for the outside and inside surfaces—metal, plywood, wood, cement, asbestos, etc.—to manufacture a sandwich panel. These panels of metal and 1-1/2 in. of foam insulation have better insulation value (R-factor 9.80) than 8 in. of brick with 1-1/2-in. metal furring and lath and plaster (R-factor 3.12) or the normal 4-in. stud partition with sheathing, siding, 2 in. of insulation and plaster board (R-factor 9.09).

Plastic foams are also used for floats and buoyancy units, for insulating pipes and ducts, and also as forms for complicated thin-shell concrete shapes which are poured on grade and then raised to final position.

Plastic Film

Plastic film is available plain or reinforced with glass fibers. Among the many diversified uses in the construction field are: as tracing paper (Mylar);

TABLE 23-9 *Plastic films*

Type of Plastic	Major Uses
Fluorocarbons	Temporary structures; air, cable, and tent structures
Polyamides	Temporary structures; protective coverings; air structures
Polyester	Drawing paper, drafting paper, printing
Polyethylene	Protective coverings; temporary enclosures; air and tent structures; dampproofing
Polyvinyls	Temporary enclosures; air, tent, and cable structures; damp-proofing

as underlayment beneath concrete slabs on earth; for moisture-proofing; as vapor barriers; for temporary enclosures and covers for protecting materials; for curing concrete, etc. With the development of air, cable, and tent-type structures, plastic films are finding ever wider use (see Table 23-9).

REVIEW EXAMINATION

1. Can the word "plastic" be used to describe plastic laminate?

2. Can a thermosetting plastic be reformed by heat?

3. Vinyl tile flooring is manufactured in what thicknesses?

4. Vinyl asbestos tile is available in what sizes?

5. What are the advantages of using plastic transparent sheet in place of glass?

6. Are plastic sheet materials as hard as glass?

7. Name three uses of corrugated plastic sheet material.

8. Name two types of plastic laminates.

FIGURE 23-3 *Foam insulating panels*

9. Where is a plastic tape used?

10. Are plastic materials used for masonry construction joints?

11. With heat, do foam plastics have adhesive qualities?

12. Name three uses of plastic film.

13. Name two types of polycarbonate sheet.

14. What is the R-factor of 1 in. of plastic foam?

ASSIGNMENT

1. Make a list of the different types of plastic sheet.

2. Make a scaled drawing showing two methods of installing glass with plastic materials.

SUPPLEMENTARY INFORMATION

Fashion Trends in Flooring

The manufacturers of vinyl and vinyl asbestos tiles and sheet vinyl are constantly creating new colors, textures, and patterns to answer consumer demands. Care should be taken that the latest and current colors, textures, and patterns chosen, are *not* a discontinued product.

Panels, Siding, and Countertops

Many 4'-0"-by-8'-0" prefabricated panel units with a variety of textures and colors, are available. Curtain wall systems 5/8" to 4" thick, with or without insulation, which include a variety of colors, textures, and finishes on the exterior and finished interior surfaces, are one of the newer plastic building materials. Plastic siding materials include siding, fascia, gravel stops, gutters, leaders, and all the necessary trim, all of which are manufactured in a variety of textures, colors, and finishes.

Complete bathtub enclosures which include tub, walls, seat, towel bars, soap dish, and ceiling are available in a variety of colors and finishes. Complete shower stall units, similar to tub enclosures are also available. A wide variety of countertops are manufactured, including complete units consisting of lavatory, back splash, and countertop, in a wide selection of colors, textures and patterns.

FIGURE 23-4   *Types of plastic pipe*

Plastic Roofing

Plastic roofing can be divided into two types: (1) those applied by spraying, rolling, brushing, and squeegeed, and (2) sheet material that is floated on or adhered with adhesives to the substrate. Urethane, polyester, vinyl, epoxy and silicone plastics are used for plastic roofing.

Plastic Pipe

Figure 23-4 shows the types of plastic pipe and methods of joining. Plastic pipe in many areas has better resistance to chemicals than metal piping, and is manufactured from several thermoplastic plastics and rubbers. Plastic pipe is used for water, sewage, drains, wastes and vents, irrigation, and industrial and chemical piping. The expansion of plastic pipe is very great and this expansion must be allowed for in both vertical and horizontal runs.

Pot Life

All plastics that consist of two or more compounds which, when mixed, produce the desired final product—for example, a sealant, caulking compound, paint, foam—have what is known as *a pot life*. Pot life refers to the length of time, once the compounds are mixed, during which the resulting compound is usable, and it can vary from a few minutes to over a half-hour. Once the pot-life time limit is passed, the compound becomes useless.

24

PLASTICS IN CONSTRUCTION

INTRODUCTION

This chapter deals with the various uses and methods of application of plastics in construction. It includes data on flooring, sheet (flat, corrugated, and V-crimp), plastic laminates, gaskets and sealants, foam, film, panels, siding, and counter tops.

TECHNICAL INFORMATION

Plastic Flooring

Plastic flooring in roll and tile form is referred to as resilient-type flooring and is applied with adhesives. In the installation of plastic-type resilient flooring the substrate must be smooth, protected from moisture and water, and without any open joints or cracks. The manufacturers of plastic resilient flooring makes bases, feature strips, and special designs for inlaying. Figure 24-1 shows various types of vinyl bases which are available in a limited range of colors.

Seamless plastic flooring is sprayed, rolled or troweled onto the substrate and the base is an intregal part of the floor. Seamless flooring is available in single colors, in a single color with colored plastic chips added, and as a terrazzo type with colored stone chips added (this type has to be machine polished).

The various types of athletic surfaces require special types of substrates for both exterior and interior surfaces and the use of special equipment, with rigid control of the entire application procedure.

Transparent, Colored, and Opaque Sheet

Plastic sheet, transparent, colored, or opaque, is installed as a replacement for glass and in various types of decorative screens, panels, and dividers. Plastic sheet is also used in skydomes, skylights, light fixtures, and simulated leaded glass.

Polycarbonate sheet, because of its high thermal expansion and contraction, demands special requirements for installation. Its advantages are that it has 20% to 30% less heat loss than glass, depending on its thickness, and is almost half the weight of glass.

Installation clearance, glazing thickness, and rabbet depth depend on size and thickness of sheet (see Figure 24-2). The type of glazing compound depends on the size of sheet (see Table 24-1).

FIGURE 24-1   *Vinyl bases*

FIGURE 24-2   *Polycarbonate windows*

TABLE 24-1 *Relation of sheet size to type of glazing compound*

	Plastic	Name*	Major Use
1.	Acrylic	Lucite Plexiglass	Skydomes, glazing, light fixtures
2.	Alkyd	Alkyd	Vehicles in paints, lacquers, and enamels
3.	Allyl	Contact adhesives	Applying plastic laminates and other sheet material to walls and surfaces
4.	Cellulose	Cellophane, Lumerith	Transparent thin sheets, artificial leather
5.	Chloroprene	Neoprene	Gaskets, sealants, and joint fillers
6.	Epoxy	Epoxies	Tough waterproof paints for walls and floors
7.	Ethyl cellulose	Household adhesives	General adhesives
8.	Latex	Latex emulsions	Water-base paints
9.	Melamines	Melamines	Plastic laminates, tableware
10.	Phenol-formaldehyde	Phenolics, Bakelite	Electrical devices, hardware, baked enamels, plastic laminates
11.	Polyamides	Nylon	Rollers, pulleys, fabrics
12.	Polycarbonate	Lexan, Merzon	Glazing
13.	Polyester	Dacron, Mylar	Fabrics; transparent tracing paper, sheets
14.	Polyethylene	Polyethylene	Dampproofing and waterproofing, sheets, pipe
15.	Polysulfide	Thiokol	Sealants, glazing compounds
16.	Polyurethane	Polyurethane, Perlon, Igamid	Insulating material, foam-type insulating material
17.	Styrene	Butadiene	Tapes, glazing compound
18.	Urea-formaldehyde	Ureas	Baked enamels
19.	Vinyl	Vinyl	Resilient flooring, gaskets, joint fillers, paint, lacquers

*Many of these are trade names and are offered as examples. No attempt is made here to be all-inclusive.

Corrugated, Shiplap, and V-crimp Sheet

Corrugated, shiplap, and V-crimp plastic sheet, because of their shape and glass fiber content, have the strength to span from 2′-6″ to 4′-6″ for a 100-lb. load, depending upon sheet shape and thickness. As a roofing for 4-to-12 and greater roof pitches, it can be easily side- and end-lapped and nailed in place with aluminum or galvanized nails. Figure 24-3 shows the various types of enclosure strips.

Plastic Laminates

Plastic laminates are applied in the shop with presses or rollers, using thermosetting adhesives

FIGURE 24-3 *Closure strips for the various types of corrugated plastic sheets*

FIGURE 24-4   *Methods of treating plastic laminates at edges*

FIGURE 24-5   *Examples of the application of plastic laminates*

or with contact adhesives. On the job, they are applied with contact adhesives, using hand rollers and special hammers (see Figures 24-4 and 24-5).

Gaskets and Sealants

Plastic gaskets and sealants are widely used in the construction field for glazing, control and expansion joints, water stops, caulking, fillers, and all types of curtain wall construction (see Figure 24-6). Sealants that consist of two components should be checked for their pot life and be installed under strict supervision.

FIGURE 24-6   *Types of plastic shapes for glazing, joint fillers, water stops, etc*

Plastic Foam

Plastic foam is used not only for the insulation of walls and roofs of structures, but also as insulation for tanks, pipes, heating and air-conditioning ducts, and perimeter insulation. Figure 24-7 shows these uses of plastic foam in the construction field.

Plastic Film

In the construction field, plastic film finds many diversified uses. Figure 24-8 shows some of these. There is widespread use of plastic film to protect materials on the job site before they are installed in the building, to protect materials already installed, and to set up temporary enclosures that enable work to continue in inclement weather and that allow concrete to cure in freezing weather.

The development of air, cable, and tent-type structures has, in turn, demanded the development of plastic film with greater strength, longer life, and the ability to control (filter) sunlight and glare.

REVIEW EXAMINATION

1. How is plastic flooring applied?
2. How is seamless flooring applied?
3. Does polycarbonate have any thermal expansion?
4. Name three types of glazing compound for polycarbonate sheet glazing.
5. What controls the strength of corrugated plastic?
6. Name three areas where plastic sheet is used.
7. Plastic two-component sealants should be checked for what?
8. How are plastic laminates applied on the job?
9. Name three insulation uses of plastic foam.
10. Where are plastic gaskets used in construction?

FIGURE 24-7 *Plastic foam in construction*

FIGURE 24-8 *Typical uses of plastic film*

ASSIGNMENT

1. Make a sketch showing the application of plastic laminate to a countertop.

2. Make a scaled drawing showing three methods of edge treatment of plastic laminates.

SUPPLEMENTARY INFORMATION

Siding, Panels, and Countertops

Plastic siding has the same design characteristics as wood siding. It is made of solid vinyl and is available in limited colors and textures. It is applied similarly to wood siding. Corner, window, door, sills, and other trim pieces are available, including fascias, soffits, gutters, and leaders.

There are two different types of panels: those for the exterior and those for the interior. Also available are complete panel (curtain wall) units to supply an exterior finish to a structure.

Each of the various types of curtain wall systems that are manufactured requires its own type of application or installation, as detailed by the manufacturer of that particular system.

Interior panels include a wide variety of decorative screens and walls. There are now bathtub and shower enclosures available as complete package units with ceilings: walls with soap dish,

251

towel bars, seat, and curtain rod; and doors or enclosures. These are available in a variety of colors and designs. The single-unit bathtub with walls and ceiling is also available. These types of package units require careful consideration: in new construction, when and how to install; in remodeling and renovating existing buildings, whether it can be brought into the building without excessive tearing down.

Solid plastic countertops for kitchens, bathrooms, vanities, bars, service counters, etc., including back splashes if required, are available in a variety of colors, textures and designs. For bathrooms they are available with integral lavatory basins. The application of these countertops only requires that the base be sufficiently strong and allowances made for securing the countertop to the base.

25

PAINTS (ORGANIC COATINGS)

INTRODUCTION

Originally, paint consisted of a natural oil (linseed oil) as a vehicle to which finely ground white solid particles of white lead (basic lead carbonate), known as pigment, were added. When properly mixed, the white lead solids were held in suspension in the vehicle. Today, however, paint is only one type of what are known as organic coatings. An organic coating forms a solid film by one of five methods: (1) absorption of oxygen, (2) solidification after evaporation of solvent, (3) heating to elevated temperatures, (4) chemical reaction of a catalyst, and (5) coalescence of latex particles.

The introduction and continuing development of synthetics and a growing variety of white paint solids plus new synthetic color pigments have brought about a complete change in organic coatings and their application. This chapter will define and explore paints, resins, driers, solvents, stains, extenders, and other types of organic coatings.

TECHNICAL INFORMATION

Paint Components

DEFINITION OF PAINT: Paint can be defined as a mixture of a vehicle and finely ground white solid particles called pigment. The vehicle is the liquid part of the paint, whereas the pigment can be considered the solid part of the paint that is held in suspension by the vehicle.

VEHICLE: The vehicle consists of the film binders (resins or natural oils) that form the film. It holds together the white paint solids and causes the paint film to adhere to the surface. The vehicle also supplies the protective and durable qualities to the film (see Tables 25-1, 25-2, and 25-3).

TABLE 25-1 *The natural resins*

Type	Source	Solvent
Damar	Oriental trees	Alcohol or turpentine
Ester gums	Glycerin, rosin	Alcohol or turpentine
Rosin	Residue from distillation of turpentine oil	Alcohol or turpentine
Shellac	Produced from the lac bug	Alcohol

TABLE 25-2 *Synthetic resins*

Type	Solvent
Acrylate	Xylene
Alkyd	Water, turpentine
Casein	Water
Chlorinated rubber	Ketone
Epoxy	Ketone, mineral spirits
Latex	Water
Phenolic	Varies with type
Silicone	Varies with type
Urethanes	Mineral spirits
Vinyl	Ketone

TABLE 25-3 *Natural oils*

Type	Solvent
Raw linseed oil	Turpentine
Fish oils	Alcohol, benzene
Safflower oils	Ether
Soybean oil	Alcohol, ether
Tung oil	Ether

TABLE 25-4 *Primary color pigments*

Color	Name	Source or Ingredient
Black	Lamp black	Carbon from burnt tars
Blue	Ultramine blue	Double silicate of sodium and aluminum
Brown	Burnt umber	Iron oxide
Green	Emerald green	Hydrated chromium oxide
Red	Cadmium red	Cadmium sulfide or barium sulfate
Yellow	Yellow ocher	Hydrated iron oxide

TABLE 25-5 *Driers*

Type	Qualities
Calcium and cobalt salts	Fast-drying; increases film hardness
Zine salts	Relatively fast-drying; increases film hardness

TABLE 25-6 *Extender pigments*

Type	Qualities Added to Paint
Barite	Better brushing
Diatomite	Gives flatness and reduces cracking
Kaolin	Strengthens film and reduces settling
Whiting	Adds gloss and increases durability of film

254

TABLE 25-7 *Solvents*

Type	Extent of Danger	Type of Vehicle
Acetate	Relatively safe	Lacquers
Acetone	Dangerous	Synthetic resins
Alcohol	Relatively safe	Shellac, some drying oils, and some natural resins
Benzene*	Toxic, dangerous	Drying oils, natural resins, and most synthetic resins
Benzine*	Relatively safe	Drying oils, natural and synthetic resins
Ketone	Dangerous	Drying oils, natural and synthetic resins
Mineral spirits	Relatively safe	Drying oils, natural and synthetic resins
Turpentine	Relatively safe	Drying oils, natural and synthetic resins
Water	Safe	Water and emulsion-base vehicles
Xylene	Dangerous	Synthetic and lacquer resins

*These are different solvents, despite almost identical spelling. Benzene is a colorless, highly flammable liquid, obtained from distillation of coal. Benzine is a flammable petroleum distillate.

PIGMENTS: Paints can be colored to almost any shade desired by the addition of color pigments, which are finely ground color solid particles (see Table 25-4).

In order to make the paint dry faster, *driers* are added. There are also a series of *extender pigments* that can be added which give the film certain improved characteristics (see Tables 25-5 and 25-6).

SOLVENTS: The solvent is the volatile portion of a vehicle which controls the viscosity of the paint or organic coating (see Table 25-7).

HIDING POWER: This refers to covering capacity or the ability to cover a surface so that nothing shows through. All white paints are graded or described on the basis of hiding-power units, which are derived from the hiding power of 1 lb. of white lead: 1 lb. of white lead mixed with linseed oil will completely cover 15 sq. ft. of a surface consisting of alternate stripes of black and white (see Table 25-8 and Figure 25-1).

From this table we can see how titanium compares to lead: a little less than 1/8 lb. of titanium dioxide will completely cover the same 15 sq. ft. of a surface consisting of alternate stripes of black and white.

TABLE 25-8 *Hiding power units of various white paint solids (pigments)*

Type of White Paint Solid (Pigment)	Hiding Power Units
Antimony trioxide	2.33
White lead (no longer used)	1
Zinc oxide	1.48
Titanium dioxide	8.16
Lithopone Zinc sulfide Barium sulfate	1.79

FIGURE 25-1 *Method of deriving one hiding power unit*

TYPES OF PARTICLE SHAPES		
TYPES	SHAPE	EFFECT ON PAINT FILM
ROUNDED	⬭	THICKNESS
NEEDLE-LIKE	▭	STRENGTH
PLATE-LIKE	⬯	RESISTANCE TO MOISTURE

FIGURE 25-2   *Paint particle shapes*

TABLE 25-9   *Types of organic coatings used in the construction field*

Type of Paint	Ingredients
Pigmented paints	Ready-mixed in containers — consists of white paint solids, color pigments, extender pigments, vehicle, and driers
Enamels	Ready-mixed in containers — consists of white paint solids, color pigments, a varnish vehicle, driers, and solvent
Varnish	Ready-mixed in containers — consists of a resin, drying oil, drier, and solvent
Lacquers	Ready-mixed in containers — consists of nitrocellulose with resins and drying oils added to improve adhesion and flexibility of film
Shellac	Ready-mixed in containers — consists of refined lac resin and alcohol
Stains	In containers — consists of dry color pigments in a vehicle of water and alcohol or drying oils

SHAPE OF WHITE PAINT SOLIDS: The shape and size of the white paint solids (pigments) play an important part in the hiding power and the smoothness, strength, thickness, and resistance to moisture of the paint (see Figure 25-2). Particle size varies in diameter from 0.0001 to 0.0060 millimeters (mm).

Types of Paint

Most paints today come ready-mixed in containers and are color-coordinated. The mixing of paint and the mixing to obtain colors on the job is almost completely nonexistent today.

The most commonly obtainable paints and solvents are shown in Tables 25-7 and 25-9.

Clear Coatings

Clear coatings are used to beautify and protect interior surfaces without hiding any of their natural appearance (see Table 25-10).

TABLE 25-10   *Clear coatings*

Type	Solvent
Epoxy	Varies with type
Lacquers	Varies with type
Shellac	Alcohol
Urethane	Mineral spirits
Varnish	Mineral spirits
Vinyl	Esters

VARNISH: Varnish is used not only as a clear transparent coating but also as the vehicle for interior pigmented (colored) enamels. In addition, it gives smoothness and leveling characteristics to the surface film.

Stains

Stains consist of a vehicle with a low pigment content and have a low viscosity, high penetrating

256

properties. They can also have preservative characteristics. There are five types: (1) water stains, (2) non-grain-raising stains, (3) oil stains, (4) exterior preservative stains, (5) pigmented stains.

Rust-Inhibiting Organic Coatings

Rust-inhibiting organic coatings are used to protect ferrous metals (except stainless steel and weathering steel) against corrosion. They are available in two types: (1) primers as a base for finish organic coatings, and (2) finish coatings (see Table 25-11).

REVIEW EXAMINATION

1. Paint is a mixture of what two components?
2. The vehicle is what part of the paint?
3. What can be added to make paint dry faster?
4. One lb. of white lead mixed with linseed oil is the basis of what?
5. Name four white paint solids.
6. Name three clear coatings.
7. Stains consist of what?
8. Name three solvents.

ASSIGNMENT

1. Make a list of the types of organic coatings used in the construction field.
2. Make a sketch of the shapes of white paint solids.

SUPPLEMENTARY INFORMATION

Dampproofing Paints

Dampproofing of foundation walls and exterior surfaces of buildings is considered painting. This is done with special paints, and the painting of interior concrete and masonry is done with cement-type coatings (see Table 25-12).

Cement-Type Coatings

Cement-type coatings consist of portland cement and lime with water as the vehicle, with or

TABLE 25-11   *Rust-inhibiting organic coatings*

Type	Color	Use
Lead chromate	Red and yellow	Prime coat
Lead oxide	Bright orange-red	Prime coat
Lead silicochromate	Gray	Prime and finish coats
Zinc chromate	Yellow	Prime coat
Zinc dust	Gray	Paints under fresh water

TABLE 25-12   *Dampproofing paints*

Type of Paint	Ingredients
Bituminous Paints	Coal-tar pitch with a solvent
Asphalt paints	Various forms of asphalt with a solvent
Cement paint	Portland cement and lime as the white paint solids, with water as the vehicle and including color pigments, extender pigments, and water repellents

without sand. They are available with color pigments, water repellents, and extender pigments.

Fire-Resistant Coatings

Fire-resistant organic coatings come in two types: (1) those that check flame spread by not supporting combustion, and (2) those that do not support combustion and will develop 2- to 4-hr. fire ratings. Type 2 coatings are called intumescent paint. When heat is applied to intumescent coatings, they swell up and stop heat transfer to the material to which the coatings have been applied.

Multicolored Organic Coatings

Multicolored organic coatings are available in which various droplets of colored paints are suspended by controlled surface tension within the paint. When applied by spray, these droplets give accent colors on a background of other colors.

Colors

The primary colors are red, yellow, and blue; secondary colors are green, violet, and orange; and tertiary colors include red-orange, yellow-orange, yellow-green, blue-green, blue-violet, and red-violet. Black and white are classified separately.

26

APPLICATION OF PAINTS
(ORGANIC COATINGS)

INTRODUCTION

This chapter explores the various methods of applying organic coatings to metal, wood, concrete, masonry, etc. Originally, painting consisted of applying the paint by brush to a surface. As the applied paint dried, a solid protective film developed. To obtain a good paint surface, it was necessary to apply from three coats (prime coat, undercoat, and finished coat) to six coats (prime coat, second prime coat, undercoat, second undercoat, under-finish coat, and finish coat). The white paint was colored by adding color pigments; it could be thinned by adding a solvent or thinner; and it could be removed by applying a solvent such as turpentine.

The development of synthetics has already caused considerable changes in the application of organic coatings. The continuing of research and development will lead to further changes in types of coatings and in their applications, which the student and practitioner should continue to investigate.

TECHNICAL INFORMATION

Painting

Painting is the word used in specifications to define the application of paint to a surface. The type of paint to be applied must be chosen not only for the decorative effect desired and its protective value but also to fit the type of surface and material to which it is to be applied.

Today, paints can completely cover a surface with only one coat, can dry within a half-hour, and the protective films can be waterproof, fire-resistant, hard and tough enough to become a floor finish, stainproof, antibacterial, and insecticidal.

In the construction field there are three methods for applying paints: (1) painting applied on the job, (2) painting applied in a mill, shop, or factory, and (3) prime coats applied in a mill, shop, factory, or on the job.

Maintenance painting is a fourth type of painting. Painted surfaces periodically require repainting, which includes cleaning and otherwise preparing the old surface for maintenance painting.

Painting on the Job

Painting on the job requires that painters not only have brushes, rollers, or spray guns (see Figures 26-1, 26-2, and 26-3) but also a series of accessories necessary to prepare the various surfaces in a correct manner prior to the application of paint (see Table 26-1).

Thinners and *solvents* are needed to thin ready-mix paint and to clean brushes, hands, etc.

Putty is needed to fill holes and cracks.

Caulking compounds are used to fill joints between materials.

Wood filler paste is used to fill pores and open grains in wood.

FIGURE 26-1   *Paint brushes*

FLAT ROLLER   TRIM ROLLER

FIGURE 26-2   *Paint rollers*

Knot-sealers are special formulations that seal knots and pitch streaks in wood to prevent staining of finish paint.

Paint and *varnish removers* of the correct type are needed to remove old paint and varnish.

Sizing materials consist of sealers for plaster, cement, concrete, and masonry materials, used to seal in the lime, which can destroy or stain the finish paint.

Mill, Shop, or Factory Painting

Shop painting is applied by various methods such as dipping, tumbling, centrifuging, spraying, and knife coating. The types of material and their

location in the building control the method of painting to be used (see Table 26-2).

Requirements for a "Good" Painting Job

All painting should be done at temperatures of 60 to 80°F. All surfaces should be clean, dry, prime-coated, sized if required, have cracks filled and rough projections removed. Knots in wood must be sealed and rough grain must be sanded smooth. In masonry, efflorescence must be removed, joints pointed, and excess mortar removed. The areas where painting is to be done must be well-ventilated. Surfaces not to be painted must be

FIGURE 26-3   *Paint spraying*

TABLE 26-1   *Methods of painting on the job*

Type of Paint	Surface Where Applied	Method of Application
Asphalt	Masonry, concrete, iron, and steel	Brush, mop
Clear finishes	Exterior wood surfaces, interior wood surfaces, and floors	Brush, spraying, roller
Dampproofing and waterproofing	Exterior concrete or masonry, above or below grade	Brush, spraying, trowel, mopping
Enamels	Interior trim and areas where cooking and moisture are present	Brush, spraying, roller
Flat-semi-flat and high gloss	Interior walls and ceilings	Brush, spraying, roller
House	Exterior wood	Brush, spraying, roller
Lacquers	Wood furniture, cabinets, shelves, etc.	Brush, spraying
Masonry	Exterior and interior stucco, cement, concrete, masonry	Brush, spraying, roller
Rust-inhibiting	Exterior and interior iron and steel	Brush, spraying, roller
Stains	Exterior and interior wood	Brush, cloth, sponge, spraying

TABLE 26-2   *Methods of mill, shop, and factory painting*

Type of Paint	Where Applied	Application
Lacquers, enamels, baked enamels	Metal furniture	Spraying and heating
Lacquers, varnishes, stains	Wood furniture	Brush, spraying
Rust-inhibiting paints	Shop priming coats	Spraying, brush, dipping
Stains	Shingles and siding	Spraying, brush
Varnishes, enamels, lacquers, stains, baked enamels	Millwork, panels, cabinet work	Spraying and heating
Varnishes, enamels, lacquers, stains, baked enamels	Plywood, sheet, and board material	Spraying, rolling, brush, dipping, heating

TABLE 26-3   *Methods of cleaning ferrous metals*

Name of Method	Where Done	Method
Flame	Shop, mill, or factory	Oxyacetylene flame
Pickling	Shop, mill, or factory	Metal submerged in phosphoric or sulfuric acid solution
Sand-blasting	Shop, mill, or factory	Jet of sand blown with compressed air
Wire brushing	Shop, mill, factory, job site	By hand on job and by machine in shop, mill, or factory
Rust remover	Job site	Applied by brush and wiped clean with cloths
Solvent cleaning	Job site	Applied by brush and wiped clean with cloths

protected, and painted surfaces should be protected until the applied paint dries.

Good painting depends on (1) the correct preparation of the surface to receive the organic coating, (2) selection of the correct organic coating for this surface, (3) use of the correct procedures for the application of the organic coating, and (4) the maintaining of correct temperature, humidity, and environmental conditions where the painting is to be done.

Painting Ferrous Metals

All ferrous metals, except stainless steel and weathering steels, require special rust-inhibiting paints and must be cleaned by special methods (see Table 26-3).

Prime coating or protective coating is required for both ferrous and nonferrous metal. Ferrous metals (other than stainless steel and weathering steels) require a prime coat to be applied by the manufacturer for two purposes: to protect the metal until it is installed, and to provide a painted surface on which a finish coat of paint can be applied on the job site (see Table 26-4).

Nonferrous metals are given a protective removable coating which is taken off when the possibility of damage or staining is no longer present at the job site.

Painting of Concrete, Masonry, Plaster, and Various Sheet, Board, and Panel Materials

The painting of concrete, masonry, plaster and the various types of sheet, board, and panel materials is for decoration only, not for the protection of the material. The exception is concrete and masonry below grade, which require dampproofing or waterproofing, and above grade to stop moisture from penetrating through the walls. The alkaline characteristics of many of these materials generally require a pretreatment (see Table 26-5).

TABLE 26-4   *Organic coatings for ferrous metals*

Type	Prime Coat	Undercoat	Finish Coat	Where Used on Ferrous Metals
Alkyd	Rust-inhibiting alkyd varnish	Same as prime coat	Alkyd, pigmented	Severe exterior weather conditions
Coal tar	Hot-applied coal tar	None	Hot-applied coal tar enamel	Installations underground and in or under fresh water
Epoxy	Rust-inhibiting epoxy	Same as prime or finish coat	Pigmented epoxy	Interior or exterior, also for resistance to alkalis and acids
Oil-base	Rust-inhibiting oil-base	Same as prime coat	Pigmented oil-base	Normal exterior weather conditions
Urethane	Rust-inhibiting urethane	Same as prime or finish coat	Pigmented urethane	Industrial finishes and for resistance to abrasion
Vinyl	Rust-inhibiting vinyl	Same as prime coat	Pigmented vinyl-alkyd	Metal immersed in fresh or salt water, and on interior for easy maintenance

TABLE 26-5   *Organic coatings for concrete, masonry, plaster and similar materials*

Type	Prime Coat	Finish Coat	Where Used
Asphalt-base (emulsion type)	Asphalt-base	Asphalt-base	Dampproofing exterior concrete or masonry walls below grade
Cement-base	Same as finish coat	Cement-base	Interior and exterior concrete, masonry, stucco, and cement plaster
Epoxy	Epoxy	Epoxy	Interior concrete floors
Resin-vehicle	Resin-base tinted same color as finish coat	Resin-base, white or tinted	Exterior and interior concrete, masonry, stucco, plaster, cement plaster; and sheet, board, and panel materials
Silicone		Silicone	Water-resistant coating for exterior concrete and masonry
Urethane		Urethane	Anti-dusting and finish for concrete floors
Varnish-base	Varnish-base	Varnish-base	Interior concrete, masonry, plaster; and sheet, board, and panel materials
Water-base	Same as finish coat	Water-base, white or tinted	Interior and exterior concrete, masonry, plaster; and sheet, board, and panel materials

Painting of Wood

In the construction field all wood requires painting or treatment of some type. All exterior and interior wood and trim which are to become the finish surfaces should be back-primed. Wood that is to be painted, stained or given a clear coating should have nail-holes, open grain and pores, holes, and cracks filled and sealed. Pitch streaks and knots should receive a coat of knot-sealer. See Table 26-6, which summarizes types of coatings and procedures.

Exterior and interior painting is generally done as two-coat or three-coat method. Each coat must be thoroughly dry before the next coat is applied.

Water-base paints require a prime or sealer coat that prevents the water-base paints from raising the grain of the wood.

Exterior staining is done with brushes, mops or squeegees, applying a single *liberally* applied coat of stain, which generally contains a wood preservative. Exterior synthetic-resin varnish requires a three-coat application.

Interior staining or bleaching of wood requires that the type of wood, type of stain, and type of finish varnish, lacquer, or wax are all compatible.

REVIEW EXAMINATION

1. Name two methods for applying organic coatings.

2. Name two surface preparations necessary before paint is applied.

3. What is the name of the coating applied by manufacturers to steel?

4. How are stains applied at on-site painting?

5. Baked enamels are applied to what?

6. Name five accessories a painter uses in applying organic coatings.

7. At what temperature should organic coatings be applied?

8. Name the two methods used for applying organic coatings with spray guns.

TABLE 26-6 *Organic coatings for wood*

Type	Prime Coat	Intermediate Coat	Finish Coat	Where Used
Alkyd	Alkyd, white for three-coat work, and tinted same color for two-coat work	Same as finish coat	Alkyd paint or enamel	Interior and exterior
Epoxy	Oil, alkyd, or epoxy	None	Epoxy	Exterior
Lacquers	Lacquer, clear or tinted	Same as finish coat	Lacquer, clear or tinted	Mill, shop, or factory applied
Latex	Latex	None	Latex, white or tinted	Exterior and interior
Oil-base vehicle	Oil-base, white for three-coat work, and tinted same color as finish coat for two-coat work	Same as oil-base finish coat	Oil-base vehicle for exterior, white or tinted; varnish vehicle for interior, white or tinted	Exterior
Stains	None	None	Oil-base latex, alkyd	Exterior and interior
Urethane	None	None	Urethane, clear	Interior and wood floors
Varnish	Clear varnish	Same as finish coat	Varnish, clear for interiors; for exteriors, spar varnish	Exterior and interior
Varnish for floors	Floor sealer	Varnish sealer	Varnish sealer	Interior floors
Vinyl	None	None	Vinyl	Interior and wood floors

9. Name three methods by which organic coatings are applied.

10. What type of organic coating is used for shop-applied prime coats?

ASSIGNMENT

1. Make a sketch showing the three different methods of applying an organic coating.

2. Make a list of materials that require a shop-applied prime coat.

SUPPLEMENTARY INFORMATION

Waterproofing and Dampproofing

Waterproofing and dampproofing organic coatings are applied by various methods, depending on the type of coating, its viscosity, and whether hot or cold application is required.

Fire-Resistant and Flameproof Paints

Fire-resistant (intumescent) and flameproof organic coatings require strict, controlled application rules and regulations, since they are able to develop a 2- to 4-hr. fire rating. Intumescent organic coatings depend on each coat to develop their hour ratings.

Multicolored Coatings

Multicolored organic coatings require strict controlled application. Generally a prime coat and undercoat are required before the multicolored coating is applied.

Spray-Gun Painting

There are two methods for applying paint with spray guns: (1) using compressed air, and (2) airless spraying using hydraulic pressure.

Special Wood Treatments

Wood and wood surfaces can be made fire resistant, flameproof, fireproof, acid resistant, and resistant to mold, rot, and insects with special organic coatings and penetrants.

27

FLOORING AND INSTALLATION OF FLOORING

INTRODUCTION

The type of flooring and the method of installation must be selected for durability, hardness, resilience, color, comfort, and maintenance. This chapter will cover the various types of flooring such as seamless, carpet, wood, tile, terrazzo, resilient, etc., and their installation.

TECHNICAL INFORMATION

Flooring

DEFINITION: Flooring may be defined as the finished surface upon which people walk and furniture is placed, and upon which materials and equipment are carried, rolled, moved, or stored.

CRITERIA FOR SELECTION: When selecting various types of flooring materials for buildings, there are specific requirements that should always be considered:

1. All types of flooring require that the surface upon which they are applied and their method of installation must be suited to correctly receive the selected flooring. For example, wood floors require that water, moisture, and dampness must be prevented from getting into and under the wood flooring. Figure 27-1 shows a method of accomplishing this by using a waterproof adhesive and installing a moisture and vapor barrier over porous fill before laying the floor.

2. Expansion and contraction should be considered not only for the flooring material itself but also for the materials and surfaces upon which the flooring is to be installed. For example; terrazzo must be subdivided with divider strips and installed on a sand bed to take care of the expansion and contraction of the terrazzo and of the material and surface upon which it rests. This prevents the terrazzo from cracking (see Figure 27-2).

3. Different levels will be required in the subfloor surfaces to meet the various depths required by different floor materials for installation. For example, quarry tile, when set in mortar, requires a depth of 1-1/4 to 2-1/2 in., whereas 1/8-in. thick vinyl asbestos tile requires none; therefore, the subsurface for the quarry tile must be depressed between 1-1/8 to 2-3/8 in. below the surface required for vinyl asbestos tile (see Figure 27-3).

4. The treatment of the joints where different types of flooring meet should be carefully detailed. For example, vinyl tile meets ceramic tile flooring as shown in Figure 27-4.

FIGURE 27-1   *Wood flooring*

FIGURE 27-2   *Terrazzo flooring*

FIGURE 27-3   *Tile flooring*

FIGURE 27-4   *Tile flooring*

5. The final finish treatments (maintenance) such as waxing, polishing, sealing, etc. must be correct for the flooring. For example, the wax used for wood floors cannot be used on asphalt tile because it has a petroleum base and petroleum products dissolve asphalt tile.

268

TYPES OF FLOORING: Flooring materials are summarized in Table 27-1 by their qualities and where they are generally used in building construction.

Methods of Installation

CARPET: The development of synthetic fibers has changed the entire concept of carpeting. Formerly, almost all carpets were manufactured from wool and other natural fibers and were made to specific sizes. Today, a single roll of 15'-0"-wide carpet can be 90'-0" long and longer, and when joined, no seam is visible.

The fibers generally used for manufacturing carpet are polyester, acrylic, nylon, and wool. The carpets with synthetic fibers can be installed both indoors and outdoors. They are resistant to color fading, mildew, rot, moth, bacteria, insects, stain, and flame. They are easily maintained and can be installed in areas of from light to heavy wear. Depending on usage, their durability varies from 5 to 15 years.

TABLE 27-1 *Types of flooring*

Material	General Area of Use	Qualities
Carpet	Where resilience, quietness, and limited durability are required. Some types will stain.	Limited durability, fairly easily maintained
Ceramic and quarry tile	Where water and moisture are present and sanitary conditions are required	Durable, hard, and easily maintained
Concrete and concrete with surface treatments	General utility areas and storage, and where there are manufacturing and industrial processes	Hard, durable, requires surface treatment to harden and eliminate dust and will stain
Resilient; asphalt, cork, rubber, vinyl, vinyl asbestos tiles, asphalt, and linoleum	Where resilience is required and where there will be slight to moderately heavy wear	From very resilient to slightly resilient (depending on type) and from poor to easily maintained (depending on type)
Paint: oil-based	General utility areas and where there will be slight wear	Limited durability, difficult to maintain, requires periodic repainting
Paint: synthetic resin-based (epoxy acrylic, etc.)	General utilities areas where there will be slight to heavy wear	Requires refinishing periodically
Seamless-epoxy polyester, oxychloric, and other types of synthetic resins	Areas where there will be slight to very heavy wear	Durable, resilient to hard, easily maintained
Steel	In areas where there are manufacturing and industrial processes and also for supporting heavy equipment	Very strong, durable, but requires periodic repainting
Stone and brick	Where there will be very heavy wear also where water and moisture are present	Durable, hard, good maintenance but will stain
Terrazzo: all types	Where there will be very heavy wear	Durable, hard, easily maintained but will stain
Wood: all types	Where there will be slight or very heavy wear (depending on type)	Fairly to very durable, relatively easily maintained, but will stain

All types of carpet must have an underlayer, either as an integral part of the carpet or as a separate material. In general there are three methods of installing carpet: stretching and tacking, adhesive, and double-faced adhesive tape (see Figure 27-5).

CERAMIC AND QUARRY TILE: This type of flooring is durable, hard, and easily maintained and is generally used in areas where water and moisture are present. There are two methods of installing this type of flooring: by the adhesive method and

by the cement mortar bed method (see Figure 27-6).

The surface upon which this type of flooring is installed should be rigid so that no bending can occur, thus avoiding cracks that may develop in the joints. Where water and moisture are present, the top of the subsurface should be waterproofed.

CONCRETE: When concrete is to be used as the finish floor surface, it must be treated with hardeners, either mixed with the concrete or applied during curing or after the concrete is cured. This is

FIGURE 27-5   *Installation of carpet*

FIGURE 27-6   *Installation of quarry and ceramic tile*

necessary because concrete, as it wears, gives off a fine dust,—that is, "dusting" occurs—which hardeners eliminate.

The concrete surface may be colored, wear-resistant, nonsparking, and nonslip. These various surfaces are achieved by the following means:

1. *Metallic oxide colors* can be mixed with the concrete or applied to the surface when it is floated, and troweled to give color.

2. *Metallic aggregates* can be applied to the surface when it is floated and troweled to give a wear-resistant surface.

3. *Metallic iron aggregates* (to give a nonspark flooring) are applied in the same manner as metallic aggregates, and the entire surface treatment is electrically grounded. Nonsparking finishes are used for areas where highly explosive or flammable materials are to be stored or used.

4. *Abrasive aggregates* are applied in the same manner as metallic aggregates to make a very nonslip surface (see Figure 27-7).

PAINTED FLOOR SURFACE: Wood and concrete have been painted for many years with oil-based paints as a finish surface flooring for cleanliness and maintenance in areas where materials are stored and in utility areas. Paint should be used only in areas where there will be very slight wear. It requires periodic repainting.

Synthetic resin based paints can be used as a finish surface flooring for areas where heavy wear will be present. These paints are hard, durable, and nonslip; they are available clear and colored, and can be applied to wood, concrete, and metal.

This type of surface flooring consists generally of two materials in separate containers—the synthetic resin and the activator. When thoroughly mixed, the end product is applied by brush, roller, or spraying and requires extensive ventilation during application because most of these paints are highly volatile and flammable. Great care should be taken that they be installed immediately once mixed because of their quick drying (known as pot life). The usual pot life is around 45 min.—

after this they cannot be used and must be confiscated and thrown away.

SEAMLESS FLOORING: This type of flooring has been installed for many years, using oxychloric cement as the cementitious material with wood sawdust, sand, and other materials mixed and applied 1/2 to 3/8-in. thick and troweled level. The finished flooring is resilient, noncombustible, nonslip, and easy to maintain. It will endure light to heavy wear.

The development of synthetic resins has resulted in a wide variety of seamless floors which can be very hard to quite resilient, also nonslip and spark-resistant. They are available in a wide variety of colors and can be used in areas where light to heavy wear will be present.

The cementitious synthetic resins generally used are epoxy, vinyl, urethane, acrylic, and neoprene. They are combined with colored plastic flakes, cork, ceramic-coated stone, and marble chips. The thickness can vary from 1/16 to 3/8 in., depending on type used. When synthetic terrazzo-type seamless floors are installed, divider strips are sometimes used but are not necessary.

One great advantage of seamless floors is that they can continue up the wall to base height, thus eliminating the entire problem of having to install the base after the floor has been laid (see Figure 27-8).

STEEL: Steel flooring is manufactured in two types, grating and steel plate. All steel flooring must be supported by light steel framing (see Figure 27-9). Steel plate is available with various surface patterns and textures to make it nonslip.

STONE AND BRICK FLOORING: All types of stone and brick for flooring are almost always set with a cement mortar bed. The stones used for flooring are marble, granite, limestone, bluestone, and slate. Of these stones, granite, bluestone, and slate are installed both indoors and outdoors, whereas

FIGURE 27-7   *Application of special surface treatments for concrete*

FIGURE 27-8 *Seamless flooring*

FIGURE 27-9 *Steel flooring*

marble and limestone are installed indoors (see Figure 27-10).

Face brick and paving brick are both used for flooring. Face brick is generally manufactured with holes; therefore, when used for flooring, only the 2-1/4-in. face can be exposed as the finish surface. Flooring brick is a dense, hard-burned, impervious type of brick that may be obtained acid-resistant, generally 8-1/2 in. long × 4 in. wide × 2-1/2, 3, and 4-1/2 in. deep (see Figure 27-11).

RESILIENT FLOORING: The various types of re-silient flooring include asphalt, cork, rubber, vinyl, vinyl asbestos, and linoleum. They are manu-factured in a wide range of colors, designs, patterns, and textures.

All the various resilient floorings are manu-factured in two forms, either as tiles, or in rolls, or both. The tile shapes are generally squares 9 × 9 in. and 12 × 12 in., in thicknesses of 1/16, 3/32, and 1/8 in. The rolls are generally 6'-0" wide and vary in length from 30'-0" to 50'-0". Their thick-nesses are 1/16, 3/32, and 1/8 in. In general the 1/8-in.-thick tile or roll is for areas where heavy wear will be present. These floorings are durable, resilient (varying from quite resilient to almost nonresilient) and easily maintained. They can be used in areas of slight to heavy wear.

The manufacturers of resilient-type flooring make bases, feature strips, and special designs for inlaying. Custom designs are also possible. As an example, on a playroom floor, checkerboard or various game markings can be installed.

When selecting a resilient type of flooring, the surface upon which it is to be applied should be smooth, have no cracks, and be protected from moisture and water (see Figure 17-12).

TERRAZZO: There are two types of terrazzo flooring, one in which portland cement is the ce-mentitious material and one in which a synthetic-type resin is the cementitious material. In both types, marble chips are added and, when cured, the surface is ground to a fine, smooth finish. Terrazzo flooring is very hard, durable, easy to maintain, and able to withstand very rough wear. The various colors are obtained by combining colored marble chips and also by coloring the cementitious material. Terrazzo is installed either at the site or as prefabricated units (see Figure 27-13).

All on-site cement-matrix terrazzo requires divider strips to stop any cracking of the finish surface (due to expansion and contraction) and any deflection of the supporting subflooring (see Figure 27-14). With the seamless type, divider

272

FIGURE 27-10 *Stone flooring*

FIGURE 27-11 *Brick flooring*

FIGURE 27-12 *Resilient flooring*

273

strips are installed only as a precaution against cracking. With the precast type, they are installed only when there is great length and changes in direction occur.

WOOD FLOORING: The various evergreen and deciduous woods used for flooring must be close-grained, hard, and wear-resistant. All wood flooring must meet the rigid rules and regulations for grading, moisture content, and kiln-drying that have been set by the Wood Flooring Manufacturers Associations. The woods generally used are oak, maple, fir, and spruce. There are three types of wood flooring: strip, thin square blocks, and solid end-grain blocks (see Figure 27-15). Strip flooring is manufactured unfinished (must be sanded and finished on job site), and prefinished (no job sanding or finishing required).

Deciduous strip flooring is manufactured quarter-sawed in thicknesses of 5/16, 1/2, 3/8, 25/32, 17/16, and 35/32-in., and widths of 1-1/2, 2, 2-1/4, 2-1/2, 3, 3-1/4, and 3-1/2 in.

The grading is controlled by the lengths. For example, *maple*, *first grade*, shall be 2'-0" and up as stock will produce; not over 30% of total footage shall be in bundles under 4'-0" in length. The grades in general are *first*, *second*, and *third*, but certain types have other grades depending on the species of wood.

Softwood strip flooring is manufactured plain-sawed, in thicknesses of 3/8, 1/2, 5/8, 1, 1-1/4, 1-1/2, 2, 2-1/2, 3, and 4 in., and widths of

TERRAZZO ON SAND CUSHION OVER CONCRETE (CEMENT MATRIX)

TERRAZZO BONDED DIRECTLY TO CONCRETE (CEMENT MATRIX)

SEAMLESS TYPE TERRAZZO (SYNTHETIC RESIN MATRIX)

PRE-CAST TERRAZZO TILE (SYNTHETIC RESIN MATRIX)

PRE-CAST TERRAZZO TILE (CEMENT MATRIX)

PRE-CAST TERRAZZO TILE (CEMENT MATRIX)

FIGURE 27-13   *Terrazzo flooring*

TERRAZZO

DIVIDER STRIP

SETTING BED

BRASS OR WHITE ZINC ALLOY

STANDARD DIVIDER STRIP

TERRAZZO

DIVIDER STRIP

PLASTIC

SETTING BED

BRASS OR ZINC ALLOY

PLASTIC DIVIDER STRIP

TERRAZZO

DIVIDER STRIP

NEOPRENE

SETTING BED

SUB-FLOOR SURFACE

BRASS OR ZINC ALLOY

EXPANSION DIVIDER STRIP

FIGURE 27-14 *Terrazzo dividing strips*

T&G SIDE MATCHED

T&G SIDE AND END MATCHED

SQUARE ENDS AND SIDES

TYPES OF STRIP FLOORING

EQUAL

$\frac{1}{4}$" TO $\frac{33}{32}$"

THIN WOOD BLOCK

SOLID END GRAIN BLOCK

TYPES OF BLOCK FLOORING

FIGURE 27-15 *Types of wood flooring*

2, 3, 4, 5, 6, 8, 10, and 12 in., bundled in various lengths and graded *select* and *common*. All strip flooring is bundled and delivered by the board foot.

Thin types of wood block flooring are pre-fabricated either from solid wood or veneers (similar to plywood). They are manufactured prefinished in different patterns and generally 9 × 9-in. and 12 × 12-in. squares.

Solid end-grain wood block flooring is installed in areas where very heavy wear will be present, such as in factories and in school shops. (see Figure 27-16).

FIGURE 27-16   *End grain solid wood block flooring*

The surface upon which all types of wood flooring is to be installed must be dry and water-proof so that no moisture or water can be absorbed by the wood (see Figure 27-17).

Wood flooring should be selected: by type of wood, as either quarter-sawed or plain-sawed, by the type of wear that it will be subjected to when installed, by color, by grain, and by the type of surface upon which it is to be installed.

2-4-1 Plywood Flooring

Comparatively new, 2-4-1-plywood flooring consists of 1-1/8″, or 1-1/4″ thick panels, 48″ × 96″, supported only around their edges. The framing, supporting the plywood generally consists of solid, built-up, or laminated wood girders spaced 48″ o.c. and supported either by a central beam, a wall or a number of piers, Fig. 27-18. The panels are nailed with 8d annularly threaded nails spaced 6″ o.c. at all panel edges. The face plies are laid perpendicular to supports and all end joints are staggered. Joints between panels are kept 1/16″ apart. Blocking under panel edges is not required because the 2-4-1 panel edges are

tongue-and-grooved to transfer bending stresses. The plywood can receive any type of floor finish.

REVIEW EXAMINATION

1. When selecting various types of flooring, are the following statements correct? (Answer *yes* or *no*.) (a) Expansion and contraction are important. (b) The method of treating the joints between different types of flooring is important. (c) The surface upon which various types of flooring are to be installed is un-important.

2. What are the three methods of installing carpet?

3. Can carpet be installed outdoors?

4. What are the two methods for installing ceramic tile and quarry tile?

5. What must be done to concrete when it will be used as a finished floor?

6. Concrete, when used as a finished floor, can be (answer *yes* or *no*); (a) colored, (b) made resilient, (c) made nonslip, (d) made nonspark, (e) made acoustic.

7. When oil-based paint is used as a finish flooring surface can it be installed in areas where heavy wear will be present?

8. What kind of wear will be possible when synthetic resin paint is used?

9. What resins are used as cementitious material in seamless flooring?

10. Steel flooring is manufactured in what two types?

11. Stone and brick flooring are installed with what setting bed?

12. Name four different types of resilient flooring.

13. Terrazzo consists of either a portland cement or a synthetic resin cementitious material and what other material?

14. To avoid cracking, what is used with terrazzo flooring?

15. Name the three types of wood flooring.

ASSIGNMENT

1. Make a freehand sketch, in scale, showing the specific information and requirements that should be considered when installing quarry and ceramic-type flooring.

2. Make a freehand sketch, in scale, showing the types of wood flooring.

FIGURE 27-17 *Wood flooring*

SECTION "AA"

FIGURE 27-18 *2-4-1 plywood flooring*

BEARING PARTITION
2-4-1 PLYWOOD
2"×6" BLOCKING

2 FRAMING ANCHORS EACH END
UNDER BEARING PARTITION

DETAIL "A"   DETAIL "B"

2-4-1 PLYWOOD
⅝" PLYWOOD STRIPPING
FOR LAMINATED GIRDERS ONLY

⅝"×4"×18"
PLYWOOD
SPLICE PL.
4"×6" OR
2-2"×6"

CUT FROM 2"×6"

CONTINUOUS
TERMITE SHIELD
WHERE REQ'D.

2"×6"

3-2"×10" NO.2 GIRDER

2"×10" BLOCKING
2"×6" SILL
½"∅ ANCHOR BOLT

DETAIL "C"

2"×4" PLATE
¼" SPACE
2-4-1 PLYWOOD
TERMITE SHIELD
2"×4" BLOCK'G
2"×6"
3"   3"

DETAIL-D

2-4-1 PLYWOOD
1⅛"
2"×6" BLOCKING

4"×4" POST
½"∅ BOLT

4"×6" GIRDERS -48" O.C.

DETAIL G

2"×6" SILL
NOTCHED
AT GIRDER

TERMITE
SHIELD

8" MIN.

2"×4" PLATE
¼" SPACE
2-4-1 PLYWOOD
1⅛"

ALLOW ½" AIR SPACE
ALL AROUND GIRDER

DETAIL "E"
IN FOUNDATION POCKET

DETAIL "F"

FIGURE 27-18 *2-4-1 plywood flooring (continued)*

FACE BRICK OR PAVING BRICK
SAND

3¾"
4" TO 8"

FINE SAND

FLAGSTONE
GRASS
¾" TO 1¼"

4" TO 8"

TOPSOIL
FINE SAND

FIGURE 27-19 *Brick or flagstone installed in sand—outdoors*

SUPPLEMENTARY INFORMATION

Brick and Flagstones

When used as flooring on the exterior, brick and flagstones are installed either with mortar as previously stated or in sand (see Figure 27-19).

Design Precautions

It is of major importance when various types of flooring are selected for a building that the sup-porting structure be considered because of the various levels or depressions that may be required for each type of flooring material (see Figure 27-20).

Wood Flooring in Large Areas

When selecting wood flooring for large areas such as gymnasiums or large manufacturing areas, there are special methods of installation, as shown in Figure 27-21.

FIGURE 27-20　*Effects of various types of flooring on supporting structure*

FIGURE 27-21　*Heavy single flooring with metal sleepers such as are used on gymnasium floors*

28

PLASTER, PLASTERING, AND SURFACE TREATMENTS

INTRODUCTION

This chapter describes plaster as a material, its various types and uses, its application, and the products manufactured from it. In building construction, plaster products represent an increasing use of this material.

The various types of special surfacing materials used on the exterior and interior, other than paint are also described, because they represent a recent technological development that is finding wide acceptance in the building industry.

TECHNICAL INFORMATION

Plaster

Plaster consists of a mixture of a cementitious material, aggregate, water, admixtures for controlling workability and setting time, and hair and fibers. There are four types of cementitious materials used to make plaster: gypsum, Keene's cement, and lime. The aggregates generally used are sand, perlite, vermiculite, and wood fibers. Plastering materials are manufactured either premixed with aggregate and additive in bags or barrels, so that only water is added at the site; or without additives in bags or barrels, with other materials separately packaged so that the mixing is done on the site. The ingredients for making plaster are shown in Table 28-1.

It should be noted that gypsum plaster is used not only as a plastering material but also to make decking, plaster board, partitions, blocks, and poured decking.

Plastering

The word "plastering" refers to the application of the various types of plaster to a surface in layers to give a smooth or textured hard surface finish which can then receive paint, wallpaper, ceramic tile, plastic laminates, textiles, etc., as final finish.

For exterior plastering, portland-type cements are used; where water and moisture are present on the interior, Keene's cement-type plaster is used; and for interior plastering, gypsum plaster is generally used.

The plaster can be applied to various types of masonry walls such as brick, structural clay tile, gypsum block, etc., either directly or onto wire lath, plaster-board lath, or other material that will give sufficient keying or bonding for the plaster. The thickness of plaster is usually 5/8 to 7/8 in. on masonry and wire lath and 1/2 in. on plaster lathing board and gypsum block.

Plaster is applied either by the two-coat or three-coat method. The first coat is called the *scratch coat*, the second coat is called the *brown coat*, and the finish coat is called *hard finish*. In two-coat work the scratch and brown coats are combined and are called the base coat, with the finish coat the same as that used for three-coat plastering (see Table 28-2).

Lath, either metal or plasterboard, is used to span the open spaces between structural framing to form a surface to which plaster can be applied. All lath must be of a type to which the plaster can bond (see Figure 28-1).

For ceilings where structural members are widely spaced and for hung ceilings, a system of small channels must be installed to which the lath can be applied (see Figure 28-2).

Before plaster is installed, grounds and screeds are employed, set in such a way that the plaster will have a level and plumb surface (see Figure 28-3). The various accessories used in plastering to take care of corners, expansion, reinforcing, changes in materials, etc., are manufactured for both two-coat and three-coat plastering (see Figure 28-4).

Plaster Products

GYPSUM BOARDS: These consist of a core of gypsum plaster containing fibers or hair sandwiched between two sheets of heavy paper, usually with sized paper on one side and unsized paper on the other. The core may include perlite or vermiculite and glass or mineral fibers, all of which increase fire resistance.

Gypsum boards, more commonly known as *sheetrock*, are manufactured in various types: regular, fire-rated (type X), backer board, insulating, vinyl-coated, sheathing, decorative and laminated for non-load-bearing partitions.

Regular sheetrock has one side with sized paper, the other unsized paper, and is available in thicknesses of 3/8, 1/2, and 5/8 in., 4'-0" wide and in lengths 6'-0" to 14'-0" in 1-ft. increments. In residential and other wood-frame construction work, gypsum boards are nailed directly to the wood frame as a surfacing material for walls and ceilings to receive paper, paint, and textiles. The

TABLE 28-1 *Plaster ingredients*

Ingredients	Type and Form	Use
Cement	Portland or portland pozzolana	Exterior and interior walls and ceilings
Fiber	Glass, hemp, sisal, or jute Clean, long, and free from tannic acid	Reinforcing plaster
Gypsum	Plaster of paris	Making gypsum plasters
	Gypsum plaster	2- and 3-coat interior
	High-strength gypsum plaster	Plasterboard, decking, block, 2- and 3-coat interior plastering
	Keene's cement	Finish for 2- and 3-coat gypsum plaster, and Keene's cement plaster
	Fibered gypsum plaster	Scratch coat
	Prepared gypsum plaster	2- and 3-coat interior
	Fire-resistant gypsum plaster	Fireproofing steel, etc.
	Acoustical plaster	Acoustical treatment for walls and ceilings
	Bonding plaster	Finish for concrete walls and ceilings
	Sand-float finish plaster	For finish of 2- and 3-coat plastering
Hair	Goat or cattle 1/2 to 2″ long. Clean and free from rust, knots, and balls	Reinforcing plaster
Lime	Hydrated lime Lime putty	Gives workability and plasticity to plasters
Sand	White or light gray fine sand, 100% passing through a No. 4 sieve	Aggregate for plasters
Water	Clean, fresh water containing no salt, sulfur, or other harmful substances	Makes cementitious materials and aggregate workable, and also combines chemically with gypsum and lime
Lightweight aggregate	Perlite or vermiculite	Imparts fire resistance to plasters

TABLE 28-2 *The thickness of plastering coats*

Three Coats	Two Coats
Scratch coat 1/2″	Base coat 1/2″
Brown coat 1/4″	Hard finish 1/8″
Hard finish 1/8″	

regular type is also used extensively in larger construction on metal partitions; it is made to adhere to rigid foam insulation on masonry walls and to prefabricated laminated sheetrock partitions (see Figures 28-5 and 28-6).

Fire-rated (type X) gypsum consists of sheetrock with one side of sized paper and the other of unsized paper; it is available in thicknesses of 1/2 in. with a 45-min. fire rating and 5/8 in. with a 1-hr. fire rating; 4′-0″ wide and in lengths 6′-0″ to 14′-0″ in 1-ft increments. This type is used in areas that require 45-min. or 1-hr. fire resistance.

Backer board consists of sheetrock with unsized paper on both sides, available in thicknesses of 3/8, 1/2, and 5/8 in., 2′-0″ wide, and 8′-0″ long. It is used primarily as a backing material to which other finish materials are applied—for example, as backing for acoustical tile applied with an adhesive.

Insulating sheetrock consists of any of the various types with aluminum foil laminated to one side. The aluminum foil acts as a vapor barrier and reflective-type insulation.

Vinyl-coated sheetrock has one side treated with a waterproof vinyl coating; it is available 3/8 and 1/2 in. thick, 4′-0″ wide, and 8′-0″ long.

WIRE LATH   EXPANDED METAL 'V' RIB LATH   EXPANDED METAL FLAT RIB LATH

FIGURE 28-1 *Lath for plastering*

FIGURE 28-2 *Installation of furring channels to receive wire lath and plaster ceiling*

FIGURE 28-3 *Application of plaster*

284

EXTERNAL CORNER BEAD   STRIP MESH   INTERNAL CORNER BEAD

CORNER MESH   CASING BEAD/GROUND   EXPANSION JOINT

FIGURE 28-4   *Plaster accessories*

CEILING JOIST

REGULAR SHEETROCK

INSULATION

SUB-FLOOR

FLOOR JOIST

REGULAR SHEETROCK
APPLIED TO WOOD FRAME

BACKER BOARD

REGULAR SHEETROCK LAMINATED TO BACKER BOARD

METAL STUD

DOUBLE 'U' CLIPS

WIRE CLIPS

BACKER & REGULAR SHEETROCK ATTACHED TO METAL PARTITIONS

FIGURE 28-5   *Details of application of sheetrock*

SHEET METAL SCREW W/WASHER SCREWED INTO METAL L

LAMINATED CORE

REGULAR SHEETROCK JOB-LAMINATED

24 GA. METAL U

FINISHED FLOOR

SECTION SHOWING TREATMENT AT FLOOR & CEILING

METAL DOOR BUCK

U-CLIP WELDED TO BUCK

CLIPS NAILED TO BUCK

METAL BUCK

CORNER BEAD

CROSS-NAILED

REGULAR SHEETROCK JOB-LAMINATED

LAMINATED CORE

CORNER DETAIL

FIGURE 28-6   *Details of prefabricated partition*

Its major use is in areas where moisture and vapor are present; it also is used as backing for adhesive-type installation of ceramic, metal, or plastic tile.

Sheetrock sheathing consists of a core treated with asphalt and the outside paper surface treated for water resistance; it is 1/2 in. thick, 2'-0" wide, and 8'-0" long. It is used for exterior sheathing for frame construction.

Decorative sheetrock has one side treated with a prefinished surface treatment (decorative paper, wood grains, etc.).

Laminated sheetrock partitions consist of two, three, or four sheets of sheetrock laminated together to manufacture prefabricated partitions (see Figure 28-6). There are various types of partition systems, both permanent and removable, using sheetrock.

Edges and finishes. The various types of sheetrock have different types of edge treatment (see Figure 28-7). The finish treatment of joints and nail indentations consists of what is known as *spackling* (see Figure 28-8).

DECKING: Gypsum plaster decking is manufactured 2-in. thick, 15-in. wide, and 10'-0"

long and generally has a metal tongue-and-groove frame at its edges. The maximum span between supports is 7'-0". Gypsum plaster decking can be cantilevered 2'-6" in its 10'-0" dimension and only 6 in. in its 15-in. dimension (see Figure 28-9).

POURED ROOFING: Poured gypsum roofing is lightweight, fire-resistant, has the advantage of setting in a half-hour, and develops enough heat to be installed in freezing weather. It is generally used for roof construction because of its setting time and light weight and also because it can easily be mixed at ground level and pumped directly to the roof. Its one disadvantage is that, if wet, it can deform; therefore, the finished roofing material should be applied as fast as possible. A poured gypsum roofing job, if well-organized, can be completely installed with finish roofing in one day (see Figure 28-10).

The wire lath generally used to reinforce poured gypsum roofs is No. 12 gauge wire, 4-in. o.c. lengthwise, and No. 12 gauge wire, 8-in. o.c. crosswise. The materials used for the permanent form depend upon the type of interior finish required. An example would be 1-in. insulating form board with acoustical tile applied with adhesive.

FIGURE 28-7   *Edge treatments for the various types of sheetrock*

FIGURE 28-8   *Sheetrock edge and corner treatments*

FIGURE 28-9　*Gypsum plaster decking*

FIGURE 28-10　*Poured gypsum roof deck*

FIGURE 28-11　*Application of surfacings*

Surfacings

"Surfacings" is the word adopted by the building industry for special types of surfacing finishes. Many of these "surfacings" consist of the same synthetic resins, adhesives, and synthetics used in paints and coatings; but when used in combination with other materials, they form new types of surface finishes. For example, epoxies mixed with cement and fine sand form a paste which can be troweled to give a waterproof, durable, colored, textured finish surface.

Surfacings can be factory- or shop-applied and job-site applied. They are available in a wide variety of finishes, textures, and colors; they can be waterproof, are easily cleanable, dustproof, and fire-retardant; they can serve as breathers (to allow moisture vapor from back-up material to be dissipated) and be resistant to shock and abrasion.

Surfacings can be brushed, sprayed, troweled, and rolled; the exposed aggregates, when used, can be seeded (embedded) or blown on (see Figure 28-11). Generally, all types of surfacings become the permanent surface in 24 hrs.

287

One can anticipate the development of new types of surfacings and special coatings, because much research is being done by manufacturers and there seems to be a general increase in the use of such surfacings.

REVIEW EXAMINATION

1. Which of the following materials are manufactured from gypsum plaster? (a) plasterboard, (b) asbestos cement board, (c) decking, (d) plaster for the exterior, and (e) partitions.

2. What type of plaster is used for the following areas? (a) exterior, (b) interior, (c) where water and moisture are present.

3. What is the thickness of plaster on masonry and wire lath?

4. Name two types of lath used for plastering.

5. Name two types of accessories used in plastering.

6. Fire-rated (type X) 5/8-in. gypsum plaster-board has what fire rating?

7. What is the finish treatment of joints and nail indentations in gypsum plaster-board called?

8. Gypsum plaster decking is 2-in. thick, 15-in. wide, and $10'-0''$ long. What is the maximum span between supports?

9. Can poured gypsum plaster roofing be installed in freezing weather?

10. Name four types of gypsum plaster-boards.

11. How are gypsum plaster-board partitions manufactured?

ASSIGNMENT

1. Make a freehand sketch to scale, showing details of installing prefabricated gypsum plaster partitions.

2. Make a freehand sketch to scale, showing details for the installation of a poured gypsum plaster roof.

SUPPLEMENTARY INFORMATION

Fireproofing Coatings

Such coatings are a special type of surfacing applied like paint; they are only 3/16-in. thick but will give a 2-hr. fire rating. These coatings, when exposed to fire and heat, expand from 3/16 to 3 in. of a foam-type insulation. This reaction is known as *intumescence.*

Bonding Qualities of Surfacings and Coatings

The bonding qualities of these new surfacings and coatings are such that they will adhere to almost any material permanently, including wood, concrete, brick, metal, and plaster.

Sheetrock Limitations

Sheetrock should not be used as a vapor barrier and it must not be stored outside for any extended length of time without proper covering. Exterior finishes such as wood siding, wood furring strips, stucco mesh, wall ties, etc., must be secured to the framing by fastening through the sheathing. Sheetrock is not recommended as a base for ceramic tile.

Metal Reinforcement for Stucco Finishes

Metal reinforcement should conform to the weight requirements as specified in Table 28-4.

TABLE 28-3   *Specifications for M.S.F. gypsum sheathing*

Size	Nominal Thickness	Maximum Framing Spacing	Approximate Weight per M.S.F.* (lbs.)
$2' \times 8'$	1/2″	24″	2000
$4' \times 8'$	1/2″	16″	2000
$4' \times 9'$	1/2″	16″	2000

*M.S.F. (Thousands of Square Feet)

TABLE 28-4 *Metal reinforcement for stucco finishes¶*

Type	Weight lbs./sq. yd.	Opening Size	Dimensions
Expanded metal lath—diamond mesh*	3.4	5/16″ × 3/8″	27″ × 96″
Stucco mesh	1.8 and 3.6	1-3/8″ × 3-1/8″	48″ × 99″
Flat rib lath	3.4	5/16″ × 3/8″	24″ × 96″
3/8″ rib lath	3.4 and 4.0	5/16″ × 3/8″	27″ × 96″ and 27″ × 99″
Wire lath woven*	1.7 (18 ga) 1.4 (17 ga)	1″ Hex 1-1/2″ Hex	3′ × 150′ rolls†
Welded wire*	1.4 (16 ga) 1.4 (18 ga) 1.9 (16 ga)	2″ × 2″ 1″ × 1″ 1-1/2″ × 2″	3′ × 150′ rolls†

*Available in plain, self-furring and paper backed types.

†Paper backed and self-furring types also available in sheet form.

¶Courtesy of Construction Principles, Materials & Methods, The Institute of Financial Education, Chicago, Illinois.

29

INSULATION AND
ACOUSTICAL MATERIALS

INTRODUCTION

Many of the insulating and acoustical materials used in the building industry are manufactured from the same raw materials. For example, fiberglass insulation and fiberglass acoustical tile are basically of the same raw material. This chapter will deal with broad basic types of insulating and acoustical materials used in the building industry. Included are flexible, loose, and rigid types of insulation and the various acoustical materials such as tiles, perforated materials, plaster, baffles, and site-assembled materials.

TECHNICAL INFORMATION

Insulation

Most materials offer some resistance to the passage of heat. Those that offer high resistance to the flow of heat are called thermal insulation or simply "insulation." Insulation is needed in all buildings that are exposed to the low temperatures of a winter season or to the high temperatures of a summer season. The more severe the heat or cold, the greater the need for insulation. Insulation primarily adds to the comfort of the individual, and saves both heating and air-conditioning costs.

RATING OF INSULATION: Standard methods of testing insulating materials have been established that give a comparison of the rate by which a given material retards the flow of heat. The rate of resistance is represented by numbers such as 6.25 and 14.29. These numbers represent thermal resistance and are known as the R-factor.

The importance of insulation as an energy-saving material has caused an important shift in terminology from U-factors to R-factors in the construction field. Today banks, mortgage brokers, building codes, etc., set R-factor ratings for exterior walls (for example, 20.0 R) or ceilings under roofs (for example, 24.0 R). It is therefore important to understand the relationship between U-factors (heat loss coefficients) and R-factors.

The R-factor is the reciprocal of a U-factor, therefore an R-factor of 25.0 is equivalent to a U-factor of 1/25.0, or 0.04. The U-factor multiplied by the area of any surface (wall, floor, or ceiling) and by the temperature difference between the inside and outside will give the heat loss or heat gain in BTUs (British Thermal Units). The formula may be stated as follows:

$$BTU = U \times TD \times A$$

in which

BTU = the required heat loss or heat gain

U = heat loss coefficient (assigned to materials)

TD = temperature difference between the outside and the inside of the room. Interior design temperature is usually taken at 70°F.

A = area of the wall, ceiling, or floor where a known temperature difference exists and where a heat loss occurs

EXAMPLE: A room has one exterior wall which is 8'-0" high × 15'-0" long, or 120 sq. ft. in area. The outside design temperature for a specified locality is, say 5°F above 0°F and the inside temperature is 70°F. The difference then is 65°F. The U-factor for the wall is assumed as 0.18. Find the BTU heat loss.

$$\frac{1}{R} = U$$

therefore

$$\frac{1}{40} = 0.025$$

$$BTU = U \times TD \times A$$

$$= 0.025 \times 65° \times 120$$

= 195 (the required heat loss which the heating unit must be able to provide)

From the above example it is obvious that the lower the U-factor or the higher the R-factor, the better the insulating qualities of the material. Table 29-1 gives sizes, R-factors, and U-factors for insulating materials, and Table 29-2 gives R-factors for some typical materials used in construction.

Types of Insulation

FLEXIBLE INSULATION: This type is usually in the form of "blankets" or "quilts," either of which may be in rolls several hundred feet long or "batts" up to 48 in. long. Becase flexible insulation should be built into the hollow spaces in walls or ceilings, the blankets or batts are sized in width to allow them to be fitted into the space between structural framing members. This form of insulation is avail-

TABLE 29-1   *Sizes, R-factors, and U-factors for insulating materials*

Type	Thickness	Width	R-Factor	U-Factor
Blanket, quilt, roll batt	3-1/2″	15″ and 23″	11.00	0.180
	6″	″ ″	19.00	0.053
	9″	″ ″	30.00	0.053
	12″	″ ″	38.00	0.026
Loose	Bag covers approximately 25 sq. ft. of 4″ thickness		3.89	0.260
Foam sheathing	1/2″	4′-0″ × 8′-0″	4.00	0.250
	5/8″	″ ″	5.00	0.200
	3/4″	″ ″	6.00	0.166
	1″	″ ″	8.00	0.125
	1-1/2″	″ ″	12.00	0.083
	2″	″ ″	16.00	0.063
Foam panels	1″	4′-0″ × 8′-0″	5.00 to 6.25	0.20 to 0.16
	1-1/2″	″ ″	7.50 to 9.38	0.13 to 0.11
	2″	″ ″	10.00 to 12.50	0.10 to 0.08
	2-1/2″	″ ″	12.50 to 15.63	0.08 to 0.06
	3″	″ ″	15.00 to 18.75	0.07 to 0.05
Foam, spray-on	1″		3.85	0.26
	3″		11.00	0.09
	3-1/2″		13.00	0.08
	5-1/8″		19.00	0.05
	6-1/2″		24.00	0.04
	8-5/8″		32.00	0.03
	10-3/4″		40.00	0.02
Perlite and vermiculite	Bag fills 50 sq. ft. of 1″ space		4.17	0.24
Foam glass	1″	18″ × 24″	2.86	0.35
	2″	″ ″	5.72	0.17
	4″		11.44	0.09
Insulating board	1/2″	4′-0″ × 8′-0″	1.39	0.72
	5/8″	″ ″	1.43	0.70
	3/4″	″ ″	2.02	0.50
	1″	″ ″	2.78	0.36
	1-1/2″	″ ″	4.17	0.24
	2″	″ ″	5.26	0.19
Insulating decking	1-7/8″	2′-0″ × 8′-0″	5.24	0.19
	2″	″ ″	5.55	0.18
	2-1/2″	″ ″	6.93	0.15
	3″	″ ″	8.32	0.12
	3-1/2″	″ ″	9.70	0.10
Reflective insulation	1″ air space with 2 reflective surfaces		1.39	0.72

TABLE 29-2   *R-factors for typical construction materials*

Material	R-Factor
Concrete block 4″	0.71
8″	1.11
Concrete, 8″	0.64
Face brick	0.40
1/2″ sheetrock	0.45
Plate or float glass	0.18
1/2″ plywood	0.60
Insulating glass	1.61
Asphalt shingles	0.45
Wood shingles	0.87
Vertical V-joint pine	0.94

able in thicknesses from 3-1/2 to 12 inches or thicker. One surface of the blanket or batt is usually covered by asphalt-impregnated paper, which serves also as a vapor barrier (see Figure 29-1, A). Metal foil is an excellent vapor barrier and is frequently used with blanket or batt insulation for that purpose.

LOOSE (FILL-TYPE) INSULATION: Loose insulation is usually delivered in bales or bags. It can be poured into place or packed by hand into the small spaces around window frames or chimneys. For example, this type of insulation is used to build up any thickness of insulation desired on horizontal surfaces (see Figure 29-1, B).

FIGURE 29-1   *Types of insulation*

RIGID INSULATING BOARD AND DECKING: The commonly used materials for rigid insulating board and decking are some form of wood or cane fiber compressed into soft boards; also, glass fibers are loosely compressed and enclosed in asphalt impregnated paper. Rigid insulating board and decking are available 2-and 4-ft. wide and 8-ft. long, 1/2″ to 3-1/2″ thick (and thicker). They may be smooth or rough, depending on whether they are to be left exposed or to be concealed (see Table 29-3 and Figure 29-1, C).

FOAM INSULATION: This type of material has both a high R-factor and inertness. It is also a vapor barrier and has other advantageous properties. Glass, urethane, polystyrene, cellulose, urea-formaldehyde, polyisocyanate and others, which are added as research continues, are the most widely used materials for manufacturing foam-type insulation. In general, approximately 95% of the volume of foam insulation consists of millions of tiny sealed cells. There are four kinds of foam insulation: rigid board, spray-on, site-applied, and insulated sandwich panels.

It is advisable before selecting a foam type insulation to check with the manufacturers as to its flame spread, fire resistance, resistance to exposure to earth, and whether it gives off any dangerous or toxic fumes either after installation or in case of a minor fire. Most important to check is the best method or methods of installation for its particular end use.

Rigid foam board is manufactured in thicknesses of 1/2 to 3 in. or thicker, from 16 to 48 in. in width, and from 4 to 10 ft. and longer in length. It can be used for sheathing, in cavity walls, on roofs, and for perimeter insulation. It can also serve as a base for plastering, and for adhering plywoods and plaster-board.

Spray-on insulation is applied to surfaces by guns that mix and atomize the foam as it is being applied.

TABLE 29-3   *Rigid insulating board and decking*

Type	Thickness (in.)	Width (ft.)	Length (ft.)	R-Factor
Sheathing	1/2, 5/8, 3/4, 1	4	8	2.06 to 2.78
Roof insulation	3/4, 1, 1-1/2, 2	2	4	2.14 to 5.26
Decking	1-7/8, 2, 2-1/2, 3, 3-1/2	2	8	5.24 to 9.70

Site-applied foam insulation is hand-mixed and applied with special applicators.

Insulated sandwich panels include doors, curtain wall units, and wall panels. The foaming mixture is injected between skins of aluminum, steel, plastic, wood, plywood, etc., and because the foaming mixtures used are of the type that adheres and bonds to these skins, an extremely strong and rigid material is produced.

REFLECTIVE INSULATION: This type of material consists of sheets of highly reflective metal foil with air spaces between. It differs from other types of insulation because the number of reflecting surfaces, not the thickness of the material, determines its insulating value. To be effective, the foil must be exposed to an air space, because the only heat that can penetrate is radiant heat which can be reflected. When so used, each reflecting surface is equivalent to approximately 1/2 in. of insulating board. When a reflecting metal foil is applied to a rigid material, it must be installed facing an air space, thereby adding to the total insulation (see Figure 29-1, D).

Acoustical Materials

SOUND: The science of controlling sound within buildings is called acoustics. Sound is a wave traveling in air. A dog barking across the street creates sound waves that travel through the air and to the ear. Sound is also transmitted by vibration through materials. Knocking on a pipe on one floor of a building will set up vibrations in the pipe that will travel up and down the pipe, creating sound waves in all the rooms where the pipe is located. Sound waves cause changes in the atmospheric pressure, and the decibel (dB) is the unit used to measure these sound pressures (see Table 29-4).

NOISE REDUCTION COEFFICIENT (NRC): The NRC of any acoustical material is the arithmetic average of its absorption coefficients at 250 to 2000 hertz (Hz) (see Table 29-5).

TYPES OF ACOUSTICAL MATERIALS: Selecting the acoustical material for effective sound absorption and transmission is becoming increasingly difficult, not only because of the many new building materials specifically designed to meet the demands for effective sound absorption and transmission but also because of the increasing knowledge in the science of acoustics. All building materials absorb sound and transmit it to some degree. Hard

TABLE 29-4   *Relative intensities of everyday noises and sounds*

Intensity of Noise	Decibels	Examples
Very faint	0–20	Whisper, patter of rain
Faint	20–40	Quiet conversation, private office
Moderate	40–60	General conversation; low radio, hi-fi, or television
Loud	60–80	Average factory, loud conversation, playground
Very loud	80–100	Noisy factory, angry conversation, very loud hi-fi
Deafening	100–200	Thunder, artillery fire, air hammer

TABLE 29-5   *Noise reduction coefficients (NRC) of some typical acoustical materials*

Type	Thickness	Noise Reduction Coefficient
Regularly perforated ceiling tile	1/2″ 1/4″	0.60–0.80 0.65–0.85
Textured ceiling tile	1/2″ 1/4″	0.40–0.60 0.45–0.75
Perforated metal pans with acoustical pads	1-9/16″	0.70–1.10
Perforated structural clay facing tile with acoustical pad	4″ or 8″	0.50–0.70
Acoustical concrete block with acoustical pad	4″ or 8″	0.50–0.75
Fabric drapes	1″	0.65–0.75
Non-Acoustical Materials		
Glazed brick		0.01–0.02
Plaster		0.01–0.05
Concrete, smooth		0.01–0.02
Glass		0.02–0.18

interior surfaces such as plaster and glass generally absorb less than 5% of the sound waves and reflect the balance. Effective absorption of sound is normally a characteristic of low-density materials, whereas dense materials are effective against sound transmission.

Sound-absorbing materials are relatively fragile and must be located so as to avoid abrasion and impact. This is one of the reasons for designing ceilings so that they assume a major role in the acoustical treatment of rooms. There are, basically, five broad categories of acoustical materials for sound absorption: (1) prefabricated, (2) "wet" or plastic-applied materials, (3) suspended baffles or "space" absorbers, (4) special site-assembled materials, and (5) drapes and carpet.

Prefabricated or *factory-finished materials* include most of the products listed in the Acoustical Materials Association (AMA) bulletin (see Table 29-6). Basically these are factory-finished products, ready for installation.

Wet or *plastic-applied materials* include acoustical plaster or mineral-type fiber products to which a binding agent is added at the time of application. They are applied in a wet or semi-plastic state, either by hand troweling or machine spraying. Acoustical plasters are combinations of special aggregates, gypsum plaster, and additives to create air bubbles. As a rule, acoustic plaster materials are covered by patents and trademarks.

Suspended baffles or *space absorbers* are prefabricated or specially designed sound-absorbing units such as flat baffles, cones, prisms, or crystalline shapes constructed of porous, sound-absorbing materials.

Special site-assembled acoustical materials and treatments are required when the interior architectural design is of a special kind—such as in a theater—or when the space requires special acoustical treatment—such as in a recording studio.

REVIEW EXAMINATION

1. Materials that offer high resistance to the flow of heat are called what?
2. The more severe the heat or cold, the greater the need for what?
3. Flexible insulation is usually in what forms?
4. What is the R-factor of 2-in. foam sheathing?
5. What is the insulation with an R-factor of 38.00?
6. Name three places in construction where foam type insulation is used.
7. Effective absorption of sound is normally accomplished by what type material?
8. There are basically how many broad categories of acoustical materials?
9. What type of noise is very loud?
10. What is the R-factor of 4 in. of foam glass?

ASSIGNMENT

1. Make a list of the five types of acoustical material.
2. Make sketches showing the installation of three types of insulation.

SUPPLEMENTARY INFORMATION

Insulation of Pipes and Ducts

Pipes are insulated to prevent heat loss, condensation (dripping), and freezing (see Figure 29-2). When water pipes are exposed to extreme cold, either in unheated portions of the structure or when built into exterior walls, they must be insulated to avoid freezing.

The dripping of water from pipes caused by condensation can be eliminated by insulation. Cold water pipes and pipes for the chilled liquid for air conditioning causes condensation and dripping and should be insulated in a similar manner. Heating pipes are insulated to prevent heat loss. The cover-

TABLE 29-6 *Classification of acoustical materials*

Types	Description
I	Regular perforated cellulose fiber tile
II	Random perforated cellulose fiber tile
III	Slotted cellulose fiber tile
IV	Textured, finely perforated, fissured, or simulated fissured cellulose tile
V	Membrane-faced cellulose fiber tile
VI	Cellulose fiber lay-in panels
VII	Perforated mineral fiber tile
VIII	Fissured mineral fiber tile
IX	Textured, finely perforated or smooth mineral fiber tile
X	Membrane-faced mineral fiber tile
XI	Mineral fiber lay-in panels
XII	Perforated metal pans with mineral fiber pads
XIII	Perforated metal lay-in panels with mineral fiber pads
XIV	Mineral fiber tile rated as part of fire-resistant assemblies
XV	Perforated asbestos board panels with mineral fiber pads
XVI	Sound-absorbent duct lining

FIGURE 29-2   *Insulation of pipes*

ing is made from cellular material in the form of a tube, split in half to allow for its installation. Rope-like insulations designed to be wrapped around the pipe are equally satisfactory. Coverings for ducts are in sheet or board form, solid or cellular.

Acoustical Treatments

The acoustical treatments for insulating against sound transmission through vibration are based on the use of dense materials such as lead and concrete or by means of isolation and vibration control. Solid concrete block 8-in. thick is a better insulator against sound transmission than 8-in. thick cellular concrete block because it is a denser material.

Commercial Insulating Materials

Commercial insulating materials are of two major categories: (1) those manufactured of fibrous, granular and foam materials, and (2) reflective metal foils separated by air spaces. The first category can be summarized as follows:

I. Materials used for insulation

   A. Fibrous

      1. Mineral wool
        (a) rock wool
        (b) glass wool
        (c) slag wool
        (d) mica

      2. Vegetable fiber

   B. Granular

      1. Mineral (vermiculite, perlite)

      2. Vegetable (granulated cork)

   C. Foam

   D. Reflective coatings applied to paper or other surfaces

The second category is also described in Chapter 30 (see Metal Reflective Insulation).

30

INSTALLATION OF INSULATION AND ACOUSTICAL MATERIALS

INTRODUCTION

This chapter deals with the application and installation of insulation and acoustical materials. There are many important conditions which must be considered for insulation (required R-factors, vapor barriers and condensation), and for acoustical materials (sound absorption, sound transmission, vibration, and location of the material).

TECHNICAL INFORMATION

Heat Loss and Insulation

Heat is lost or gained in buildings in three ways: conduction, convection, and radiation. An example of this is the sun striking a solid brick wall on the south side of a building. The rays of the sun heat up the outside brick surface and this heat is transferred through the brick wall by conduction. Once the inside face of the brick wall becomes warm, it heats the air next to it by convection; and finally, as the wall gets warmer and warmer, it radiates heat into the interior room space, similar in its action to the radiant heat of the sun.

Insulation is used to resist the heat loss or gain in structures. Insulating an attic space presents such a problem. In ceilings with un-insulated attic space, the ceiling beams are generally 8- or 10-in.

deep and therefore 6 or 9 in. of flexible insulation can be installed with R-factors of 19.00 and 30.00, respectively.

EXAMPLE: An attic space used for living space where flexible insulation is to be installed in the spaces between the roof rafters. Figure 30-1 shows how to obtain an R-factor larger than 28.00 for the attic living space.

Installation of Insulation

Flexible insulation in rolls or in batts is generally installed between vertical studs in exterior walls, and between roof, floor, and ceiling rafters and beams. The various thicknesses that are available all have different R-factors. In a 4-in. wood or metal stud exterior wall, only 3-1/2 in. of flexible insulation can be installed. This gives only 11.00 R; therefore, more insulation may be needed to meet governing R-factor requirements.

Rigid insulation made from some sort of wood, cane, or reprocessed paper is used as an insulating material where small R-factors are required. Foam-type rigid insulation is generally used where large R-factors are necessary.

Rigid fiber decking, because of its ability to span up to 4 ft., its finished surface on one side, and its R-factors up to 9.70, is used extensively in construction in areas where roof beams are exposed and where the temperature does not fall below 40°F.

FIGURE 30-1   *Insulation of a livable attic room*

FIGURE 30-2   *Applications of foam board insulation*

Rigid foam board insulation is installed as combination sheathing and insulating material to which interior finish or to-be-finished materials can be applied with adhesives, and as perimeter and cavity-wall insulation (see Figure 30-2).

Foam insulation is also extensively used for pipes, tanks, and ducts and for prefabricated air-conditioning ducts (see Figure 30-3).

Spray-on foam insulation can be applied with guns and installed between studs, rafters, beams, etc., where it can penetrate inaccessible areas. Foam insulation also can be injected into other-

FIGURE 30-3   *Applications of foam insulation*

wise inaccessible areas such as spaces between walls, windows, and door frames, cavity walls, open areas in curtain wall construction, and the cells in concrete block, etc.

EXAMPLES: Figure 30-4 gives details of various methods of insulating exterior walls made of different materials.

Metal Reflective Insulation

This type of material is used as a part of or attached onto another material, and is used both as a vapor barrier and as reflective insulation. In large deep-freeze installations, reflective insulation used for walls and ceiling may have as many as eight highly reflective metal surfaces and seven air spaces.

Vapor Barriers

The formation of frost on the inside faces of windows in cold weather is an example of water vapor in a room condensing on the glass because of a temperature change. This can generally be eliminated by using storm sash, which actually is another means of insulation because of the introduced air space. Water vapor can pass through most building materials, and in cold weather it may con-

FIGURE 30-4   *Examples of exterior walls using various types of insulation showing their R-factors*

dense within the wall structure. Such condensation may, in time, lessen the value of the insulation and also may cause paint and building materials to deteriorate. A vapor barrier, a membrane through which water vapor cannot pass, is essential to prevent moisture from reaching the insulation and causing condensation.

Metal foils make excellent vapor barriers, as do asphalt-treated felts, treated laminated papers, and polyethylene film of 0.002 or 0.004-in. thickness.

The vapor barrier should always be located on the warm side of the wall, depending on geographic location. In southern Florida the exterior of the walls is generally warm, whereas in North Dakota the room or the inside of the walls is generally the warm side. Elimination of the possibility of condensation (formation of water) that can cause damage is the reason for using vapor barriers.

Acoustical Materials

Sound-absorbing materials are relatively fragile except for drapes and carpets, which have a comparatively short life span before they must be replaced. There are, basically, five broad categories of acoustical materials for sound absorption; (1) prefabricated, (2) spray-on or trowel-on mate-

rials, (3) suspended baffles or "space" absorbers, (4) special site-assembled materials, and (5) drapes and carpet.

PREFABRICATED SOUND-ABSORBING MATERIALS: These are factory-finished materials ready for installation. Figure 30-5 illustrates some of these acoustical materials and the methods by which they can be mounted onto a ceiling. The acoustic tile or panel can be applied to a ceiling by means of adhesives, or nailed to wood furring strips.

Suspended acoustical ceilings are installed by providing various systems of grids, consisting of supporting channels or angles to which are attached various types of Ts, Zs, splines, etc., for supporting the tiles or panels (see Figure 30-6).

Figure 30-7 shows the installation details of perforated sound-absorbing materials.

SPRAY-ON OR TROWEL-ON ACOUSTICAL MATE-RIALS: These are very fragile, since they consist of filler and a binder with additives to create minute air bubbles so that the surface becomes a sound absorbing material. This type of acoustical treatment is generally applied only to ceilings.

Special site-assembled acoustical materials and *treatments* are shown in Figure 30-8.

FIGURE 30-5 *Acoustical materials and types of mountings*

CONCEALED "Z" TYPE SUSPENSION SYSTEM

"H" & "T" SUSPENSION SYSTEM

FIGURE 30-6 *Suspension systems for acoustical units*

FIGURE 30-7 *Perforated sound absorbing materials*

REVIEW EXAMINATION

1. What material provides an effective moisture barrier?

2. What is one method of applying acoustical tile to a concrete or gypsum board ceiling?

3. What type of structural facing tile is acoustical?

4. Do air-conditioning ducts require acoustical treatment?

5. Does a crawl space in a building need insulation?

6. Name two methods of installing machines that vibrate.

7. Name a method by which a partition wall may be sound-insulated.

8. What masonry materials have acoustical characteristics?

9. What type of insulation material is used in cavity walls?

10. Do pipes in exterior walls have to be insulated?

ASSIGNMENT

1. Make sketches showing three methods of fastening acoustic tile to a ceiling.

2. Illustrate by sketch two types of special site-assembled acoustical treatments.

SUPPLEMENTARY INFORMATION

Drapes and Carpets

Drapes are installed as sound-absorbing materials over large glass areas or in front of highly sound reflective wall surfaces. Carpet, a natural sound-absorbing material, is installed on floors and

FIGURE 30-8   *Architectural materials used for sound absorbing treatments*

walls for acoustical treatment; it has even been used on ceilings for the same purpose.

Insulating and Soundproofing of Ducts

Heating, air-conditioning, and ventilating ducts can transmit sound from one area to another and therefore must be soundproofed. This can be accomplished by installing a sound-absorbing material on the inside of the duct. Also, by the choice of the material, the duct can be insulated and soundproofed at the same time (see Figure 30-9).

FIGURE 30-9   *Insulating and sound-proofing ducts*

Masonry Acoustical Units

Various acoustical masonry units are available in which the surface has been textured and given a porous type of finish so it becomes a sound-absorbing material. Others use perforations or slots backed with sound-absorbing pads, or just various types of slots (see Figure 30-10).

FIGURE 30-10   *Acoustical masonry units*

31

ROOFING AND SIDING

INTRODUCTION

Roofing and siding are exposed to the damaging rays of the sun, rain, snow, sleet, ice, and wind. In order to make them weatherproof and waterproof, all of the natural elements have to be taken into consideration when roofing or siding material is selected and installed. This chapter deals with the various types of roofing and siding material, including wood, asbestos-cement, metal, asphalt, glass, built-up roofing, and plastic, as well as with the methods of installing these materials on buildings.

TECHNICAL INFORMATION

The climate where the building will be constructed must be carefully considered in selecting the type of roofing and siding materials to be used. For example, Miami has no snow, sleet, or ice and a short rainy season, but it also has long periods of hot clear days with very intense sunlight and a hurricane season with winds up to over 90 mph. Las Vegas has no snow, sleet, ice, or rain and winds up to only 40 mph, but it has almost continuous days of intense sunlight. Portland, Maine has rain, sleet, large quantities of snow and ice, winds as high as 60 mph, and only a month of intense bright sunlight.

Roofing

Roofing may be defined as the method or materials used to make a roof weathertight and waterproof. All types of roofing materials are figured by the *square*, which is 100 sq. ft. (see Figure 31-1).

ROOF PITCH: Roofs upon which roofing materials are applied can be divided into two main categories:

TABLE 31-1   *Types of materials used for roofs with pitches over 3 to 12*

Type of Material	Type of Roofing
Aluminum	Shingles; plain and corrugated sheet
Asbestos-cement	Shingles; plain and corrugated sheet
Asphalt	Shingles and strip shingles
Clay tile	Shingles
Copper, lead, stainless steel, terne plate, zinc	Sheet
Corrugated wired glass	Corrugated
Galvanized steel	Corrugated and plain sheet
Roll roofing	Rolls
Slate	Shingles
Steel	Baked enamel coated shingles
Wood	Shingles

(1) roofs with pitches of 3 to 12 and greater; and (2) roofs with pitches less than 3 to 12 ranging down to flat (see Figure 31-2). The materials used for the two categories are shown in Tables 31-1 and 31-2.

Roofs with pitches of 3 to 12 and greater quickly drain off the water from rain, snow, and sleet; therefore they do not have to be completely waterproof. In like manner, the steeper the pitch the less chance there is for high winds to lift off the materials except under extreme conditions, such as during hurricanes. In climates where there will be heavy snowfall it is advisable to use pitches of 6 to 12 and greater so that the snow will immediately slide off and not collect on the roof in large quantities and then, in a thaw slide off and create a hazard for people below. For roofs in this category, only the intense sunlight and the wind must be carefully considered.

TABLE 31-2   *Types of materials used for roofs with pitches less than 3 to 12 to flat*

Type of Material	Type of Roofing
Asphalt or tar	Built-up, 10- to 20-year guarantees
Canvas	Rolls
Copper, lead, stainless steel, and ternplate	Rolls
Plastic	Rolls, liquid, foam, and paint
Roll roofing	Rolls

TABLE 31-3   *Exposure of wood shingles for various roof pitches*

Type of Shingle	Length	Exposure for 5 to 12 Pitch and Greater	Exposure for 3 to 12 to 4 to 12 Pitches
Dimension and random	16″	5″	3-3/4″
	18″	5-1/2″	4-1/4″
	24″	7-1/2″	5-3/4″
Hand split	25″ to 27″	7-1/2″ to 8″	Cannot be installed

Shingles

Shingles are manufactured as single units or in units simulating single shingles from 3′-0″ up to 6′-0″ in length. These various types are manufactured of wood, slate, clay tile, asbestos-cement, asphalt, aluminum, and special coated steel.

Wood shingles are single shingles and are manufactured in three types: dimension, random, and hand split (see Figure 31-3). They are installed either on solid sheathing or on wood strips (see Figure 31-4). The exposure varies with the roof pitch (see Table 31-3).

Slate may be laid on wood strips spaced the same as slate exposure or on solid sheathing with 15-lb. felt first applied. Slate colors are blue-gray, black, gray, purple, green, and red (see Figure 31-5).

Clay tile roofing (shingle) can only be used on roofs with pitches 4-1/2 to 12 and greater. Clay tile shingles are made from the same clay as used for bricks and manufactured by the soft-mud and dry-press methods. They are generally a red color but can be ordered with colored glazes in a wide variety of colors (see Figure 31-6). Clay tile roofing is manufactured in various types, such as Spanish, Mission, French, English, Norman, and Scandia.

Asbestos-cement shingles are made from portland cement and asbestos fibers, which act as reinforcing. They are available either plain or striated or with a wood textured surface, and in a variety of colors. Roof pitches 3 to 12 and greater are required (see Figure 31-7). There are two other types of asbestos-cement shingles—Dutch lap and hexagonal, which give a different design to the roofing.

PITCHED ROOF

FLAT ROOF

15 × 40 × 2 = 1200 SQ. FT.

$$\frac{1200 \text{ SQ. FT.}}{100 \text{ SQ. FT.}} = 12 \text{ SQUARES}$$

50′ × 80′ = 4000 SQ. FT.

$$\frac{4000 \text{ SQ. FT.}}{100 \text{ SQ. FT.}} = 40 \text{ SQUARES}$$

FIGURE 31-1   *Roofing material units*

→ ALL TYPES OF SHINGLES, CORRUGATED SHEETS AND METALS

→ ASPHALT STRIP SHINGLES AND METALS
→ ROLL ROOFING
→ ALL ASPHALT, TAR OR PLASTIC TYPE ROOFING AND METALS THAT CAN BE SOLDERED OR WELDED

FIGURE 31-2   *Diagram showing the general types of roofing materials used for various roof patches*

FIGURE 31-3 *Types of wood shingles*

FIGURE 31-4 *The two methods of installing wood shingles*

$$EXPOSURE = \frac{LENGTH - HEAD\ LAP}{2}$$

FIGURE 31-5 *Size, shape, and installation of slate shingles*

FIGURE 31-6 *Size, shape, and installation of clay tile roofing (shingles)*

FIGURE 31-7 *Size, shape, and installation of asbestos cement shingles*

Slate, clay tile, and asbestos-cement shingles are very heavy materials and therefore the supporting structure should be designed to receive this extra load. Asbestos-cement shingles vary in weight from 265 to 585 lbs. per 100 sq. ft. (square), slate weighs 700 to 810 lbs. per 100 sq. ft., and clay tile weighs 900 lbs. per 100 sq. ft.

Asphalt individual and *strip shingles* are manufactured in various colors and in weights ranging from 210 lbs. to 345 lbs. per square (100 sq. ft.), and also in various degrees of fire resistance. They are installed on roofs with pitches of 3 to 12 and greater, and they must be installed on solid sheathing. In order to overcome high winds they can be obtained with special tabs of adhesive near the butt end (see Figure 31-8). Single asphalt shingles are manufactured in hexagonal types and also in a Dutch-lap type.

Aluminum and *steel shingles* are both available with various colored baked enamel, vinyl, or special organic coatings. These shingles are similar to clay tile shingles in form and shape.

Roll Roofing

Asphalt roll roofing is manufactured in rolls 36 in. wide and in lengths of 36'-0" to 48'-0". The exposure surface is a colored mineral surface and the remaining surface is plain. This roofing is used for roof pitches from 1 to 12 to 4 to 12 (see Figure 31-9).

Corrugated Roofing

Corrugated asbestos-cement, wire glass, plastic, and metal are used for roofs with pitches of 3 to 12 and greater. They are joined at the sides by lapping the corrugations (except wire glass) and are generally end-lapped 6 in. They all require predrilling for holes (except the plastic type), and all methods of attaching should allow slight movement; therefore, they are never tightly attached (see Figure 31-10).

SINGLE ASPHALT SHINGLE

3 TAB AND 2 TAB HEXAGONAL ASPHALT STRIP SHINGLES

FIGURE 31-8   *Size, shape, and installation of asphalt shingles*

FIGURE 31-9   *Size, shape, and installation of roll roofing*

FIGURE 31-10 *Corrugated roofing materials*

Corrugated steel, aluminum, glass, asbestos-cement, and plastic are manufactured in various shapes of corrugations and thicknesses of the materials.

Metal Roofing

The metals, copper, lead, stainless steel, aluminum, and ternplate are used for roofs with pitches of 3 to 12 and greater. The methods of installation are similar, and attachments, screws, and nails must be of a type compatible with the metal used for roofing. For example, copper nails are to be used with copper roofing and aluminum nails with aluminum roofing (see Figure 31-11). Roofs with pitches ranging from 3 to 12 to flat require that wind, waterproofing, drainage, snow, sleet, ice, and intense sunlight must be carefully considered.

The metals that can be easily soldered or welded are used for roofs that are flat and up to 2 to 12 pitches. The metals used are copper, lead, zinc, terneplate, and stainless steel (see Figure 31-12).

When using any metal for roofing, care should be taken that all the materials in contact with the metal or used for installing the metal will not set up a galvanic action that will corrode or disintegrate the metal roofing or the materials in contact with metal or the nails, screws, clips, etc. used in installing the metal—for example, aluminum roofing with stainless steel gutter (see Figure 31-13).

Built-Up Roofing

Asphalt and *tar built-up roofing* consists of alternate layers of either asphalt- or tar-saturated felts (paper) and hot or cold asphalt or hot tar (known as pitch). Each layer of felt and asphalt or tar is called a ply. This type of roofing is designated as 3-ply, 5-ply, etc. The first layer is not considered a ply because it consists of one or two layers of unsaturated felt, nailed down to the substrate. This layer is of utmost importance because it is the method of bonding (holding down) the built-up roofing to the substrate. Generally a 4-ply built-up roof consists of one ply of unsaturated

STANDING SEAM
(USED FOR VERTICAL SEAMS, RIDGES AND GABLE ENDS)

CLEATS 12" O.C.

BATTEN SEAM
(USED FOR VERTICAL SEAMS, RIDGES AND GABLE ENDS)

CLEATS 12" O.C.

SINGLE LOCK SEAM
(USED FOR HORIZONTAL CROSS SEAMS)

DOUBLE LOCK SEAM
(USED FOR HORIZONTAL CROSS SEAMS)

CROSS SEAM
(USED FOR STEEP PITCHES)

NAIL

CROSS SEAM
(USED FOR LOW PITCHES)

CONTINUOUS CLEAT SOLDERED IN PLACE

NAIL

EXPANSION JOINT

ALLOWANCE FOR EXPANSION

SINGLE LOCK AND DOUBLE LOCK SEAMS
(USED WITH CLEATS FOR ROOFS WITH 6 TO 12 PITCH OR GREATER)

CLEATS 18" O.C.

CLEATS 18 O.C.

FIGURE 31-11 *Seams and locks for metal roofing*

CONTINUOUS SOLDERED JOINT

CLEATS 2'-0" O.C.

SOLDERED SINGLE LOCK SEAM

CLEAT WELDED TO ONE SHEET

CONTINUOUS WELD

CLEATS 2'-0" O.C.

CLEAT WELDED TO ONE SHEET THEN BOTH SHEETS WELDED WITH CONTINUOUS WELD AND THEN BENT OVER

FIGURE 31-12 *Methods of joining metal roofing on flat or roofs with pitches up to 2 to 12*

ALUMINUM ROOFING

ALUMINUM CLIPS

STAINLESS STEEL GUTTER

S.S. NAIL

S.S. TUBE

WHERE ALUMINUM AND STAINLESS STEEL COME INTO CONTACT THEY MUST BE ISOLATED EITHER BY HEAVY COATINGS OF ASPHALT PAINT OR PLASTIC WASHERS

FIGURE 31-13 *Detail of stainless steel gutter and aluminum roofing*

311

felt and four plies of saturated felt and pitch. To protect the plies from intense sunlight, a finish surface of slag or stone chips is applied. Built-up roofing is applied to roofs that are flat and with pitches up to 2 to 12 (see Figure 31-14).

Canvas has been used successfully for residential roof terraces and decks for many years. The solid sheathing is given a heavy coat of white lead and the canvas is applied in strips lapped 2 in. at joints and secured with copper tacks at lapped edges. When installed, two coats of exterior oil base paint are applied.

Plastic types of roofing were first developed to meet the new roof forms designed with reinforced concrete, such as thin shell domes. These new roof shapes were not adaptable to the then-existing types of roofing materials.

Plastic roofing materials are manufactured as single-ply, single-ply combined with foam-type insulation, spray-on, roll-on, trowel-on, brush- or mop-on, and float-on. In all cases the type of substrate must be checked so that the type of plastic roofing to be installed will permanently bond (adhere) to the substrate. In general, a substrate that has a high moisture content or high absorption rate requires special treatment when a plastic type roofing is to be applied (see Figure 31-15).

These roofing materials have led to the development of a completely new set of flashing and expansion joint details (see Figure 31-16). In general, most plastic-type roofing materials are neoprene, silicone, synthetic rubbers, urethane, and adhesives based on the same material as the roofing.

They are manufactured in various sunfast colors, and all the various flashing and expansion joint materials and devices are available.

Siding

Many roofing materials are also used for siding, among them wood, slate, asbestos-cement, and asphalt shingles. Types of siding materials include those which are applied over a sheathing, prefabricated panels including exterior facing, insulation, and interior finish (see Table 31-4).

TABLE 31-4   *Siding materials*

Material	Available Forms of Siding	
Aluminum	Shingles	Siding, corrugated siding and prefabricated panels
Asbestos-cement	Shingles	Siding, corrugated siding, panels, prefabricated panels
Asphalt	Shingles and strip shingles	Various textured siding materials
Plastic		Siding, panels, and prefabricated panels
Slate	Shingles	
Steel	Shingles	Siding, (with protective colored coating), corrugated siding, panels, and prefabricated panels
Wood	Shingles	Siding boards and various finished plywood panels
Zinc		Corrugated siding

FIRST PLY ONE OR TWO LAYERS OF UNSATURATED FELT

THREE PLY 20 YEAR BOND BUILT-UP ROOFING

FIGURE 31-14   *Built-up roofing*

FIGURE 31-15   *Installation of various types of plastic roofing*

FIGURE 31-16   *Flashing and expansion joints used with plastic types roofing*

ALUMINUM SIDING: Aluminum siding is manufactured in various types: horizontal (wide and narrow design) and vertical (V-joint or board-and-batten design). It is available 0.025 in. thick, in a wide variety of colors, either baked on or a synthetic type paint finish (see Figure 31-17).

Aluminum industrial siding is manufactured in sheets from 3′-0″ to 30′-0″ in lengths, in widths of 3′-5-5/8″, 1′-7-1/2″, and others depending on manufacturer. These types of siding are available as prefabricated panels with insulation and interior finish (see Figure 31-18).

ASBESTOS-CEMENT SIDING: Asbestos-cement panels are manufactured in sheets 1/8 and 3/16-in. thick, 4′-0″ wide, and 4′-0″, 8′-0″, 10′-0″, and 12′-0″ long, in various colors. They must be predrilled for nailing (see Figure 31-19).

Asbestos-cement siding in large single strips 12″ × 4′-0″ long are predrilled and installed the

FIGURE 31-17   *Aluminum siding*

FIGURE 31-18   *Industrial aluminum siding shapes, sizes, and methods of attaching onto materials of buildings*

FIGURE 31-19   *Installing asbestos cement sheets as siding material*

same as shingles. They are manufactured in a wide range of colors.

Asbestos-cement sandwich panels consisting of an insulation-type board with two sheets of 1/8-in. asbestos-cement panels bonded to both sides are used for checking, curtain walls, and exterior walls for residences.

STEEL SIDING: This is manufactured in many shapes similar to aluminum, with various types of protective surface finishes. These panels can be single sheet or a combination of sheet and backing insulation, or a complete prefabricated panel with exterior and interior finish having an insulating material sandwiched between.

WOOD SIDING: Wood is manufactured in horizontal siding in various shapes and in boards for vertical siding (see Figure 31-20).

REVIEW EXAMINATION

1. Roofs with pitches from 3 to 12 and greater are required to be what?

2. Roofs with pitches from 3 to 12 to flat are required to be what?

3. The climate of the area where a building is to be constructed should be checked for what six things before selecting roofing material?

4. What are the two categories of roofs upon which roofing materials are applied?

5. What are the three types of wood shingles?

6. When installing slate, clay tile, or asbestos-cement shingles on a roof, what should first be considered regarding the supporting structure?

7. What should asphalt strip shingles have to overcome high winds?

8. Asphalt roll roofing can be installed on roofs with what degree of pitch?

9. Corrugated type roofing materials other than glass are joined at their sides by what?

10. Metals, when used for roofing on roofs with pitches 3 to 12 and greater are joined at vertical seams, ridges and gable ends with what?

11. Metals, when used for roofing on roofs with pitches of 3 to 12 and greater are joined at horizontal or cross seams with what?

12. Built-up roofing consists of layers called what?

13. Plastic-type roofing materials are installed by what three methods?

14. When using metals for roofing materials, why should care be taken with materials in contact with the metal or used for installing the metal?

15. What qualifications must metals used for roofs that are flat and up to 2 to 12 pitches have?

16. Name the roofing shingles that are also used as siding.

17. Is metal siding, either aluminum or steel, manufactured as complete prefabricated panels with inside and outside finishes and insulation?

BEVELED   NOVELTY   SHIPLAP

HORIZONTAL SIDING

SHIPLAP

"V" JOINT

BOARD & BATTEN

VERTICAL SIDING

VERTICAL BOARD AND BATTEN

PLYWOOD SIMULATING VERTICAL SIDING

VERTICAL JOINT OF PLYWOOD WITH A BATTEN

SHIPLAP   LAPPING   METAL Z

HORIZONTAL PLYWOOD JOINTS

FIGURE 31-20   *Types of wood siding*

ASSIGNMENT

1. Draw a freehand diagram of roof pitches ranging from 0 to 12 to 8 to 12 and list the various types of roofing material used for various roof pitches.

2. Draw freehand, to scale, the flashing and expansion joint details for plastic-type roofing materials.

SUPPLEMENTARY INFORMATION

Substrate

This is the term to describe the material upon which roofing materials are to be applied.

Wood Shingle Designations

There has been established by shingle manufacturers a system to designate the thickness of wood shingles (see Figure 31-21).

Slag

A nonmetallic waste product obtained from the smelting of ferrous metals, slag is the remaining material from the metal ores after the metal has been extracted. In granular form it is used as topping for built-up roofing, in powdered form it is used in masonry cements, and in the manufacture of portland blast-furnace slag cements.

Copper Roofing

When copper is used as a roofing material, care should be taken that any water running or dripping from it will not come in direct contact with other materials, because copper, when exposed to the weather, will develop a bright green protective coating that can run and stain other materials.

TCS Roofing

Terne-coated stainless steel is a nickel-chrome stainless steel covered on both sides with terne alloy (80% lead, 20% tin). It does not need maintenance if properly installed and has proven itself for decades; it will outlast virtually any building on which it is applied.

The terne coating on TCS is anodic to stainless steel, which means that the terne will sacrifice itself to protect the core metal. It is therefore recommended for use in severe industrial and chemical environments.

THE BUTT OF FOUR (4) SHINGLES = 2" DESIGNATION 4/2

THE BUTT OF ONE (1) SHINGLE = ½" DESIGNATION 1/½

FIGURE 31-21   *Thickness designations of wood shingles*

32

WINDOWS AND DOORS

INTRODUCTION

This chapter deals with the various types of wood and metal windows such as double-hung, projected, casement, awning, and others. Details of installation, architectural symbols, glazing, and the various finishes available for wood or metal windows are discussed. This unit also deals with the various types and kinds of doors, their installation, hardware, architectural symbols, and operation identifications.

TECHNICAL INFORMATION

Windows

Windows originally were used for admitting daylight and later for ventilation. Perhaps the first ventilating window was the casement type because it required the simplest type of hardware—only pivots, a simple latch, and a bar of metal to hold it open. Today we have a great variety of window types and with the increasing use of air-conditioning, the provision for ventilation is becoming almost unnecessary, and the window is returning to what it originally was—a means of admitting daylight.

Generally all wood or metal stock windows are standardized as to sizes and are manufactured as complete units that include hardware, weatherstripping, operating mechanism, etc., come glazed or unglazed, and are ready to be installed in a building. They are manufactured to receive window glass, 1/4-in. thick plate or float glass, 1/4 in. special glass, or insulating glass. They also may be obtained with screens and storm sash.

Windows are manufactured in four categories based on their use in building construction: residential, commercial, industrial, and monumental. All types have established standards that have been developed by window manufacturers' associations and institutes, U.S. Department of Commerce, American Standards Association, and other city, state, and federal agencies.

In architectural elevation drawings (see Figure 32-1), standard symbols are used to show the various types of ventilation (window swings).

Test data are available for all types of wood or metal windows—included are horizontal and vertical loads, air infiltration and wind, torsion tests for projected and awning types, and water resistance. When a window type and grade have been selected to meet the design requirements in a building, obtaining test data and details from various manufacturers of this type and grade of window enable the selection of the correct type, grade, and manufacturer.

All types of windows, when assembled and ready to be delivered to a building under construction or to warehouses and distributors, receive a factory-finishing treatment. This treatment may be either protective, preservative, permanent finish, or a base for painting, staining, or other type of finish (see Table 32-1).

WOOD WINDOWS: Standards governing the production of wood windows have been established for double-hung, casement, sliding, and awning windows. These standards cover materials, sizes, frame, sash, check rails, hardware, operating mechanisms, weatherstripping, and screens and storm sash. The standards require that all wood parts receive preservative treatment against fungi, insects, and water.

Other types of wood windows include picture (fixed), bay or bow window, modular units, cellar windows, and various other types and operating systems.

TABLE 32-1   *Factory finishes and permanent finishes for windows*

Type of Window	Factory Finish	Permanent Finish Job- or Factory-Applied
Wood	Preservative against fungi, insects, and water	Paint, stain, vinyl, or aluminum
Steel	Shop prime coat or corrosion-resistant prime coat	Paint, baked enamel, vinyl
Aluminum	Protective coating	Smooth to high polish, colored anodized finishes, and baked enamel
Stainless steel	Protective coating	Colored, smooth to high-polish finishes

FIGURE 32-1 *Window types and standard architectural symbols to show types of ventilation operation*

Most wood windows are manufactured as complete units ready to be installed, but are also available as separate sash and frames. They may be obtained with screens, storm sash, single glaze, double glaze or with insulating glass.

Ponderosa pine, kiln-dried to a moisture content of 6 to 12% is the wood generally used in the manufacture of wood windows. Of all wood window types, the double-hung window is the most widely used. The details in Figure 32-2 show an elevation of a double-hung wood window indicating that details were taken at the head section (A), the meeting rail (B), the sill section (C), the muntin

(D), and the jamb section (E). Although the sash for most residential windows is 1-3/8 in. thick, commercial and institutional sash are 1-3/4 in. thick. Insulating glass 1/2-in. thick can be used with 1-3/4-in. sash; however, 2-1/4-in. sash is recommended for 3/4 and 1-in. insulating glass because these thicknesses are too heavy for 1-3/4-in. sash.

Glazing for wood windows should be done with a wood glazing-type compound, knife consistency, or extruded plastic-type gaskets. All glass should be bedded with the same material if a glazing compound is used (see Figure 32-3). All

319

HEAD
(A)

2⅜ 1⅛ ¾ 1¾ ⅜ 1¾ 1¾

(B)

1"

3½"

SILL
(C)

TYPICAL HEAD & SILL
SECTION OF DOUBLE HUNG
WOOD WINDOW

(A)
(D)
(B)
(E)
(C)

ELEVATION OF DOUBLE
HUNG WOOD WINDOW

DOUBLE INSULATING
GLASS - MUNTIN

MUNTIN
(D)

SPRING
BALANCE

CAULKING

JAMB SECTION
(E)

FIGURE 32-2   *Window details*

NAIL

BED APPLIED
TO RABBET
BEFORE GL.
IS SET

INTERIOR

STOP BEAD

GLAZING POINT
FACE PUTTY

INTERIOR

GLAZING COMPOUND

ZIPPER GASKET

INTERIOR

GASKET TYPE

FIGURE 32-3   *Glazing details in 1-3/8″ sash*

320

exterior nails that cannot be set should be aluminum or stainless steel, and all other exterior nails that can be set and puttied should be hot-dipped, galvanized steel or aluminum.

STEEL WINDOWS: All types of steel windows are manufactured as a complete unit including hardware, weatherstripping, and operating mechanism, but they are always site-glazed.

Standards have been established regarding sizes, material, weatherstripping, hardware, glazing, and operating mechanism for residential, commercial, industrial, and monumental windows. These standards are based upon use. For example, the windows used for an industrial building do not have to meet the rigid requirements that are established for a hospital or a library.

Figure 32-4 shows the installation of a steel window in a typical commercial building. Note the anchor fasteners used at head, jamb, and sill.

Because all steel windows are to be site-glazed, the correct method of glazing should be selected. Steel windows are manufactured with interior or exterior glazing with or without stop beads (see Figure 32-5).

ALUMINUM WINDOWS: Aluminum extrusions are used to manufacture all the various types and grades of aluminum windows. The alloys most

generally used are 6063-T5 and 6063-T6. These alloys have tensile strength in excess of 22,000 psi, which is the minimum set by the Architectural Aluminum Manufacturer's Association (AAMA). A minimum of 0.062 in. has been established for material or section thickness. Joints are either welded or fastened by mechanical means. All hardware, operating mechanism, weatherstripping, fasteners, anchors, etc., must be of a metal that is compatible or isolated from aluminum so that no galvanic action can occur. Aluminum-to-aluminum contact, where parts move against one another, is not permitted.

Extrusions allow for various small grooves, projections, etc. to be formed, which make possible a snap-on type of glazing stop bead (see Figure 32-6).

Details of an aluminum double-hung window installed in a typical commercial building are shown in Figure 32-7.

STAINLESS STEEL WINDOWS: A limited number of manufacturers produce types and grades of stainless steel windows. Stainless steel is available in various finishes ranging from highly polished to a dull sand-textured finish. It is highly corrosion-resistant and exceptionally strong in thin gauges. Stainless steel sheets in gauge Nos. 16, 18, 20, and 22 of alloy types 202, 302, and 430 are generally

FIGURE 32-4 *Installation of steel window in a typical commercial building*

FIGURE 32-5 *Glazing for steel windows*

CAULKING COMPOUND
OR EXTRUDED PLASTIC
MATERIAL OR GASKET — SNAP ON GLAZING BEAD

SINGLE GLAZING — INSULATING GLASS

WEATHERSTRIPPING GROOVE

SNAP ON GLAZING BEAD

FIGURE 32-6 *Snap-in glazing beads*

FOAM INSULATION

HEAD

SILL

FOAM INSULATION

JAMB — MULLION

FIGURE 32-7 *Detail of an aluminum double hung window*

used. Figure 32-8 shows a jamb section of an awning type window.

As with other metals, all hardware, operating devices, fasteners, anchors, etc. should be of a metal compatible with stainless steel so that no galvanic action can occur.

STORM WINDOWS: Storm windows are available as a complete unit consisting of window frame, movable sash, single glazed or double glazed, and including screen and complete weatherstripping. In general, they are double-hung of aluminum, steel, and stainless steel.

Doors

Doors are primarily used for exterior entrances and exits from a building and to close off or subdivide areas within a building. The materials most generally used in the manufacturing of doors are wood, steel, aluminum, stainless steel, glass, fabrics, and plastic. Doors can be identified by their method of opening, such as swinging, folding, sliding, bypassing, overhead, revolving, and rolling (see Figure 32-9).

The most widely used doors are the swing type. To establish a uniform method of denoting the swing and establishing a set of standards, the hardware manufacturers set specific names that are used when facing swinging doors (see Figure 32-10).

In general, doors are site-installed (although several types are available as a complete preassembled unit including frame, door, and hardware) and therefore it is necessary to select the type of finish hardware to be used such as butts (hinges), pulls, push plates, knobs, latches, locks, closers, etc. The various locations and dimensions for finish hardware have been standardized, as shown in Figure 32-11.

FIGURE 32-8 *Jamb of stainless steel awning type window*

WINDOW SILL

EXTERIOR

INTERIOR

WINDOW STOOL

SINGLE SWING   DOUBLE SWING   PAIR OF SWINGING DOORS

OPEN   CENTER PIVOT   FOLD UP

CLOSED   SIDE HINGED   SWING UP

BY PASSING   CENTER PIVOT   ROLL UP
VERTICALLY   FABRIC

BY PASSING   FOLDING   OVERHEAD

REVOLVING

CONCEALED POCKET

EXPOSED POCKET
SLIDING

SIDE ROLLING

FIGURE 32-9 *Types of doors identified by their opening action*

RIGHT HAND   LEFT HAND   DOUBLE ACTING   PAIR   RIGHT HAND   LEFT HAND
                                                    REVERSE BEVEL REVERSE BEVEL

FIGURE 32-10 *Specific names used when facing swing type doors*

Building codes require certain doors to be fire-resistant. Doors are available in various ratings such as 1/2-hr., 1-hr., etc., to meet these fire-rating requirements.

WOOD DOORS: Wood doors are manufactured for both interior and exterior use. They are available in the following standard dimensions: 1-3/8 and 1-3/4-in. thickness, 6'-8" and 7'-0" in height and widths, from 1'-10" to 3'-0" in 2-in. increments. Exterior doors are generally 1-3/4 in. thick, made with waterproof adhesives, and treated against decay, fungi, and insects, whereas interior doors generally are 1-3/8 in. thick (1-3/4 in. where heavy use will be encountered), made with nonwaterproof adhesives, and not treated for decay, fungi, and insects. Wood doors are also manufactured with fire ratings, acoustical treatment, and x-ray shielding.

Figure 32-12 shows various wood swing-type doors. They are manufactured in different ways such as with solid wood, solid wood core with wood veneers, hollow core with wood veneers, and various core materials with wood veneers (see Figure 32-13).

Wood constructed doors are used for folding (flush or panelled), overhead fold-up (flush or panelled), sliding (flush or panelled), bypassing (flush or panelled), and side-rolling (small strips of solid wood) type of doors.

STEEL DOORS: The greatest use of steel doors in building construction is for interior doors requiring fire ratings and for entrance and exit doors with or without fire ratings.

Fire ratings, based on The Standard Building Code, are as follows: *class A*, 3 hrs. minimum; *class D*, 1-1/2 hrs. minimum; *class D*, 3/4 hr.

FIGURE 32-11   *Location of typical finish hardware for all types of doors*

FIGURE 32-12   *Wood swing type doors*

FIGURE 32-13 *Construction details of wood doors*

FIGURE 32-14 *Various types of steel door construction*

minimum; *class E*, 3/4 hr. minimum; and *class F*, 3/4 hr. minimum. Steel doors are available in the same types as swing-type wood doors (see Figure 32-12) and also as overhead roll-up, fold-up and swing-up, sliding, revolving, and bypassing. They are usually manufactured of 14, 16, 18, or 20-gauge cold-rolled steel with all joints welded and ground smooth; 10, 12, and 14 gauges are used for reinforcing channels and angles and as reinforcing for hinges, closures, locks, etc., (see Figure 32-14).

ALUMINUM DOORS: In building construction, aluminum doors are used for entrance doors, which include the frames, and for interior swing-type doors where no fire ratings are required. They are used for swing-type, bypassing, revolving, overhead, and sliding doors.

They are generally manufactured from 6063-T5 aluminum alloy; joints are welded or mechanically secured and meet standards established by the National Association of Architectural Metals Manufacturers; they are available in the same types as wood swing-type doors (see Figure 32-12).

Figure 32-15 shows details of a typical aluminum entrance door, transom, and side lights.

Aluminum doors for interior work are manufactured by various different methods, as shown in Figure 32-16.

325

ELEVATION

SECTION I-I

HEAD

MULLION

SILL

SECTION 2-2

SECTION 3-3

SECTION 5-5

SECTION 4-4

FIGURE 32-15   *Aluminum entrance door with transom and side lights*

ALUMINUM TRIM

ALUMINUM TRIM

ALUMINUM TRIM

ALUMINUM TUBE

ALUMINUM REINFORCING CHANNEL

TEMPERED HARDBOARD WITH ALUMINUM FACING OR PLASTIC LAMINATE

TEMPERED HARDBOARD WITH ALUMINUM FACING OR PLASTIC LAMINATE

TEMPERED HARDBOARD WITH ALUMINUM FACING OR PLASTIC LAMINATE

HONEYCOMB TYPE CORE

HONEYCOMB OR MINERAL CORE

HONEYCOMB TYPE CORE

FIGURE 32-16   *Interior aluminum doors*

FIGURE 32-17 *Typical tempered glass swing type door*

Aluminum fire-rated doors, which consist of a fire-resistant core with aluminum laminated to the faces and edges, are now available with various fire ratings.

GLASS DOORS: Tempered glass is used for swing-type doors and revolving doors. This kind of glass requires that all pivots, locks, holes, etc., be part of the casting when the tempered glass is manufactured. Figure 32-17 shows a typical elevation and section of a tempered glass door.

STORM DOORS: In order to control heat loss or heat gain, many types of storm door combinations are available. These include single glazed; double glazed (which must be plastic or tempered glass); fixed or removable glazed areas (for screen insert in summer); and weather stripped or not weather stripped. The frames are manufactured of wood, steel, aluminum and stainless steel.

5. Are steel windows delivered to a building construction site glazed or unglazed?

6. Do the aluminum window specifications of the Architectural Aluminum Manufacturer's Association require a minimum tensile strength of (a) 22,000 psi, (b) 27,000 psi, or (c) 35,000 psi?

7. What is a minimum required material thickness for aluminum windows?

8. Name four types of doors identified by their opening action.

9. Do swing-type doors have specific names used to denote the swing?

10. Are there standards for locating finish hardware for doors?

11. Wood doors are manufactured in what two standard thicknesses?

12. Are steel doors labeled for fire rating?

13. What is the aluminum alloy used in the manufacturing of doors?

REVIEW EXAMINATION

1. Name the four window categories by their use.

2. Are the vast majority of wood windows (a) double-hung, (b) casement, or (c) projected?

3. What is the wood almost universally used for wood windows?

4. What is the moisture content permitted in standard wood windows?

ASSIGNMENT

1. Sketch five door types in elevation.

2. Sketch five window types in elevation showing swing designations.

3. Sketch the symbolic representation of the following doors:

   (a) Swing, two types

   (b) Folding, three types

   (c) Overhead, three types

SUPPLEMENTARY INFORMATION

Door Frame and Door Buck

All doors have a frame into which they are hung or installed. This is known as the door frame or door buck. The buck must not only be of the size and type to meet the architectural design requirements but also must meet the requirements for the joining of the door and frame to the materials into which it is to be installed.

As a general rule, the buck is of the same material as the door—a wood door requires a wood buck, a steel door a steel buck, etc. A significant change to this rule must take into consideration that door and buck must be of compatible materials so that no chemical or galvanic action can occur. For example, a steel buck with an aluminum door for exterior entrances would set up a galvanic action whereby the aluminum would be destroyed.

Figure 32-18 illustrates various types of wood bucks with wood doors. Two of the jamb sections are for interior doors where plaster-board is shown on both sides and where ceramic tile on plaster board on one side with wood panelling on the other.

The exterior jamb sections include insulation between the walls, outside sheathing, and siding or brick veneer.

Figure 32-19 shows various types of steel bucks with wood or steel doors.

The jamb sections shown in Figure 32-19 indicate metal bucks anchored into a concrete block wall, a concrete block wall with plaster finish and ceramic tile applied with adhesives, concrete block with structural facing tile, and an exterior wall with brick and concrete block.

Figure 32-20 illustrates aluminum door frames or bucks and how they are set into a structural facing tile wall and into a solid masonry wall with granite facing.

Figure 32-21 shows a stack and bumper jamb and a head section through a folding partition. These partitions are available with manual operation or electrical motorized operation. While the partition is in motion a 5/8-in. clearance is allowed between the bottom of the partition and the finished floor. The acoustical floor seals are automatically actuated by the final closing action of the partition and will also lock the partition firmly in place without the use of floor bolts or floor locks.

MID-TERM OR END-TERM
REVIEW EXAMINATION—CHAPTERS 22–32

1. What must the minimum clearance between the edges of plate glass and its frame be?

2. Before glass is installed into a wood frame, how should the wood be treated?

FIGURE 32-18 *Typical wood door frames (bucks)*

FIGURE 32-19 *Jamb details of steel door bucks*

FIGURE 32-20 *Jamb details of aluminum door bucks*

FIGURE 32-21 *Folding partition*

3. What is elastic glazing compound made from?

4. Glass block walls cannot be used for what type of walls?

5. When glass block is installed in a masonry or steel frame opening, what is the size limitation?

6. Heat-strengthened glass is generally used in what kind of walls?

7. What type plastic is used in the manufacture of skydomes?

8. Vinyl flooring is manufactured in rolls and in tile form. What sizes of square tiles are available?

9. Translucent corrugated plastic sheets are used in the construction field for what purpose?

10. Polyurethane and polystyrene plastics produce a pre-formed and foamed type of insulation. What is the U-factor for 1-in.-thick preformed plastic insulation?

11. What is the maximum size manufactured for a silvering, mirror-glazing type of plate glass?

12. What is the liquid part of the paint known as?

13. What is the solvent for shellac?

14. What is the hiding power of the type of white paint solid known as zinc oxide?

15. The best results in painting are achieved when the paint is applied between what temperatures?

16. What does the word "length," when used in relation to varnish, mean?

17. What do the plate-like particle shapes in white paint solids (pigments) increase?

18. What is one method of cleaning ferrous metals?

19. Which type of metals receive a protective removable coating that is taken off when the possibility of damage or staining is no longer present?

20. What must be provided when 9 × 9 in. wood block flooring is installed directly onto a concrete slab on grade?

21. In order to provide for the expansion and contraction of terazzo flooring, what is it necessary to do?

22. Where in a building should terrazzo flooring be installed?

23. What must the surface be upon which ceramic and quarry tile flooring is to be installed?

24. When concrete is to be used as the finish floor surface, what must it be treated with?

25. After a concrete floor is floated and troweled, what can now be applied to give a hard, durable, and wear-resistant surface?

26. What are the cementitious materials used in applying seamless flooring?

27. What is the most common of the hardwoods used for strip flooring?

28. What cementitious material is used for exterior plastering (such as stucco)?

29. What is usually the thickness of plaster applied on masonry and wire lath?

30. In a three-coat plaster job, what is the second coat called?

31. What are gypsum plaster-boards commonly known as?

32. What is gypsum plaster board with unsized paper on both sides known as?

33. Poured gypsum roofing is lightweight, fire-resistant and has the advantage of setting in what amount of time?

34. The wire lath generally used to reinforce poured gypsum roofs is of what gauge?

35. Which of the following U-factors, or heat loss coefficients, has the highest heat flow: (a) 0.18; (b) 0.24; or (c) 0.34?

36. To find the BTU heat loss through a wall, one must multiply the U-factor by the area of the wall by what?

37. All types of roofing materials are figured by what factor?

38. In climates where there will be heavy snowfall, it is advisable to use roof pitches greater than what?

39. What is the roofing material that weighs from 700 to 810 lbs. per 100 sq. ft?

40. What are the shingles that are made from portland cement and asbestos fibers?

41. Asphalt roll roofing is used on roofs with pitches from what minimum to what maximum?

42. For what use is terneplate an excellent material?

43. Terneplate is very reactive with what metal?

44. What was probably the first ventilating window?

45. What is the wood used in the manufacture of most wood windows?

46. In the manufacture of aluminum windows, the frames, sash, and mullions are produced by what process?

47. What is the minimum tensile strength of the alloys used in aluminum windows as required by the AAMA?

48. Swing-type and revolving glass doors require what kind of glass?

49. The fire rating for a class A steel door is how many hours?

50. How are folding partitions operated?

appendix

METRICATION

THE INCH-POUND AND METRIC SYSTEMS

The two systems of weights and measures that have been used most extensively throughout the world are the inch-pound system and the metric system. The inch-pound system was evolved in Great Britain as the British Imperial System, but Britain has now changed to the metric system. The United States is one of a few nations that still uses the inch-pound system, also known as the U.S. Customary System.

The *metric system*, used almost exclusively for scientific work, is also called the International System. It coordinates the measurements of length, area, volume, and mass into one decimalized system. Except for moving the decimal point, the metric system requires no conversion from unit to unit as does the inch-pound system. For example, the conversion from inches to feet, or ounces to pounds, does not exist in the metric system.

The principal unit of *length* in the metric system is the *metre*. The symbol for metre is (m). The common metric units of length are the millimetre (mm), used for small dimensions, the centimetre (cm) for average dimensions, the metre (m) for large dimensions of objects, and the kilometre (km) for longer distances.

This can be stated as follows:

for what used to be measured in fractions of inches, use millimetres (mm).

for what used to be measured in inches, use centimetres (cm).

for what used to be measured in yards, use metres (m).

for what used to be measured in miles, use kilometres (km).

METRIC CONVERSION ACT

The Metric Conversion Act of 1975 set the United States firmly on a metric course. Learning the metric system now will help bring about a smooth transition to metric usage.

WHY CHANGE TO THE METRIC SYSTEM?

The metric system is used throughout the world for two principal reasons: it is a simple system and it is a decimal system. British educators claim that, because of the simplicity of the metric system, doing calculations in metric saves 15% of math class time over use of the inch-pound system of measurement.

An all-metric world creates stronger ties between countries in the areas of government relations, economics, industry, commerce, international relations, and international trade.

METRIC UNITS FOR LENGTH

The prefixes for subdivisions and multiples of the metre are: milli-METRE = 1/1000; centi-METRE = 1/100; deci-METRE = 1/10; METRE = 1; deka-METRE = 10; hecto-METRE = 100; and kilo-METRE = 1000.

Simply stated, the foregoing can be expressed as follows:

1	milli-METRE (mm)	=	0.001	METRE
1	centi-METRE (cm)	=	0.01	METRE
1	deci-METRE (dm)	=	0.1	METRE
1	METRE (m)	=	1	METRE
1	deka-METRE (dam)	=	10	METRES
1	hecto-METRE (hm)	=	100	METRES
1	kilo-METRE (km)	=	1000	METRES

Not all subdivisions and multiples of the metre are commonly used commercially. Those commonly used for length are:

millimetre (mm)

centimetre (cm)

metre (m)

kilometre (km)

ACTUAL METRIC LENGTH MEASURES

The actual visual size of a millimetre, a centimetre, and a decimetre can be seen on the metric rule (Figure A-1). The millimetre is the smallest division on the rule. Ten millimetres equals 1 centimetre, the distance from 0 to 1 on the reverse side of the scale. Ten centimetres is equal to 1 decimetre, or 100 millimetres. Ten decimetres equals 1 metre, which cannot be shown full size on a page of book size. The reverse side of the rule shows centimetres up to 20. Each division is 1 centimetre. The rule has 20 centimetres.

THINK METRIC

To visualize metric measures, one must think metric. Almost everyone in this country can visualize the size of U.S. coins. The old silver dollar is the largest coin; the half-dollar is smaller but larger in diameter than the quarter. The nickel is smaller in diameter than the quarter but larger in diameter than the dime. The penny is larger in diameter than the dime but smaller than the nickel. This is relatively easy to visualize because of our familiarity in use and handling of money.

To visualize the size or the diameter of the coins in metric dimensions, note that the dollar coin, shown full size in Figure A-2, has a diameter of 37 millimetres (37 mm) or 3.7 centimetres (3.7 cm). The half-dollar coin has a diameter of 30 millimetres (30 mm) or 3 centimetres (3 cm). The quarter measures 24 mm or 2.4 cm in diameter. The nickel measures 21 mm or 2.1 cm in diameter. The penny measures 18 mm or 1.8 cm in diameter, the dime measures 17.5 mm or 1.75 cm in diameter, and the Susan B. Anthony dollar coin measures 26 mm or 2.6 cm.

NOTE: In converting from millimetres to centimetres, the next larger unit of measure, point off one digit to the left.

PRACTICE READING METRIC MEASURES

Fill in the proper subdivisions of the given metric measures, or write them on a separate sheet of paper, as shown in Table A-1. For the given 37.5 cm, the number of millimetres, decimetres, and

FIGURE A-1

FIGURE A-2

TABLE A-1   *Practice reading metric measures*

Milli-metres, mm	Centi-metres, cm	Deci-metres, dm	Metres, m
375	37.5	3.75	0.375
		183	
			2.57
3673			
	137.7		
		25.4	
102			
		96	
			0.015

TABLE A-2   *Ideal metric masses of persons 20 to 30 years old*

Height without Shoes (mm)	Mass without Clothes (kg)
Men	
1626	60
1676	64
1727	68
1778	72
1829	76
1880	79
Women	
1575	52
1626	55
1676	58.5
1727	62
1778	65
1829	70

metres are given. Fill in the blanks for the other measures given.

METRIC UNITS FOR MASS

The standard or principal unit of *mass* is the *gram.* The symbol for gram is g. The common units of mass are the milligrams (mg), the centigram (cg), and the kilogram (kg).

Masses over 1000 kilograms are expressed in tonnes (t). Where applicable, however, mass may be expressed in any multiple of the gram.

The prefixes for subdivisions and multiples of the gram are as follows:

1	milli-GRAM (mg)	=	0.001	GRAM
1	centi-GRAM (cg)	=	0.01	GRAM
1	deci-GRAM (dg)	=	0.1	GRAM
1	GRAM (g)	=	1	GRAM
1	deka-GRAM (dag)	=	10	GRAMS
1	hecto-GRAM (hg)	=	100	GRAMS
1	kilo-GRAM (kg)	=	1000	GRAMS
1	TONNE (t)	=	1000	KILOGRAMS

Not all subdivisions and multiples of the gram are commonly used commercially. Those commonly used for masses (weights) are:

milligram (mg)

gram   (g)

kilogram   (kg)

tonne   (t)

See Table A-2 for common mass measurements expressed in metric units.

METRIC UNITS FOR VOLUME

The standard unit of *volume* is the *cubic metre* (m^3). A common unit is the litre, which is $0.001 \ m^3$. The symbol for litre is the capital letter ell, or L. A common metric unit of volume is the millilitre (mL). One teaspoon equals 5 millilitres; one tablespoon equals 15 millilitres.

In measuring cups, use millilitres or litres, where each cup equals 240 millilitres or 0.24 litre.

The prefixes for subdivisions and multiples of the litre are as follows:

1	milli-LITRE (mL)	=	0.001	LITRE
1	centi-LITRE (cL)	=	0.01	LITRE
1	deci-LITRE (dL)	=	0.1	LITRE
1	LITRE (L)	=	1	LITRE
1	deka-LITRE (daL)	=	10	LITRE

All subdivisions and multiples of the litre are not commonly used commercially. Those commonly used for volume are millilitres (mL) and litres (L).

THE METRE BOARD

In the metric system there is a unique relationship among the metre (length), the kilogram (mass), and the litre (volume). This can best be understood through the *metre board* (Figure A-3).

FIGURE A-3   *The metre board*

1000 GRAMS OR
1 KILOGRAM

500 GRAMS

200 GRAMS

FIGURE A-4   *The metre/litre cube*

MILK

1-LITRE

FIGURE A-5   *One litre of milk fits into a 10 cm cube*

The metre board is 1 metre long, which is 10 decimetres long, which is 100 centimetres or 1000 millimetres long. Its width is 1 decimetre or 10 centimetres or 100 millimetres. Its thickness is 1 centimetre or 10 millimetres. At each decimetre, scored lines divide the board into 10 equal decimetres. At one end, 1 decimetre is scored, forming 10 lines of 1 centimetre in two directions, creating a waffle effect.

If the metre board were to be disjointed at the decimetre scored lines and neatly stacked up as shown in Figure A-4, a cube is formed. Each piece of the metre cube has its mass adjusted to exactly 100 grams, so that the whole has a mass of 1 kilogram or 1000 grams. Similarly, 1 litre of milk requires a container size of 7 cm × 7 cm × 20.41 cm high, containing a total of 1000 cm³ (cubic centimetres). This is the amount of milk that will fit in a cube that is 10 cm × 10 cm × 10 cm or in a container that is 1000 cm³. The metre cube and the litre cube are the same—hence the expression metre/litre cube (Table A-3; see also Figure A-5).

TABLE A-3 *The metric litre cube*

1 cubic decilitre	(1 × 1 × 1)	=	1 litre
2 cubic decilitres	(2 × 2 × 2)	=	8 litres
3 cubic decilitres	(3 × 3 × 3)	=	27 litres
4 cubic decilitres	(4 × 4 × 4)	=	64 litres
5 cubic decilitres	(5 × 5 × 5)	=	125 litres
10 cubic decilitres	(10 × 10 × 10)	=	1000 litres
13 cubic decilitres	(13 × 13 × 13)	=	2197 litres

TEMPERATURE

Prefixes are not commonly used with *temperature* measurements as they are for length, mass, and volume. Temperatures in *degrees Celsius*, as compared with the familiar Fahrenheit temperatures, are given in Table A-4.

TABLE A-4 *Celsius/Fahrenheit equivalencies*

Celsius	Fahrenheit
0°C =	32°F (freezing point of water)
10°C =	50°F
20°C =	68°F
30°C =	86°F
37°C =	98.6°F (normal body temperature)
40°C =	104°F
100°C =	212°F (boiling point of water)

In translating from Fahrenheit to Celsius, use the following formula:

$$°\text{Celsius} = °\text{Fahrenheit} - 32 \div 1.8$$

The visual difference between the Celsius and the Fahrenheit scale is clearly illustrated by the two thermometers shown in Figure A-6.

THE INTERNATIONAL SYSTEM (SI)

The General Conference on Weights and Measures, held in Paris (1960) gave formal approval to the *Système International d'Unités*, better known under the internationally accepted abbreviation of *SI*, which is an extension and simplification of the traditional metric system founded in France during the French Revolution. The SI system is more understandable and a simplification of the older metric system (see Table A-5). The Conference agreed on:

Basic SI Units

Derived SI units

Supplementary SI units

TABLE A-5 *The SI system*

Physical Quantity	SI Unit	Symbol
Basic SI units (partial list)		
Length	metre	m
Mass	kilogram	kg
Time	second	s
Electric current	ampere	A
Thermodynamic temperature	kelvin	K
Amount of substance	mole	mol
Luminous intensity	candella	cd
SI derived units (partial list)		
Angular acceleration	radian per second squared	rad/s^2
Angular velocity	radian per second	rad/s
Area	square meter	m^2
Density	kilogram per cubic meter	kg/m^3
Energy, work, quantity of heat	joule	J
Force	newton	N
Pressure, stress	pascal	Pa
Volume	cubic meter	m^3
SI supplementary units		
Plane angle	radian	rad
Solid angle	steradian	sr

Many benefits have come from the change to SI metric units. For instance, the Canadian grain trade is saving $6 million a year by not having to make so many paper conversions from pounds to bushels. They now do all measuring and pricing on the basis of the tonne (1000 kg). Projected to the U.S. economy, such use of metric would provide a saving of about $60 million to the grain trade.

THE METRE STICK

The *metre stick* looks like an ordinary yardstick except that it is a little longer. Where the yardstick is 3 ft. or 914.4 mm long, the metre stick is 1000 mm long, a difference of 85.6 mm. A good method of learning to read metric measurements is to use the metre stick and measure things around you, such as the height of a door knob, the width of a door, or the height of the kitchen table.

BOILING POINT OF WATER — 212°
200°
190°
180°
170°
160°
150°
140°
130°
120°
110°
100°
90°
80°
70°
60°
50°
40°
FREEZING POINT OF WATER — 32°
30°
20°
10°
0°

180 DIVISIONS

FAHRENHEIT

100° BOILING POINT OF WATER
90°
80°
70°
60°
50°
40°
30°
20°
10°
0° FREEZING POINT OF WATER

100 DIVISIONS

CELSIUS

FIGURE A-6 *Thermometers*

EXPRESSING DATES AND TIME

The expression of calendar dates and time is in a sense a form of measurement.

In the past there have been two general practices of expressing *dates*—a European writes 2 July 1982 whereas most U.S. citizens write July 2, 1982. Provided that the month is spelled out in full or with the first three letters, there is no problem of understanding. The difficulty arises when an all-numerical expression is used, so the examples above become 2-7-82 and 7-2-82, respectively.

The issue has been discussed by the International Standardization Organization (ISO) and they have published standards governing the expression of dates.

Basically, the ISO standards call for the expression of dates in descending order, always using two digits for the month and date to provide for the continuing sequence year–month–day by adding digits for hour–minute–second.

When only numbers are used, the ISO method should be used as follows:

1982-07-02

If a *time* element is required, it should be added to the date using only the 24-hour clock:

1982-07-02-14:27

Seconds can also be added in the following manner:

1982-07-02-14:27:02.4

The acceptance of the ISO method should lead to uniformity when only numbers are used, and it is particularly convenient for computer data processing.

THE 24-HOUR CLOCK

The advantage of the 24-hour clock (Figure A-7) over the 12-hour A.M.–P.M. clock is in the fact that is causes less confusion.

In the *24-hour clock system* the hours from midnight to noon are the same as in the 12-hour

337

THE 24 - HOUR CLOCK

FIGURE A-7   *The 24-hour clock*

system. After that, the P.M. time is the usual time plus 12. For example: at 2:30 P.M., the 24-hour clock will read 12 + 2:30 = 14:30. Similarly, at 7:00 A.M., the 24-hour clock will read 7:00. The hour of 8:00 P.M. will read 20:00 on the 24-hour clock. Spoken expressions are: "The concert begins at twenty-one thirty" (21:30). "Change the baby at zero twenty" (00:20). "Dinner is served at nineteen hundred" (19:00).

Although the 24-hour clock is not a part of the metric system, it has, nevertheless, been found useful in our country as well as many other countries for scheduling purposes. Among its users are the National Weather Service, the Federal Aviation Administration, the U.S. military services, and police departments.

INTRODUCTION

When adding, subtracting, multiplying, or dividing metric numbers of different prefixes, first change one prefix to correspond to the other.

A number expressed in centimetres cannot be added, subtracted, multiplied, or divided by a number expressed in metres. The metres must be changed to centimetres, or the centimetres to metres.

METRIC ADDITION

PROBLEM 1:   Add the following and express the sum in metres.

1376 mm + 364 cm + 19.750 m

SOLUTION:

    1376 mm =   1.376 m
     364 cm =   3.640 m
  19.750 m = 19.750 m
    _____
         24.766 m   answer

PROBLEM 2:   Add the following and express the sum in millimetres.

0.265 cm + 89 mm + 1.320 m

SOLUTION:

    0.265 cm =   2.65 mm
       89 mm =   89.00 mm
     1.32   m = 1320.00 mm
    _____
         1411.65 mm   answer

PROBLEM 3:   Add the following and express the sum in centimetres.

137 mm + 1.570 m + 19.75 cm

SOLUTION:

      137 mm =   13.70 cm
    1.570   m = 157.00 cm
   19.75   cm =   19.75 cm
    _____
         190.45 cm   answer

PRACTICE PROBLEMS:

Add and find metres: 376 cm + 246 mm + 4 m
    centimetres: 1285 mm + 19.6 m + 14 cm
    millimetres: 23 cm + 16.67 mm + 1.2 m

METRIC SUBTRACTION

PROBLEM 1:   Subtract the following and find the number of centimetres.

67.75 mm from 2.5 m

SOLUTION:

     2.5 m   = 250.000 cm
   67.75 mm =   6.775 cm
    _____
         243.225 cm   answer

PROBLEM 2:   Subtract the following and find the number of millimetres.

2750 mm from 4.5 m

SOLUTION:

4.5   m = 4500 mm
2750 mm = 2750 mm
_____
             1750 mm   answer

PRACTICE PROBLEMS:

Subtract and find mm: 140 cm from 1.5 m
          find cm: 7.66 cm from 8660 mm
          find m: 106 cm from 2.7 m

METRIC MULTIPLICATION

PROBLEM 1:   Multiply the following and find the number of square metres.

39.7 cm by 1.5 m

SOLUTION:

39.7 cm = 0.397 m
1.5   m =   1.5 m
_____
          0.596 m^2 answer

PROBLEM 2:   Multiply the following and find the number of square centimetres.

2367 mm by 2.6 m

SOLUTION:

2367 mm = 236.7   cm
2.6 m   = 260   cm
_____
          61542 cm^2 answer

PRACTICE PROBLEMS:

Multiply: 3.07 m by 507 cm
         16.76 cm by 2000 mm
         2.875 m by 18.9 cm

METRIC DIVISION

PROBLEM 1:   Divide the following.

0.595 m ÷ 150 cm

SOLUTION:

0.595 m ÷ 1.5 m = 0.397 m   answer

PROBLEM 2:   Divide the following.

2.6 m ÷ 2367 mm

SOLUTION:

2.6 m ÷ 2.367 = 1.09 m   answer

PRACTICE PROBLEMS:

Divide: 15.56 cm ÷ 120 mm
        3.5 m ÷ 1250 mm
        1.8 m ÷ 14 cm

METRIC SQUARE MEASURE

In the metric system of measurements not all of the multiples and subdivisions are used commercially. Those ordinarily used for length are kilometre (km), metre (m), centimetre (cm), and millimetre (mm). For area, the square metre, the square centimetre, and square millimetre are most often used.

Calculations, for capacity, using metric units over customary units are greatly simplified. This can best be illustrated by a comparison problem.

PROBLEM: What is the area of the floor of a room with the following dimension, 14′-6″ × 18′-8″?

Conventional Method:

The area is found by multiplying the width by the length of the room. Since feet and inches, or mixed numbers, cannot be multiplied, it becomes necessary to first reduce them to a common unit expression, which, in this case, may either be feet or inches. If it is to be inches, multiply the 14 ft of the 14′-6″ dimension by 12 and add the 6 in.

(14 × 12) = 168 + 6 = 174 in.

Similarly, multiply the 18 ft of the 18′-8″ dimension by 12 and add the 8 in.:

(18 × 12) = 216 + 8 = 224 in.

By multiplying the length in inches by the width in inches, the square inches are found. Thus:

$174 \text{ in} \times 224 \text{ in} = 38{,}976 \text{ in.}^2$

If the square feet of the room are to be found, divide the square inches by 144, or:

$$38.976 \div 144 = 270.6 \text{ or } 271 \text{ ft.}^2$$

If the square yards are to be found, divide the square feet by 9, or

$$271 \div 9 = 30 \text{ yd.}^2$$

Metric Method:

Multiply the width by the length of the room in metres. The length, 5.69 m (18'-8") multiplied by the width, 4.42 m (14'-6"), is equal to 25m². It can be seen that computations by the metric system are easier, take less time, and greatly reduce the chance of error.

Square measure is illustrated in Figure A-8. The large square is the actual size of 1 square decimetre. One square decimetre is equal to 100 square centimetres. One square decimetre is also equal to 1/100 or 0.01 of a square metre.

One decimetre is also equal to 10,000 square millimetres. Each side of the square decimetre has 10 centimetres or 10 × 10 = 100 square centimetres, or each side of the square decimetre has 100 millimetres or 100 × 100 = 10,000 square millimetres.

$$1 \text{ square decimetre (dm}^2) = \quad 0.01 \text{ m}^2$$
$$1 \text{ square decimetre (dm}^2) = \quad 100 \text{ cm}^2$$
$$1 \text{ square decimetre (dm}^2) = 10,000 \text{ mm}^2$$

FIGURE A-8   *Square measure*

FIGURE A-9   *Squaring metric shapes*

We can further say:

100 square millimetres (mm²) = 1 square centimetre (cm²)
100 square centimetres (cm²) = 1 square decimetre (dm²)
100 square decimetres (dm²) = 1 square metre (m²)

PRACTICE FINDING AREAS IN METRIC MEASURE

PROBLEM 1:   Find the area of each of the illustrations shown in Figure A-9, A to D). The answers are: (A) 25 cm²; (B) 42.75 m²; (C) 18 cm²; (D) 1089 cm².

PROBLEM 2:   Assume the illustration in Figure A-10, A to be the floor plan of a building. The ceiling height is 2.6 m. Find the total wall area in square metres (m²).

PROBLEM 3:   Find the area in square metres (m²) of the three wall surfaces, minus the glass areas, shown in Figure A-10, B.

PROBLEM 4:   Find the total area in square metres (m²) of lot 119, Figure A-10, C, by first finding each triangle, I, II, and III, separately.

PROBLEM 5:   A builder purchased lots shown in Figure A-10, D. Determine the number of square metres (m²) purchased.

LOT 119

FIGURE A-10 *Finding metric areas*

METRIC CUBIC MEASURE

Figure A-11 shows the actual size and relation between metric measures of length, volume, and mass.

The cube shown measures 10 × 10 × 10 cm, which is equal to 1000 cubic centimetres, or a mass of 1 kilogram. The figure that represents 1 millilitre (mL) is also 1 cubic centimetre (cm^3). One cubic millimetre of water has a mass of 1 gram (g).

To change: cubic millimetres (mm^3) to cubic centimetres (cm^3), move the decimal point three figures to the left:

$$9\ 000\ 000\ \text{mm}^3 = 9\ 000\ \text{cm}^3$$

To change: cubic centimetres (cm^3) to cubic decimetres (dm^3), move the decimal point three figures to the left:

$$9\ 000\ \text{cm}^3 = 9\ \text{dm}^3$$

To change: cubic decimetres (dm^3) to cubic metres (m^3), move the decimal point three figures to the left:

$$9\ \text{dm}^3 = 0.009\ \text{m}^3$$

FIGURE A-11 *The metric cube*

341

To change: cubic centimetres (cm^3) directly to cubic metres (m^3), thereby eliminating the cubic decimetre, move the decimal point six places to the left:

$$2\,500\,000 \text{ cm}^3 = 2.5 \text{ m}^3$$
$$1\,500\,000 \text{ cm}^3 = 1.5 \text{ m}^3$$
$$875\,000 \text{ cm}^3 = 0.875 \text{ m}^3$$

Therefore:

$$18\,000\,000 \text{ mm}^3 = 18\,000 \text{ cm}^3 = 18 \text{ dm}^3 = 0.018 \text{ m}^3$$
$$15\,000 \text{ cm}^3 = 15 \text{ dm}^3 = 0.015 \text{ m}^3$$
$$9650 \text{ dm}^3 = 9.650 \text{ m}^3$$
$$135\,000 \text{ cm}^3 . = 0.135 \text{ m}^3$$

1000 cubic millimetres (mm^3) = 1 cubic centimetre (cm^3)
1000 cubic centimetres (cm^3) = 1 cubic decimetre (dm^3)
1000 cubic decimetres (dm^3) = 1 cubic metre (m^3)

To find the number of cubic metres in a container that measures 100 cm by 100 cm by 100 cm, multiply the three dimensions:

$$100 \text{ cm} \times 100 \text{ cm} \times 100 \text{ cm} = 1\,000\,000 \text{ cm}^3$$

Since $100 \text{ cm}^3 = 1 \text{ dm}^3$, divide $1\,000\,000$ by 1000:

$$\frac{1\,000\,000}{1000} = 1000 \text{ dm}^3$$

Since $1000 \text{ dm}^3 = 1 \text{ m}^3$, divide 1000 dm^3 by 1000:

$$\frac{1000}{1000} = 1 \text{ m}^3 \quad \text{answer}$$

The formula above can be simplified by immediately changing the centimetres to metres:

$$100 \text{ cm} = 1 \text{ m}$$

Therefore:

$$1 \text{ m} \times 1 \text{ m} \times 1 \text{ m} = 1 \text{ m}^3$$

FIND CUBIC CONTENT

PROBLEM 1:   Find the cubic centimetres in a board that measures 10 cm $\times$ 10 cm $\times$ 1 m long (100 cm).

SOLUTION:

$$10 \text{ cm} \times 10 \text{ cm} \times (1 \text{ m}) \text{ or } 100 \text{ cm} = 10\,000 \text{ cm}^3$$

PROBLEM 2:   Find the cubic centimetres of a piece of lumber that measures 4 cm $\times$ 8 cm $\times$ 2.5 m long.

SOLUTION: First change the 2.5-m length to 250 cm. Then:

$$4 \text{ cm} \times 8 \text{ cm} \times 250 \text{ cm} = 8000 \text{ m}^3 \quad \text{answer}$$

PROBLEM 3:   Find the cubic metres in 30 pieces of beam that measure 5 cm $\times$ 20 cm $\times$ 1200 cm.

SOLUTION:

$$5 \text{ cm} \times 20 \text{ cm} \times 1200 \text{ cm} = 120\,000 \text{ cm}^3 \text{ or } 0.120 \text{ m}^3$$

Then:

$$0.120 \text{ m}^3 \times 30 = 3.6 \text{ m}^3 \quad \text{answer}$$

PROBLEM 4:   Find the cubic metres of five posts that measure 15 cm $\times$ 15 cm $\times$ 3.5 m long.

SOLUTION:

$$15 \text{ cm} \times 15 \text{ cm} \times 350 \text{ cm} = 78\,750 \text{ cm}^3$$

Then:

$$0.078 \text{ m}^3 \times 5 = 0.39 \text{ m}^3 \quad \text{answer}$$

PROBLEM 5:   In Figure A-12, find the volume of concrete in cubic metres (m^3) that the concrete form will hold.

Procedure:

Find the volume of the entire shape by multiplying the length by the width by the height, or $4.5 \times 3.0 \times 1.68$ m. Next, find the volume of the inner shape by multiplying $3.5 \times 2.0 \times 1.68$ m. Subtract the volume of the inner shape from the outer shape to get the remaining volume, which is the volume of the concrete. The answer is 10.92 m^3.

RULES CONSISTENT WITH SI PRACTICES

Length

On drawings use metres (m) and millimetres (mm) for measurements of length. For long dimensions use kilometres (km). On drawings delete all unit symbols: use 360, not 360 mm; 2.180, not 2.18 m. Decimalized expressions, taken to three decimal places, always indicate metres, such as 2.920, 0.625, or 0.019, (all in metres).

FIGURE A-12 *Concrete form*

Area

The preferred unit for area is the square metre (m^2). Give large areas in square kilometres (km^2), small areas in square millimetres (mm^2). The area of building products may be expressed by linear dimensions, such as 50 mm × 100 mm, or 400 × 600. It is preferred practice to indicate the width dimension first and the height second.

Volume and Fluid Capacity

The preferred unit for measurement of volume in construction is the cubic metre (m^3); units for fluid capacity (liquid volume) are the litre (L) and the millilitre (mL). The litre is equal to one thousandth of a cubic metre (m^3) or 1 cubic decimetre (dm^3).

Flow

Flow rates are expressed in cubic metres per second (m^3/s), litres per second (L/s), or cubic metres per hour (m^3/h).

Temperature and Temperature Interval

The SI base unit of temperature is the kelvin (K), and is used in expressing both the thermodynamic temperature and the temperature interval. Wide use is also made of the degree Celsius (°C) for the expression of ambient temperature levels and for temperature intervals.

A temperature expressed in degrees Celsius is equal to the temperature expressed in kelvins less 273.15. There are no negative (minus) temperature values in the kelvin scale.

Use the kelvin (K) in compound units involving temperature or temperature internals.

Mass and Force

SI uses explicit and distinctly separate units for "mass" and for "force."

CONCRETE TAKEOFF BY THE UNIT METHOD

The unit method implies the finding of concrete quantities in tabular form. If two walls or footings, for example, are alike in length, height, and thickness, they are known as two units. In Figure A-13, for example, the north and south walls are the same length, height, and thickness. The east and west walls are of the same length, height, and thickness.

In finding the cubic meters of concrete for walls and the cubic metres of concrete for footings, proceed as shown on Table A-6. By multiplying the units by the length, height, and thickness in centimetres, the result is cubic centimetres (m^3). To find the cubic metres, divide by 1 000 000, or move the decimal point six places to the left.

343

DIMENSIONS IN METRES AND MILLIMETRES

FIGURE A-13   *Concrete take-off*

TABLE A-6   *Tabular takeoff (unit method)*

Item	Number of Units	Length (cm)	Height (cm)	Thickness (cm)	cm³	m³
Wall						
N–S	2	610	183	30	6 697 800	
E–W	2	397	183	30	4 359 060	
					11 056 860	11.05
Footing						
N–S	2	640	30	60	2 304 000	
E–W	2	367	30	60	1 321 000	
					3 625 000	3.62

TABLE A-7   *Tabular takeoff (unit method)*

Item	Number of Units	Length (m)	Height (m)	Thickness (m)	m³
Wall					
N–S	2	6.10	1.83	0.30	6.69
E–W	2	3.97	1.83	0.30	4.36
					11.05
Footing					
N–S	2	6.40	3.0	6.0	2.30
E–W	2	3.67	3.0	6.0	1.32
					3.62

The north and south walls are two units of the same length (610 cm), the same height (183 cm), and the same thickness (30 cm). Multiply the figures:

The footing quantities are found similarly.

If the dimensions are given in metres, the tabular takeoff shown in Table A-7 will result.

$$\text{N–S}: 2 \times 610 \times 183 \times 30 = 6\ 697\ 800\ cm^3$$
$$\text{E–W}: 2 \times 397 \times 183 \times 30 = 4\ 359\ 060\ cm^3$$
$$11\ 056\ 860\ cm^3 \text{ or } 11.05\ m^3$$

MEASUREMENT CONVERSIONS

LENGTH

1 inch = 25.4 mm
1 foot = 0.3048 m
1 yard = 0.9144 m
1 mile = 1.609 km

MASS

1 pound = 0.454 kg
1 U.S. short ton = 0.9072 tonne

CAPACITY OR VOLUME

1 ft.^{3} = 0.028 m^3
1 yd.^{3} = 0.764 m^3
1 liquid quart = 0.946 litre
1 gallon = 3.785 litres

AREA

1 ft.^{2} = 0.092 m^2
1 yd.^{2} = 0.836 m^2
1 acre = 0.404 hectare (ha)

HEAT

1 BTU = 1055 joule (J)
1 BTU/hr. = 0.293 watt (W)

TABLES

TABLE A-8   *List of symbols*

Symbol	Unit	Quantity
mm	millimetre	Length
cm	centimetre	
m	metre	
km	kilometre	
mm^2	square millimetre	Area
cm^2	square centimetre	
dm^2	square decimetre	
m^2	square metre	
km^2	square kilometre	
cm^3	cubic centimetre	Volume
dm^3	cubic decimetre	
m^3	cubic metre	
mg	milligram	Mass
g	gram	
kg	kilogram	
t	tonne	
°C	degree Celsius	Temperature
K	kelvin	
s	second	Time
rad	radius	Plane angle
N	newton	Force
kN	kilonewton	
J	joule	Energy, work, quantity of heat
kJ	kilojoule	
MJ	megajoule	
W	watt	Power, heat flow rate
kW	kilowatt	
Pa	pascal	Pressure
kPa	kilopascal	
mPa	megapascal	

TABLE A-9   Conversion table

0.001 inch	= 0.025 mm
1 inch	= 25.400 mm
1 foot	= 30.48 cm
1 foot	= 0.3048 mm
1 yard	= 0.9144 mm
1 mile	= 1.609 km
1 in.^{2}	= 6.4516 cm^2
1 ft.^{2}	= 0.0929 m^2
1 yd.^{2}	= 0.8361 m^2
1 acre	= 0.4047 ha
1 mile^2	= 2.590 km^2
1 in.^{3}	= 16.387 cm^3
1 ft.^{3}	= 0.028 m^3
1 yd.^{3}	= 0.7647 m^3
1 U.S. oz.	= 29.57 mL
1 U.S. pint	= 0. 4732 L
1 U.S. gal.	= 3.785 L
1 ounce	= 28.35 g
1 pound	= 0.4536 kg
1 short U.S. ton	= 0.9072 tonne
1 lb./in.^{2}	= 0.0703 kg/cm^2
1 mile/U.S. gal.	= 0.4251 km/L
1 degree Fahrenheit	= −17.2°C
1 lb./ft.^{2} × 0.04788	= kilopascal (kPa)
1 lb./in.^{2} × 6.89476	= kilopascal (kPa)
1 BTU × 1.05506	= kilojoule (kJ)
1 degree Fahrenheit × $(t_F + 459.67)/1.8$	= kelvin (K)
1 degree Celsius × $t_C + 273.15$	= kelvin (K)

TABLE A-10   Wire gauge of ferrous and nonferrous wire*

Gauge Number	Ferrous American Steel Wire Gauge		Nonferrous American Wire Gauge	
	mm	in.	mm	in.
00	8.407	0.3310	9.266	0.3648
0	7.785	0.3065	8.252	0.3249
1	7.182	0.2830	7.348	0.2893
2	6.668	0.2625	6.543	0.2576
3	6.190	0.2437	5.827	0.2294
4	5.723	0.2253	5.189	0.2043
5	5.258	0.2070	4.620	0.1819
6	4.877	0.1920	4.115	0.1620
7	4.496	0.1770	3.665	0.1443
8	4.115	0.1620	3.264	0.1285
9	3.767	0.1483	2.906	0.1144
10	3.429	0.1350	2.588	0.1019
11	3.061	0.1205	2.304	0.0907
12	2.680	0.1055	2.052	0.0808
13	2.324	0.0915	1.829	0.0720
14	2.032	0.0800	1.628	0.0641
15	1.829	0.0720	1.450	0.0571
16	1.588	0.0625	1.290	0.0508
17	1.372	0.0540	1.151	0.0453
18	1.207	0.0475	1.024	0.0403
19	1.041	0.0410	0.912	0.0359
20	0.884	0.0348	0.813	0.0320

*Inches × 25.4 = millimetres.

TABLE A-11 *Conserving water use in litres and gallons**

Activity	Normal Use	Conservative Use
Shower	95 litres 25 gallons Water running	15 litres 4 gallons Wet down, soap up, rinse off
Tub-bath	136 litres 36 gallons Full	38 to 45 litres 10 to 12 gallons Minimal water level
Dish washing	114 litres 30 gallons Tap running	19 litres 5 gallons Wash and rinse in sink
Toilet flushing	19 to 26 litres 5 to 7 gallons Depends on tank size	10 to 23 litres 4 to 6 gallons Using tank displacement bottles
Automatic dishwasher	60 litres 16 gallons Full cycle	26 litres 7 gallons Short cycle
Washing machine	200 litres 60 gallons Full cycle, top water level	100 litres 27 gallons Short cycle, minimal water level
Brushing teeth	4 litres 1 gallon Tap running	2 litres 1/2 gallon Wet brush, rinse briefly
Washing hands	8 litres 2 gallons Tap running	4 litres 1 gallon Full basin
Outdoor watering	40 litres/min. 10 gal./min. Average hose	Lowest priority: can be eliminated

TABLE A-12 *Metric paper sizes: A-series*

Size Designation	Metric* Dimensions (mm)			Customary Equivalents (in.)		
	W	×	L	W	×	L
A0	841	×	1189	33.11	×	46.81
A1†	594	×	841	23.39	×	33.11
A2	420	×	594	16.54	×	23.39
A3	297	×	420	11.69	×	16.54
A4	210	×	297	8.27	×	11.69
A5	148	×	210	5.83	×	8.27
A6	105	×	148	4.13	×	5.83
A7	74	×	105	2.91	×	4.13
A8	52	×	74	2.05	×	2.91
A9	37	×	52	1.46	×	2.05
A10	26	×	37	1.02	×	1.46

*In the halving process, odd numbers divided by 2 are rounded down to the nearest whole millimetre.

†A decision must be made as to whether the A1 sheet dimensions of 841 by 594 mm will apply to the outside edges, thus reducing the drawing area, or whether an oversized A1 sheet will be required such that these dimensions may apply to the borderlines.

Source: *Metric Manual*, U.S. Department of the Interior, Bureau of Reclamation.

TABLE A-13 *Metric paper sizes: B-series**

Size Designation	Metric Dimensions (mm)			Customary Equivalents (in.)		
	W	×	L	W	×	L
B0	1000	×	1414	39.37	×	55.67
B1	707	×	1000	27.83	×	39.37
B2	500	×	707	19.68	×	27.83
B3	353	×	500	13.90	×	19.68
B4	250	×	353	9.84	×	13.90
B5	176	×	250	6.93	×	9.84
B6	125	×	176	4.92	×	6.93
B7	88	×	125	3.46	×	4.92
B8	62	×	88	2.44	×	3.46
B9	44	×	62	1.73	×	2.44
B10	31	×	44	1.22	×	1.73

B-size: The basic size (B0) of the B-series has an area of $\sqrt{2}\,m^2$. The ratio of length to width is the same as that for the A-series, $\sqrt{2}$.

Source: *Metric Manual*, U.S. Department of the Interior, Bureau of Reclamation.

TABLE A-14   *Metric paper sizes: C-series**

Size Designation	Metric* Dimensions (mm)			Customary Equivalents (in.)		
	W	×	L	W	×	L
C0	917	×	1297	36.10	×	51.07
C1	648	×	917	25.53	×	36.10
C2	458	×	648	18.03	×	25.53
C3	324	×	458	12.72	×	18.03
C4	229	×	324	9.02	×	12.72
C5	162	×	229	6.36	×	9.02
C6	114	×	162	4.49	×	6.36
C7	81	×	114	3.18	×	4.49
C8	57	×	81	2.24	×	3.18
C9	40	×	57	1.57	×	2.24
C10	28	×	40	1.10	×	1.57

**C-size:* the basic paper size (CO) of the C-series has an area of $\sqrt[4]{2}\,\mathrm{m}^2$, which equals 1.189 m². The ratio of length to width is $\sqrt{2}$.

Source: *Metric Manual*, U.S. Department of the Interior Bureau of Reclamation.

ANSWERS

Chapter 1

1. legal description, survey
2. size, easements, lot, block, and section numbers
3. architectural survey
4. taxes, building costs, site improvement, legal fees, utilities, insurance, landscaping and planting, professional services, mortgages
5. architectural, structural, mechanical, site planning and landscaping considerations
6. yes
7. yes
8. architectural, structural, and mechanical considerations
9. architect, Clerk-of-the-Works, and building department inspectors
10. architect
11. contract drawings and specifications
12. punch lists

Chapter 2

1. rock
2. rock masses detached from the ledge of which they originally formed a part
3. gravel
4. 1/4
5. decayed rock
6. hardpan
7. 80
8. 10
9. coarse dry sand, or hard clay
10. hardpan or hard shale, loose rock and hard rock
11. detached rock particles 1/4 in. to 3 in. in size, rounded and waterworn
12. test pit, loading platform, test borings
13. loading platform
14. load on platform times B/A + B
15. load of building per sq. ft.
16. 7200 lbs.
17. 1200 lbs.
18. 4; 24, 24
19. 18,000 lbs.
20. 3/4 in.
21. 60%
22. reduced load
23. log of test borings
24. 133,333 lbs.

Chapter 3

1. underneath the street
2. 4, 9
3. gas, electricity, telephone
4. public sewer
5. water
6. syphoned off
7. telephone and electricity
8. soil stack receives the discharge of the water closet
9. private sewage disposal system
10. public sewer or private sewage disposal system
11. shores
12. cap all utilities
13. removal of topsoil
14. backfill
15. the exertion of less pressure against the foundation walls

16. must be filled with concrete
17. sheet-piled and braced
18. bracing deep pits for columns
19. keeping an excavation dry during the placement of the foundation
20. clean earth

Chapter 4

1. footing
2. mat, raft or boat; column or pier; wall
3. 6in. to 8 in.
4. Douglas fir, Southern pine
5. precast, cast-in-place
6. mandrel
7. 8 to 10 in.
8. 20 ft.
9. concrete
10. 3 to 25
11. billet
12. cement grout
13. 5/8
14. billet
15. welded together
16. plain poured concrete, concrete block, reinforced concrete

Chapter 5

1. the house drain and house sewer
2. pitched type roofs
3. cast iron
4. area of roof to be drained
5. 75 ft.
6. 150
7. trap seal
8. 1.00
9. 42
10. 67

Chapter 6

1. lime, gypsum, portland cement, and masonry cements
2. dolomite limestone
3. hydrated lime
4. plasticity, workability, and water-holding capacity
5. gypsum
6. gypsum
7. Keane's cement
8. lime, silica, iron oxide, and alumina
9. standard, high early strength, modified, low heat and sulfate-resisting
10. 45 min, 10
11. 1 cu. ft., 94 lbs.
12. mortars, I and II
13. seamless flooring, terrazzo
14. asphalt concrete, paving and asphalt blocks

15. strength, durability
16. water–cement ratio
17. consistency, plasticity, workability
18. consistency
19. 1/5 to 1/4
20. millions of tiny air bubbles
21. adding abrasive aggregates

Chapter 7

1. tongue-and-groove boards, plywood, metal, synthetic materials
2. 1″, 2″
3. 1/2″ to 3/4″
4. fiberglass, steel, or special reinforced paper
5. allowing it to flow over long distances, and by excessive spading or vibrating
6. washed off
7. covering surface with wet burlap, by sprinkling periodically, by covering slabs with sand or earth that is kept moist
8. 72 hrs.
9. the loss of water
10. 300 ft.

Chapter 8

1. steel rods, or wire mesh
2. 6000
3. 150,000
4. 1-way, 2-way, flat slab 2-way, flat slab 4-way
5. metal, paper
6. width 15 to 32 in., length 4 to 10 ft.
7. 2 to 3
8. 15 to 50
9. curtain walls
10. deflection

Chapter 9

1. soft-mud, stiff-mud, dry-press
2. water-struck
3. sand-struck
4. 2-1/4″ × 3-3/4″ × 7-3/4″
5. 5th, 6th, or 7th
6. burning in the kiln
7. SW, MW, NW
8. false
9. face, side, cull, end, bed, and bed
10. 75%

Chapter 10

1. A, B, and C
2. property specifications and proportion specifications
3. 3/8″ and 1/2″

4. A = required area in sq. ins. P = load in lbs. per sq. in., and fc = compressive strength of brick work
5. expansion joint
6. premolded, mastic, and metal
7. vertical coursing, horizontal coursing
8. weatherstruck, flush, round-rodded, V-shape
9. raked, troweled, beaded, stripped
10. 200'-0"

Chapter 11

1. 75%
2. load-bearing walls, partitions and non-load-bearing partitions
3. end construction, side construction
4. LBX, LB
5. FTX, FTS
6. false
7. false
8. large sizes
9. load and non-load-bearing walls and partitions, fireproofing, backup, foundations
10. solid, hollow
11. A, B
12. where hard, durable, easily maintained surfaces are required
13. fireproofing steel, non-load bearing partitions

Chapter 12

1. LBX, LB
2. 20'-0"
3. false
4. yes
5. FTX, FTS
6. 1/4"
7. yes
8. calculated
9. weight, color, texture, coefficient of heat transmission, strength, denseness
10. no
11. yes
12. cracking
13. dense water-resistant concrete block, surface should be treated with a waterproofing material (stucco) and painted with waterproof-type paint
14. false
15. adhesion, anchor

Chapter 13

1. igneous, sedimentary, metamorphic
2. dimension (cut) stone, rubble stone (ashlar type), flagstone, monumental stone, crushed stone, stone dust
3. marble, slate, soapstone
4. granite

5. 7/8"
6. aggregate for concrete, asphaltic concrete, terrazzo, precast concrete panels, artificial stone, surfacing treatment for buildings
7. 1/4"
8. dust-press, plastic
9. 6" square
10. standard, seconds
11. nonvitreous, semivitreous, vitreous, impervious
12. trim tiles

Chapter 14

1. dimension (cut) stone, rubble stone, flagstone
2. granite, limestone, marble
3. nonstaining, nonstaining waterproof
4. 7/8"
5. masonry backup, concrete backup, joining veneers, steel and ceiling
6. granite, limestone
7. granite, slate, limestone, bluestone, sandstone, soapstone
8. ceramic tile
9. ceramic mosaic
10. cement mortar, adhesive

Chapter 15

1. oak, maple, birch, walnut, cherry
2. pine, spruce, fir, hemlock, redwood, cedar, cypress
3. house construction—joists, studs, rafters
4. yard lumber, structural lumber, factory or shop lumber
5. flooring, dressed and matched, lumber, siding, subflooring, sheathing
6. less than 2 in. thick and 8 in. or more in width
7. 1-1/2" × 7-1/4"
8. plank
9. select and common
10. grade A and B suitable for natural finish, grade C and D some defects—can be covered with paint
11. classes 1, 2, 3, 4, 5
12. 5 in. or more in thickness, and 8 in. or more in width

Chapter 16

1. "face," "back"
2. crossbands
3. veneer, solid wood or lumber core, particle board core
4. exterior, interior
5. 4 × 8 ft.
6. 5/16"
7. shiplap
8. core
9. standard, tempered, low density
10. pulp, chips, fibers
11. holding power of the nails
12. insulating, acoustical

Chapter 17

1. the strength of the member
2. 1" to 2"
3. 1 ft
4. 2-1/4", 2-3/4", 3" 3-3/4", 4"
5. 30 to 100 ft.
6. wide spans
7. does not require ties, special foundations, or buttresses
8. the steel beams
9. roofing clear spans
10. bow string truss

Chapter 18

1. 4 in
2. bridal iron (joist hangers)
3. wood bents
4. door head, jamb, sill
5. balloon, braced, western or platform, modern braced
6. western or platform

Chapter 19

1. ferrous, nonferrous
2. yes
3. they corrode
4. galvanic action
5. iron, carbon
6. hard, strong, and corrosion-resistant
7. structural framing, reinforcing for concrete, forms for concrete, hollow metalwork, miscellaneous and ornamental metalwork
8. corrosion resistance
9. flashing, roofing, screens, tubing
10. tin
11. zinc
12. flashing, copings, roofing, bathroom accessories, hardware, galvanizing

Chapter 20

1. structural, hollow metal, miscellaneous metal, ornamental, windows, doors, curtain walls, partitions, flashing
2. masonry
3. rolled steel sections
4. reinforced concrete slab, steel decking, metal pan, open-web joists, reinforced concrete slab on top of structural steel
5. ferrous and nonferrous
6. loose lintels, built into masonry structural shapes, stairs, railings, fences, gratings, ladders, access doors
7. ornamental metalwork

8. facing type, prefabricated type, grid type, structural type
9. less thickness, lightweight, saves time in construction, adds rentable floor area, saving in heat and air conditioning losses and less air infiltration
10. concealed, exposed
11. copper, aluminum, zinc, lead, stainless steel
12. stainless steel
13. aluminum, steel

Chapter 21

1. sand, soda, and lime
2. AA, A, and B
3. both sides
4. rolling, sand-blasted, etched with acid, and special-type roller
5. 3 to 5 times
6. by metal or glass
7. 42%
8. total radiant heat of the sun
9. 7/8", 24
10. both sides
11. decorative panels and sidewalks
12. 144 sq. ft

Chapter 22

1. glazing
2. setting blocks and spacers
3. glazing compound
4. 1/4 points
5. thoroughly dried and rough projections removed
6. 40° F
7. prime painted
8. no
9. 3/8" expansion strips
10. lapping, attaching, condensation

Chapter 23

1. no
2. no
3. 1/16", 3/32", 1/8"
4. 9" × 9", 12" × 12"
5. will not break
6. no
7. porch roofs, screen walls, clerestory windows
8. general-purpose, for forming radii and curves, and cigarette-proof
9. glazing
10. yes
11. yes
12. tracing paper, moisture-proofing, roofing, flashing, waterproof membranes

13. single sheet and laminated sheet
14. R-7.15 to 9.09

Chapter 24

1. adhesives
2. sprayed, rolled or troweled
3. yes
4. elastic, silicones, two-part polysulfide
5. the shape, thickness, and glass fibers
6. glazing, skydomes, light fixtures
7. pot life
8. contact adhesive
9. perimeter, sandwich panels, and wall
10. precast concrete panels, glazing, control and expansion joints

Chapter 25

1. vehicle, white paint solids (pigment)
2. liquid part
3. driers
4. the hiding power unit
5. antimony oxide, white lead, zinc oxide, titanium dioxide, lithopane, zinc sulfide, barium sulfate
6. epoxy, lacquers, shellac, varnish, urethane, vinyl
7. dry color pigment in a vehicle
8. acetate, acetone, alcohol, benzene, benzine, ketone, mineral spirits, turpentine, water, xylene

Chapter 26

1. applied at job; applied at mill, shop or factory; prime coats applied in the mill, shop, factory or on the job
2. clean, dry, prime-coated, sized cracks filled, rough projections removed
3. prime coating
4. brush, cloth, sponge
5. metal furniture
6. putty, caulking compounds, wood filler paste, knot sealers, paint and varnish removers, sizing material, thinners and solvents
7. 60 to 80°F
8. air, airless
9. brush, roller, spray gun
10. rust-inhibiting paints

Chapter 27

1. (a) yes, (b) yes, (c) no
2. stretching, adhesive, tape
3. yes
4. mortar base, adhesive
5. hardened, dust-proofed
6. (a) yes, (b) no, (c) yes, (d) yes, (e) no

7. no
8. heavy
9. epoxy, vinyl, urethane, acrylic, neoprene, oxychloric cement
10. gratings, plate
11. cement mortar
12. asphalt, vinyl, cork, vinyl asbestos, rubber, linoleum
13. marble, granite, or limestone chips
14. divider strips
15. strip flooring, thin wood block, solid end-grain block

Chapter 28

1. (a) yes, (b) no, (c) yes, (d) no, (e) yes
2. (a) cement plaster, (b) gypsum plaster, (c) Keene's cement
3. 5/8"
4. wire lath, gypsum plaster lath
5. internal and external corner beads, casings, expansion joints, strip mesh, corner mesh
6. 1-hr.
7. spackling
8. 7'-0"
9. yes
10. regular, fire-rated, backer board, decorative, insulating, vinyl coated, sheathing, laminated
11. 2, 3, or 4 sheets of plaster board laminated together

Chapter 29

1. thermal insulation
2. insulation
3. blankets, batts
4. 10.00 to 12.50
5. 12" of flexible insulation
6. cavity-wall, perimeter, fill-in for the voids of concrete block
7. low density materials
8. four
9. very loud hi-fi, noisy factory or angry conversation
10. 11.44

Chapter 30

1. metal foils
2. adhesives
3. perforated structural facing tile
4. yes
5. yes
6. mounted on pads or suspended
7. stagger studs with sound-absorbing material wrapped between them
8. acoustical concrete block and acoustical structural facing tile
9. rigid foam insulation
10. yes

Chapter 31

1. weathertight
2. waterproof
3. sun, rain, snow, sleet, ice, wind
4. roofs with pitches of 3 to 12 and greater, roofs with pitches less than 3 to 12 until they are flat
5. random, dimension, hand-split
6. design for extra load
7. adhesive tabs
8. 1 to 12 to 4 to 12
9. lapping of corrugations
10. standing seams and batten seams
11. single lock, double lock
12. plies
13. single ply, single ply with foam-type insulation, spray-on, roll-on, trowel-on or brush-on or mop-on
14. galvanic action
15. must be easily soldered or welded
16. asbestos-cement, asphalt, slate, wood
17. yes

Chapter 32

1. residential, commercial, industrial, monumental
2. double-hung
3. Ponderosa pine
4. 6 to 12%
5. unglazed
6. 22,000 psi
7. 0.062
8. swing, overhead, sliding, revolving, by-passing, folding, side-rolling
9. yes
10. yes
11. 1-3/8″, 1-3/4″
12. yes
13. 6063-T5

MID-TERM AND END-TERM
REVIEW EXAMINATIONS—CHAPTERS 1–6

1. conduct soil tests
2. the architect
3. owner
4. he checks all materials
5. rock
6. gravel
7. sand
8. 1 ft.
9. peat
10. 10 tons
11. 1 ton
12. building code (in area where building is to be constructed)
13. four times the design load

14. 60% of settlement under proposed load
15. 7200 lbs.
16. 1800 lbs.
17. to locate the elevation of sound rock
18. bedrock
19. public utilities
20. rural areas
21. house sewer
22. soil stack
23. 7-1/2 gal. per min.
24. six-fixture units
25. telephone and electric power
26. prevents breakage of house trap seal
27. prevents breakage of fixture trap seal
28. 12″ square, 1′-6″ deep
29. 350 ft.
30. cap or cut off gas, sewer, and water pipes
31. shores
32. inclined position
33. dry-pack
34. trench excavation
35. sheet piling
36. to keep excavation temporarily dry until foundation is installed
37. sand and gravel
38. the nature of the soil
39. 36° 53′
40. 4–6 ft. apart
41. raft or boat footing
42. cast-in-place concrete pile
43. roof area to be drained
44. 4″ per hr.
45. 15 sq. ft.
46. dolomite limestone
47. at manufacturer's plant
48. 45 min.
49. high early strength
50. coal
51. strength
52. water–cement ratio
53. consistency
54. 1/4
55. 7
56. air-entraining agents
57. fill
58. 45 min.
59. normal, moderate, high early strength, low heat, sulfate-resisting
60. as the cementitious material combined with aggregates to make paving

MID-TERM OR END-TERM REVIEW
EXAMINATION—CHAPTERS 7–13

1. wire, she bolt, tapered, he bolt, flat, pull out, drive wedge
2. by engineers

3. forms for columns
4. concrete slabs poured on grade and when cured jacked up to floor levels
5. two and four ways
6. one and two ways
7. concrete slabs are poured on grade and tilted up into a vertical position
8. $6'' \times 12''$
9. pine
10. steel, paper, plastic
11. excessive tamping or vibrating, correctly depositing
12. improper mixing
13. covering surface with wet burlap, sand, straw or special papers, wetting periodically
14. temperature changes
15. loss of water
16. elastic joint filler
17. use fairly rich mix
18. 18 hrs.
19. reinforcing rods, wire mesh
20. curtain walls
21. brick
22. high quality of mechanical perfection
23. 2200 psi
24. rate of water absorption of brick
25. natural clays
26. load-bearing
27. 3/8 in. and 1/2 in.
28. expansion joint
29. flush
30. 200 ft. long
31. 0.0000031″
32. mastic
33. soluble salts which are in the brick
34. 75%
35. fireproofing, back-up, furring, load-bearing, and non-load bearing
36. concrete block
37. structural clay tile
38. type A
39. 20 ft.
40. 1/4″
41. cracking
42. igneous stone
43. 6000 to 14,000 psi
44. as a filter
45. 170 lbs./cu. ft.
46. terrazzo-type flooring
47. dark green and black
48. reddish and yellowish colors
49. gray, green, and blue
50. gray and buff

MID-TERM OR END-TERM REVIEW EXAMINATION—CHAPTERS 14–21

1. granite
2. nonstaining

3. dampproofed, so no moisture can develop
4. 4 anchors
5. cement mortar, adhesives
6. cleavage plane
7. softwood
8. green
9. air, kiln
10. yard, structural, factory or shop
11. $1\text{-}1/2'' \times 3\text{-}1/2''$
12. light frame construction
13. select, common
14. dressed and matched
15. fungi
16. creosote
17. building construction
18. cabinet work, furniture, millwork
19. interior, exterior
20. $4' \times 8'$
21. 3/8″
22. 5/16″
23. core
24. 5/8″ to 3″
25. 1 to 2″
26. 24 ft.
27. 60 ft. in 1-ft. increments
28. parabolic, Tudor, Gothic
29. platform
30. balloon, braced
31. flexibility
32. 9/32″
33. galvanic
34. 2.7
35. 8.89
36. nonferrous
37. cast iron
38. structural steel framing
39. tin
40. brass
41. by gauge number
42. structural steel framing
43. exposed, concealed
44. 85%, 95%
45. sand, soda, lime
46. insulating glass
47. 0.47
48. 1 lb.
49. wire glass
50. 1.12

MID-TERM OR END-TERM REVIEW EXAMINATION—CHAPTERS 22–32

1. 1/8″
2. painted with a prime coat
3. processed oil and white paint
4. bearing walls or partitions
5. 144 sq. ft.
6. curtain walls

7. acrylic plastic
8. 9 × 9 in. and 12 × 12 in.
9. porch roofs, screen walls, clerestory, windows
10. 0.16, 0.20
11. 10′ × 20′
12. vehicle
13. alcohol
14. 1.48
15. 60 to 80°F
16. ratio of oil to resin
17. resistance to moisture
18. flame, pickling, sand-blasting, wire-brushing, rust remover, solvent cleaning
19. nonferrous metals
20. vapor barrier under slab and a waterproof adhesive
21. install divider strips
22. when there will be heavy wear
23. rigid
24. hardeners
25. metallic aggregates
26. oxychloric cement, epoxy, vinyl, urethane, acrylic, and neoprene
27. oak
28. portland-type cement
29. 5/8″
30. brown coat
31. sheetrock
32. backer board
33. 1/2 hr.
34. 12 gauge
35. 0.34
36. the temperature difference
37. the square
38. 6 to 12
39. slate
40. asbestos-cement shingles
41. 1 to 12 to 4 to 12
42. roofs
43. steel
44. casement
45. Ponderosa pine
46. extrusion
47. 22,000 psi
48. tempered
49. 3 hrs.
50. manually or motorized

INDEX

A

Accessories for brickwork, 116–17
Accessories for masonry units, 143
Accessories for stone, 154–55
Acoustical masonry units, 304
Acoustical materials, 295–96, 302
 prefabricated or factory finished, 296, 302–3
 special site-assembled materials and treatments, 296, 302, 304
 suspended baffles, 296, 302–3
 wet- or plastic-applied, 296, 302
Acoustical treatments, 297
Admixtures, 70–71
Adobe brick, 107
Aggregates, 67–68
 aggregate combinations, 67, 69–70
 aggregate size, 67, 69–70
Air-entrained agents, 67–68, 70
Air-entraining concrete, 67
Alluvial soil, 11
All-weather wood foundation, 193, 196, 199
Aluminous cement, 72
Aluminum, 205–6
 doors, 325–27
 shingles, 309
 siding, 313–14
 windows, 321–22
Anchors for stone, 155
Angle of repose, 37
Architectural services fees, 7
Architectural survey, 3, 6
Area drains, 53–54
Asbestos-cement shingles, 307–9
Asbestos-cement siding, 313–14
Asphalt, 63
 pavement, 72
 shingles, 309
Auger borings, 10, 19–20

B

Backfilling, 32
Backfilling around foundations, 35
Banked earth slopes, 37–38
Bar spacing, 47
Bearing capacities of soils, 12
Bending plywood, 178
Bluestone, 151
Boat footing, 40
Bonding of surfacings and coatings, 288
Boulders, 10–11

Bracing, 33
Branch plumbing lines, 27
Brass, 206
Brick, 100–7
 accessories for brickwork, 116–17
 bonds, 102–4
 grades, 100–1
 hardness, 103
 physical requirements, 101–2
 shapes and names of cut brick, 107–8
 sizes, 101–3
 special brick shapes, 102–3
 types, 100–1
 veneer, 103–4
 wall construction, 105
Brick cavity wall with steel frame, 114, 116
Brick veneer with frame backing, 114–15
Brick veneer with metal stud backing, 114–15
Brick wall with reinforced concrete, 118, 121
Brick with concrete block back-up, 118, 120
Bronze, 206
Brownstone, 146
Building process, 2
Built-up roofing, 310, 312–13
Bulb-tee system, 97–98

C

Canvas roofing, 312
Carbon steels, 207
Cast and wrought iron, 203–4
Cast-in-place piles, 44
Catch basin, 54
Cavity wall, 116, 137
Cement, 62–63, 67, 71–72
Cement brick, 107
Ceramic mosaic tile, 150
Ceramic veneer, 130–31, 140–42
Certificate of occupancy, 5
Clay, 10–11
Clay tile shingles, 306–8
Clerk-of-the-works, 5
Color of stone, 151
Colors, 257
Column pier footing, 41
Commercial insulating materials, 297
Common brick, 100–2
Com-ply wall studs and floor joists, 177–78
Computing cut and fill, 37–38
Concrete, 64–98
 admixtures, 70–71
 air content test, 67
 consistency, 64